PRAISE FOR *THE ESSENTIAL G*
TELECOMMUNICATIONS, SIXTh ~~EDITION~~

"Dodd's The Essential Guide to Telecommunications *provides the history and context that make a fundamental underpinning of modern business more accessible to technologists and businesspeople alike. This new edition of her primer is an essential reference in the continuously evolving communications landscape."*

> —Tom Hopcroft, President and CEO,
> Mass Technology Leadership Council

"Annabel Dodd's book is a clear guide and big-picture view of technologies and industries. It is an up-to-date guide for anyone who wants to be familiar with important innovations and key technologies. This is truly an industry bible for mobile, Internet, and networking services."

> —Hiawatha Bray, Technology Reporter,
> *The Boston Globe*

"Ms. Dodd's aptly titled The Essential Guide to Telecommunications *has been my bible for all things telecom since my days as an AT&T transmission network engineer nearly twenty years ago. Exhaustively and meticulously researched, concisely written for lay folks and techs/engineers alike, this book aids me in my current role as an IT Support Technician II when discussing new technology with our telecommunications department. Thank you to Ms. Dodd for keeping us all current!"*

> —Todd Garbarini, IT Support Technician II
> Commvault Systems, Inc.

*"*The Essential Guide to Telecommunications *is probably one of the most useful and well-written books on our telecom bookshelf. Annabel Z. Dodd does a great job of capturing a snapshot of the current telecom industry. Even those with little or no technical training should be able to understand the text. This is the perfect book for salespeople who want to learn more about the products and services they are selling, or for those who just want to keep up to date on the latest in telecom technology."*

> —William Van Hefner, President,
> Vantek Communications, Inc.

"Ms. Dodd continues to provide an excellent and thorough text on the telecommunications industry. As in her previous editions, she presents a good balance of technical and business-related information that is readily understandable by anyone with an interest in this key component of today's business environment. In her new edition, she has captured many of the recent changes in this dynamic field, which will affect every company in the years ahead. I strongly recommend her book to anyone who wants a better understanding of telecommunications."

> —Joe McGrath, VP, Sage Pharmaceuticals, Inc.

"Annabel Dodd has a unique knack for explaining complex technologies in understandable ways. This latest revision of her book covers the rapid changes in the fields of broadband, cellular, and streaming technologies; newly developing 5G networks; and the constant changes happening in both wired and wireless networks. She also explains the consolidation going on in the industry, the impacts of social media, and software control and virtualization of provider networks. This book is a must-read for anyone wanting to understand the rapidly evolving world of telecommunications in the 21st century!"

—David Mash, Retired Senior Vice President for
Innovation, Strategy, and Technology
at Berklee College of Music

The
Essential
Guide to
Telecommunications

Sixth Edition

Annabel Z. Dodd

Boston • Columbus • New York • San Francisco • Amsterdam • Cape Town
Dubai • London • Madrid • Milan • Munich • Paris • Montreal • Toronto • Delhi • Mexico City
São Paulo • Sydney • Hong Kong • Seoul • Singapore • Taipei • Tokyo

For information about buying this title in bulk quantities, or for special sales opportunities (which may include electronic versions; custom cover designs; and content particular to your business, training goals, marketing focus, or branding interests), please contact our corporate sales department at corpsales@pearsoned.com or (800) 382-3419.

For government sales inquiries, please contact governmentsales@pearsoned.com.

For questions about sales outside the U.S., please contact intlcs@pearson.com.

Visit us on the Web: informit.com

Library of Congress Control Number: 2018967285

ISBN-13: 978-0-13-450679-1
ISBN-10: 0-13-450679-0

2 2019

To Bob, Judy, Nancy, Laura, Steve, Bobby, Elizabeth, Julia, Gabriel, Ari, Michael, Moses, Delancey, and Harry

Contents

Part II
Industry Overview and Regulations   123

Preface

When *The Essential Guide to Telecommunications* was first published in 1997, broadband and cellular networks were many times less complex. Voice calls were carried separately from data traffic, and e-mail required arcane commands and was used mostly at universities. The federal government had recently deregulated telecommunications and opened it to competitors. Deregulation opened voice and data networks to new competitors. These competitors competed with established providers for subscribers by offering lower prices. This competition drove innovation and resulted in the build-out of high-speed fiber-optic networks. Large incumbents responded with their own network improvements and lowered prices. A similar pattern occurred in cellular networks after 1999.

In the years since 1997, most small and medium-sized and even some large competitors were either acquired by large incumbents or went out of business. These incumbents also acquired other large providers that were formerly part of the Bell system. The result of these mergers is that today's telecommunications, cellular, and cable TV markets have far fewer competitors: mainly AT&T, CenturyLink, Comcast, and Verizon. Partly as a result of minimum competition, prices for broadband services are higher compared with most of the world.

Social networking, cloud, and Office software conglomerates Amazon, Facebook, and Microsoft have built large, cloud-located networks of data centers. Their services have disrupted commerce in each of their fields. Microsoft operates one of the four largest cloud services in the United States. It offers a platform on which developers customize Microsoft applications for enterprise customers. Additionally, their Teams service is used by enterprises to make low-cost international voice calls and video conference calls and collaborate on joint projects.

Google, which was started by Stanford graduate students, operates the largest search service in the United States. The founders used software to search the web and keep repositories of web site addresses. It quickly became an enormous company, whose popularity grew through word of mouth. They are now a huge conglomerate that earns billions of dollars each year through the advertising on their site.

Amazon was started by Jeff Bezos. Its cloud-based retail service is another example of a business that has had an enormous impact. Brick and mortar retailers have lost millions of dollars, chains have gone out of business, and many have closed a number of their stores. Amazon is still innovating with its home automation offering Alexa, its fast turnaround delivery service, its purchase of Whole Foods, and its entrance in drug deliveries for hospitals.

And AT&T and Verizon are building large fiber networks and cellular infrastructure to carry new generations of mobile networks. T-Mobile and Sprint are building out their cellular networks as well.

However, the number of choices consumers and enterprise customers have for their Internet access and broadband services as well as their mobile services has decreased and will shrink more if T-Mobile is granted permission to acquire Sprint's cellular network. If the Sprint acquisition is approved, the number of mobile operators for nationwide coverage will shrink from four to three. This is a significant change, one that may lead to higher prices for the students and young people that flock to T-Mobile for its low prices.

New 5th generation mobile networks promise to support higher data rates than ever before. However, these upgrades are costly, and require thousands of additional cell sites and antennas, particularly in downtown urban areas with large amounts of foot traffic. Mobile providers are additionally upgrading current 4th generation cellular networks. Both of these efforts will support higher speeds, some up to a gigabit per second. As capacity on mobile networks increases, they will support streaming video and, in some cases, broadband links to residential subscribers' homes.

Because of the greater capacity in mobile networks, many young people and students depend wholly on mobile networks for messaging, streaming, and social network access. Teens and twenty-somethings for the most part use Snapchat and Instagram (part of Facebook) social networks rather than Facebook and Twitter. Snapchat is newer, launched in 2011, and appeals to young people for its more visual service where users upload videos and photos, rather than biographies and other written material as on Facebook and other social networks.

Streaming services were first envisioned by Reed Hastings, the CEO and founder of Netflix. Netflix initially mailed DVDs to subscribers in iconic red envelops and stated at the time that Netflix would stream TV shows and movies when Wi-Fi became robust enough to support video traffic. Netflix is a disruptive service that changed user behavior and disrupted traditional sales of DVDs and movie theaters. Streaming caused Blockbuster, the largest seller of DVDs, which had outlets on every corner, to go out of business and movie theaters had to close many of their theaters due to fewer people going to movies. Netflix is now an international business with service in nearly 200 countries.

A core strategy of Netflix, Hulu, Amazon, and their competitors is to attract subscribers by offering popular TV shows and movies. Netflix was initially able to license the TV series and movies it offered from content providers such as Disney, Time Warner, and Universal Studios. As these companies started offering their own streaming services or were bought by larger companies, for example, AT&T and Comcast, less content became available for competing streaming providers. As a result, Netflix, Amazon, and others have poured billions of dollars into creating original content to attract subscribers. Content is a critical factor in people's decision to either drop cable TV or subscribe to smaller cable TV packages.

Software is the driving force in managing today's broadband and LAN (local area networks) networks. Broadband networks controlled by software are referred to as wide area software defined networks (W-SDNs). SDNs are also implemented in enterprise networks. Both implementations are controlled from central terminals programmed with commands that direct traffic to avoid routes with outages and congestion. Software is used to manage complex high-capacity broadband networks. Functions previously installed on proprietary hardware can be abstracted in non-proprietary hardware. These network functions include routers, servers dedicated to security, and gateways that translate between networks that use different protocols. Another way that networks are enabled to carry more traffic is the network equipment connected to fiber-optic cabling that enables gigabit and even terabit data rates. A terabit is equal to a thousand gigabits.

Networks that connect people have made the world smaller and opened up communications worldwide. However, the common protocols used on the Internet where everyone is connected to everyone else means that networks are inherently open to hackers who use these common protocols as a way to hack into organizations' networks.

Organizations large and small have experienced security breaches. Some breaches have resulted in the loss of millions of peoples' private information including their social security numbers. In addition, security breaches have cost enterprises millions of dollars in bad publicity and stolen intellectual property. To avoid major hacking attacks, enterprises hire outside consultants, and strengthen their security staff. They also educate users to the danger of opening attachments from people they don't know. These phishing emails contain malware able to contaminate entire networks. However, there is no 100 percent guarantee that any of these steps will protect an organization from a determined hacker. But organizations with strong security recover faster, and detect attacks more quickly.

Register your copy of *The Essential Guide to Telecommunications, Sixth Edition*, on the InformIT site for convenient access to updates and corrections as they become available. To start the registration process, go to informit.com/register and log in or create an account. Enter the product ISBN (9780134506791) and click Submit. Look on the Registered Products tab for an Access Bonus Content link next to this product, and follow that link to access any available bonus materials. If you would like to be notified of exclusive offers on new editions and updates, please check the box to receive e-mail from us.

Acknowledgments

Thank you to all of the many people that took the time to share important information about technology and government regulations. Staffs at the FCC and the Massachusetts Department of Telecommunications and Cable provided clear explanations of national and state regulations. Marketing Consultant David Gitner was a terrific source of information on storage systems. Geoff Bennett, Director, Solutions and Technology at Infinera, provided clear information about fiber-optic multiplexers, and Mike Quan, cofounder of Boston 360, illuminated information about virtual reality. James Chapman, Senior Product Manager at Ipswich, spoke with me about network management systems. Bob Xavier, Director, Systems and Networks at Berklee College of Music, gave me a tour of Berklee's IT department and discussed the issues involved in managing merging IT systems when colleges merge.

As always, Carly Premo Mello, IT Director, and Jamie V. Schiavone, Network Manager for Framingham, Massachusetts, discussed the challenges of managing security and storage networks. Joe Mulvey, IT director for Newton, Massachusetts, and his staff spent time discussing their broadband, Wi-Fi, and IT structures and gave me a tour of their data center. Mark Roberts, the Chief Marketing Officer at the former Shortel (now Mitel), discussed specialty applications using VoIP technology. All of these people provided insights into real-world issues.

Thank you also to Fernando Mousinho, Cisco Systems Director of Product Management for Endpoints, for his lucid explanation of Cisco Systems' office products and video conferencing services. Many thanks to Dave Parks, former Director of Segment Marketing at Ciena Corporation, for his generosity in providing information on Ciena's broadband hardware and software. Dave has been an enormous source of information for earlier editions of my book as well as for this sixth edition as has Joe McGrath, VP of Information Technologies, Sage Therapeutics. Thanks to Kevin Klett, VP of Product Management & Marketing at 128 Technology for his lucid explanations of their stateful routing software.

Thanks to Rick Swiderski, VP and General Manager at NEP Group, for his informative discussions of the challenges facing rural telephone companies. His first-hand knowledge was tremendously helpful. Thanks also to Kurt Raaflaub, head of strategic solutions marketing at ADTRAN. Kurt and his staff provided important information on the use of copper cabling connections to fiber cabling to bring high-speed broadband to rural areas. Glenn Axelrod of Axelrod Broadcast Solutions illuminated the details behind multiplexing technologies used in cable TV networks. Sal Tuzzeo at Nielsen discussed consumer trends in viewing television. Thanks as well to Joanta Stanke, Research Director at Point Topic Ltd,, for her information and graphic on Internet access patterns worldwide. Special appreciation to Mohammad Zulqarnain, Distinguished Architect of Global Solutions at Verizon Communications. Mohammad illuminated the important features and advantages of software defined networks. He further provided examples of how enterprises and branch offices are deploying the technology.

A special thank you to Tom Case, Chief Information Officer for the town of Lexington Massachusetts, who met with me and discussed the day-to-day issues involved in designing and maintaining municipal networks. A thank you also to Donna Drudik and Jim Thompson, California 911 Telecommunications Engineers, for discussing the importance and time criticality for handling calls to 911 emergency centers. Jim also provided information on technologies used for deploying emergency telecommunications services for handling text messages, mobile, and landline calls at emergency call centers. Thanks to Ben, vice president of security for a major financial company. Ben illuminated the challenges and technologies deployed to protect enterprises from hackers. And appreciation to Keith Wise for valuable assistance with the Study Guide.

And finally, thank you to the many people I spoke with that preferred to not have their names used. I appreciate the information each of you shared. Most importantly, thank you to my husband Bob Dodd who read everything I wrote multiple times and provided common sense advice on how to improve sections to clarify important concepts.

About the Author

Photo courtesy of Annabel Z. Dodd

Annabel Z. Dodd is on the faculty at Northeastern University's School of Professional Studies, where she teaches courses on data networks in the Master's Degree Program in Informatics. In addition to her university teaching, Annabel presents seminars to organizations worldwide. Her webinar on LTE Essentials for USTelecom attracted over 900 people.

Annabel has been an adjunct professor in the Master of Science in Technology Management program at the State University of New York at Stony Brook, where she taught in a joint program with The Institute of Industrial Policy Studies, Seoul, South Korea. In addition, the Fundación Innovación Bankinter selected her to participate in their Future Trends Forum in Madrid in 2004, 2005, and 2007. Formerly in marketing at New England Telephone (now Verizon Communications) and Telecommunications Manager at Dennison Manufacturing Company (now Avery Dennison), Dodd was honored by the Massachusetts Network Communications Council as Professor of the Year. *The Essential Guide to Telecommunications* has been translated into nine languages since its first edition, which was published in 1997.

Part I

Fundamentals, Data Centers, and IP PBXs

1 Computing and Enabling Technologies

In this chapter:

Capabilities discussed in this chapter are the basis of important technologies used by residential and business customers on a daily basis. They enable:

- the Internet to store vast amounts of data
- millions of people to simultaneously access the Internet
- cellular networks to handle ever-increasing amounts of traffic
- storage devices to hold massive amounts of data

High-powered computer chips are the building blocks of innovation in the twenty-first century. Their increased memory, speed, and 8-core processing capabilities along with smaller size have made possible innovative technologies affecting industry, personal productivity, and connectivity. Decreases in chip sizes enable people to carry computers in the form of smartphones in their pockets. Computing power, previously only available in personal computers and large centralized computer servers, is now used in smartphones and tablet computers.

For the most part, these electronics and networks have been available for most of the twenty-first century. However, innovations in the speed, capacity, and amount of memory on computer chips have resulted in higher capacity fiber-optic networks and denser storage systems.

High-capacity virtualized servers that store multiple operating systems and applications in a single device in less space, as well as high-capacity broadband networks, are the basis of highly reliable cloud computing. Moreover, fiber networks link cloud data centers together so that if one data center fails, another one automatically takes over.

In an effort to more flexibly store applications, cloud companies and large enterprises use *containers*. Like virtual servers, containers don't require that each application be held in its own dedicated physical server. Containers break applications into multiple parts so that each part can be modified without changing an entire application. With virtualized servers, entire applications need to be rewritten for every change. The software running containers is usually open source, free software. The hardware is often lower-cost commodity servers.

The growth in capacity and reduced price of broadband networks have made access to images, music, television series, and movies available to millions of people via broadband networks powered by innovations in computer chips, multiplexing, and compression. The images and videos are stored and accessed from high-capacity computers. The computers, often located in the cloud, hold movies and TV shows offered by services such as Netflix and Hulu.

Computing and enabling technologies have spurred the increased use of cloud computing and streaming movies. Cloud computing has now evolved to a point where many companies and individuals use it, but there are nevertheless challenges for large organizations that use cloud computing. IT staff need skills suited to monitoring and transmitting applications to the cloud and making sure that applications previously accessed from onsite data centers are compatible with each cloud provider's infrastructure.

Another enhancement enabled by increased speed and memory in chips is *machine learning*. Machine learning is the ability of chips with powerful memories to "recognize" patterns of images and changes in order to "learn" how to perform particular tasks. For example, machines can learn to recognize clues in medical images to diagnose medical conditions that previously required skilled physicians to analyze.

For the most part, the technologies and protocols discussed here are not new. Rather, they are more powerful and many of them have been refined to support additional applications. This is the case with the growing use and availability of cloud computing and fiber-optic networks by all segments of developed nations.

FIBER-OPTIC AND COPPER CABLING ....

The three technologies discussed in this section—fiber-optic cabling, multi-core processors, and memory—are the building blocks of modern networks. They enable networks to carry more information faster. Decreasing memory costs have led to affordable personal computers and the ability to store vast amounts of information, accessible via fiber-optic–based networks at lower costs.

Fiber-Optic Cabling: Underpinning High-Speed Networks

Without fiber-optic cabling, modern high-speed data networks would not be possible. Fiber-optic cabling is the glue connecting all high-speed networks to the cloud, and to other continents. Fiber networks are located between cities; undersea in oceans; within cities; and on university, business, and hospital campuses. Sophisticated equipment and computer chips are enabling fiber networks to keep up with the growing demand for capacity on broadband networks.

Demand for bandwidth is a result of cloud computing, subscribers streaming movies and television shows, online gamers, real-time coverage of live sporting events, and international news. People expect instant access to breaking news, social networks such as Facebook, QQ, and Weibo, and entertainment. (Chinese company Tencent owns QQ and a different Chinese company, Sina owns Weibo.) Fiber-optic networks support broadband connections to the Internet, which enable streaming TV services such as Netflix and Amazon; streaming music providers including Apple Music, Pandora, and Spotify; and social networks. The world has gotten smaller and businesses and people expect to be able to remain connected wherever and whenever they want.

Because of dropping prices of installation and lower maintenance costs, network providers including AT&T, Verizon, and CenturyLink are increasingly connecting fiber-optic networks to apartment buildings and even individual homes. Traffic on fiber-optic cabling is not limited to these networks. It is also growing in cellular networks that use fiber-optic cabling to carry data- and video-heavy smartphone traffic between antennas and mobile providers' data centers in mobile networks. Fiber networks also carry traffic from cellular networks to the Internet.

Cloud computing is the main reason for the growing demand for capacity on fiber networks. Most students, residential customers, corporations and governments use cloud computing to access some or all of their applications. Fiber-optic networks connect much of the world to applications located in the cloud. Demand for capacity on networks is expected to continue growing as more organizations, developing countries, individuals, and governments use cloud-based applications and stream movies and television shows.

In an interview, Geoff Bennett, Director of Solutions and Technology at the fiber-optic networking company Infinera, stated:

> *Nothing else has the transmission capacity of optical fiber, and that's why fiber powers the Internet. There is no technology on the horizon that could replace it.*

Information Content Providers: Heavy Users of Fiber

Google, Amazon, Microsoft, and Facebook are information content providers. Information content providers generate enormous amounts of traffic over fiber-optic networks in locations worldwide. Information content providers build and operate massive data centers connected to high-bandwidth fiber-optic networks that carry streams of data to and from millions of subscribers. The data centers are connected to other information content providers' data centers as well as to the Internet. Facebook operates its data centers in much of the world. Two of its data centers are located in Luleå, a city on the northern coast of Sweden. The data centers in Luleå are linked to each other by fiber-optic networks as well as to a network of Facebook data centers throughout Europe. Infinera built these fiber-optic networks for Facebook. Other fiber-optic providers in addition to Infinera are Ciena, Huawei, and Nokia.

Nearness to customers to minimize delays and assure the availability of power are two of the criteria information providers consider when selecting locations for their data centers. To get closer to subscribers and large business clients, Internet content providers locate data centers in large cities as well as locations near plentiful electricity sources such as in Luleå, Sweden. Sweden offers the advantage of requiring less power for cooling because of its cold climate. Google has bought many buildings in New York City and other major cities so that it can be closer to its many customers in these cities. This minimizes delays in responses to users that access Google.

Fiber links to duplicate data centers enable cloud-based data centers to function even if one of their centers is disabled due to an equipment or software malfunction or a natural disaster such as a hurricane. Fiber links importantly enable cloud-based data centers to continuously back up their entire sites in real time to ensure that customer data is not lost during a disaster or malfunctions. The duplicate data center may be hundreds of miles away or nearby within the same city.

Each data center that is linked to another data center and to subscribers has redundant fiber cabling connected to their facilities so that if one group of fiber cables is damaged or cut, the other is still intact. For example, one bundle of fibers may be located on the eastern side of their building and another on the western side. Duplicate power sources are also installed at these data centers.

Splitting Capacity of Individual Fiber Strands into Wavelengths

Dense wavelength division multiplexers (DWDMs) add capacity to individual strands of fibers connected to fiber strands by dividing each fiber into numerous channels called *wavelengths*. See Figure 1-1 below. Dense wave division multiplexers divide the fiber into wavelengths using frequency division multiplexing, where each stream of light uses a different frequency within the fiber strand. In some networks, each wavelength is capable of transmitting a 100Gb stream of light pulses.

The distance between the highest parts of each wavelength equate to the wavelength sizes. Wavelengths are so small that they are measured in *nanometers*. A nanometer equals one billionth of a meter. A nanometer-sized object is not visible to the human eye. A fiber-optic cable is smaller than a strand of hair or thinner than a sheet of paper.

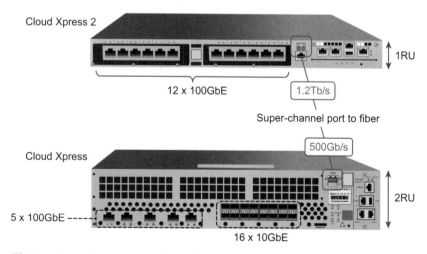

Figure 1-1   Representation of dense wavelength division multiplexers used for connections between data centers. (Based on image courtesy of Infinera)

The Cloud Xpress is a first generation 500Gbps Dense Wavelength Division Multiplexer that supports an aggregate speed of 500Gbps. The newer second generation Cloud Xpress 2 is smaller and faster. Its capacity is 1.2 terabits per second and requires only one RU (rack unit), about 1.75 inches (44.45 millimeters) high in a 19-inch wide computer rack. The older Cloud Xpress takes up 2RU, essentially two vertical shelf units.

Lasers—Lighting Fiber

Lasers (Light amplification by stimulated emission of radiation) are the source of light on long-distance fiber networks and on fiber networks within cities. A laser turns light pulses on and off over fiber cables. Most outside fiber-optic cabling is connected to lasers for generating their light pulses. Due to improvements in manufacturing and chips, lasers are so small that they are now available as computer chips integrated into line cards connected to fiber-optic cables.

Super Channels—For Even More Capacity

Super channels are an advanced form of dense wavelength division multiplexing. Super channels essentially mix multiple gigabit per second wavelengths together to achieve higher gigabit or terabit speeds on a single circuit card. In some systems, one wavelength can transmit at 100Giga bits per second. For example, a fiber used for sending can combine five 100Gbps wavelengths to transmit at 500Gbps. The fiber sending in the other direction can transmit at 500Gbps, equaling a total of a terabit of capacity. Thus, super channels enable fiber to reach terabits (1,000 gigabits) of capacity.

Coherent fiber optics is one of the technologies that enable high bandwidth transmissions above 40Gbps. Coherent fiber transmissions achieve high bandwidth by the use of error correction bits in transmitted light pulses, and in lasers located in receivers. At the receiving end, receivers are equipped with lasers tuned to the exact same frequency and shape as the transmitted wavelength. Each wavelength has an associated laser in the receiver in fiber-optic networks that optical network providers build.

Receivers use sophisticated algorithms to correct for impairments in the signals sent from lasers associated with each wavelength. Coherent transmission is an important enabler of high bandwidth transmission in long-haul networks because increasing the speed of transmissions causes additional impairments. Long-haul networks are those connecting cities, and countries. Undersea fiber-optic cables that connect continents to each other are also examples of long-haul networks.

Half Duplex: Sending and Receiving on Separate Cables

Fiber-optic cables are *half duplex*. Each fiber cable is capable of sending in one direction only. Consequently, a separate fiber strand is needed for sending and a different fiber for transmitting back in the other direction. In other words, each strand of fiber can send signals in one direction only.

In contrast, copper cabling is *full duplex*. Within buildings a single copper cable is connected to each computer and printer. This single cable is used both to send and receive signals. Moreover, cable modems and routers within people's homes require just one copper cable to both send and receive e-mail messages and files to and from the Internet. See Table 1-1 for examples of half vs. full duplex.

Table 1-1   Half Duplex vs. Full Duplex

Half and Full Duplex	Type of Cabling for Each	Where Deployed
Half duplex	Separate cables for sending and receiving	Locations with fiber or copper cabling
Examples of half duplex	Fiber networks	Fiber optic cabling in large data centers
		Fiber optic cabling between floors in many apartment buildings and businesses
		Fiber optic networks between and within cities
Full duplex	Send and receive on same	Locations with copper cabling
Examples of full duplex	Copper cabling-based networks	Cables to homes, desktop computers, and printers

Amplifiers vs. Regenerators

Although signals on fiber-optic cabling travel longer distances than those on copper cabling, the signals do fade; they weaken over long distances. In addition to fading, imperfections in the form of noise impedes the signals over distances. See Table 1-2 for a comparison between amplifiers and regenerators. Thus, equipment must be added to fiber-optic networks both to boost the signals when they fade and eliminate the noise. Amplifiers and regenerators do these tasks.

Table 1-2 Amplifiers vs. Regenerators

	Distance when Needed	Function	Cost Comparison
Amplifier	80 to 120 kilometers (49 to 74.4 miles)	Boosts optical amplitude of all wavelengths when they fade	Lower cost
Regenerator	3,000 to 4,000 kilometers (1,860 to 2,480 miles)	Removes noise and other impairments. Regenerates each wavelength separately	More costly than amplification

Amplifiers are needed in fiber-optic networks every 80 to 120 kilometers (49 to 74.4 miles). They boost the signals' amplitude on all the wavelengths of an entire fiber in one operation. Amplitude refers to the height of a signal at the highest point of the wavelength. Amplitude is similar to a unit of loudness or strength.

Regenerators are needed less frequently than amplifiers, about every 3,000 to 4,000 kilometers (1,860 to 2,480 miles). Regeneration is more costly than amplification because each wavelength must be regenerated individually rather than regenerating the entire fiber and all the wavelengths in one operation.

Fiber-Optic Cabling—No Electromagnetic Interference, Smaller and Lighter than Copper

In contrast to copper cabling, fiber-optic networks have more capacity and they can carry the signals longer distances without amplification. In addition, fiber-optic networks are less costly to maintain once they are installed. This is because bits are carried on non-electrical light pulses. These pulses are analogous to the light emitted by quickly turning a flashlight on and off. Because the pulses are non-electrical, there is no resistance from electromagnetic interference (EMI).

Resistance associated with EMI in networks made up of copper cabling causes fading over relatively short distances of about 2 miles. This is analogous to water pressure from a hose weakening over short distances. Consequently, amplifiers are needed every mile and a half to 2 miles to boost electrical signals carried on copper-based networks. *The absence of resistance from electrical interference is fiber's main advantage over copper cabling.* Moreover, once installed, amplifiers must periodically be replaced and maintained.

Because data on fiber-optic cabling is carried as non-electric pulses of light, amplification is only needed after 80 to 120 kilometers (49 to 74.4 miles). This means that in many short fiber runs to homes or apartment buildings, no amplification is needed. In long-haul networks, those between cities, states, and countries, fewer amplifiers are required to boost optical signals after they have faded than are required in copper networks.

The non-electric light pulses on fiber-optical cabling can travel about 400 kilometers, or 248 miles, before having to be regenerated. This is another savings in labor because fewer technicians are needed to install regenerators. This lowers the cost for network providers who lay miles of fiber between cities, within cities, and under the ocean. In short fiber runs, regeneration is not needed if the cable runs are less than 4,000 kilometers.

Lighter and Smaller than Copper Cabling

In addition to the absence of electrical interference, fiber-optic cabling is lighter and smaller than copper cabling. Because of its size, it takes up less space than copper cabling in conduits (hollow pipes in which cables are run) that are located under streets. This is important in large cities where conduits are often stuffed and at capacity with older copper cabling. A university in downtown Boston wanted to connect two buildings by running fiber-optic cabling under a public street between its buildings. This was a problem because there was no space left in the existing underground conduit that was already filled with copper cabling. The university needed to get permission from the city's authorities to dig up the street to add a new conduit, and they had to pay for digging up the street in addition to the cost to lay a new conduit for the fiber-optic cabling between their two buildings.

If the conduit had fiber cabling, it's likely that space would have been available because of fiber's smaller diameter.

More Capacity than Copper Cabling

A significant advantage of fiber-optic cabling is its enormous capacity compared to copper cabling and mobile services. Light signals on optical cabling pulse on and off at such high data rates that they are able to handle vastly greater amounts of information than any other media and the capacity can be multiplexed into wavelengths. See Table 1-3 for a comparison of copper and fiber optic cabling.

In older networks, once high-quality fiber is installed in trenches, newer lasers and dense wavelength division multiplexing can be added to increase its capacity to handle the growing amounts of traffic, including high-definition video transmitted along its routes.

Dark Fiber

Because of the high cost of laying fiber underground and digging trenches, organizations that build new fiber optic networks often lay more fiber than they need when they build the original network. They don't add fiber multiplexers or lasers needed to "light" the fiber on the extra fiber pairs. This fiber that does not have multiplexers or lasers connected to it is referred to as *dark fiber.* It has not been "lit" with equipment such as lasers needed to operate the fiber. See Figure 1-2 for an example of dark fiber.

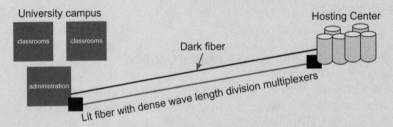

Figure 1-2   A fiber-optic cable with DWDMs and dark fiber.

For example, a university in the Northeastern United States installed two fiber runs to a hosting center where many of their computer servers were located. They added dense wavelength division multiplexing (DWDM) to one fiber run, and left the second one as an alternate route to their hosting center, to be used in the event of a cable cut in the main fiber pairs.

Table 1-3   Summary of Fiber-Optical Cabling Compared to Copper Cabling

Characteristic	Fiber-Optical Cabling	Copper Cabling
Diameter	Thin as a strand of hair	Larger diameter—Needs more space in conduits
Capacity	Higher—Non-electrical pulses so no electromagnetic interference	Lower—Electromagnetic interference causes resistance to signals
Weight	Light	Heavier
Distance before amplification needed	80 to 120 kilometers (49 to 74.4 miles)	2.4 to 3.2 kilometers (1½ to 2 miles)
Installation costs	Higher labor cost	Lower—Less skill required
Maintenance costs	Lower—Less equipment needed to boost signals	Higher—More equipment to maintain
Security from eavesdropping	High—Need to physically break cable; easy to detect	Low—Can attach a monitor without cutting cable
Half duplex or full duplex	Half duplex—A separate fiber for sending and receiving	Full duplex—Can send and receive on same cable

Infinera: A Vertically Integrated Fiber-Optic Manufacturer

Infinera, headquartered in Sunnyvale, California was founded in 2000 and was initially funded by venture capital companies. In 2007, the company raised an additional $300 million in an initial public offering. During the years between 2000 and 2005 when Infinera developed their fiber-optic technology, there was a glut of fiber-optic capacity. However, by the time they first began shipping their products in 2005, the glut was ending.

Infinera's goal in designing their products was to enable network providers to bring up denser fiber-optic capacity in a single operation. They have a fully vertical operation where they manufacture and sell all the components needed for an optical network. Infinera designs and manufactures all of their own components including chips, dense wavelength division multiplexing, receivers, circuit boards, and fiber-optic cabling.

Their networks were designed from the beginning so that a large number of wavelengths could be brought up and put into service in a single operation by network providers.

When Infinera started shipping their products in 2005, all of their fiber-optic equipment was made for long-haul networks connecting cities, countries, and continents. In 2015 they purchased Transmode, a company that specialized in metro wavelength division multiplexing within cities. Transmode additionally provided fiber networks to mobile carriers for connections between their towers and data centers and between mobile networks and the Internet.

Infinera is able to achieve the density they offer because of the photonic chips they manufacture. Photonic chips send data within the chip via light pulses because electrical impulses in non-photonic chips have electrical magnetic interference that slows down signals. Another innovation is that their chips are built using indium phosphide instead of silicon, which Infinera feels provides the exacting transmissions required in their high-speed optical components. All the processing in their chips is done using multicore, parallel mode processors.

Single-Mode vs. Multi-Mode Fiber

There are two main types of fiber: single-mode and multi-mode. Single-mode fiber is smaller, is more expensive, and supports higher speeds than multi-mode fiber. Measuring approximately the same diameter as a strand of human hair, it is used mainly in carrier networks and in undersea cabling.

The fact that single-mode fiber carries light pulses faster than multi-mode fiber can be explained by a geometric rule: A straight line is the shortest distance between two points. Light travels faster in a straight line than if it zigzags along a path, which is precisely what happens to light waves if they reflect, or "bounce," off the inner wall of the fiber strand as they travel. These zigzag paths also cause the signals to attenuate, lose power, and fade over shorter distances. The narrow core results in a narrower angle of acceptance. The small angle of acceptance of single-mode fiber keeps the light signal from bouncing across the diameter of the fiber's core. Thus, the straighter light signal travels faster and has less attenuation than if it had a bouncier ride through the core.

When the light pulses travel in narrower paths, fewer amplifiers are needed to boost the signal. Single-mode fiber can be run for 49 to 74 miles without amplification (boosting). In contrast, signals on copper cabling need to be amplified after approximately 1.5 miles. For this reason, telephone companies originally used fiber for outside plant cabling with cable runs longer than 1.2 miles. However, the demand for higher capacity and the lower maintenance costs have resulted in carriers running increasing amounts of fiber cabling directly to homes and buildings.

The main factor in the increased expense of single-mode fiber is the higher cost to manufacture more exact connectors for patch panels and other devices. The core is so small that connections and splices require much more precision than does multi-mode fiber. If the connections on single-mode fiber do not match cores exactly, the light will not be transmitted from one fiber to another. It will leak or disperse out the end of the fiber core at the splice.

Multi-mode fiber has a wider core than single-mode fiber. The wider core means that signals can only travel a short distance before they require amplification. In addition, fewer channels can be carried per fiber pair when it is multiplexed because the signals disperse, spreading more across the fiber core. Multi-mode fiber is used mainly for LAN backbones between campus buildings and between floors of buildings.

Another factor in the expense of installing fiber cabling systems is the cost of connector standardization. Three of the main connector types are the Straight Tip (ST), the MT-RJ, and the Little Connector (LC). Each type of connector requires specialized tools for installation, and both factory- and field-testing. Technicians perform field-testing prior to installation to ensure that the connectors meet factory specifications. It's critical that connectors match up exactly to the fiber so that signals don't leak. If the connectors don't exactly match up to the fiber, signal loss impairs the fiber's performance.

Fiber-Optic Cabling in Commercial Organizations

Because fiber is non-electric, it can be run in areas without regard to interference from electrical equipment. However, due to its higher installation cost, fiber within buildings is used most often in high-traffic areas. These include:

- Within data centers
- Between buildings on organizations' campuses
- Between switches in *backbone* networks. A backbone connects switches to each other and to data centers. Backbone networks are not connected to individual computers—only to servers and switches.

Fiber-optic cabling fiber itself requires more care in handling and installation than copper. For example, it is less flexible than copper and cannot be bent around tight corners. However, given its greater capacity and cost savings in ongoing maintenance, developers install fiber between floors in large office buildings and between buildings in office complexes. See Figure 1-3 for an example of fiber-optic cabling in enterprises. The fiber-optic cabling within commercial organizations is for the most part multi-mode rather than single-mode because of multi-mode's less stringent installation requirements. Moreover, multi-mode capacity is adequate for commercial buildings' bandwidth requirements.

Figure 1-3 Examples of fiber-optic cabling used in telephone company networks. (Photo by Annabel Z. Dodd)

There are two reasons why fiber is typically more expensive than copper to install:

- The electronics (multiplexers and lasers) to convert electrical signals to optical signals, and vice versa, are costly.

- Specialized technicians, paid at higher levels, are required to work with and test fiber cabling.

The multiplexers and interfaces between fiber-optic cabling and copper cabling in the customer's facility require local power. This adds a point of vulnerability in the event of a power outage.

Fiber-optic cable is made of ultra-pure strands of glass. The narrower the core that carries the signals, the faster and farther a light signal can travel without errors or the need for repeaters. The cladding surrounding the core keeps the light contained to prevent the light signal from dispersing, that is, spreading over time, with wavelengths reaching their destination at different times. Finally, there is a coating that protects the fiber from environmental hazards such as rain, dust, scratches, and snow.

An important benefit of fiber-optic cabling is that eavesdropping is more difficult because the strands have to be physically broken and listening devices spliced into the break. A *splice* is a connection between cables. Splices in fiber-optic cables are easily detected.

Copper Cabling in Enterprises

Improvements in copper cable have made it possible for unshielded, twisted-pair cabling to transmit data rates at speeds of 100Gbps in Local Area Networks (LANs). Previously, these speeds were only attainable over fiber-optic cabling. This is important because the interfaces in most computer devices are compatible with unshielded, twisted-pair (UTP) cabling, not fiber-optic cabling. Connecting this gear to fiber requires the cost and labor to install devices that change light signals to electrical signals, and vice versa. Figure 1-4 depicts copper cabling in enterprises: four pairs of wires enclosed in a sheath. Each pair consists of two strands of wire twisted together— a total of eight strands of cable, arranged by color: purple with white, orange with white, green with white, and brown with white.

Figure 1-4   Unshielded twisted-pair cabling used within enterprise buildings. (Photo by Annabel Z. Dodd)

UTP copper and fiber-optic cables are the most common media used in enterprise LANs. Because of improvements in the speeds, capacity, and distances wireless signals can be transmitted, wireless media is replacing copper cabling in some office buildings. Wireless services based on the 802.11 (Wi-Fi) protocols are discussed in Chapter 7, "Mobile and Wi-Fi Networks."

Characteristics of media have a direct bearing on the distance, speed, and accuracy at which traffic can be carried. For example, thin copper wire carries data shorter distances at lower speeds than thicker, higher-quality copper.

In corporate networks, UTP is the most prevalent medium used to link computers, printers, and servers to wiring closets on the same floor. This is referred to as the horizontal plant.

Fiber is capable of carrying vastly more traffic than copper. However, it is more expensive to install and connect to devices in LANs than UTP, and thus it is generally used in high-traffic connections between the following:

- Wiring closets

- Floors (the risers)

- Buildings on campuses

The key characteristic that makes fiber suitable for these high-traffic areas is that it's a non-electric medium. Fiber exhibits superior performance because, unlike copper, it does not transmit electric signals that act like an antenna and pick up noise and interference from nearby electrical devices.

Connecting Fiber to Copper

In enterprise networks, when fiber is connected to copper cabling at locations such as entrances to buildings, at wiring closets, or in data centers, equipment converts light pulses to electrical signals, and vice versa. This requires converters called transmitters and receivers. Transmitters also are called *light-source transducers*. If multiplexing equipment is used on the fiber, each channel of light requires its own receiver and transmitter. Transmitters in fiber-optic systems are either Light-Emitting Diodes (LEDs) or lasers. There are several reasons for this:

- LEDs cost less than lasers. They are commonly used with multi-mode fiber.

- Lasers provide more power. Thus, less regeneration (amplification) is needed over long distances.

- At the receiving end, the light detector transducers (receivers) that change light pulses into electrical signals are either positive intrinsic negatives (PINs) or avalanche photodiodes (APDs).

- LEDs and PINs are used in applications with lower bandwidth and shorter distance requirements.

Electrical Property—Disadvantage of Copper Cabling

Signals transmitted via copper react to electrical interference or "noise" on the line. Power lines, lights, and electric machinery can all inject noise into the line in the form of electric energy. This is why interference from signals such as copiers, magnetic sources, manufacturing devices, and even radio stations can introduce noise and static into telephone calls and data transmissions. One way to protect copper cabling from noise and *crosstalk* introduced by nearby wires is to twist each insulated copper wire of a two-wire pair. Noise induced into one wire of the twisted pair cancels an equal amount of noise induced in the other wire of the pair. Crosstalk occurs when electrons that carry the conversations or data along a copper pair cross over, or "leak," on to other nearby wire pairs.

Another electrical property of copper wire is resistance. Resistance causes signals to weaken as they are transmitted. This is referred to as attenuation. Attenuation is the reason signals on copper cable in the outside network need to be boosted on cable runs of more than approximately 1.5 miles. Thus, the dual inherent impairments of interference and resistance are the key factors that limit copper's performance. See Table 1-3 for the differences between copper and fiber cabling

Copper Cabling Standards: Higher Capacity, Exacting Installation, and Connections

Cabling standards have been created to support ever-higher speeds, carry multimedia traffic, and ensure that organizations can purchase cabling and connectors from diverse manufacturers without risk of incompatibility. Each cabling standard includes defined tests that should be performed when cables are installed to ensure that it and all of the connectors perform to their specifications.

Every new standard needs to be compatible with all lower standards. This allows applications that operated over lower-category cabling systems to operate on higher categories, as well. The biggest problems organizations face with cabling systems are that they are not always properly installed and tested to meet standards. This results in either lower-than-expected data rates or inconsistent reliability.

Each of the standards specifies not only the cable itself, but all of the connections including jacks (outlets), plugs, and cross-connects in wiring closets. Cross-connects provide outlets on each floor where cabling from individual devices is connected. The floor cabling, also referred to as the horizontal plant, is connected to the riser cabling, which is the cabling connections between floors. See Figure 1-5 for an example of copper cabling in enterprises. The riser cabling is connected in the building's main wiring closet and to other buildings within a campus.

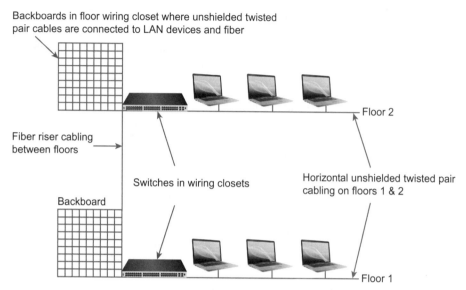

Backboards in floor wiring closet where unshielded twisted pair cables are connected to LAN devices and fiber

Floor 2

Fiber riser cabling between floors

Switches in wiring closets

Horizontal unshielded twisted pair cabling on floors 1 & 2

Backboard

Floor 1

Figure 1-5 Riser and horizontal cabling connections in a wiring closet.

Standards also specify the network interface card (NIC) in printers and computers from which a cable connects the device to the jack (outlet). The Telecommunications Industry Association (TIA) rates twisted-pair cabling and connection components used inside buildings.

Unshielded Twisted-Pair Copper Cabling Standards

Category 3 UTP cabling—often referred to as simply "CAT 3"—is rated as suitable for voice transmission, but it is only suited for older type phone systems. It is rarely used in new installations. Categories 5, 5e, 6, and 6a, are the commonly deployed cabling system standards for UTP. Organizations often use Category 6a to support 10Gbps speeds in their data centers, and Category 6 for the rest of their facility. New cabling infrastructure is installed using categories 7 or 7a. Moreover, this same cabling plant is generally used for both voice and data. Category 7 and 7a cabling are based on a standard ratified by the International Organization for Standardization (ISO). The following is a synopsis of the major UTP categories. Category 8 was approved by the Telecommunications Industry Association (TIA) in May 2017.

- **Category 5** *Supports speeds of up to 100Mbps for 100 meters (328 feet) over UTP.* It was the first ratified standard for megabit Ethernet transmissions. It consists of four pairs of eight unshielded copper wires. Category 5 has been superseded by Category 5e.

- **Category 5e** *Supports 1Gbps speeds at distances of 100 meters (328 feet).* Higher speeds are attainable because the cabling and connectors are manufactured to higher standards. There are more twists per inch in the cabling than that specified for Category 5.

- **Category 6** *Supports 1Gbps speeds at 100 meters (328 feet).* At shorter distances, it handles 10Gbps speeds. A higher twist rate, heavier cabling, and a metallic screen around the entire cable protect it from ambient noise. Insulation material (usually plastic strips) is placed between each of the four pairs to reduce crosstalk between the wires.

- **Category 6a (augmented)** *Supports 10Gbps Ethernet transmissions of up to 55 meters (180 feet).* This is possible because the stricter standards result in less cross talk between adjacent cables. Lower speeds are supported for up to 100 meters (330 feet).

- **Category 7** *Supports 10Gbps speeds up to 100 meters (330 feet).* High performance at longer distances is possible because there is foil shielding around each pair of wires and an overall metal foil shield around the entire cable. It must be installed with different components and connectors from those for Categories 5 through 6a to accommodate this shielding. It can also be installed with the same type of connectors specified in earlier standards; however, it will not transmit 10Gbps traffic as far as the 100 meters (330 feet) achieved with the appropriate connectors.

- **Category 7a** *Supports 40Gbps speeds up to 50 meters and 100Gbps up to 15 meters.* It is similar to Category 7. It requires shielded twisted-pair cabling with shielding around the entire cable. It is widely available and is often used in new cabling installations. The standards for connections are more exacting than those in Category 7. The shielding in Category 7a guard against electromagnetic interference (EMI). Shielding must be extended to all connections within the cabling system to attain gigabit speeds. This requires a special insert into every RJ45 jack in the building. RJ45 jacks are outlets used to plug cables into. The designation RJ stands for registered jack.

- **Category 8** *Supports 25Gbps and 40Gbps speeds up to 30 meters.* The shielding and connectors are not compatible with Categories 7 and 7A. The TIA approved Category 8 cabling in 2017. Category 8 cabling is capable of supporting high-bandwidth transmissions between servers in data centers because of its stringent shielding and connector requirements. This is less costly than using fiber-optic cabling. The standard specifies both F/FTP (foil-shielded twisted-pair cabling) where the entire bundle of four pairs of cable is surrounded with one shield. The other option is foil-shielded twisted pairs (S/FTP) where each of the four pairs is shielded individually.

CHIPS—BUILDING BLOCKS OF THE DIGITAL AGE....

Chips, short for microchips, are integrated processors and memory found in computers, cellular devices, electronic toys, wristwatches, thermostats, airplanes, cars, trucks, and automated devices people and machines interact with daily. Multi-core chips have up to eight cores, each of which is able to process information simultaneously, in real time. Chips are the basis of the digital age.

Faster multi-core processors are an integral part of the high-speed electronics used on fiber-optic, Wi-Fi, and cellular networks. They enable these networks to process multiple streams of signals simultaneously. They are also at the core of network switches, continually transmitting increasing amounts of data at ever-higher speeds. Additionally, these processors facilitate the capability of personal computers, set-top boxes, and smartphones to handle graphics and video transmitted via the Internet.

Chips now incorporate up to 64-bit processing (the ability to process data in chunks of 64 bits), which means that they process data faster. Chips are now able to process *petabytes* and *exabytes* of information. One petabyte equals 1,000,000,000,000,000 bytes or 1,000,000,000 gigabytes. An exabyte equals 1,000,000,000,000,000,000 bytes. Moreover, they are small and inexpensive, and use only small amounts of power. The size of chips is shrinking at the same time that more processors can be packed into personal computers and other electronic devices.

Low power consumption results in longer battery life in mobile devices. ARM chips are designed by semiconductor firm ARM Holdings, Plc., and are available to electronics manufacturers who pay a licensing fee plus royalties up front for each chip designed. ARM is part of SoftBank Group Corp., which is headquartered in Japan.

Other chip makers include Broadcom, Nvidia, Intel, Qualcomm, NXP, and Micron. Figure 1-6 is an example of a Nvidia X-1 chip. Facebook and Alphabet subsidiary Google are developing chips as well. Facebook will use its chips in servers located in their data centers.

Figure 1-6 The Nvidia Integra Xi chip is about the size of a thumbnail. It was the first chip Nvidia used for self-driving car technology development. (Image courtesy of Nvidia)

Machine Learning

Memory and processing power in chips enable machine learning and in the future will enable artificial intelligence. Although the terms are often used interchangeably, there is a difference between machine learning and artificial intelligence. Machine learning uses microchips to compare stored images to new images to detect anomalies and patterns of data. It can be thought of as computerized pattern detection in existing data and identification of similar patterns in future data. Microchips compare billions of images and phrases and words to find anomalies and to perform tasks formerly done by people.

For example, graphic processing units (GPUs) chips are able to process and store complex mathematical algorithms that represent images. Google is training its machine learning system to recognize a picture with a car in it. The machine learning system is shown a large number of pictures with a car in it. Telling the system if there is a car in the picture or not enables the computer to later recognize the visual qualities associated with cars. Machine learning is also used in facial recognition software used by police departments.

Artificial intelligence solves problems by using reasoning, logical deduction, searching, and trial and error. Artificial intelligence has the ability to imitate a human brain's functions. Although media articles claim that certain applications and cloud computing services use artificial intelligence, they are actually powered by machine learning. Artificial intelligence applications that mimic human intelligence are not currently available.

The following are examples of machine learning:

- Mass General Hospital in Boston's radiology department is planning to use Nvidia's graphical processing units on chips to analyze a library of 10 billion x-rays, CT scans, and MRI images that will be compared with new images to identify images indicating the presence of cancer and Alzheimer's.

- Medical applications analyze large amounts information in medical journals and textbooks to assist physicians in making a diagnosis.

- In the future, self-driving cars and trucks may replace all or some taxi and truck drivers because chips with image recognition will detect vehicles and pedestrians on roads as well as traffic signals and signs.

- At Amazon warehouses, automation enables robots to take products off shelves and give them to employees to package for shipping. The robots retrieve four times as many products hourly as employees.

- Speech recognition systems from Nuance recognize words based on previously learned patterns of frequencies. Nuance software for individuals and businesses is programmed to recognize spoken words. Nuance also develops specialized applications such as one used by Radiologists to write reports.

- Home digital assistants such as Amazon's Echo and Alphabet's Google Home respond to users' spoken commands based on data previously collected.

- Banks use machine learning to track and investigate anomalies in claims and transactions to find fraudulent activities.

- The military deploys robots to find and defuse unidentified explosives so that personnel are not injured.

Machine learning enabled by powerful chips already has a major impact on work and job efficiency. Machine learning will continue to affect jobs that involve repetitive tasks and those needing stored information to make decisions.

PACKETIZED DATA ....

All Internet traffic, and the vast majority of high-speed data network traffic, is sent in *packets*. And increasingly, traffic that carries residential traffic in neighborhoods is also arranged in packets. Putting data into packets is analogous to packaging it in envelopes. Packet switching was developed by Rand Corporation in 1962 for the United States Air Force and utilized in 1969 in the Advanced Research Projects Agency (ARPANET) of the Department of Defense. ARPANET was the precursor to today's Internet. The Department of Defense wanted a more reliable network with route diversity capability. Developers envisioned greater reliability with packet switching in the ARPANET, where all locations could reach one another.

Packet networks are more resilient and can better handle peak traffic periods than older networks, because diverse packets from the same message are routed via different paths, depending on both availability and congestion. In a national emergency such as the September 11, 2001 attacks in the United States on the Pentagon in Washington, DC, and the World Trade Center in New York City, the Internet, which is a packet network, still functioned when many portions of the older public voice and cellular networks were either out of service or so overwhelmed with traffic that people could not make calls.

If one route on a packet network is unavailable, traffic is rerouted onto other routes. In addition, unlike older voice networks, the Internet does not depend on a few large switches to route traffic. Rather, if one router fails, another router can route traffic in its place.

Per Packet Flexible Routing

Packet networks can handle peak congestion periods better than older types of net-works because traffic is balanced between routes. This ensures that one path is not overloaded while a different route carries only a small amount of traffic. Sending data from multiple computers on different routes uses resources efficiently because packets from multiple devices continue to be transmitted without waiting until a single "heavy user" has finished its entire transmission. Thus, if one route is congested, packets are transmitted on other routes that have more availability.

Routers in packet networks are connected to each separate route in the network. They have the ability to check congestion on each leg of the journey connected to them and send each packet to the least congested route. As shown in Figure 1-7, packets from the same message are transmitted over the different routes.

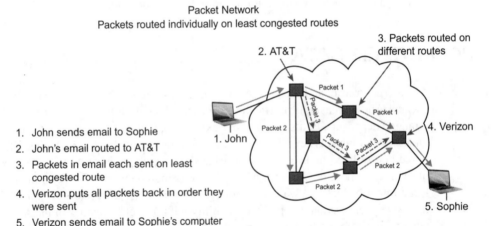

1. John sends email to Sophie
2. John's email routed to AT&T
3. Packets in email each sent on least congested route
4. Verizon puts all packets back in order they were sent
5. Verizon sends email to Sophie's computer

Figure 1-7   Three of the packets of an e-mail from John to Sophie take different paths through the network.

Packet Contents: User Data vs. Overhead

Each packet is made up of user data; data bits, digital voice or video, and specialized header information, such as addressing, billing, sender information, and error correct-ing bits. See Figure 1-8 for an example of a data packet. Error correction might indi-cate if the packet is damaged, if the receiver is ready to start receiving, or if the packet has been received. The end of the packet contains information to let the network know when the end of the packet has been reached. Header, end-of-packet data, and other signaling data are considered overhead. User data (also referred to as the payload) is the actual content of the e-mail message or voice conversation.

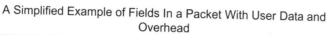

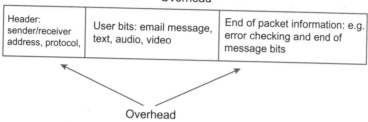

Overhead

Figure 1-8 *User data vs. overhead addressing and end-of-packet bits in packets.*

Throughput

Throughput is the amount of user information transmitted, not the actual speed of the line. The disadvantage of frequent error messages and other protocol-related bits is that overhead bits often consume large amounts of bandwidth. Throughput only measures actual user data transmitted over a fixed period of time. It does not include header bits. Protocols with many bits for error control messages and other types of overhead have lower throughput. Technologies such as Deep Packet Inspection and Traffic Shaping are used to mitigate the effect of delays associated with these protocols. (See the section "Traffic Shaping," later in this chapter, for more information.)

So, What Are Carriers and ISPs?

At one time, the term "carrier" referred to local telephone companies, such as Verizon Communications, that carried voice and data traffic for consumers and commercial organizations. Now, all companies that provide outside cabling or mobile infrastructure and operate networks are generally referred to as carriers. These include cable television operators, cellular telephone companies, long distance providers and traditional local telephone companies. Cable TV operators, mobile carriers, and traditional local telephone companies transmit voice, data, and television signals as well as providing connections to the Internet. To complicate matters further, carriers are also referred to as operators and providers.

ISPs at one time provided the connections to the Internet and information services over a carrier's cabling, and sometimes provide the switching infrastructure needed to access the Internet. ISPs also provide e-mail hosting and other services over a carrier's infrastructure. In everyday usage, the terms carriers and ISPs are used for all types of providers. This is due to the fact that telephone companies such as AT&T as well as traditional ISPs provide access to the Internet, e-mail services, and e-mail addresses to customers.

DEEP PACKET INSPECTION: MONITORING, PRIORITIZING, AND CENSORING TRAFFIC ....

In order to manage the networks they operate, companies and carriers need information about traffic patterns. They monitor security, congestion, and whether there is too much capacity. Enterprises, healthcare organizations, and universities monitor outgoing traffic to safeguard privacy and intellectual property such as patents, social security numbers, formulas for new drugs, and details on new technologies. An important tool in managing both enterprise and telephone and cellular company's networks is deep packet inspection.

Deep Packet Inspection (DPI) accomplishes this by analyzing the contents of packets transmitted on network operators' landline and mobile networks. DPI can examine the content in the headers of packets as well as user content. It inspects and looks for patterns in header information, such as error correction, quality of service, and end-of-message bits, and sometimes the e-mail messages themselves.

Large, modern packet networks typically carry a mix of rich media traffic, including television, movies, game, voice, and music streams, as well as data. Faster processors and more affordable memory have led to DPI switches and software that enable carriers, large universities, and enterprises to manage congestion in real time as well as offer new services on these diverse mobile and landline networks.

Depending on how it's configured, DPI equipment can monitor the header only or the header plus the user data (payload) of e-mail and instant messages. Capturing the payload of a message is referred to as *data capture*. Data capture can be used to store messages for later scrutiny or to scan messages in real time. Either function requires high-speed processors and massive storage archives.

Deep packet inspection is one tool that organizations, telephone companies, and governments use to manage traffic in the following scenarios:

- On a specific carrier's Internet networks
- Between residential customers and their carriers
- On mobile networks
- Between enterprise locations
- On enterprise links to the Internet
- Within the internal networks of an enterprise

In addition to the above functions, deep packet inspection is used to censor messages critical of governments.

DPI in Organizations: Protecting Confidential Information

Organizations use Deep Packet Inspection to block access to specific non-business-associated web locations such as Facebook (the social network site) to cut down on unnecessary traffic on their networks and increase employee productivity. Importantly, they also use Deep Packet Inspection to protect their networks against hackers.

Private organizations use DPI to ensure that intellectual property is not leaked. For example, it may monitor outgoing traffic for keywords. Healthcare and educational institutions that collect private information such as social security numbers or student information monitor outgoing traffic to ensure privacy of patients and students, to be in compliance with privacy regulations.

Universities, for example, have applications with DPI capabilities enabling them to block outgoing e-mail containing students' social security numbers and student identification numbers from all computers except those few computers in, for example, human resources or registrars' computers that need to collect the information.

Moreover, because DPI software can detect packet content as well as header bits, it is one way to recognize malware hidden within for example graphics in PDF documents.

Governments Monitor: Terrorism, Web Access, and Unfavorable Comments

Governments often request that their countries' wireless and wireline telephone companies monitor and/or censor e-mail messages that they might consider harmful. DPI can be used, for example, to track terrorists or people critical of the government. They may also request that telephone companies block access to particular web sites. Governments additionally request that telephone and cellular companies monitor networks for terrorism suspects and other criminal acts such as disseminating child pornography.

Governments do this to block access to web sites they consider detrimental to their goals. For example, at one time the Chinese government blocked access to certain web sites in the United States including Google. In August 2016, Turkey blocked access to Facebook, PayPal, YouTube, and Twitter, in response to a failed military coup. ·

However, some citizens figure out ways to circumvent efforts to block them from reaching particular web sites. One method they use is to create a VPN (virtual private network) to directly access a web site.

Carriers, Networks: Categorization and Billing

DPI is an application that can potentially be used by carriers to discriminate against competitors' traffic. For example, using DPI, a carrier can slow down or block traffic generated by competitors' services. See Chapter 6, "The Internet," for information on network neutrality. Network neutrality refers to carriers treating their own and competitors' traffic in an equal manner.

DPI further enables telephone companies to categorize traffic in real time to prioritize particular applications or traffic from their own subscribers. T-Mobile and Sprint both announced plans to allow cellular subscribers unlimited video streaming.

DPI systems have the capability to exchange information with a carrier's billing system to support specialized offerings for data plans covering e-mail, songs, games, video, and web browsing. A carrier might offer plans in which customers are allowed to use 3Gb of data for a fixed price, with metered pricing kicking in on anything over 3Gb.

Metered pricing is a billing practice in which customers are charged by usage, rather than a flat rate, for unlimited or predetermined amounts of minutes or data bits. In some broadband networks, carriers *throttle* certain customers' transmission if they use more bandwidth than the carrier has allotted or if there is congestion. This has happened in broadband and cellular networks even with customers who are on unlimited usage plans.

For example, carriers have slowed down subscribers' traffic if they are considered "bandwidth hogs." In particular, these subscribers might watch 10 hours of video a day and be among the top users of bandwidth capacity in a carrier's network. Carriers want to ensure that a few users don't cause undue congestion for other subscribers.

Alerts to Customers with High Usage

A customer's cellular carrier sent the subscriber text alerts notifying her that her voice usage exceeded her plan's number of minutes. This happened during a medical crisis when her husband was hospitalized and many family members and friends called asking for updates on the patient's condition.

The customer was charged $60 extra for the additional calls. DPI lets carriers track subscribers' usage. Computers in their data centers are programmed to automatically send text messages notifying customers when they're near and over their plans' data and voice usage.

Traffic Shaping: Prioritizing Traffic

Deep Packet Inspection can provide information on network conditions because of its capability to see more fields in packets than only the "send to" address. Discerning only a packet's address is analogous to looking at the address of an envelope. DPI provides the capability to determine which application the packet is using by examining patterns within packets. It can distinguish Voice over Internet Protocol (VoIP) traffic from data, gaming, and video traffic. Carriers use traffic shaping to prioritize particular types of traffic.

Giving certain types of traffic priority over other types is referred to as *traffic shaping*. Traffic shaping can be used to prioritize and deny access to the network by types of traffic, e.g. music vs. data or video, and traffic from particular organizations. Traffic from healthcare providers or companies that pay extra fees might be given higher priorities than other traffic.

DPI software develops a database of patterns, also referred to as *signatures*. Each signature or pattern is associated with a particular application such as peer-to-peer music sharing or protocols such as VoIP. It can also be associated with traffic from certain hackers or even terrorists attempting to launch malicious attacks with a goal of disrupting Internet or government sites. The DPI software matches its own database of patterns found in packets to those associated with particular applications, and network attacks.

DPI software can be installed in stand-alone switches connected to an ISP or carrier's network or as part of routers or firewalls. Routers are used to connect traffic to the Internet as well as to select routes to other networks. *Firewalls* are hardware or software that is designed to protect networks from hackers by looking for and blocking unusual header information and known viruses and to detect outgoing messages with confidential and private information.

DPI vs. Stateful Inspection

Stateful inspection refers to the ability to look at packets in real time as they are transmitted. Both DPI and Stateful Inspection examine packet headers in real time. However, only DPI has the ability to look at both the actual data bits users send and receive. Because it only examines the headers, Stateful Inspection is faster than DPI.

Both Stateful Inspection and DPI are used to screen out malicious packets as they enter networks. However, DPI is slower because it looks at both the header and content in packets. Because it looks at both the data content and the header data, DPI is better at catching known malicious code.

Stateful inspection is better suited to screening for packet storms caused by denial of service attacks, when hackers try to overwhelm a network by sending it millions of packets per second. Because of their different capabilities, many companies use both DPI and Stateful Inspection.

COMPRESSION ....

Compression is a technology that reduces the size of video, data, image, and voice files so that they take up less space in networks and on hard drives in computers. Compression has the same effect as a trash compactor that reduces the amount of space trash consumes. Compression shrinks the size of files without materially changing images or text. The benefit of compression is that it dramatically decreases the amount of network capacity (bandwidth) needed to transmit high definition TV, music, and movies.

Compression additionally facilitates the ability of companies to store video files, and large databases can use less disc space on computer storage systems. The ability to store more information using less computer capacity has led to companies, governments, social networks, and marketing organizations storing petabytes of data.

Additionally, compression has drastically changed the entertainment business, sports viewing, online games, and has led to the formation of new business models including streaming media companies, specialty set-top boxes such as Apple TV and Roku, and video productions of online video ads.

Compression increases throughput, the amount of user data or video transmitted, without changing the actual bandwidth (capacity) of the line. In other words, it takes fewer bits to transmit a movie, but the bandwidth of the network is the same. A given amount of bandwidth is able to transmit more user information, TV, audio, and video, with fewer bits.

At the receiving end compressed files are de-compressed, re-created, in the exact images as before they were transmitted or at a slightly lower quality. Text is re-created exactly as it was before it was compressed so that numeric information or product information is not altered. However, when it's received, compression might re-create video and voice in varying degrees of lower video resolution or voice quality with acceptable, often barely noticeable, alterations. Certain critical files such as MRI and x-ray images are decompressed without losing any quality.

There are a number of standardized compression *algorithms* (mathematical formulas used to perform operations such as compression) that enable compressed text and video to be transmitted in a format that can be easily decompressed at the receiving end. The following is a list of commonly used compression protocols:

- UHD is used for Ultra High Definition TV

- 8K UHD is a video compression standard that compresses files to 4320p *progressive* lines of *non-interlaced* vertical display. Progressive video displays odd and even lines in video at the same time. *Interlaced* displays show all the even lines and then all the odd lines.

- HDR (High Dynamic Range) has a higher range of luminosity, which results in greater color contrast and improved color accuracy. Netflix is now streaming some shows in HDR to subscribers with broadband bandwidth between 16 and 20Mbps.

- Various *MPEG* standards are used to compress and decompress audio and video. MPEG stands for Moving Picture Experts Group.

- MPEG-4 is a standard used mainly for streaming and downloading compressed video and television.

- AAC *Advanced Audio Coding* is Apple's proprietary compression used in iTunes and Apple Music. It is part of the MPEG-4 standard.

- Most Windows-based personal computers store and transmit files using *WinZip* compression. It is available for MAC computers as well. It can compress a group of files into one "package."

See Table 1-4 in the "Appendix" section at the end of this chapter for a more complete listing of compression standards.

Streaming: Listening and Viewing without Downloading

For the most part, when people watch television and movies on the Internet, the content is streamed to them. They do not own or keep copies of what they're viewing. The ability to stream high-quality music, TV shows and movies has drastically changed the music and entertainment industries. This ability is a result of advancements in compression. While some people own CDs and DVDs, ownership and rentals of DVDs and ownership of CDs have shrunk considerably due to the ease of streaming and downloading music, movies, and television shows over the Internet.

Streaming is different from downloading. Downloading requires an entire file to be downloaded before it can be viewed or played. With streaming, the user can listen to music in real time, but cannot store it for later use. Spotify, Pandora One, Google Play Music, and Apple Music each offer streaming music services. With streaming music, subscribers are able to listen to more targeted choices, often without ads, than that offered on AM and FM radio. Most music sources charge a monthly subscription fee for the ability to listen to music without hearing ads.

In addition, most free music services are streamed at a lower quality than paid streaming music services. For example, Pandora free services stream music at 64 Kbps, and Spotify's streams at 160 Kbps. Pandora's paid subscription streams at 192 Kbps and Spotify's streams at up to 320 Kbps. Apple Music has no free subscriptions, only paid ones where listeners stream music from Apple's library of 300,000 songs at 256 Kbps using AAC (Advanced Audio Coding) compression.

Because many young people have too many songs to store on their smartphones, they store their music in the cloud. In addition to gaining storage capacity, they can stream their songs wherever they are as long as they have access to the Internet. Moreover, if they lose or change devices, they can access their music from other devices.

Streaming and downloading music has caused the music industry and artists' royalties to shrink considerably. Customers now buy their music primarily from online sources such as iTunes and listen to songs on their smartphones. This has caused sales of CDs to shrink because people want to buy just a favorite song from particular artists. They often choose not to buy a CD because they may like only one or two of the songs. Illegal free music downloads are still occurring from sites such as LiveWire.com. According to Hannah Karp's March 30, 2017, article "In a First, Streaming Generated the Bulk of Annual Music Sales" in the *Wall Street Journal*, in 2016 streaming music made up 51 percent of the total music revenue in the United States. This was the first time that streaming sales accounted for the majority of music revenue compared to CDs and music downloads.

The combination of free downloads and the drastic decreases in CD sales have resulted in lower royalties to musicians. Popular singers now depend on concert sales for the majority of their income because for the most part, young people simply buy individual songs online. Or they stream music and don't own copies of all the songs to which they listen.

Compression: The Engine behind TV over the Internet

Compression used on video and multimedia streamed over the Internet has transformed how people get their entertainment. Television and movies at sites such as Hulu (a joint venture of Disney; and Walt Disney Company's ABC Television Group, with 60 percent; Comcast with 30 percent, and AT&T with 10 percent of Hulu.) and Netflix enable individuals to stream high quality movies, TV, sports events, and news from the Internet. Viewers now expect to view even high quality real-time sporting events over their broadband connections. To take advantage of these expectations, broadcasters and cable TV companies such as AT&T include broadband streaming in their product mix and strategy planning.

In another nod to this capability, new television sets have the capability to connect directly to the Web so that people can stream and watch broadband programming more easily on their high-definition, digital televisions. These changes have been made possible by advancements in compression, home Wi-Fi technology, and improved broadband connections.

Innovative Compression Algorithms—Fewer Bits, Higher-Quality Images

FLIF, GFWX, and PERSEUS are examples of compression software that compress images at higher speeds, achieve higher quality images, and require less bandwidth when compressed images are transmitted over broadband networks than older compression standards. All of the above compression methods were introduced in either 2015 or 2016.

FLIF compression, which stands for Free Lossless Image Format, shrinks the size of files dramatically. FLIF as the name states is *Lossless*. Lossless refers to the fact that files are stored at the same quality as the original image. Another feature of FLIF is that it is progressive. As images are downloaded, a preview appears so that people see a preview of the image before it is fully downloaded. Because it is lossless, FLIF is suitable for all types of images including MRIs, photographs, and art. FLIF is available without cost or royalties under GNU General Public License.

GFWX, Good, Fast Wavelet Codec, was developed by Graham Fyffe at the University of Southern California to store large amounts of video. It encodes and decodes videos faster than earlier compression standards. It can store videos in *lossy* and lossless formats. With lossy formats, bits deemed non-essential are eliminated when the video is stored. Images on DVDs are stored in lossy formats.

V-NOVA's PERSEUS compression software is based on the premise that there is a lot of spare digital processing capacity in the multiprocessing chips that process the complex mathematical algorithms that are the basis of this compression. PERSEUS compression is encoded in parallel rather than sequential, serial lines of code. The complex mathematical algorithms coded in hierarchical, parallel streams take advantage of the multiprocessing capabilities in digital devices such as set-top boxes, video games, mobile devices, computers, and storage systems where processors can simultaneously process complex mathematical algorithms encoded in parallel streams.

According to V-NOVA's co-founder Guido Meardi, the fact that compression enormously shrinks the number of bits needed to transmit data will enable mobile networks to carry vast amounts of video and rich media applications. This is particularly important in countries with older cellular networks not built to transmit bandwidth-heavy video and medical images. Compression that vastly shrinks the number of bits required for medical imaging could bring telemedicine to people in countries with predominantly older cellular networks. V-NOVA's compression is being deployed in Nepal where doctors collaborate over their older cellular network with radiologists in New York City on interpretation of MRIs and x-rays.

Compression Applications

- Streaming TV in India—FastFilmz, an Indian streaming TV provider similar to Netflix, uses PERSEUS compression to stream standard definition (SD) TV compressed down to 128 kilobits per second to customers with 2nd generation cellular service. Currently, about 70 percent of consumers in India have 2G cellular service. The 9 percent of customers in India with 3G cellular are able to receive high definition (HD) that requires only 2.5 to 3.5Mbps rather than 9Mbps. Prior to FastFilmz's use of V-NOVA's PERSEUS two thirds of people in India could not receive any streaming video because of 2G's low capacity.

- Concentration camp survivors' testimony—At the University of Southern California, GFWX compression is used to manage storage of videos compiled by the New Dimensions in Testimony project. The videos are clips of remembrances by survivors of World War II concentration camps. The U.S. Army Research Laboratory and the USC Shoah Foundation sponsored the project.

Plug-Ins for Software Upgrades and Decompression

The use of plug-ins enables compression applications to transmit upgrades to devices using their software. Plug-ins are small programs used to ease sending upgrades to devices. Plug-ins can additionally decode compressed images and files sent over networks, thus avoiding the need to install hardware at customers' sites to decompress received files such as images, videos and text.

 A *plug-in* is a small computer file that enables a computer application to work with and receive changes from its parent program. Programmers encode plug-ins at the sending and receiving ends of applications such as browsers and compression software. An example of how a plug-in is deployed is Netflix transmitting plug-in upgrades when they upgrade their software. In a similar way as Netflix, PERSEUS transmits any changes to its software via plug-ins sent to customer devices. V-NOVA and Netflix can tweak their software without requiring customers to make any changes because the changes to the plug-ins are transparent to end-user devices, e.g. set-top boxes, smartphones, computers, and cameras used for virtual reality applications.

Using Codecs to Compress and Digitize Speech

Speech, audio, and television signals are analog in their original form. Analog signals are transmitted in waves; digital signals are transmitted as on and off bits. Before they are transmitted over digital landlines or wireless networks, codecs compress (encode) analog signals and convert them to digital bits. Codecs sample speech at different amplitudes along the sound wave and convert it to a one or a zero. At the receiving end, decoders convert the ones and zeros back to analog sound or video waves.

Codecs are located in cellular handsets, telephones, high-definition TV transmitters, set-top boxes, televisions, IP telephones, and radios. Codecs also compress voice in speech recognition and voicemail systems. With compression, codecs do not have to sample every height on the sound wave to achieve high-quality sound. They might skip silence or predict the next sound, based on the previous sound. Thus, fewer bits per second are transmitted to represent the speech.

Virtual Reality—Immersive Experiences

Virtual reality (VR) is the use of specialized software and hardware to produce video that creates an immersive experience for people that play video games, and watch videos, sporting events, and movies. The goal of virtual reality is to create the illusion that people watching movies and sporting events are actually at the event rather than watching from a remote location. They are virtually experiencing it. For example, the experience of watching someone climb a mountain via VR can give the viewer a sense of the peril and freezing temperature experienced by the climber. As a result of this immersive experience, virtual reality movies that depict assaults on people or scenes of destruction caused by war or natural disasters may create empathy for people viewing these videos.

Virtual reality (VR) is a technique for capturing immersive images and videos. For example, people can see the cruise ship or resort in VR to help select a vacation venue. Images captured in virtual reality formats have far greater detail than available on traditional photos and videos. The viewing angle is also larger, and not limited to just a TV screen.

Rather, the video image appears to be all around viewers. High-quality cameras and viewing devices are needed to view, transmit, and decode 100- or 120-degree images. Special software can also be used to "stitch" a few cameras together to create wide virtual reality images. In the future, social networks might allow people to upload posts in virtual reality formats.

According to Mike Quan, Co-Founder of Boston-based Boston 360:

> *Social media has connected us. Virtual reality provides people the opportunity to experience another person's life, almost to see it through someone else's eyes. It's the ultimate telepresence.*

Head Mounted Displays for Viewing Virtual Reality Content

Viewing virtual reality content requires special headsets called *head mounted displays* (referred to as HMD or goggles) with high-powered lenses and controls that enable users to focus in on parts of the video and to tilt the video. Additionally, a virtual reality app (small application) must be downloaded to their smart phone to enable virtual reality formats. The app in combination with a head mounted display enables people to watch high definition videos in a virtual reality format.

Depending on the headset, users can control how they see the video with a physical remote or their hands. For example, moving their hands or their phone in a certain direction enables them to look at the video sideways. The virtual reality software on their smartphone or PC combined with the headset provides an immersive experience so that users feel as though they are actually within the movie. VR headsets are commonly connected to PCs so that users can play video games on their computers in a virtual reality format.

Compression software, multifunction graphical processing chips, increases in memory capacity, and financial backing from companies that see potential profits from virtual reality all enable virtual reality development. For example, graphical processing chips process large chunks of video, and powerful compression software means fewer bits need to be transmitted to create virtual reality images. Samsung, Facebook's Oculus Rift, Sony, Dell, Leap Motion, and Google manufacture virtual reality headsets. See Figure 1-9 for an Oculus Headset.

Figure 1-9   A VR headset. (Photo by cheskyw/123RF)

Open Source software developer Unity provides a 3-D software tool for creating virtual reality applications that a majority of the about 2 million virtual-reality developers use to develop virtual reality applications. In addition, Google, Facebook, Apple, and Amazon are developing virtual reality capabilities for their smartphones and web sites.

The most commonly used virtual reality applications are video games. Additional applications under development or in use include:

- Live televised sports events that people with headsets and compatible smartphones can view. VR provides 360-degree views of sporting events from all angles: front, sides, and back.

- Training professional athletes with simulation of tactics.

- Real estate applications where prospective buyers see homes for sale without actually having to travel to each home.

- A remodeling virtual reality application being tested by Loews that enables customers to envision how remodeling projects will look.

- Social network posts that enable people to connect with each other in a more personal way using posts in virtual reality formats to share experiences and feelings.

- Medical training that involves virtual reality videos for operating nurses and anatomy courses where students use VR to learn anatomy and gain "firsthand" knowledge of steps in medical procedures.

- Drones with high-quality cameras that capture images on the ground in virtual reality format.

Technical and Content Availability Challenges

One of the current issues with virtual reality is that it can create nausea in viewers. This is because people turn their heads faster to look at images than current frame rates can process these view changes. Because of this delay, people don't see what they expect to see. As the technology matures, this issue should be resolved.

Another challenge is the need for additional content in virtual reality formats. Developers are waiting for additional VR users and buyers are often reluctant to purchase head mounted displays and download apps until more virtual reality content is available.

Additionally, current cellular networks don't have the capacity to support virtual reality. VR requires either direct connection to broadband or Wi-Fi connected to broadband Internet links. Thus, it is limited to indoor use. Next generation 5G networks may have the capacity to support virtual reality. See Chapter 7, "Mobile and Wi-Fi Networks," for information on 5G technologies.

Augmented Reality

Augmented reality, on the other hand, adds pictures of animated characters or other images to what users see when they look around them. Augmented reality requires specialized apps on smart phones, but not always specialized headsets or headsets resembling eyeglasses. The mobile game Pokémon Go, which was released in 2016, is an example of the use of augmented reality (AR). Pokémon Go, a joint effort of Niantic Labs, Nintendo, and Pokémon Company as reported in the July 12, 2016, *Wall Street Journal* article, "What is really behind the Pokémon Go Craze," by July of 2016, was the most profitable game on Google and Apple's app stores up until that time.

Augmented reality needs smartphones' cameras, GPS, and position sensors. Position sensors rely on accelerometers within smartphones. All new smartphones are equipped with accelerometers able to detect how users tilt their smartphones. For example, are they tilting them sideways or straight up? Accelerometers enable smartphone viewers to modify the angle at which they view images.

Augmented reality is used in manufacturing and product assembly. In one example, workers wear special glasses such as Google Glasses that flash images of instructions and diagrams sent from computers to the glasses with directions for the next steps in processes. In this way, workers don't have to interrupt their work to read instructions.

INCREASING NETWORK CAPACITY VIA MULTIPLEXING...

Multiplexing combines traffic from multiple devices or sources into one stream so that they can share a circuit or path through a network. Each source does not require a separate, dedicated link.

Like compression, companies and carriers use multiplexing to send more information on wireless airwaves, fiber networks, and internal Local Area Networks (LANs). However, unlike compression, multiplexing does not alter the actual data sent. Rather, the multiplexer at the transmitting end combines messages from multiple devices and sends them on the same wire, wireless, or fiber medium to their destination, whereupon a matching device distributes them locally.

One important goal is to make more efficient use of the most expensive portion of a carrier's network so that the carrier can handle the vast amounts of traffic generated by devices such as smartphones and computers. Multiplexing is also used by enterprises that link offices together or access the Internet by using only one circuit (a path between sites) rather than paying to lease multiple circuits from their provider. The two most commonly used types of multiplexing are time division and statistical.

Time-Division Multiplexing

Time-Division Multiplexing (TDM) is a digital multiplexing scheme that saves capacity for each device or voice conversation. Once a connection is established, capacity is saved even when the device is idle. For example, if a call is put on hold, no other device can use this spare capacity. Small slices of silence in thousands of calls in progress result in high amounts of unused network capacity. This is the reason TDM is being replaced in high-traffic portions of networks by VoIP technologies, in which voice packets are interspersed with data and video traffic more efficiently, without wasting capacity. Thus, network capacity is not wasted during pauses in voice or data traffic.

Statistical Multiplexing: Efficient Utilization via Prioritization of Network Services

Statistical multiplexers do not guarantee capacity for each device connected to them. Rather, they transmit voice, data, and images on a first-come, first-served basis, as long as there is capacity. Ethernet, the protocol used in local area networks, Wi-Fi networks, and broadband networks is an example of statistical multiplexing. Unlike time division multiplexing, statistical multiplexing is asynchronous. A particular amount of capacity is not dedicated to individual devices. Rather, capacity is allocated asynchronously, on demand, when requested in an uneven manner.

Statistical multiplexers can be used in a Wide Area Network (WAN) to connect customers to the Internet. It is also the most common method of accessing LANs within buildings. The Ethernet protocol uses statistical multiplexing for access to LANs. On Ethernet LANs, if more than one device attempts to access the LAN simultaneously, there is a collision and the devices try again later. Ethernet gear and software is used for LAN access and is located in each network-connected device, such as a printer, computer, or security monitor.

Statistical multiplexers support more devices and traffic than TDMs because they don't need to save capacity when a device is not active. Carriers sell WAN Internet access via carrier Gigabit Ethernet offerings, supporting a range of speeds from 10Mbps to 100Gbps. If there is a surge in traffic, such as during peak times, the carrier can temporarily slow down traffic. However, because Gigabit Ethernet's statistical multiplexing has the capability to prioritize traffic, customers who contract for more costly, high-priority service can obtain higher capacity than customers with lower-priority service during traffic spikes.

Other types of multiplexing in addition to statistical multiplexing include dense wavelength division, a form of frequency division multiplexing which divides traffic among frequencies in fiber-optic networks to increase the fibers' capacity. Dense wavelength division multiplexing is discussed in the section below on fiber optical cabling.

Bytes vs. Bits: Measuring Capacity and Speed

Federal and state requirements mandating retention of e-mail, financial, and other documents as well as corporations retaining all of their files rather than filtering out just what is needed have resulted in computer data storage in the petabytes range. A petabyte equals 1,000,000,000,000,000 characters or 1,000 gigabytes.

People often use the terms "bits," and "bytes" interchangeably. Their meanings, however, differ significantly. Bits per second (bps) refers to the actual number of bits sent in a given time from point A to point B, or the number of bits transmitted each second. It is also represented as millions of bits per second (Mbps), gigabits per second (Gbps), and terabits per second (Tbps). Simply put, it is the number of bits that can be transmitted in 1 second.

Bps (with a capital "B") stands for bytes per second by convention. Speeds are represented by the bps acronym. Here are some examples:

- Gigabit Ethernet, used in carrier and enterprise networks, can carry data at speeds of one gigabit per second (1Gbps) to 100 gigabits per second (100Gbps).
- Terabit speed routers deployed on the Internet are capable of transmitting at a rate of 1,000 gigabits or 1 terabit; 10 terabits per second = 10,000,000,000,000 bps.

Bits organized into groups of 8 bits are bytes. Each byte can be a letter character, punctuation, or a space. Computer hard-drive capacity is measured in bytes, but speeds on digital lines are measured in bits transmitted per second. Bytes stored on computer drives and large servers are stored in digital form.

To summarize, a byte is a character made up of 8 bits. A bit is an on or off electrical or light pulse.

USING PROTOCOLS TO ESTABLISH A COMMON SET OF RULES ....

Protocols enable disparate devices to communicate by establishing a common set of rules for sending and receiving. For example, TCP/IP is the suite of standard protocols used on the Internet with which different types of computers, running a variety of operating systems, can access and browse the Internet. The fact that TCP/IP is simple to implement is a prime factor in the Internet's widespread availability.

The fact that protocols used on the Internet are available for free in their basic form and work with a variety of browsers, operating systems, and computer platforms makes them attractive interfaces for enterprises, hosting, and cloud-computing sites that support remote access to services such as Microsoft Office documents. A web-based interface compatible with many types of computers and operating systems enables enterprises to support software at a central site.

Installing software at a central site minimizes support requirements. When an IT department supports applications such as the Office suite that are installed on each user's computer, it must download software and updates to every computer and ensure that each has a compatible hardware platform and operating system. By locating the software at a central site rather than on each user's computer, updates and support are simpler. In addition, fewer IT employees are required to maintain servers with applications on them in remote offices.

However, many of these frequently used protocols are structured in such a way that they add a great deal of overhead traffic to the Internet and enterprise networks. This is because these protocols require numerous short signaling messages between the user and the Internet for functions such as identifying graphics, checking for errors, and ensuring correct delivery and receipt of all the packets.

The following protocols are used on the Internet and on corporate networks that have a web interface to information accessible to local and remote users.

- **Ethernet**   This is the most common protocol used in corporate LANs. It defines how data is placed on the LAN and how data is retrieved from the network. Wi-Fi wireless networks are based on a different form of Ethernet.

- **Hypertext Markup Language (HTML)**   This is the markup language used on the Internet and on enterprise networks. Employees who write web pages for their organization often use it. HTML commands include instructions to make text bold or italic, or to link to other sites. Instructions, known as tags (not visible on Internet documents), are bracketed by opening and closing angle brackets (< and >), otherwise simply known as the less-than and greater-than symbols. Tags indicate how browsers should display the document and images within each web page. For example, <bold> is a command for bolding text. Tags are delivered along with the web page when users browse the Internet and access information through web interfaces at enterprises. They are good examples of overhead bits.

- **Hypertext Transfer Protocol Secure (HTTPS)**   This is a protocol used to transfer data over the Internet and other networks in a secure fashion by encrypting data. It provides protection from hackers. It can authenticate (verify) that the network connected to is not spoofed, meaning it is the network that it purports to be and that another network has not intercepted a communication intended for a different site.

- **Extensible Markup Language (XML)**   This is another markup language based on elements surrounded by tags that identify fields requiring user input. The tag <name> is an example of a tagged label; it is not visible to users. Other variable labels might include quantity, address, age, and so on. Firms can analyze responses provided by visitors to a site who fill out online surveys. Tagged responses can be sorted by fields such as geography or age. XML enables computers to automatically process responses collected online or in specialized applications such as purchasing and ordering functions in businesses. The protocol-related tags and labels identifying fields in XML create the many extra overhead bits transmitted along with documents containing XML commands.

- **Simple Object Access Protocol (SOAP)**   This enables communications between programs on different operating systems such as Windows and Linux by specifying how to encode, for example, an HTTP (Hypertext Transfer Protocol) header and an XML file. It eliminates the requirement to modify infrastructures to process HTTP and other communication transport protocols on networks.

PROTOCOLS AND LAYERS ....

When describing their products' capabilities, organizations often refer to the OSI layers. In the 1970s, the International Organization for Standardization developed the *Open Systems Interconnection* (OSI) architecture, which defines how equipment from multiple vendors should interoperate. *Architecture* refers to the ways that devices in networks are connected to one another.

Although not widely implemented because of its complexity, OSI has had a profound influence on telecommunications. The basic concept underpinning OSI is that of layering. Groups of functions are divided into seven layers, which can be changed and developed without having to change any other layer. (See Table 1-5 in the "Appendix" section at the end of this chapter for a complete list of layers.) LANs, public networks, and the Internet's TCP/IP suite of protocols are based on a layered architecture.

An understanding of the functionality at each layer of the OSI provides an understanding of the capability of particular protocols and equipment. Examples of the layers include the following.

- **Layer 2: Switches**   This layer corresponds to capabilities in the *Data Link Layer*, functioning as the links to the network. However, Layer 2 devices cannot choose between multiple routes in a network. Layer 2 switches are placed in wiring closets in LANs and route messages to devices within their LAN segment. See Figure 1-6 for an illustration of how this works.

- **Layer 3: Switches and Routers**   Layer 3 corresponds to the *Network Layer*. These devices can select an optimal route for each packet. Routers select paths for packets on the Internet and route messages between networks.

- **Layer 5: Encryption Protocols**   These are *Session Layer* protocols that reorder data in packets by using complex mathematical algorithms to keep data private.

- **Layer 7: Deep Packet Inspection (DPI)**   DPI services include *Application Layer* capability. DPI can look into packets to determine the application of the data within them.

Knowing the capabilities in each layer helps in understanding the protocol and equipment capabilities being described.

VIRTUALIZATION: SPACE, COST, AND MAINTENANCE EFFICIENCIES.................................

The term "virtual" refers to entities such as networks or servers that provide the functions of the physical devices that they are emulating. A virtual machine is software with the functionality of a computer. Server refers to single servers performing the functions of multiple servers. To illustrate, multiple *virtual machines* can exist within a single server, with each virtual machine performing the functions of a single server.

 NOTE Servers are computers used for specialized tasks such as managing document traffic to printers and storing applications.

Without server virtualization, each server in a data center would support only a single operating system. Virtualization enables each server to run multiple operating systems, with each operating system running multiple applications. Each operating system running multiple applications is a *virtual machine*. This reduction in the number of servers required to support vast numbers of applications made virtualization a key building block for cloud computing.

Technical advances have enabled virtualization to make it possible for large enterprises and cloud computing providers to consolidate servers. Supporting more than one operating system on a single physical server requires large amounts of processing power. However, with the development of powerful multi-core processors, parallel-computing streams can perform multiple computer instructions simultaneously.

Virtualization host operating software from companies such as VMware, Inc. (VMware was developed by EMC, which is now owned by Dell) and Microsoft allocate and manage computer resources such as memory, hard-disk capacity, and computer processing between the operating systems and applications on a server. Virtualization management software simplifies data center operations by providing the ability to allocate more resources in a data center from a single interface.

Server sprawl can be a problem when many applications are replicated on diverse servers. It is often a challenge to manage the large number of virtual machines located within a data center.

Scalability and Energy Savings

Carriers, ISPs, enterprises, and developers adopt virtualization as a way to save on energy, computer memory, staffing, and hardware costs. Installing applications on multiple virtual computers on each physical server decreases the number of physical servers required. It also ensures that there is less wasted capacity than on physical servers used for a single application, often using only 10 percent of the physical server's capacity. This makes data centers more scalable. Applications can be installed more easily, without adding extra hardware. Rather, a new virtual machine can be added to a physical computer that has spare capacity until the physical server is at between 70 percent and 80 percent of capacity.

In addition, having fewer computers to run applications results in less space used and lower facility cooling costs. Although individual servers running virtual operating software are more powerful and require more cooling than less-powerful servers, the reduction in the total number of physical devices results in overall energy efficiency.

Virtualization—Enabling Cloud Computing

Virtualization is a major enabler of cloud computing. Server virtualization refers to a single physical server with multiple operating systems and applications. Prior to server virtualization, each unique operating system required its own physical server. Virtualized servers enable multiple operating systems as well as multiple applications to reside on the same server.

Large cloud providers commonly have multiple data centers that maintain replicated copies of all data. If a data center becomes disabled, another can easily take over its functions. Virtualization makes it less costly and complex for providers to support multiple data centers in different physical locations. This results in a reduction of physical services, less electrical power, and less cooling, thus lowering providers' energy costs.

Moreover, virtualization enables data centers to support multiple developers by providing a virtual computing platform for each developer while he is logged on to a virtual machine. Multi-core processors enable multiple developers to simultaneously log on to the same physical server. When a developer logs off from his area of the server, computing power is freed up for other uses.

Because of security and privacy concerns, large companies often do not want their applications and files on the same physical servers as those of other organizations. In these instances, they can elect to reserve a group of servers for their own use. Amazon refers to this feature as a *Virtual Private Cloud*. Other providers offer similar features. Not surprisingly, there is an extra monthly fee associated with this service.

MANAGING VIRTUALIZATION.................................

Organizations can realize many benefits by implementing virtualization capability in servers and storage networks. They also take on challenges managing them in complex environments.

Managing Memory, Virtual Machines, and Disk Storage in Virtualized Data Centers

Server virtualization has many benefits, including saving money on electricity, heating, and cooling. However, there are challenges in large data centers. One such challenge is managing memory in the host physical servers. Newer operating systems installed on host servers have more code and require more memory to operate. IT staff members allocate memory to applications on virtual machines by using VMware's Hypervisor software. Staff members need to monitor applications' memory usage so that servers can be upgraded or applications moved to other hosts if memory in the current host is not adequate. If this isn't done, applications will run slowly and response times on individual user computers will be degraded.

New servers are equipped with eight CPUs—quite literally, eight CPU chips on a single host server. However, as the amount of processing needed to run programs grows, even this is not always adequate for the virtual machines installed on them. Programs that have sound and video are "fatter," with more code, which requires additional CPU overhead. It's difficult to estimate under these conditions the amount of CPU power that's required for applications running on virtual machines.

In addition, disk storage is being used up at a faster rate. Users now routinely store MP3 files in their e-mail inboxes. In data centers where user files and e-mail messages are archived, this can deplete spare storage in Storage Area Networks (SANs) at a faster rate than planned. Thus, storage, memory, and processing requirements should be monitored. In large, complex data centers, it can sometimes be easier to monitor and manage single physical servers rather than virtual machines and storage.

In small organizations, managing memory, storage, and CPU usage is not as complex. With only three or four physical servers, it's not as difficult to track and manage resource allocation.

Server Sprawl

Server sprawl is the unchecked proliferation of virtual machines on physical host servers. (Virtual machines are also referred to as *images*.) Managing server sprawl in large data centers is a major challenge. Because it's easy to install multiple images of applications on virtualized servers, the number of applications can escalate rapidly. Data centers that previously had 1,000 servers with 1,000 applications can potentially now have 8 images per physical server and 8,000 applications to manage.

Another cause of server sprawl occurs when an application is upgraded. To test the application before it's upgraded, management creates an image of the application, upgrades the image, and then tests the upgrade on a small group of users before making the upgrade available to all users. However, often the original and the upgraded application are left on the physical server, which further contributes to sprawl. To complicate matters further, if either the original or the upgraded version is moved to a different physical server, it can be difficult to determine that there is a duplicate. Containers, which are discussed below, are also vulnerable to sprawl.

Containers: A Newer Form of Server Virtualization

Containers are servers with a single operating system shared by multiple small programs. Like server virtualization, containers enable a single physical server to hold multiple applications and components of applications.

Unlike virtualized servers in which each virtual machine (each application) requires a separate operating system, applications in containers share a single operating system. See Figure 1-10 for a comparison between containers and virtualized servers. This enables containers to hold many more applications than virtualized servers. This is because in virtualized servers, each application has an operating system and also a virtual copy of the hardware that runs the virtual machine. Thus, each operating system uses memory and server capacity.

In contrast, container technology's use of a single operating system is an efficient use of memory and disk space. Because of this, containers hold many more applications than virtual servers. Netflix alone has over 500 micro services in its containers located in Amazon's and Google's data centers in the United States and Europe.

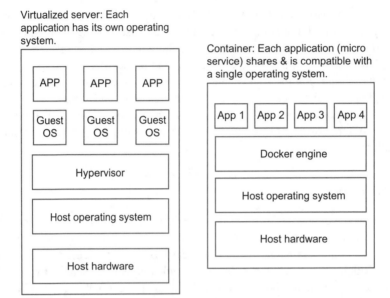

Figure 1-10   *A comparison of virtualized servers and containers.*

Containers are used to hold small, related programs that are referred to as micro services. For example, Netflix and LinkedIn might use containers to differentiate and manage each of the many services they offer customers without having to change programming for other services. This is efficient when organizations need to modify just part of their offerings. With containers, programmers don't need to alter their entire application, just a particular piece of it: a micro service. For this reason, applications in containers are less complex to modify. Thus, if there's a change in one service, programmers need only modify that particular micro service.

Factors in Choosing between Containers and Virtualization

Enterprises might choose virtualized servers when they have applications that require a variety of operating systems in a single physical server. This is because containers support only a single operating system per server.

Organizations that switch to containers from virtualized servers need to rewrite their applications so that they're compatible with the open source operating systems used with containers and with the container platform, e.g. Docker. Examples of these open source operating systems are: Red Hat, Linux, Ubuntu, and Rocket. Windows operating systems can also be used in containers. There is no cost for using open source software, but a company may need to hire a programmer with the skill to rewrite the programs for compatibility with their container's operating system.

Container applications are installed on *bare metal servers*, which have only a single operating system. Many containers are installed on cloud platforms such as those provided by Amazon and Rackspace. Private equity firm Apollo Global Management LLC owns Rackspace.

Each container is located on a private server dedicated to a single organization. Multiple customers do not share containers in the cloud. This is an advantage for customers who want to be assured that the total capacity of the server is reserved for their applications. They are isolated from traffic, also referred to as noise, from other customers' traffic, which may use much of the physical server's resources.

Applications on containers located in the cloud or in large data centers are accessed via application program interfaces (APIs), small programs that translate between programs in the containers and those in the data center from which staff access the programs in the container. APIs are used by both developers and end-users. Accessing an application is referred to as *pulling an image* (an application) *down*.

Security Challenges with Containers

Because there is only one operating system in containers, if that one operating system is hacked, the entire container with its large number of micro services is likely to be damaged. Thus IT staff need to be extra vigilant about who is allowed to access each container. Additionally, installing certain applications as read-only will also protect against hackers damaging micro services on containers.

Docker: A Container Software Platform

Docker software was developed as open source, free software. It is a software platform that enables developers to write applications compatible with containers. Docker is a set of software tools for coding, testing, and running applications on Linux- and Windows-based containers. The Docker company offers paid consulting and container set-up services as well as the open source Docker software.

THE CLOUD: APPLICATIONS AND DEVELOPMENT AT PROVIDERS' DATA CENTERS ....

Cloud computing refers to the paradigm by which computing functions, document storage, software applications, and parts of or all of a data center are located and maintained at an external provider's site. Businesses use cloud computing to more quickly develop applications and to eliminate the need to maintain and update applications. Companies additionally can use the cloud to dramatically shrink the size of their data centers. Start-ups and small businesses often eliminate them altogether and rely solely on cloud services.

Cloud computing is based on a distributed architecture structure where providers' data centers are duplicated in multiple geographic locations. See Figure 1-11 for distributed cloud data centers. Cloud providers generally build duplicate data centers that are connected to each other by high capacity fiber optic cabling. For example, they may have data centers on the west coast, on the east coast, and a few in the central or western states. The goal of connecting the data centers with fiber-optic cabling is that if one data center fails, a duplicate data center can take over operations.

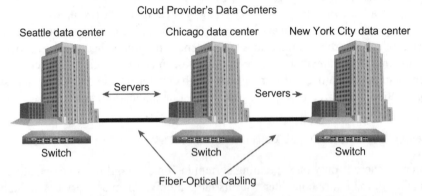

> ➤ Three distributed cloud data centers connected together with fiber-optic cabling.
> ➤ Switches at each data center transmit back up data to the others so data is not lost in the event of a failure

Figure 1-11 Cloud computing distributed data centers connected by fiber-optic cabling.

Organizations now have choices about where applications are located. They can place applications at:

- A hosting center where companies often place their own computers and manage them remotely. The hosting company is responsible for:
    - Security
    - Broadband links to the hosting site
    - Sustainability in the event of power outages and natural disasters.
- Purchasing rights to software with installation at their own data centers
- On the cloud where a provider manages the hardware and the application software

When cloud computing was first introduced, it was wildly popular with small start-ups that wanted to avoid investing in computer hardware because of growth uncertainties. However, larger businesses were more cautious about moving applications to the cloud because of concerns about privacy, security, and loss of control over applications. Cloud computing is now widely recognized by organizations of all sizes as a legitimate way of managing and developing applications. However, there are still concerns over security. There are additionally challenges involved in moving applications to the cloud and controlling runaway usage costs associated with the cloud.

Private vs. Public Cloud Service

Depending on their privacy and security requirements, organizations choose private or public cloud services. With private cloud service, the organization's server is not shared with any other organization. This ensures customers that there is no interference from other customers' applications, which might have large amounts of traffic into the server.

With public cloud service organizations, applications are on servers used by other customers. They share the capacity of the physical server with other customers. This is more commonly used than private cloud service, which is more costly.

Cloud Computing Fees

The pricing structure for most cloud-computing providers is typically based on the number of transactions and the number of users for a given application. Customers that contract with providers for e-mail or other data applications pay by the hour or by the gigabyte for CPU (computer processing unit) gigabytes consumed. In addition, cloud providers often charge an implementation fee, and might charge developers who use their platform to develop applications for bandwidth consumed on the provider's Internet connections.

Rationale for Cloud Computing

There are many reasons why organizations adopt a cloud-computing strategy. When cloud computing was first available, most of these reasons revolved around the desire to carry out IT functions more cost-effectively with fewer capital outlays. A small start-up company, for example, might not have the resources to hire staff and purchase computing hardware. No onsite software to maintain, fewer servers, and less technical staff required for maintaining and upgrading applications were all motivations for moving applications to the cloud. In fact, smaller companies of fewer than 200 or 300 employees may have only a single server to support because most of their applications are located in the cloud.

Using a service such as Amazon Web Services or Google Apps (offered by Amazon and Google, respectively) for computing and archiving data saves start-up costs with fewer financial risks. If the business grows, it won't outgrow the hardware that it purchased earlier. Conversely, if the business fails or slows down dramatically, it doesn't have an investment in hardware and software with little resale value or one that might be too sophisticated for its changing needs. It is also useful in supporting IT in acquired companies and gearing up for spikes in usage.

The cloud is additionally a way for concerns, particularly start-ups, to develop and test applications before making them available to staff or customers. The following is an example of how a new company used cloud computing to test the viability of their planned applications. The start-up rented 50 client computers and one server with four application programs and one database machine from Amazon for 0.50¢ an hour to test their application without having to invest in hardware. Without the ability to test applications on Amazon, their start-up costs would have been prohibitive because they would have had to lease 50 computers plus 1 for a database.

Large enterprises were initially interested in cloud computing because there was a perception that it would be less costly than hiring additional staff as well as purchasing and supporting hardware and software for new applications. With cloud computing there is no capital investment. Companies pay usage per person, in a similar manner to renting a car.

Cost savings are not always the main advantage or impetus for using cloud computing. While capital and staff expense are lower with cloud computing, monthly usage costs can balance out these savings so that businesses don't spend less money on overall IT services. Usage fees from employees' extra computing and data access can eliminate expected savings as employees use more computing resources than initially envisioned.

Both large and small organizations look to cloud computing to maximize their attention and assets on core missions. They may consider some IT applications to be utilities better managed by IT experts at cloud companies. For example, they may use Microsoft Azure's cloud-based Office applications for word processing, collaboration, presentations and spreadsheets to avoid managing and upgrading these applications. With Office in the cloud, upgrade responsibilities are taken care of at Microsoft's data centers.

An important advantage of cloud computing is the speed at which new applications can be implemented in the cloud. This can equate to competitive advantages. For example, customer service or sales application can increase sales revenue. Faster access to company analytical data about sales and customers are other examples of how the speed of developing applications can help businesses grow or retain current customers. In fact, while saving money may be the initial motivation, it is often not the key advantage of using cloud computing. Agility in business operations, the ability to launch strategic applications, and the ability to scale and shrink as required are stronger motivations for using the cloud. The following is a quote from an IT Director in the Boston area:

> *We ordered Oracle one day and the next day it was launched in the cloud. Without the cloud it would have taken three months and additional staff time. When we purchase new software, we always look for applications that are cloud ready.*

Three Categories of Cloud Services—Layers in the Cloud

There are three generally agreed upon but sometimes overlapping classifications of cloud computing offerings. It's not unusual for providers to offer more than one of these types of services.

The classifications are as follows:

- **Software as a Service (SaaS)**   Application developers manage and develop specific applications for enterprises. Enterprise and residential customers pay monthly fees to use these applications, which are generally accessed via a web browser interface.

- **Platform as a Service (PaaS)**   Providers make their hardware and basic application suite available to developers and enterprises that create specialized add-on applications for specific functions.

- **Infrastructure as a Service (IaaS)**   Developers create applications on basic computing and storage infrastructure owned and supported by cloud providers. This is the hardware used by developers.

SaaS

Software as a Service is the most frequently used cloud service. Organizations that want to avoid the staff time needed to develop, test, and roll out new applications often use Software as a Service. With SaaS, new applications can be can be implemented more quickly than if the customer implemented them on their own servers. They can turn to developers to write them or simply use existing cloud-based applications.

Customers are attracted to Software as a Service because the cloud provider manages applications, the operating systems on which applications are installed, the virtualization in the server, servers, storage, and broadband connections between users and the applications. The customer's responsibility is porting applications to the cloud, and monitoring the billing and usage. Many SaaS providers offer applications, such as Salesforce.com and NetSuite, used by business and commercial organizations.

Salesforce.com offers its customer relationship management (CRM) services for managing relationships concerning customers and sales prospects. Its software can be used to automate writing sales proposals. It also profiles and targets customers based on these profiles. NetSuite, owned by Oracle, offers businesses an end-to-end software suite that includes CRM, inventory, and e-commerce applications that integrate web sales with back-office functions such as billing and accounts receivable.

Young people and adults as well use SaaS applications in their personal lives. For example, students in particular back up their music on sites such as iTunes. The following is a quote from a Chinese exchange student in the Boston area:

> *I use the cloud to back up my music. I like being able to listen to my music from all of my devices. And, I don't have to worry about running out of space on my smartphone.*

Services for residential customers, such as the Office-like Google Docs suite, the document-sharing service DropBox, the backup service Carbonite, and social media sites LinkedIn and Facebook are examples of Software as a Service.

PaaS: Cloud-Based Data Centers with Specialized Software

Platform as a Service providers manage the operating system, servers, virtualization, storage, and networking within their data centers. They provide data centers with specialized software to enterprises and application developers. For example, one PaaS provider, Microsoft, currently maintains massive data centers in the United States, Europe, and Asia. The Microsoft Azure platform is available to developers to customize applications that they in turn offer to their customers. Both Salesforce.com and NetSuite sell directly to developers as well as to business customers. The services Salesforce.com and NetSuite sell to developers are considered PaaS offerings because developers use the platforms to customize and support software for their own customers.

An enterprise customer can also create applications directly on Azure, or use standard office software such as word processing and spreadsheet applications as well as productivity applications such as web conferencing and calendaring, and then later port them to Azure. By using applications housed on Azure, organizations eliminate the complexity of supporting in-house applications. Azure also offers storage facilities to developers and enterprise customers. A bank can store a year's worth of records on Azure to which each of its customers and their own staff have access.

Akamai Technologies maintains platforms focused on e-commerce that are deployed on 1450 public networks worldwide, where it hosts web sites for major enterprise customers. Web applications located on these servers generate massive amounts of multimedia Internet traffic, such as games, map generation, search, and dealer/store locators. Akamai intercepts this web traffic for its customers and sends it to its destination on the fastest available route.

Akamai's security services are available at each of the public networks in which its equipment is installed. These services include security that protects sites from distributed Denial of Service (DoS) attacks. Distributed DoS attacks simultaneously send thousands of bogus messages or messages containing viruses to networks in coordinated attacks from computers in multiple locations around the world. If one of its sites does become disabled, Akamai has the ability to run its applications at other locations.

IaaS: Infrastructure as a Service

With Infrastructure as a Service, customers manage their applications, their data, the operating system, and middleware for applications located at a cloud provider. The cloud provider manages the servers, virtualization, data storage, and networking within their own data centers so that an adequate number of users can reach the applications within the data center.

 NOTE Middleware is a piece of software used between application programs and other software such as database managers. It is used to mediate the differences between operating systems and applications so that they operate together. It essentially mediates the differences between pieces of software. In cloud computing, middleware mediates the differences between onsite software being moved to the cloud and the computing environment at the cloud provider's data center.

Amazon: The Gorilla of Cloud Computing

Amazon is the largest cloud provider in the United States. In addition to its computing infrastructure for developing applications, it offers storage. Interestingly, Netflix, its competitor for streaming media services, is a major customer. Netflix stores its movies on Amazon servers. Thus, when Netflix customers in the United States stream movies and TV shows, they access the shows from computers located in Amazon's data centers. Amazon has expanded into applications such as databases and analytics to analyze usage statistics of applications on its site. Its HSM security encryption services is designed to protect the security of files located on Amazon's infrastructure.

Other major cloud providers include Microsoft Azure, IBM, Salesforce.com, Rackspace, Google, and Oracle. Rackspace offers hosting in addition to its cloud service. With hosting, customers supply their own servers (computers) and additionally manage the software on their servers. The following is quote from a staff member at a small organization that uses Amazon EC2:

> My company is a start-up. We rent 50 client computers, one server machine with a LAMP (Linux, Apache, MySql, PHP) package and one database machine for just 0.50¢ per hour. There are many features in Amazon to customize the environment according to our requirements.

Spinning Applications to the Cloud

When organizations talk about moving applications to the cloud, they use the term spin. They spin applications up to the cloud over broadband links between their site and the Internet. When transmitting applications over broadband links to the cloud, companies often protect these transmissions from eavesdroppers and interception by creating Virtual Private Networks (VPNs). The VPN creates a secure link between the cloud and the customer by encrypting the data and providing a way to securely decrypt (re-create) the data at the receiving end.

Encryption is the process of using a mathematical formula to reorder bits so that they are unrecognizable to equipment that doesn't have the "key" to decrypt the data into readable data. The VPN also ensures that the data exchanged is formatted so that it is not blocked by firewalls at either end. A firewall is a software application that all incoming transmissions must pass through. Firewalls are programmed to accept only certain transmissions and to block known viruses. The software used to spin applications to the cloud makes the addressing formats compatible between the cloud's infrastructure and the customer's data center, and vice versa.

Another complication of spinning applications to the cloud is that many users access applications from mobile devices. Companies have to figure out how to get applications to them when they're not sitting at their desk. Two issues are that the mobile user may be accessing an application from a location with poor mobile coverage and from a device with a small screen that makes it difficult to actually view the data easily.

Moving applications from data centers to the cloud can involve rewriting them or changing internal processes. For example, operating systems and addressing schemes used by a particular cloud provider might be different from those utilized by its customer. Addressing schemes can include formats such as IP addresses assigned to databases and applications, and Media Access Control (MAC) addresses for individual computers. In addition, compatibility between the two infrastructures is important, because applications that reside on a provider's infrastructure interface might not be compatible with its customers' databases.

Regulations and the Cloud

Various state and national regulations mandate that organizations in fields such as banking, healthcare, pharmaceutical, and government retain files for specified lengths of time. In addition to archiving information with cloud providers, organizations often use these providers as a lower-cost emergency backup in the event that their data is destroyed in a natural disaster, fire, or computer hacking incident. Enterprises can store up to 1 petabyte (PB) of data in servers that are often as large as a refrigerator. These servers consume large amounts of energy and take up a great deal of space.

Computers used for storage are now also able to take advantage of efficiencies attained by virtualization. Data stored in different database formats (for example, Microsoft SQL vs. Oracle) can be stored on the same physical computer by using virtualization able to separate files by operating system. Thus, the databases of various customers can be stored on the same storage server, resulting in server consolidation, both for storage and for running applications.

Security in the Cloud

Security is a major concern when organizations move applications to the cloud. While cloud services are often more secure than those provided at small and medium-sized companies that don't have the resources to hire top security staff, they are not without risks. Cloud applications in which large numbers of customers access the application are the most vulnerable to hacking attacks.

There is often a conflict between making sites easy to access and having sufficient authentication requirements to protect against intrusions. According to Alert Logic, a cloud security and compliance firm headquartered in Houston, Texas, sites with high amounts of financial, health, and other personal information are at particular risk. Information gleaned from hacking these sites can be sold for millions of dollars. Moreover, because of their high-profile, large cloud providers are particular targets.

The cloud's most vulnerable link is often the staff and customers that access cloud-based applications. Important ingredients in protecting against hacker attacks are customers that shield the secrecy of their log-on credentials. Consumers that use cloud services may share their log-on credentials with friends or log in from public Wi-Fi where their passwords and user IDs may be stolen. Many public Wi-Fi services in cafes and other public areas don't provide encryption, making these transmissions vulnerable to being hacked, and people's log-on credentials can be stolen while they are transmitted over the air.

To avoid being hacked, companies require employees to log in with strong passwords and multi-factor authentication. An example of multi-factor authentication might be a password and a token that generates a unique code that users type into their computer when they log into the cloud. These organizations may also mandate encryption on transmissions sent from mobile devices.

As a further step, organizations may lease security appliances (computer hardware with specialized software) or security software from companies such as Amazon and Alert Logic. In addition to its HMS security application, Amazon and other cloud security companies such as Threat Stack offer a software application with assessment tools to evaluate applications' vulnerability to hackers, anomalies in workflow, and compliance with industry standards.

Finally, it's up to customers to monitor and update applications and browsers in the cloud to avoid possible security breaches. Customers can request reports in the form of security logs from their cloud provider so that they or their consultants can audit their applications for security breaches. Logs that indicate spikes in usage may be indicative of a denial of service attack where overwhelming amounts of traffic are sent to a site, making it difficult or impossible for legitimate users to access these applications. Furthermore, hackers may introduce viruses that destroy data files into cloud-based applications or steal a company's private information via hacking attacks.

Shadow IT—Departments Independently Signing up for the Cloud

In large companies it's not unusual for staff in various departments to sign up for cloud services that fit the particular needs of their department without prior approval from the IT (Information Technology) staff. If the department stores intellectual property or confidential information in the cloud, they may not have the expertise to manage the security needed for access to the cloud. They may not use strong passwords or authentication. This is an ongoing challenge for large businesses where individual departments may feel that IT does not respond quickly enough to their needs.

Fewer IT Employees; Different Skills—DevOps

When cloud applications are moved to a cloud provider's data center, companies need fewer staff to manage them. An organization that formerly required five people to manage its Enterprise Resource Planning (ERP) application may need only a single person to manage it once the application is in the cloud.

However, the skills necessary to support cloud-based applications are different from those used to manage traditional onsite data center-based applications. The skill most often in demand when large and medium sized companies move applications to the cloud is *DevOps*, short for development operations.

The term DevOps refers to developing, provisioning (installing), and managing software. In companies that have applications in the cloud it means application development, spinning applications up to the cloud, and monitoring cloud-based applications. DevOps staff are involved in the planning relating to which applications to port to the cloud, tracking security or reasons for delays when accessing cloud-based applications, monitoring access to the cloud, and integration of cloud applications with business processes. Importantly, DevOps staff collaborate with other IT personnel and with management to determine organizations' needs and then develop applications compatible with the cloud.

Compatibility with the Cloud

All applications are coded to a particular operating system, and operating systems are dependent on the resident hardware characteristics. These applications may not be coded to operate on all cloud platforms. Without changes, some applications might not be compatible with hardware located in a provider's data centers. The addressing formats also need to be compatible between the cloud's infrastructure and the customer's data center, and vice versa. Addressing schemes can include formats such as IP addresses assigned to databases and applications, and Media Access Control (MAC) addresses for individual computers. Without changes, some applications might not be compatible with hardware located in a provider's data centers. Software, transparent to customers and cloud providers is required to create compatibility between operating systems, hardware, and applications.

A common practice is for customers to program their applications using a *stack* of open source *LAMP* programs (Linux, Apache, MySql, PHP), packages located, for example, on Amazon. Stacks are programs that work together. Linux is an operating system, Apache is an HTTP program for transferring data, PHP is a programming language. Perl and Python are also used instead of PHP. LAMP programs may be grouped together in container servers.

Moving applications from data centers to the cloud can involve rewriting them or changing internal processes. In addition, compatibility between the two infrastructures is important, because applications that reside on a provider's infrastructure interface might not be compatible with its customers' databases.

APIs, (Application Programming Interfaces) transparent to customers and cloud providers, create compatibility between operating systems, hardware, and applications. This enables different software programs to communicate with each other. Most companies use APIs to spin applications to the cloud.

Some applications are not architected for the cloud. Standard web browser interfaces are used with APIs to access cloud-based applications. Before applications are spun up to the cloud, organizations test access to them with multiple web browsers to make sure they will be compatible with all staff even when staff are traveling or accessing them from home computers where a variety of browsers might be installed. If organizations want something more sophisticated than a web user interface, they might bring them in-house rather than putting them in the cloud.

Monitoring Runaway Costs, Service Logs, and Congestion on Transmissions to the Cloud

Managing cloud-based operations is an ongoing task. It involves the following:

- Monitoring costs
    - Are costs increasing in line with business growth?
    - If not, what is causing the increase?
    - Are particular staff or departments using an unnecessary amount of computer resources?
- Tracking congestion on broadband links connected to the cloud
    - Is higher capacity needed?
    - Is there too much capacity?

- Monitoring cloud providers' reports on outages or other glitches
- Checking out user complaints
  - Are broadband links congested or are complaints coming from people accessing the cloud remotely using their cable modems or public Wi-Fi services that don't have adequate broadband bandwidth?
- Making sure that cloud applications are compatible with users dialing in from mobile devices
- Making sure that providers are adhering to contractual obligations for uptime, availability, and security

Integrating Applications Located at Different Providers

There are now web applications that enable companies to integrate or synchronize applications with each other when they are located at multiple cloud providers' sites. This enables companies to compare data located at different cloud providers' sites. This is helpful when applications from the same company need to be on different specialized providers' cloud-based data centers. Oracle, Microsoft, and Salesforce.com are examples of providers who offer cloud services for applications such as Microsoft's Azure, and Oracle's database services for specialized data centers.

Integration is often needed to develop meaningful information. For example, the sales department may need sales figures compared to financial data. If the financial data is at, say, Amazon, and data for sales is at Salesforce.com, it may be difficult to determine the gross margins on products. If, for example, a NetSuite—mid-sized ERP—application is at Amazon, the sales department can see how many widgets were sold at Salesforce.com, but not gross or net profit on each or inventory data on their NetSuite application.

There could be one database in the cloud for Oracle, one for a NetSuite, and one for manufacturing, in separate clouds. Each cloud is a silo that needs to "talk" to the other applications. If Salesforce.com and NetSuite are at different clouds, each will have a different database. The solution is for applications in separate clouds to be linked together. This is not currently possible.

In the pharmaceutical industry, document workflow management that tracks drug development is needed for regulatory approval of new drugs. Product safety must be documented; safety results, pricing, and the name of the drug are all required reports. Pharmaceutical companies must report on problems such as the adverse effects of drugs and what caused them as well as product packaging issues such as tampering with over-the-counter drugs in retail outlets. While people in the same company may be able to add to reports fairly easily, having staff from other organizations access this information on the cloud complicates security because of log-on and authentication requirements.

Because of security concerns, collaboration on product development between multiple companies is a challenge when using the cloud. Because businesses are worried about security, they build all kinds of barriers around accessing this data. So organizations that need to collaborate with other companies may keep some applications in-house so they can control access more easily when collaborating with other organizations.

Keeping Up with Automatic Updates

Without cloud computing, IT departments have the challenge of updating applications on their own as updates become available. Some of these updates are security patches for newly discovered viruses. A *virus* is a piece of computer code that is developed by hackers to damage and/or steal computer files. As new viruses are discovered manufacturers and developers provide application updates to customers. These updates are not always applied automatically. It's at the discretion of IT staff as to when to install updates and whether to test updates before making them available to corporate staff.

When applications are in the cloud, cloud software automatically applies updates. This can be disruptive as the user interface may be changed or customers may not be informed in advance about an upgrade that affects how users interact with an application. For example, users may have been trained to access information in a database a certain way or to use particular commands in a spreadsheet application. Additionally, and more critically, a staff person's computer operating system and hardware needs to be compatible with updates. This can be a problem with older computers and operating systems.

Provider "Lock-in"—Moving Applications between Providers

Often, organizations that consider using the cloud for particular applications are concerned about portability. Customers may wish to change providers because of factors such as costs and service. Others may want to move from a more limited hosting environment to a fuller service cloud provider.

Another layer of complexity is that all applications are coded to a particular operating system, and operating systems are dependent on the resident hardware characteristics. Without changes, some applications might not be compatible with hardware located in a provider's data centers. A healthcare company moved its applications from Rackspace's hosting environment to Amazon. The transition required 6 months of recoding software and Application Programming Interfaces to make them compatible with Amazon's data centers. It additionally involved training staff on how to access applications on Amazon.

Various consultants and developers offer software or consulting services to assist customers in moving applications between providers.

Privacy Internationally—Data Transfers

When organizations move applications to the cloud, they are required to follow privacy and security regulations mandated by governments for specific industries, particularly healthcare and finance. All countries have rules about guarding private information located in the cloud and personal information transferred to data centers in other countries.

In the United States, healthcare organizations are required to follow HIPAA (Health Insurance Portability and Accountability Act) rules on protecting the privacy of people's medical records. Retailers are bound by PCI DSS (Payment Card Industry Data Security Standard) regulations. Government agencies need to follow the 2002 Federal Information Security Management Act (FISMA), legislation that defines security practices to protect government information, as well defenses against natural or man-made threats. Financial firms have specific privacy and security regulations as well.

Adhering to the myriad of rules internationally in different countries often means that companies with a presence in, say, the U.S. and the European Union need to establish separate data centers that adhere to Europe's privacy and security rules. The same holds true in Asia and Pacific Rim countries. Moving that information to other countries is also subject to privacy rules.

The EU–U.S. Privacy Shield

Prior to 2015, the European Union and the United States Department of Commerce had agreed upon ways to protect European Union citizens' information stored in United States companies' cloud centers in both the United States and Europe. In 2015, in response to a privacy suit filed against Facebook, the 28-country European Union's highest court, the European Court of Justice, invalidated the earlier EU–U.S. Safe Harbor agreement that set out terms for companies in the United States to transfer cloud-based data containing personal information about European Union members to data centers in the United States. The 2015 ruling requires United States companies moving files out of Europe that contain information about Europeans to follow EU privacy guidelines.

The European Union and the United States Department of Commerce came to a new EU–U.S. agreement in 2016 on updating privacy regulations to protect European data. The agreement, called the *Privacy Shield*, took effect on August 1, 2016. Its requirements are more stringent than those in the Safe Harbor agreement. However, many experts expect even these regulations to be challenged in court.

In addition, some U.S. companies are slow to update their privacy clauses to comply with the new regulations. Some of this slowness is because of the uncertainty about the Privacy Shield. There are concerns that the EU Court of Justice will overturn it as not being strict enough. Other organizations see adherence to the Privacy Shield stipulations as a competitive edge in competing for business in the European Union.

At any rate, a new set of privacy regulations, the General Data Protection Regulation, took effect in May 2018. It includes a "right to be forgotten" provision that states that people's personal data should be deleted when citizens request the right to be forgotten.

Establishing Cloud-Based Data Centers Abroad

Companies, particularly small and medium sized ones, often solve the challenge of establishing cloud-based data centers in other counties by signing agreements with providers familiar with various international rules for hosting their data centers in other countries. Data storage company Box's partnership with IBM and Amazon to host other cloud companies' data centers outside of the United States are examples of this type of agreement. For now, companies are hosting data centers in Europe even though rules on privacy and security are not 100 percent clear.

Cloud Summary: Rationale and Challenges

The use of cloud computing application development, application management, and IT services in general has become a widely accepted practice in commercial and for-profit companies. There are however, a number of challenges in managing cloud computing and adapting applications for the cloud. Security and privacy are major concerns. Small and medium-sized companies recognize that cloud companies for the most part have more skilled staff to manage security and privacy. Large companies with the resources to manage security better than smaller companies, are careful not to place highly confidential or strategic files in the cloud. There is never a 100 percent guarantee that a cloud company won't be hacked or have an outage. However, it is generally accepted that the advantages for most applications need to be weighed against security and privacy concerns.

Cloud computing advantages include faster time to market that enables companies to implement new, strategic applications in less time with fewer staff. However, staffs and consultants with different skills from those required to manage in-house applications are required to move applications to the cloud. This can be an issue where there is a shortage of employees with these skills. Moreover, total cost of running IT services may not be lowered by using the cloud because of usage fees that often increase over time.

Major implication of using cloud computing is the fact that local area networks within buildings and broadband networks carry an exponentially increasing amount of traffic. Moreover, these networks are more critical than ever as many computing functions are not possible without broadband and in-house network links. Thus, it behooves companies to have network backup plans and redundancy in the event of failures in their networks.

SUMMARY...

The rapid pace of innovation and technological advancements is powered by computer chips that are faster and smaller and have increased memory and processing power. Chips are the engines in personal and business computers and all electronic devices including wristwatches, headsets, printers, fitness gear, televisions, set-top boxes, thermostats, and newer vending machines. Much of this gear is connected to broadband networks.

Broadband networks transmit data, voice, and video over high-capacity fiber-optic cabling. Dense wavelength division multiplexers, with powerful chips, connected to fiber in broadband networks enable broadband networks to carry many more streams of traffic simultaneously. The small chips within multiplexers take up less space, but enable transmissions from multiple devices to be carried simultaneously on single strands of fiber cables.

Compression and multiplexing gear are key elements in advanced gigabit per second packet networks connected to homes, commercial organizations, and businesses. Compression is an important technology that uses advanced mathematical algorithms to shrink the number of bits needed to transmit high-definition video, music, text messages, and voice. The most widely used cloud applications enabled by compression and multiplexing are the social networks whose subscribers upload and stream music, video clips, and photos to and from Facebook, Snapchat, Spotify, LinkedIn, and others. Amazon's cloud computing, streaming media, and retail sales is another factor in increased traffic on broadband networks.

Compression, multiplexing, high capacity networks and computer chips additionally enable cloud computing. Cloud computing has a large impact not only on how IT departments manage their applications. It also is a factor in how consumers manage their own storage requirements for photos and music. Young people in particular consume such high amounts of music and photos that their personal devices often don't have the capacity to store them all. Thus, they too use cloud computing for the ease of accessing their music and documents from anywhere there is broadband and from any device.

Compression is the key enabler of virtual and augmented reality. Chips used to compress images in virtual reality have graphical processing capability that can process large chunks of graphical data. Currently, online gaming is the most frequently used application for virtual reality. It enables high-density images that provide immersive experiences for gamers. In the future, virtual reality will also be used for applications such as training, education, and commerce.

APPENDIX ....

A Comparison between Analog and Digital Signaling

Speed or frequency on analog service is stated in hertz (Hz). A wavelength that oscillates, or swings back and forth between cycles, 10 times per second has a speed of 10Hz or cycles per second. A cycle starts at a neutral place in the wavelength, ascends to its highest point, descends to its lowest point, and then goes back to neutral. Lower frequencies are made up of longer wavelengths than higher frequencies.

Analog telephone signals are analogous to water flowing through a pipe. Rushing water loses force as it travels through a pipe. The farther it travels in the pipe, the more force it loses, and the weaker it becomes.

The advantages of digital signals are that they enable the following:

- **Greater capacity**   The ability to mix voice, video, photographs, and e-mail on the same transmission enables networks to transmit more data.

- **Higher speeds**   It is faster to re-create binary digital ones and zeros than more complex analog wavelengths.

- **Clearer video and audio**   In contrast to analog service, noise is clearly different from on and off bits, and therefore can be eliminated rather than boosted along with the signal.

- **Fewer errors**   Digital bits are less complex to re-create than analog signals.

- **More reliability**   Less equipment is required to boost signals that travel longer distances without weakening. Thus, there is less equipment to maintain.

Table 1-4   Compression Standards and Descriptions

Compression Standard	Description
H.264	An International Telecommunications Union (ITU) standard used widely for video conferencing systems on LANs (local area networks) and WANs (wide area networks).
G.726	A family of standards for voice encoding adopted by the ITU. It is used mainly on carrier networks to reduce the capacity needed for VoIP (Voice over IP).
IBOC ·	*In-band, on-channel* broadcasting that uses airwaves within the AM and FM spectrum to broadcast digital programming. IBOC is based on the Perceptual Audio Coder (PAC). There are many sounds that the ear cannot discern because they are masked by louder sounds. PAC discerns and discards these sounds that the ear cannot hear and that are not necessary to retain the observed quality of the transmission. This results in transmission with 15 times fewer bits. PAC was first developed at Bell Labs in the 1930s.
JPEG	A *Joint Photographic Experts Group* compression standard used mainly for photographs. The International Standards Organization (ISO) and the ITU developed JPEG.
MPEG-2	A *Moving Picture Experts Group* video compression standard approved in 1993 for coding and decoding video and television images. MPEG-2 uses past images to predict future images and color. It then transmits only the changed image. For example, the first in a series of frames is sent in a compressed form. The ensuing frames send only the changes. A frame is a group of bits representing a portion of a picture, text, or audio section.
MPEG-3	MPEG-3 is Layer 3 of MPEG-1. MPEG-3, also referred to as MP3, is a standard for streaming audio and music. MPEG-3 is the compression algorithm used to download audio files from the Internet. Some Internet e-commerce sites use MPEG so that potential customers who have applications that use compression software can download samples of music to decide if they want to purchase a particular song.
MPEG-4	MPEG-4 is a standard for compression, which defined coding on audio and video.

Table 1-5 OSI Layers

OSI Layer Name and Number	Layer Function
Layer 1: Physical Layer	Layer 1 is the most basic layer.
	Layer 1 defines the type of media (for instance, copper, wireless, or fiber optic) and how devices access media.
	Repeaters used to extend signals over fiber, wireless, and copper networks are Layer 1 devices. Repeaters in cellular networks extend and boost signals inside buildings and in subways so that users can still take advantage of their cellular devices in these otherwise network-inaccessible locations.
Layer 2: Data Link Layer	Ethernet, also known as 802.3, is a Layer 2 protocol. It provides rules for error correction and access to LANs.
	Layer 2 devices have addressing information analogous to Social Security numbers; they are random but specific to individual locations.
	Frame Relay is a Layer 2 protocol previously used to access carrier networks from enterprises.
Layer 3: Network Layer	Layer 3 is known as the routing layer. It is responsible for routing traffic between networks that use IP network addresses. Layer 3 has error-control functions.
	Layer 3 is analogous to a local post office routing an out-of-town letter by ZIP code while not looking at the street address. Once an e-mail message is received at the distant network, a Layer 3 device looks at the specific address and delivers the message.
Layer 4: Transport Layer	Layer 4 protocols enable networks to differentiate between types of content. They are also known as content switches.
	Layer 4 devices route by content. Video or voice transmissions over data networks might receive a higher priority or quality of service than e-mail, which can tolerate delay.
	Filters in routers that check for computer viruses by looking at additional bits in packets perform a Layer 4 function.
	Transmission Control Protocol (TCP) is a Layer 4 protocol.
Layer 5: Session Layer	Layer 5 manages the actual dialog of sessions. Encryption that scrambles signals to ensure privacy occurs in Layer 5.
	H.323 is a Layer 5 protocol that sends signals in packet networks to set up and tear down, for example, video and audio conferences.
Layer 6: Presentation Layer	Layer 6 controls the format or how the information looks on the user's screen.
	Hypertext Markup Language (HTML), which is used to format web pages and some e-mail messages, is a Layer 6 standard.
Layer 7: Application Layer	Layer 7 includes the application itself plus specialized services such as file transfers or print services. HTTP is a Layer 7 protocol.

2 Data Centers and LANs, Storage, and IP Private Branch Exchanges

In this chapter:

INTRODUCTION ....

IT management is in a race to keep up with growing demand for capacity on local area networks (LANs) and storage systems. The growth in the amount of traffic on LANs that results in congestion is due to the growing number of employees

- Accessing data that is in the cloud
- Uploading data to the cloud
- Downloading data from the Internet
- Holding videoconferences with remote and local colleagues
- Using collaboration software to share and edit documents related to joint projects

The above factors add to the increasing volume of data traversing the LANs.

In addition to more voice, data, and video transmitted on LANs, there are requirements for additional capacity on storage systems. Some of the needs for additional storage can be attributed to the fact that regulations in certain industries require businesses to save data for 3 or more years. Examples of industries with retention requirements include

- Medical device and pharmaceutical companies
- Hospitals
- Retailing
- Financial firms
- Government agencies

Even organizations without as many requirements to retain data are finding it necessary to add more storage space for data related to customer information, product specifications, research projects, and employee data. In addition, the cost for storage is decreasing, which allows organizations to store more data.

Data centers are centralized locations for housing software applications. Because of the growing dependence on the cloud to store and manage applications, enterprise data centers are shrinking in physical size. Placing applications in the cloud takes the burden of monitoring, patching, and upgrading applications away from staff in corporate data centers. It additionally reduces the load on organizations to have mechanisms to protect applications from power outages, brief power interruptions, and natural disasters such as hurricanes and tornadoes.

Cloud services allow small companies to operate without a data center, and most of the medium-sized companies only require two or three servers. For small and large organizations alike, cloud services provide many of the management tasks previously performed by in-house technical staff. However, even with cloud services, IT staff is needed to monitor security and secure access to applications in the cloud.

Employees often bring expectations for capacity, accessibility, and user-friendly interfaces from their experience as residential customers. Residential customers can easily access Facebook, Snapchat, and Google from mobile devices and laptops. Employees expect the same level of service for work-related computing tasks. They anticipate the applications they access to be always available, easy to use, and accessible from mobile devices and remote locations. This is an ongoing challenge for IT personnel and management.

Organizations are meeting these staff expectations through unified communications, collaboration software, and easy-to-access desktop video conferencing. Unified communications is the ability to access company directories and voice mail messages from within a single e-mail inbox. Collaboration software, which mimics Google Docs and Box services, enables employees to share documents, edit documents written by other staff, and keep up-to-date on group projects. Telephone system manufacturers such as Mitel and Cisco often include these applications and capabilities in their systems' platforms.

To meet staff expectations for access to applications, organizations are taking steps to prevent delays and ensure continuous uptime. They are investing in higher capacity switches to transmit growth in LAN traffic, and LAN monitoring software to quickly spot and resolve equipment and software glitches.

WHAT IS A LAN? ....

A LAN is a local network owned by an enterprise, a commercial organization, or a residential user. The purpose of a LAN is to allow employees and residential users to share resources. For example, without a local area network, each person would need his or her own printer, router, switch, and applications. The LAN enables employees to share high-speed printers, routers, modems, Wi-Fi equipment, and broadband services to reach the Internet, and to receive incoming and make outgoing calls. Without a LAN, each user would additionally require her own connection to the Internet. In short, costs would be sky-high and staff would be burdened with arranging all their own access to services.

Table 2-1 is a partial list of devices connected to LANs. Growing numbers of "connected" devices is adding tremendous traffic to LANs. It is additionally increasing the criticality of LANs. Each device on a LAN is referred to as a *node*. The size of a LAN is often described as the number of nodes on that LAN.

Table 2-1   Devices (Nodes) on LANs

Routers	Security cameras
Printers	Wi-Fi equipment
Switches	Telephones
Personal computers	Cable modems
Thermostats	Video conferencing equipment
Electronic white boards for meetings	Security alarms
Lights	Equipment to manage lighting
Fire alarms	Factory automation systems
Shared applications	Projectors
Wireless devices connected to Wi-Fi	Bar code scanners in retail locations
Cash registers	LAN monitoring software
Storage networks	Databases
Televisions	Set-top boxes including Apple TV and Roku

SWITCHES, MEDIA, AND PROTOCOLS IN LANS.......

Switches have been described as "goes into, goes out of." Requests for access to applications including e-mail go "into" switches and the responses to these requests are transmitted "out of" switches.

LANs are made up of Layer 3 (also referred to as core or backbone) switches and Layer 2 switches.

- Layer 3 core or backbone switches

  - Transmit messages between buildings on a campus.

  - Are connected to other Layer 2 and to Layer 3 switches.

  - Are not connected to nodes.

  - Carry the highest amount of LAN traffic.

- Layer 2 switches

  - Are connected to nodes (devices) on floors.

  - Carry less traffic than Layer 3 switches.

Copper, Wi-Fi, and fiber media tie nodes and switches together into a network.

Layer 3 Switches—Transmitting Data between Switches and Data Centers

Layer 3 switches are large-capacity switches that transmit data between Layer 2 switches and centralized applications in data centers. Layer 3 switches are also referred to as *core* or *backbone* switches. They tie together buildings located in, for example, hospitals, universities, and enterprise campuses. Core switches are not connected directly to end-users' devices. A backbone switch has connections to multiple switches and to routers, but not to LAN nodes listed in Table 2-1. On large LANs, if a link to a core switch is down, the backbone switch can often route traffic around the disabled switch to a functioning switch.

IP Addresses in Layer 3 Switches

Layer 3 switches are called Layer 3 because they route messages to devices via their IP address. Layer 3 devices are considered Network Link nodes equipment. Layer 3 Network Link switches send messages *only to other switches* and routers, not to nodes such as printers and individuals' devices. All networks including broadband, cellular and the Internet, have Layer 3 switches for transmitting data and voice within backbone networks. See Chapter 1, "Computing and Enabling Technologies," for backbone networks.

Layer 2 Switches—Links to Nodes

In LANs, Layer 2 switches are located in wiring closets on individual floors. The switches typically have between 8 and 24 *ports* with a dedicated port for each device connected to them. Each port is connected to users' computers, Wi-Fi access points, printers, and other LAN nodes. Because each device is cabled to its own dedicated port, messages they transmit are not broadcast to all users. For example, a manager is able to send the same e-mail or video to staff on various floors. These messages are sent only to the designated recipients, not to each person working on these floors. This avoids flooding each device with traffic for other nodes.

 NOTE In data communications parlance, a *port* is an interface into which a cable is plugged for linking a computer to another device (a laptop to a display), or to link devices to switches and networks.

MAC Addresses in Layer 2 Switches

Layer 2 switches send packets to devices based on their Media Access Control (MAC) address. Each device connected to a LAN has a MAC address. Layer 2 devices are considered Data Link equipment. They typically support up to 40Gbps speeds. If a port fails, the device connected to it loses its connection to the LAN. See Figure 2-1 for switches in wiring closets. This represents a single point of failure to the devices connected to them. If the switch crashes, all of the 16 to 24 devices connected to it are out of service. But the nodes connected to Layer 2 switches in other wiring closets don't lose service.

Many Layer 2 switches are an industry-standard 19 inches wide for rack mounting and are typically housed in freestanding equipment racks with horizontally positioned blades. Circuit boards are often referred to as *blades* when they are dense, such as when they have many ports. Switches can be wall-mounted in wiring closets that don't contain other equipment.

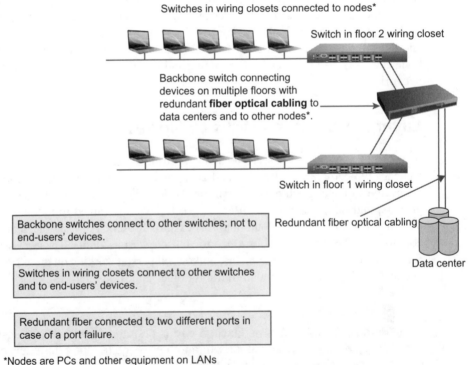

Switches in wiring closets connected to nodes*

Switch in floor 2 wiring closet

Backbone switch connecting devices on multiple floors with redundant **fiber optical cabling** to data centers and to other nodes*.

Switch in floor 1 wiring closet

Backbone switches connect to other switches; not to end-users' devices.

Redundant fiber optical cabling

Data center

Switches in wiring closets connect to other switches and to end-users' devices.

Redundant fiber connected to two different ports in case of a port failure.

*Nodes are PCs and other equipment on LANs

Figure 2-1   A switch located in a wiring closet.

The Criticality of Layer 3 vs. Layer 2 Switches

LAN backbones where core switches are located carry the highest volume of an organization's traffic. Backbone switches are more critical in supporting staff communications than switches in wiring closets. If a backbone switch fails, every Layer 2 switch plus the nodes connected to each wiring closest switch are out of service. In contrast, if a Layer 2 switch crashes, the only nodes that lose service are the 8 to 16 or 24 devices connected to it. Moreover, the cost to purchase redundant Layer 2 switches is high because there are so many of them. In a five-story building, there could be a total of 40 Layer 2 switches in wiring closets and only six in the backbone. See Figure 2-2 for switches in LAN backbones.

There are instances, however, when high-level employees such as CEOs are connected to a dedicated Layer 2 switch. In these cases, components within the wiring closet may be duplicated to avoid outages. In addition, IT staff closely monitor these senior employees' equipment connections so that if they do break down, they can be repaired or quickly replaced.

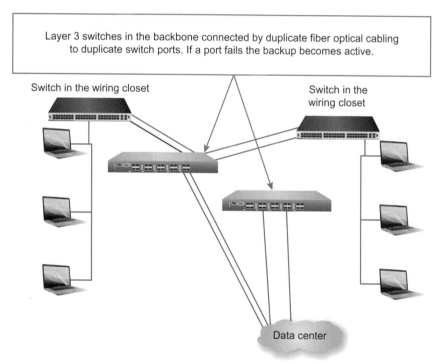

Figure 2-2   Switches in LAN backbones.

Layer 3 Switch Redundancy in the Backbone

Because core Layer 3 switch failures impact many nodes in networks, there are often redundant Layer 3 switches. Medium- and large-sized organizations often have redundant switches in their backbone network so that if one switch is out of service traffic can be rerouted to a different Layer 3 switch.

In addition to or instead of having redundant switches in backbones, components within each core switch can be duplicated, particularly those components such as power supplies that fail more frequently than other components. And importantly, there may be redundant switches within data centers. When either of these two things is done, there are rarely LAN outages.

Organizations consider a variety of levels of redundancy for core switches, including the following:

- Purchase of a separate, duplicate switch that can take over if one fails.

- Installation of redundant power supplies in the switch. (A power supply converts AC power to the low-voltage DC power required by computers.) Switches are inoperable if the power supply fails.

- Installation of redundant blades in the switch. Each blade (also referred to as a *card* or *circuit board*) supports a megabit or gigabit capacity Ethernet port.

40/100Gbps Ethernet Switch Standards

The Institute of Electrical and Electronics Engineers (IEEE) approves Gigabit Ethernet standards such as a 40/100Gbps and higher capacities. Most organizations currently use the 40Gbps switches. However, for organizations whose networks support web sites with extremely high traffic, this is actually too slow. To support ultra-high levels of web site traffic, they deploy 100Gbps Ethernet switches. Facebook's needs for bandwidth are so large that they have developed source switches that support 400Gbps. They've made the design available to other organizations. They've additionally stated their intention to develop a switch with thirty-two 400Gbps ports.

When IT staff discuss the capacity of their LAN networks, they refer to them by the capacity of their switches. So organizations with 40 Gbps switches state their LAN as a 40Gbps or 40 Gig network. Here is one IT staff member's comment:

> "We used to have a 10 Gigabit network. But, because of the increase in our LAN traffic, we upgraded to 100 Gigabits."

User Errors—A Major Challenge

In a company located in China, an employee mentioned to the IT Director that the LAN was running unusually slow. The IT Director checked the network monitor, but could not see an equipment failure. He did find an unusual amount of traffic at one switch. Initially, he was concerned that the cause was a computer virus. He started unplugging devices from the network in case the virus had spread. When he unplugged a cable from one switch, the LAN traffic speeded up.

When he traced where the cable from that switch was plugged, he found that the other end of the cable was plugged into the same switch rather than a different one. This solved the problem because a loop storm had been created where data traveled in a circle between the two ports on the switch. Later, an employee e-mailed him and told him he saw a cable lying on the floor and so plugged it into another port of the same switch.

Virtual Local Area Networks for Specialized Treatment

A Virtual Local Area Network (VLAN) comprises devices such as personal computers, physical servers, IP phones, and wireless telephones whose addresses are programmed as a group in Layer 2 switches to give them higher priority or special privileges, or to segregate them from the rest of the corporate network for higher security. Although they are programmed as a separate LAN and treated like a separate LAN in terms of privileges, they are not necessarily connected to the same switches. Some computers are put into VLANs so that they can access secure files such as healthcare records.

VLANs are used to provide special features to nodes. For example, video conferencing or LAN-connected telephones may receive priority over e-mail traffic because delays in video may result in distorted images whereas e-mails are not time sensitive and delays in sending or receiving messages are not noticeable.

IP telephones and video conferencing units that send voice in packets over networks and wireless LAN devices are often programmed into their own VLANs. These devices allow only certain types of equipment, such as other telephones or video conferencing equipment, to communicate with them.

Media-Connecting Nodes to LANs

In information technology and telecommunications, media refers to cabling and wireless services that connect devices to each other, to buildings and ultimately to individuals.

Examples of media are: copper, fiber-optic cabling, and wireless on cellular and Wi-Fi networks. Copper is used most often between individual wired computers and the wiring closet on each floor. Fiber is often used to transmit data between floors and within the data center to transport the heavy concentrations of traffic. Because of its light weight and large capacity, fiber is deployed where there is the heaviest amount of traffic. See Chapter 1 for a discussion of fiber and copper cabling. Copper cabling is used most often to connect nodes to LANs. (The term devices are used synonymously with nodes.) Wireless of course is used for Wi-Fi. See the section on Wi-Fi in Chapter 7, "Mobile and Wi-Fi Networks."

Increased Bandwidth Needs on LANs

A number of factors are causing the amount of traffic on local area network to increase exponentially. These include increasing amounts of data-intensive centralized computing and requirements for additional storage. Another factor is the growing dependence on accessing content in the cloud. The staff's cloud traffic transits LANs to reach databases located in the cloud and in companies' data centers. And to a greater extent than ever before, video traffic streamed and downloaded from the cloud, the Internet, and from on-site videoconferences is adding to LAN congestion and the need for larger pipes.

Other factors adding to LAN congestion are:

- Large graphics file attachments such as PowerPoint files.

- Daily backups to databases of entire corporate files.

- Web downloads of long, continuous streams of images, audio, and video files.

- Access by remote and local employees to applications and personal files on centralized servers and storage devices.

- Web access, during which users typically have four or more windows open concurrently. Each open web page is a *session*, an open communication with packets traveling between the user and the Internet.

Here's a quote from an IT Director at a university:

"We never have enough capacity on our local network or storage space in our storage area network."

Protocols for Communications in LANs

All devices connected to LANs use network protocols to access the LAN. They communicate with other devices and applications, which might be located on the same floor, on another floor, in another building, or even on an organization's LAN located on another continent. By providing a uniform way to communicate, LANs simplify the process of linking devices, applications, and networks together. Ethernet is the most common of these protocols. Other specialized protocols are used to access Storage Area Networks.

The Ethernet Open Standard for Network Access

Ethernet is an 802.3 open-standard protocol, approved by the Institute of Electrical and Electronics Engineers (IEEE), a non-profit standards body. Devices such as personal computers and printers use it to access the LAN and to retrieve packets from wired and wireless LANs. Each device on an Ethernet LAN has an address, referred to as its Media Access Control (MAC) address. Layer 2 switches in wiring closets use the MAC address to send messages to other LAN-attached devices.

Ethernet is the first LAN access scheme that was widely adopted. Because it is based on an open standard, it is broadly available from different manufacturers. In the 1980s, departments within companies began to use Ethernet to link their computers together over coaxial cables to share software applications, such as accounting and financial tracking packages as well as printers. In the 1990s, lighter-weight, lower-cost unshielded, twisted-pair (UTP) cabling became available on new UTP cable standards on LANs. This greatly simplified installing and moving computers on LANs because of the lighter weight and flexibility of UTP cabling. See Table 2-2 for additional LAN protocols, devices and terms.

Ethernet is an *asynchronous* protocol. Asynchronous protocols do not specify a specific start and stop time for each packet of data. All devices connected to the network attempt to send whenever they are ready.

Ethernet's simplicity makes it straightforward to connect equipment to networks. All that's required are computers with Ethernet interfaces (ports) for an Ethernet cable, a Network Interface Card (NIC), and Ethernet software to link devices to switches in wiring closets. Because of the uncertainty of traffic volume at any given point in time, Ethernet networks are often configured to run at no more than half of their capacity.

NOTE *Frames* serve the same function as packets. They surround user data with addressing, error checking, and other protocol-related bits. The term "frame" is used in lower-level protocols, such as Ethernet, which is used for communicating within LANs connected to the same switch in the wiring closet. *Packets* refer to data configured for transmission between LANs and on the Internet by using TCP/IP.

Using TCP/IP as a Linking Protocol

Ethernet is a way for individual frames to access LANs and for computers to retrieve frames from local networks, whereas TCP/IP is used to tie LANs together and to route packets *between* networks as well as to and from the Internet. As the need arose to tie LANs together for e-mail and file sharing, compatibility between LANs from different manufacturers became a problem. The TCP/IP suite of protocols became a popular choice for overcoming these incompatibilities and for managing the flow of information between LANs.

Routers were developed to send data between individual LANs, and between LANs and the Internet and other networks. Routers send packets to individual networks based on their IP address. IP addresses are assigned to individual networks and servers that run software applications.

Software Defined Networks in LANs

As more varied applications, data from storage networks, cloud data, and Internet traffic is transmitted across LANs, large organizations need to have more control over how various applications are transmitted. For example, video files and real-time transactions require a higher priority than for example, e-mail.

In addition, IT managers are under pressure to keep the staff lean and productive. At the same time, they need the ability to quickly adapt to changes and to add and delete features and applications. This is often difficult with current local area network infrastructure where prioritizing traffic results in complicated management of that traffic.

It may be difficult to add new services because of the need for backward compatibility with older applications and equipment. This is particularly true in large conglomerates often made up of a variety of subsidiaries and departments, many of which have different applications and requirements.

Features of Software-Defined Networks

As the name implies, software-defined networks are controlled by software rather than hardware. The software is located in a central controller in off-the-shelf, general-purpose computers. The controller has policies in software that define how packets are forwarded. The control plane distributes policies that the controller transmits to it. The data plane is made up of tunnels that carry data to endpoints. Endpoints are also referred to as nodes, devices connected to the LAN.

The key advantage of distributing policies to endpoints is that endpoints do not need to continuously communicate with a central controller because the policies are forwarded as they change with instructions on how to treat data that is transmitted by the endpoints. These policies have instructions on how to treat traffic during peak times. The endpoints do not need to send data back to a central point for instructions because they are automatically sent to the endpoints whenever there are changes in policies. Thus, LANs can respond dynamically in real time, to changing traffic patterns, congestion, and outages. For example, if one route is congested or out of service, data is automatically transmitted on other routes.

Dependence on a Central Controller—The Need for Redundancy

Controller redundancy is important in SDNs because no new policies can be transmitted to endpoints if the links to the central controller or the central controller itself is out of service. Once service is reestablished, controllers automatically transmit policies that were programmed during the outage to endpoints.

Flexibility

Changes can be implemented rapidly because many changes in software-defined networks do not require additional hardware. Changes are made by programming new policies in central controllers. Changes should of course be tested in isolated parts of the network or data centers before they are implemented. See Chapter 4, "Managing Broadband Networks," for software-defined network technologies on broadband links.

Network Operating Systems

LAN Network Operating System (NOS) software is located on specialized computers called *file servers* in the LAN. File servers provide shared access to programs on LANs. A NOS—also referred to as simply the operating system (OS)—defines consistent ways for software to use LAN hardware and for software on computers to interoperate with the LAN. LAN operating system client software is located on each device connected to the LAN.

The way PCs request access to services such as printers, e-mail, and sales applications located on servers is defined by operating systems. A network operating system also defines how devices access shared applications and the network. A NOS further controls how icons are displayed on computers' "desktops." Examples of network operating systems include Novell, Windows Server 2010, Windows Server 2016, Sun Solaris 10, and Linux.

Client software (software on nodes) is installed on individual devices. Examples of client software on PCs include Windows XP, Windows 8, and Windows 10. Apple computers use various operating systems such as OS10.5 and OS10.14.2. Often when client software on Windows and MAC computers are upgraded, older Office and other applications need to be upgraded. Features in the upgraded operating system may not be compatible with older word processing and spreadsheet software.

Data Centers—Centralized Locations for Housing Applications

A data center is a physical location where an organization or cloud provider's data applications are centralized. This includes LAN operating systems, e-mail servers, security software on dedicated servers or appliances, voice telephony, storage area networks, databases, and accounting applications. See Figure 2-3 for a depiction of a data center. An *appliance* is a server dedicated to a specific software function such as email and security. Applications including e-mail are housed in servers, powerful computers accessed by authorized staff. Switches in data centers transmit traffic to individual applications in the data center.

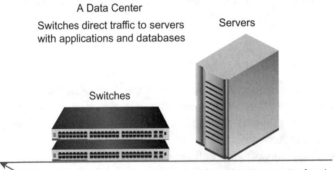

Figure 2-3   A data center.

Data centers come in a variety of sizes. They can be located in an organization's branch as well their headquarters. They are also at cloud providers' sites. For example, a small to medium-sized company may have a data center with only a few servers if the bulk of their applications are located in the cloud. Large organizations with multiple sites may have data centers and applications in branch offices as well as at headquarters. Or branch office staff may remotely access information in a centralized data center at headquarters or at a cloud provider's data center.

Hyper cloud providers—the very largest providers; Amazon, Facebook, Google (part of Alphabet), and Microsoft have large data centers spread all over the world. As cloud computing proliferates, an increasing number of applications previously at enterprise data centers are now at hosting and cloud providers' data centers. According to a *Wall Street Journal*, April 10, 2017, online article, "A New Arms Race for Tech" combined capital expenditures at Amazon, Microsoft, and Alphabet's Google increased 22 percent in 2016 compared to 2015.

Protecting Data Centers

Cloud providers and social networks have multiple, duplicated large data centers dispersed around the world. Many of them are exact duplicates of each other in the event that one of their data centers is destroyed by a natural disaster or other disaster. As discussed in Chapter 1, duplicate data centers are for the most part connected by fiber-optic cabling. Capacity in fiber cabling and the electronics connected to it have the capacity to back up data continuously in real time or at the end of the day.

Telephone companies and cellular providers all have data centers. These data centers manage services and applications such as voice mail and messaging that they offer customers. In addition, these companies deploy roomfuls of technicians to remotely monitor and manage their networks. This is done from data on technicians' screens in these data centers. Cellular and telephone companies' data centers monitor and manage:

- Connections to other networks

- Connections to subscribers

- Conditions in their own networks

- Tracking customers' voice and data usage

- Billing software with information on each subscriber's voice and data usage and voice and data plan

- Security

- Switches used for voice calling

- E-mail servers

The Impact of Cloud Computing on Data Centers

Although the criticality of and reliance on applications and databases is increasing, many data centers are shrinking in physical size. When cloud computing was first introduced, mainly small and medium-sized organizations trusted it enough to use it for the majority of their applications. As time went on, more organizations began trusting the cloud and transferring more of their applications and development to cloud platforms. This resulted in smaller data centers and fewer tech staff required to operate data centers because a number of applications are located in the cloud and often managed by the cloud provider. A data center in an organization with most of its applications in the cloud might consist of only a few servers.

Hosting vs. Cloud Services

Hosting companies such as Markley Group and Rackspace provide secure locations where enterprise organizations store applications. Customers can place their own servers at the hosting site. Cambridge-based Harvard University keeps a server with applications for medical research at the Markley Group's facility in downtown Boston. Researchers access their server remotely for computing related to their research. Markley supplies the physical security, security from hackers, cooling, and "hardened" building construction to protect their facility from natural disasters such as hurricanes and earthquakes.

Cloud companies sell multi-tenant platforms (servers) where customers can spin applications up to or down from the cloud. Providers offer more granular, finer tuned services. For example, customers can control the days and hours their applications are available, the amount of cloud security they require, and whether to pay extra for their own, private server. They have the ability to more granularly measure and control computing power and usage on their applications. Cloud providers also offer Service Level Agreements (SLAs) that spell out guarantees of up-time and other performance criteria. Typically, hosting companies charge flat monthly fees and cloud providers' charges are metered, based on monthly computer usage.

Often an organization will consolidate applications that are not in the cloud into central data centers that were previously located in numerous remote offices and department. Centralization and streamlined data center operations are enabled in large part by storage, server, and switch virtualization. Increased broadband network capacity is another key enabler of centralized data centers.

Environmental Controls in Data Centers

Virtualization and cloud computing have decreased the number of physical servers needed in data centers. However, each physical server requires more cooling due to more powerful, octal processors that generate more heat than dual or single processors. This increases electricity costs needed for cooling these powerful servers.

Designing cooling, power, and *Uninterrupted Power Supply* (*UPS*) systems that distribute power are so complex that organizations often hire consultants to design cost-effective environmental controls. An uninterrupted power supply provides power for the short time before gas-generated backup power kicks in. Increasing or decreasing the number of people in the data center will further impact cooling needs.

In addition, there are different cooling requirements for equipment located at the bottom of racks vs. equipment located at the top. The type and amount of lighting also impacts cooling requirements. Energy consultants offer consulting services aimed at designing cost-effective energy and power systems for data centers.

Taking Steps to Ensure Adequate, Lower-Cost Power

To save money on electricity, some large enterprises have applied for and received permission from the United States Federal Energy Regulatory Commission (FERC) to become wholesale providers of electricity. By doing so, they can purchase bulk supplies of power at low rates. In addition to saving money on power purchases, this ensures that they have an adequate supply of electricity for their own power needs. Examples of companies that have been approved by FERC to purchase bulk supplies of electricity include Google, Exxon Mobile, Kimberly-Clark Corporation, Alcoa, Tropicana, and The Dow Chemical Company. None of these companies have stated an interest in reselling electricity on a retail basis.

While it's not expected that smaller organizations will follow this route, this does point out the efforts that large, multisite firms will take to ensure an adequate supply of electricity at the lowest possible rates. To further ensure a steady supply of power, companies also purchase power from multiple power generating companies over different power feeds. In addition, electric rates and adequate sources of power often factor into decisions of where to locate data centers. For example, Facebook has two data centers located in Sweden, partly to cut down on cooling costs.

Resiliency in Data Centers: Continuous Operation

A key task in designing data centers is determining which devices or elements represent single points of failure that have the potential to put the entire data center out of service. Power cuts and interruptions, fire, and natural disasters such as hurricanes all have the potential to shut down computer operations. Human error is also a common cause of failures.

Data centers are often located in out-of-the way spaces within buildings, particularly if there is a shortage of office space. Thus, it's not uncommon for data centers to be located in basements. In low-lying areas this is a problem because of the danger of flooding the data center and destroying the equipment. Although most data centers have raised floors, floods in these areas are nevertheless a problem.

Enterprises and carriers with mission-critical data centers must decide where to spend money on redundancy and protection from catastrophic failures. See Figure 2-4 for an example of failover during a data center failure. Because loss of an uninterrupted power supply can bring down a data center, many organizations consider redundant UPS and backup electric generator service. This can mean two UPS's and backup generators connected to the same electrical feed or the more costly option of two electrical feeds, each with its own UPS.

Organizations with two electrical feeds generally arrange that each enter the building in separate conduits and separate building entrances. If one electrical cable is cut, the data center will fail over to the other one. This is expected of hosting and cloud providers and other critical infrastructure suppliers.

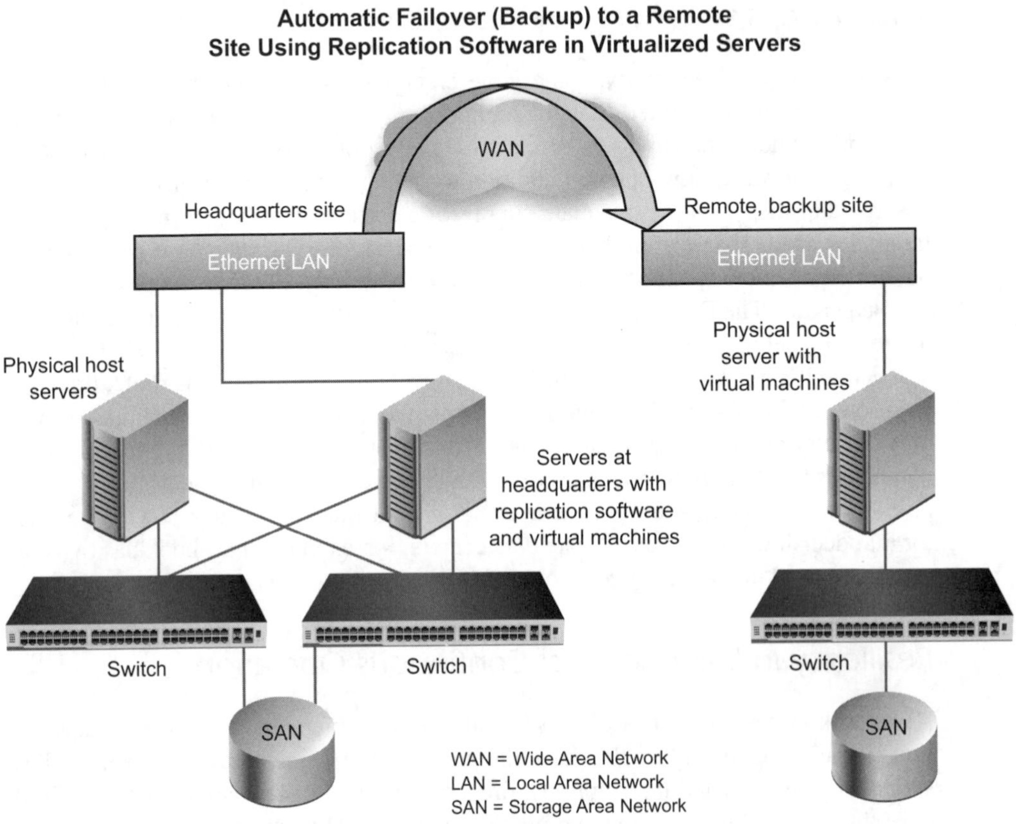

Figure 2-4   Automatic failover to a remote site.

An even more costly option is to lease or build a second, backup data center. The backup may be at a providers' site or may be owned and operated by the enterprise.

Storage Systems—Managing Petabytes of Data

Organizations use storage systems to access information for daily transactions and to archive backup copies of computer files and databases on hard drives controlled by servers with specialized software. They are used by online as well as brick-and-mortar stores that need access to credit card and customer service data to authorize purchases and resolve customer complaints.

Biopharmaceutical companies use storage systems in their refinement of and development of new drugs. They can change the amount of particular chemicals they add to drug formulations and track how each alteration changes how drugs' effectiveness is impacted by each input. These changes are tracked over time. The ability to track massive amounts of data during drug development is speeding the time to develop and improve drugs' effectiveness.

According to a chemist at a bio-tech firm:

> *"The decline in costs of mass storage has greatly impacted our research and development. We can purchase huge amounts of storage to help us analyze how changing inputs to drugs during development results in chemical changes."*

Telephone and cable TV companies store massive amounts of customer billing and usage data. Their customer service representatives access much of this information when customers call with questions about bills or to make changes to their service. Other critical functions of data in storage systems are to detect patterns of financial fraud, authorize credit card transactions, and increase the speed of stock trading by supplying near real time access to changes in stocks and bonds trades.

Without access to customer and organizational data, organizations cannot manage daily operations efficiently. Small and medium-sized organizations store databases and back up files in the cloud or on standard on-site computers. Larger organizations, however, require storage systems to manage the large number of requests to access and input information to complex storage systems. The level of complexity of storage systems is such that in large data centers, a specialized staff manages the storage.

Examples of organizations that use and manage their own large storage systems to collect and manage data are cloud providers, and large commercial entities. In particular, government agencies, municipalities, healthcare organizations, financial firms, and large universities as well as streaming media companies store enormous amounts of information. Faster processors, powerful IP fiber-optical networks, and lower-cost, large capacity disk storage and faster memory enable storage systems to provide near real time access to immense amounts of information. Typically, these storage systems are located at off-site data centers or in the cloud.

Large enterprises and data centers operated by cloud providers deploy storage systems with servers (computers) that run special-purpose programs that monitor and manage access to storage, memory chips, and disks that store information required to operate their businesses. The information is in the form of text, databases, video, and audio records.

In contrast to local and broadband networks that measure capacity in bits, storage systems measure capacity of the massive amounts of data stored in *bytes*. Each byte is made up of 8-bit characters. Large storage systems typically hold petabytes of information. A petabyte equals 1,000,000,000,000,000 bytes or 1,000,000,000 gigabytes.

Measuring Performance—Input–Output Operations per Second

Input–Output Operations per Second (IOPS) is measured by how long it takes to access data from user devices. It's the time elapsed between requesting the data, transmitting the data, and receiving the data—in other words, the movement of data between the data storage network and the requesting or sending computer. Current storage systems are capable of close to 1 million inputs–outputs per second. Each request for data uses a protocol that issues a request and receives either an acknowledgment or a negative acknowledgment if the request is refused. The transmission of the requested data is also referred to as the *time in flight*.

Storage Components

All storage systems are made up of servers with specialized programs to manage and monitor the memory in disk drives and flash memory. The programs on servers also handle access to storage. Newer storage systems are composed of standard off-the-shelf computers. Storage systems additionally require fiber-optic cabling links between the storage area network and LANs and broadband networks. Traffic on the links may be routed via specialized protocols.

Memory—Flash vs. Spinning

Memory in storage systems is complex and can be architected, or put together, a number of different ways. The data stored is held either in spinning disks or flash memory. Some storage systems use a combination of both spinning disks and flash memory. Spinning disk memory is held in drives made up of metal platters with magnetic coating on which data files are stored. See Figure 2-5 below to see a spinning disk for data storage. A read-write arm attachment accesses data on the hard drive while it is spinning.

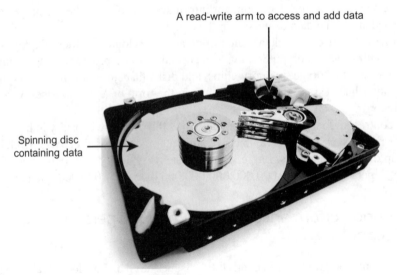

A read-write arm to access and add data

Spinning disc containing data

Figure 2-5 *A spinning disk for data storage. (Photo by olegdudko/123RF)*

Another option in addition to spinning discs is to use flash memory. Flash memory consists of interconnected flash memory chips in which data is stored. Flash memory has the advantages of being faster to access and requiring less electricity. However, after a finite amount of times that data is "written" onto flash memory, it will physically wear out. Some storage systems contain both types of memory and others consist of all flash memory. Kaminario, EMC's DSSD, and Quorum are examples of companies that offer storage systems made entirely of flash memory. Infinidat offers a hybrid system with flash memory for the most frequently accessed data and spinning discs for the rest of the data. NetApp sells both hybrid and all-flash storage.

There is disagreement in the industry over which approach, flash memory vs. spinning disks, is best. Often flash memory is used for data that is accessed more frequently and spinning disks for archived and less frequently requested data.

Storage Redundancy—Preventing Data Losses

The criticality of data requires that storage systems write data to multiple disks. If one disk fails, the data is not lost because it is stored in a redundant disk. In addition to redundant discs within the same storage system, data center operators and cloud computing providers may duplicate the entire storage system in another location. Connections between the main storage and the duplicate system enable real-time updates in the backup system. In this way, if a natural disaster such as a flood or hurricane destroys an entire data center, all data is up to date and preserved.

Frequently, only the changes in files are backed up every night. As LANs and WANs became more powerful, SANs began using *disk mirroring* to back up files in real time. Disk mirroring is the process of simultaneously writing data to backup and primary servers so that all recent changes are saved and up-to-date, in the event of a failure during working hours.

 A town in Massachusetts has a duplicated as well as main storage area network. A hacker attacked their main storage system by encrypting all of its data. (With encryption, mathematical algorithms rearrange data into a different format. A key is required to decrypt the data back to its original format.) The hacker refused to decrypt the data unless the town paid a ransom. However, the town refused to pay the ransom because they were able to replace the encrypted data with data from the backup storage system. Nearby towns without a backup storage network did pay a ransom to have their data decrypted.

Storage Area Networks—Centralized File Access

Storage area networks (SANs) enable the entire organization to share files so that people do not need their own, personal database. Having an adequate number of channels into the servers connected to storage systems is a critical step in avoiding delays because of congestion in data look-up requests. See Figure 2-6 for an example of a storage area network.

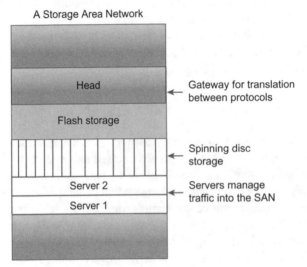

Figure 2-6 A storage area network.

The Fibre Channel group of SAN open protocols was designed for the heavy traffic generated in data-intensive networks. It is a point-to-point protocol, wherein data is transferred directly from one point (a computer) to another point (disk storage). Because of its capability to transfer large amounts of data at high speeds, large companies use Fibre Channel. It is the costliest SAN option.

The Fibre Channel over Ethernet (FCoE) protocol was approved by ANSI in 2009. It was developed so that Fibre Channel SANs could communicate with Gbps Ethernet networks without translating between Ethernet and Fibre Channel protocols. The goal is to simplify structures and communications in data centers.

Other, less costly, SANs include:

- iSCSI (Internet small computer system interface), which is a newer, less costly all-IP protocol suited for small and medium sized companies

- NAS (Network attached storage) systems, which are connected to devices via a specialized server containing file sharing software. NAS is compatible with Ethernet protocols

Hyper-Converged Infrastructure

Hyper-converged infrastructure (HCI) in data centers simplifies data center infrastructure and provides the ability to manage storage, computing, development and testing, remote offices, and other services from a single point by combining storage, applications, and networking on commodity, off-the shelf appliances. HCI is available from most equipment manufacturers. If not using off the shelf servers, HCI requires that all the data center hardware be from the same manufacturer.

HCI is software-controlled infrastructure. Centralized software is used to manage the entire HCI infrastructure and prioritize streams of data. The software application (the controller) monitors and controls the data center and creates logs of traffic, and outages. The error reporting software is centralized.

The goal of hyper converged infrastructure is to provide enterprises a way to scale up or down without a major forklift. HCI came into prominence as a way to save money by emulating cloud infrastructure in private and commercial companies. Compression and deduplication are used in storage equipment so that data can be stored using less disk space. Compression uses complex algorithms to shrink the size of data. See Chapter 1 for more about compression. Deduplication removes redundant data from stored and transmitted files. Additionally, it streamlines protocols that require acknowledgments and negative acknowledgments after each stream of data transmitted.

The Impact of Virtualized Hardware Failure

Because multiple software applications run on each physical server, virtualization increases each physical server's criticality. If one server fails, multiple applications and business processes are disrupted. Moreover, server virtualization results in the centralization of more applications, such as collaboration, video and audio conferencing, and accounts payable and accounts receivable software being centralized within data centers rather than located in remote departments. Thus, in multi-site organizations, failures affect multiple sites and departments.

Redundancy is a key consideration in organizations where computing is critical for operations. *Hot standby* is one option for redundancy. Hot standby refers to the capability of one piece of equipment to automatically take over the function of a failed unit, without human intervention. One way to achieve this is to provide alternate paths if one switch fails. Another option is to use replication software, which is used in virtualized servers to back up all files to a hot standby location that can handle all computing if the main site crashes.

Managing Users' Computers via Virtual Desktops

Desktop virtualization, also called Virtual Desktop Integration (VDI), refers to the phenomenon of users' applications and desktop images being held in central servers in data centers or in the cloud. Staff access their desktop images and applications from screens on their desktop or from mobile devices.

This relieves IT staff from troubleshooting software, applying patches to software, and upgrading software on employees' computers, which occupies a considerable amount of time. Moreover, ensuring that desktop and laptop computers don't contaminate networks with viruses is a complex and time-consuming task. End users who install unknown programs or inadvertently open e-mail attachments that contain viruses can unwittingly bring computer networks to their knees.

In addition, users today are mobile. They access their applications and documents from all types of mobile devices—laptops, desktop computers, tablets, and smartphones. In addition to providing portability and security, desktop virtualization ensures that users are able to access applications that require, for instance, Windows or others that operate on Mac operating systems.

All of these factors plus improvements in desktop virtualization and lower costs for VDI are pushing an interest in desktop virtualization by large enterprises. With desktop virtualization, users have a screen, and keyboard. A connector box linked to their computer is tied to a centralized server that runs desktop virtualization software as in Figure 2-7. Users' desktops are hosted in the central server as software.

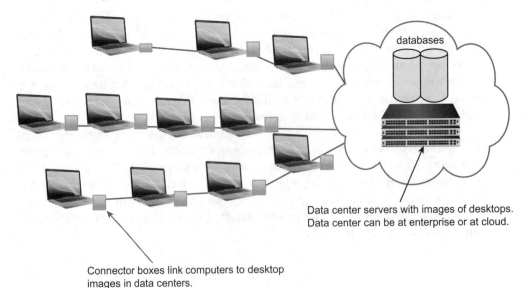

Connector boxes link computers to desktop images in data centers.

Data center servers with images of desktops. Data center can be at enterprise or at cloud.

databases

Figure 2-7   An example of desktop virtual integration (VDI).

When a user turns on his screen, he sees an image of his desktop, complete with icons. Virtual Desktop Integration is referred to as *thin-client* technology because very little intelligence is needed at the end user's device. The user's equipment is referred to as the client. Organizations such as Dell, Citrix Systems, Inc., LISTEQ, Microsoft, Nimboxx, Oracle, and VMware supply desktop virtualization software.

In the past, when Virtual Desktop Integration was tested, most organizations that installed it experienced unacceptable delays in accessing centralized files and applications because of inadequate LAN capacity. Improvements in LAN capacity have eliminated these delays. Another factor inhibiting implementation is the fear that if a remote user wants to work on centralized files, and she is somewhere without an available broadband connection, productivity gains in centralizing applications and any modifications to the files will be lost.

Multiple Operating Systems on Desktop Computers—Testing and Flexibility

Software developers and IT staff use desktop virtualization on computers with multiple operating systems to test new applications as they are developed or before they are provided to an organization's staff. They do this by trying out the new software with a variety of operating systems such as Linux, Windows, and Mac operating systems to determine if the application is compatible with each of these operating systems. They additionally can test newer and older versions of these operating systems with various applications before making them available to internal staff or customers.

Desktop virtualization can be installed on individual computers. A person with a Mac computer may wish to run a program that works only on Windows operating systems. To run a Windows program that is not available for Mac computers, they install the Windows operating system on a computer capable of supporting dual operating systems, and activate it to run the Windows-compatible application. A personal computer or laptop with adequate memory and processing power is required to avoid slowing down the computer with the use of dual operating systems.

In addition to testing operating systems, IT staff also test upgraded versions of web browsers for compatibility with Mac, Windows, and other computer operating systems.

Access to the Internet and Other Broadband Networks via Routers

Routers connect enterprise networks to the Internet, a carrier's network, and other corporate sites, based on the IP address stored in the router's memory. If a LAN-connected device such as a printer or PC is moved from one LAN to another, the router table must be updated or messages will not reach that device. The fact that routers transmit packets by IP address rather than individual device MAC addresses is one reason they are considered Layer 3 devices. Routers are critical. If they fail, all access to the Internet and other sites is lost. Because of this criticality, organizations typically purchase backup routers. They can balance the traffic between the two routers or keep a backup router on hand, which can be installed quickly in the event of a primary-device failure.

The devices that connect internal networks to a carrier's public networks are considered *edge devices*. Routers are defined as edge devices because they connect sites to the Internet via dedicated links, such as Carrier Gigabit Ethernet service. For more on Carrier Gigabit Ethernet, see Chapter 5, "Broadband Network Services." In cellular networks, cell phones and smartphones are edge devices that connect users to either the Internet or other mobile devices.

Network Functions Virtualization

Enterprises are starting to implement previously hardware-based network devices as software on their network. For example, routing and switching functions may be represented as software in commodity, x86 servers.

Additional Router Functionality

Beyond simply acting as a connection point to the Internet, routers can provide other functionality, including the following:

- **Firewall**   Routers can screen incoming and outgoing traffic.

- **Deep Packet Inspection (DPI)**   DPI can manage internal traffic. See Chapter 1 for more information about DPI.

- **Encryption protocols**   Routers employ IPsec and other protocols for sending packets over the Internet securely. Encryption is the use of complex algorithms to mathematically reorder bits in frames and packets.

- **Carrier Gigabit Ethernet**   See Chapter 5 for more information about Carrier Gigabit Ethernet.

- **Video Digital Signal Processor (DSP)**   This is used for conferencing services.

- **Wi-Fi**   A wireless service for branch and small offices that allows users to connect wirelessly to the router for Internet access.

- **Session Initiation Protocol (SIP)**   SIP support permits trunking for Unified Communications (UC) functions such as presence and instant messaging with other sites and VoIP calls.

- **Quality of Service (QoS)**   This prioritizes voice and video in the WAN. Voice and video are assigned tags that classify them with a higher priority than perhaps e-mail bits.

These services are located on specialized circuit boards, or blades, within the router. Multiple services can be located on the same blade, which can have more than one processor.

 NOTE *Blade servers* hold blades that are arranged vertically and housed in racks in data centers. In contrast to horizontal circuit boards, vertical arrangements such as this conserve space and can share power supplies, fans, and cabling, thus consuming less energy. In addition, applications can be added or removed without taking the server out of service.

Software to Monitor LAN-Connected Devices

Small data centers with only one or two physical computers holding virtual computers are generally easier to manage than data centers with perhaps 20 applications installed on 20 physical servers. However, there is a learning curve for managing numerous physical servers, each running multiple operating systems and applications. It involves keeping track of which physical server each image resides on as well as the application's address. For large data centers, it is often easier to manage physical servers, where each one can be physically observed, than to manage an array of applications on virtual computers.

However, in economic downturns, organizations are often reluctant to invest in software used to track LAN traffic and uptime. New applications critical to operating an organization's core operations have a priority in resource allocation.

Impact on IT When Organizations Merge

On January 19, 2016, the Boston Conservatory of Music and the Berklee College of Music announced an agreement to merge. At the merger, Berklee's name became simply Berklee and the Conservatory was renamed the Boston Conservatory at Berklee. Berklee is a global university with a campus in Valencia and programs internationally including in Canada, China, India, and Latin America. Although the Boston locations are a few blocks from each other in downtown Boston, the close proximity of the Boston Conservatory to Berklee did not preclude disparities in hardware and software.

Bob Xavier, former IT Directory of the Boston Conservatory, was appointed the IT Director for the merged entity. Xavier's goal was to simplify and streamline the infrastructure as key elements in ensuring uptime. The secondary goal was to make technology investments that promote the institution's business values.

Per Xavier, an immediate need was to put in place consistent processes to manage change and implementation, and to develop compatible software applications. According to Xavier,

"We are being strangled by the weight of supporting so many incompatible systems and applications."

For example, Berklee and the Boston Conservatory had incompatible student systems. Berklee had a student system called Colleague, and the Conservatory had PowerCampus Student. Student systems are software packages used to manage the majority of tasks around students. These include admissions, financial aid records, human resources, tuition bills, and course registrations.

According to IT director Bob Xavier, the number one priority for Berklee is the ability to be nimble so that the University can keep up with technological changes and requirements. Four years before the merger, the Boston Conservatory made a strategic decision to push all applications and processes to the cloud or to hosting centers. They wanted to "get out of the data center business." The rationale is that it's easier to be nimble and flexible without the burden of upgrading hardware in data centers when technology inevitably changes. Xavier is in the process of continuing the push to the cloud for the combined entity.

Incompatibility between browsers, computers, and applications is another area where the school is working toward standardization and compatibility. Not all of cloud and hosted applications are compatible with every browser used at the school. The university would like to see more standardization in browsers so that cloud and hosted applications work more smoothly and can be tested with just a single browser. In addition to these differences, some staff and faculty have PCs and others have Mac computers.

Currently the IT department feels that none of the systems scale, adequately to support both universities. They are not designed to be functioning globally, across time zones. The university is now working to align all of these incompatibilities and limits. Xavier predicts that this will be a 3-year process.

Monitoring LANs—What's Up? What's Down?

To properly operate large networks, a good suite of management tools is required. Moreover, because problems can occur in switches, servers, and storage, the best management suites are those that are capable of diagnosing and viewing all of these devices. Visibility across these three sectors is complicated by the fact that in many data centers, different manufacturers supply the switches, servers, and storage. One solution is to use third-party suites of management software that are capable of monitoring equipment supplied by more than one manufacturer.

The purpose of monitoring software is to notify IT staff about the status of LAN infrastructure. For example, are there outages? Where are the outages? Is congestion delaying traffic? Monitoring software is important on local area networks because LANs and data centers are critical to the functioning of today's organizations. Companies deploy monitoring software to alert them to outages and provide reports and charts on the percentage of outages and congestion on, for example, switch ports and routers.

LAN monitoring software includes visual information on servers with web interfaces. Charts indicate the status of various devices so that IT staff can clear the problems by having information on web-like browser interfaces indicating where the outages are that affect each LAN segment. IT staff receive email, text, and audible alerts to notify them that there are outages. LAN monitoring software can be installed on servers at customer sites or in the cloud.

Cloud based and on-site monitoring packages are sold and maintained by the software developer, resellers, and managed service providers. Developers of monitoring software include: Cisco, Hewlett Packard, ipswitch, NetBrain, PagerDuty, PRTC-Paessler, and NagiosCore.

Setting Up the System—Time Consuming, Complex

The most challenging, time-consuming part of implementing a network monitoring system is inventorying all the equipment on site. This takes about a day to accomplish. The following is a list of some of the equipment that needs to be monitored:

- Personal computers

- Printers

- Security monitors

- Switches

- Routers

- Storage devices

- Security monitors

- Servers

- Wi-Fi gear

While LAN monitoring software can be used for Wi-Fi gear, specialized Wi-Fi monitoring software from Wi-Fi manufacturers can monitor these networks in more detail. If Wi-Fi gear is included in non-specialized monitoring software, then components of Wi-Fi networks need to be inventoried. In addition to inventorying each piece of LAN hardware, monitoring software needs to be aware of which devices are connected to each other. For example:

- To which switch and/or alternate router is each router wired?

- To which printer is each computer connected?

Other information in databases includes:

- What are all the switches to which each port is connected?
- To which backbone switch is each wiring closet connected?
- What is the IP address of each device on the network?

NOTE Organizations assign a private IP (Internet Protocol) address to each piece of gear connected to their network. IP addressing is a protocol that specifies the format of addresses on the Internet. Organizations use this numbering scheme for addressing specific devices on their LANs. The format is a series of numbers: xxx.xxx.xxx.xx that indicate the part of the LAN and the address of each device. When messages are addressed to external locations, software within the LAN translates the private IP address to a public IP address assigned to them by their carrier. Private IP addresses are required because the amount of public IP addresses is limited and because it would be almost impossible for the entire world to coordinate the details of assignment of public IP addresses to individual components of local area networks.

Keeping Up with Changes—An Ongoing Challenge

The biggest challenge of operating monitoring software is keeping up with changes. As departments grow or shrink or change locations, monitoring software needs to be aware of the changes and update their software. Much of this is done automatically using discovery. Discovery is a feature of monitoring software that "discovers" new and changed devices by tracking their IP addresses. However, it is not 100 percent accurate.

Reports and Alerts—Pings: "Are You There?"

Monitoring software determines if equipment is up by sending continuous *pings* to all of the equipment in the network. Ping software consists of small software programs that expect a response to each of their messages. It's analogous to sending a message that says "are you there?" If the equipment sends a response to the ping, the monitoring software assumes that the gear is operational and that the network is operational. Because ping responses are only 80 percent accurate, IP staff must investigate further if a response is not received from a ping.

Almost all computers have ping software. Telephone companies' and computer companies' technicians commonly ping the equipment at customers' locations as a first step in determining if there is a problem in their remote equipment or, in the case of telephone companies, their outside network. For example, when a customers place a service call to their telephone company or computer vender, the technician may say, "The problem must be in your equipment because there is no problem in our network or equipment," or if there is no response to the ping the technician may say, "We see a problem and will dispatch a technician."

Alerts—24 Hours a Day, 7 Days a Week

IT staff monitor enterprise networks around the clock. Monitoring systems are able to check cloud-based applications as well as LAN gear. They are able to access their cloud applications' HTTP (Hypertext Transfer Protocol) addresses from within browsers to determine if they are able to log into applications. Monitoring software can be programmed to alert staff of outages via e-mail, text messaging, and audible alerts. If key cloud-based applications or parts of the network such as e-mail or the entire network are down, they notify staff after hours as well as during work hours.

Organizations define which devices should trigger alerts. Alerts are often programmed differently after hours than during the day. For example, only issues that adversely affect the entire network may trigger an alert after hours. After hours, if on call IT staff can't clear the problem remotely, they may be expected to come into work to try to resolve the problem during off hours so that the network is available the next morning.

Monitoring software is close to 100 percent accurate, but there are occasionally false positives and false negative alerts. In a similar way to, for example, strep throat or cancer screenings where false positives mistakenly indicate the presence of cancer or strep, with false positives, the system thinks there's an outage. A false negative is when an outage occurred, but the monitoring system didn't see it. With false negatives, the software falsely thinks the gear is up, and IT staff is not notified of an outage.

Per Jim Chapman, Product Manager at Lexington, Massachusetts-based monitoring software developer, Ipswitch:

> *"Companies would rather not get any false readings from their monitoring systems. But, if they do get a false reading, which happens from time to time, they would rather get false positives than false negatives. With a false negative, an outage is ignored and thus not resolved."*

Charts and Graphs

As indicated in Figure 2-8, charts and graphs provide visual "pictures" of the health of the local network. They further indicate congestion on ports within switches and routers. Moreover, monthly summaries are available indicating, for example, total percentage of time the network was up. This is especially important to IT and corporate management because outages negatively impact productivity, and may slow the time to market of new and upgraded products.

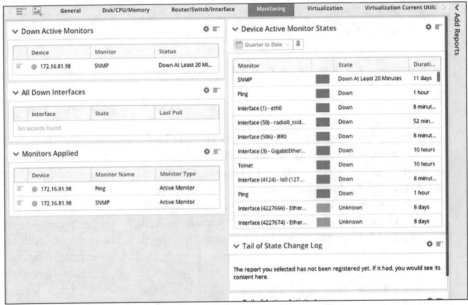

SNMP: Simple Network Management Protocol transports pings.
SSID: Service Set Identifier: Acts as a password identifying Wi-Fi devices
Gigabit Ether: Gigabit speed switches connected to the LAN
Eth: Ethernet devices on the LAN
BRO: A specialized broadband connection
Telnet: Ports that support remote access

Figure 2-8 A graphic indicating the status of LAN gear. (Screenshot of Ipswitch © 2018 Ipswitch Corporation)

LAN Monitoring Software in the Cloud

Monitoring software located in the cloud is able to access customers' networks by using agent software called a *collector* connected to firewalls. The collector polls gear such as servers, switches, and router ports on the local network and sends the results back to the cloud-based software. For providers of monitoring software, cloud-based systems have the benefits of faster set-up for each customer. This is because once the basic software is configured, only new customer information needs to be entered into the software. All customers have close to the same features, thereby simplifying the set-up and the software.

In addition, LAN monitoring suppliers receive a continuous stream of income from customers' subscriptions. In contrast, with on-site sales, there is a one-time payment for the software and an approximate 12 percent of the purchase price annual maintenance fee.

Cloud provider customers' advantages are that they avoid a one-time purchase price and the day-to-day maintenance of the software. Rather cloud providers' customers pay monthly fees based on the size of their systems. Customers whose systems are in the cloud are provided with a console with a browser interface so they are able to receive indications of what's up and what's not and print charts and graphical summaries of the status of their gear.

Monitoring software located in the cloud needs the capability to monitor diverse customers located in different locations and distinguish, for example, Customer A from Customer B. This capability is provided by multi-tenant software. Multi-tenant software is able to organize the software by individual companies.

IP PBXS—VOICE, VIDEO, AND UNIFIED COMMUNICATIONS...

Software for IP phone systems is located on servers that use industry-standard operating systems and often open-source protocols. They don't require a great deal of space and voice is considered another application in the data center.

The use of voice telephony in business and commercial organizations is declining as staff rely increasingly on messaging and e-mail services to communicate. As a matter of fact, some high-tech companies such as Alphabet do not supply most employees with telephones. Rather, these employees use e-mail and text messages to communicate with each other and the outside world. If they do need to speak with someone, they use their own cell phone. Most high-tech companies do provide some voice capabilities in conference rooms equipped with audio and videoconferencing gear so that employees can collaborate with each other and with partners.

However, companies that don't provide telephones at every desk do give each customer support center agent a telephone or computer with voice calling capabilities. They use them to speak with customers and/or partners whose questions and issues can't be resolved via text, chat, or e-mail. Sophisticated customer support centers may provide the flexibility for agents to exchange text-based chat, and text messages in addition to speaking directly with callers whose issues can't be resolved via online chats or text messages. Contact centers are also used to make outgoing telemarketing calls.

IP Telephone Systems—Voice and Applications on LANs

When organizations purchase new phone systems, they buy IP-based systems for a number of reasons. Today, employees routinely conduct their day-to-day communications by using e-mail, collaboration tools, and instant messaging. Thus, there is not the level of concern regarding the use of one network (the LAN) for both voice and data in the event of a LAN crash. For the most part, voice is used for discussions about complex topics as well as for audio and video conferences. It is also used for time-sensitive purposes such as reporting fires and other emergencies. These outgoing calls can be made on mobile phones as well as office phones.

IP-based voice and data traffic is carried over the LAN. IP PBX systems are easier to maintain and can be more easily integrated with all types of conferencing and contact centers. Moreover, the quality of voice carried on LANs is generally quite good. This is also due to improvements in LAN capacities. In addition, LAN reliability is such that downtime is no longer a concern of any substance.

While the initial cost of many IP telephone systems is no less expensive than older-style phone systems, ongoing support costs are lower. In addition, sharing centralized applications such as audio and video conferencing and contact center services with remote offices is less complex than it was in older systems.

IP Telephony Manufacturers

Makers of voice telephone systems such as Avaya, Inc. and Mitel Networks Corporation once dominated the market for telephone systems. However, the advent of IP telephony, wherein voice and data are carried on the same network, presented an opportunity to companies such as Cisco Systems and Microsoft that previously sold only data equipment and software.

Microsoft's VoIP product Microsoft Teams replaces Skype for Business. Teams is a cloud based suite of applications such as voice, email, and collaboration between staff. Teams also includes integration with Office 365, a package of software for spread sheets, word processing and presentations. Microsoft has stated its intention to continue its Skype service for consumers and small businesses.

Manufacturers and software developers of IP-based telephone systems include the following:

- Avaya Communications
- Cisco Systems, Inc.
- Microsoft
- Mitel Networks

- Nexmo (part of Vonage)

- Polycom

- RingCentral

- Mitel

- Tropo

- Twillio

- Vertical

IP TELEPHONY—CONVERTING VOICE SIGNALS TO DIGITAL DATA ....

Converged phone systems convert analog voice signals to digital bits, compress that data, and then bundle the compressed, digitized bits into packets, essentially transmitting voice as data packets. Data, voice, and video packets often share the same LAN infrastructure (cabling and switches) as that used for normal data traffic. However, voice and video require special treatment. They need to be sent in real time. Impairments such as delay and packet loss caused by network congestion are often not noticeable with data traffic. However, these problems noticeably degrade voice and video quality.

Thus, network capacity is critical for sustaining voice quality. Greater LAN capacity and faster Digital Signal Processors (DSPs) as well as protocols for Quality of Service (QoS) enable local data networks to carry high-quality voice and video. Even though voice quality is generally good in IP systems, the aforementioned problems can occur. Therefore, packets with voice and video are given priority over packets containing bits that are less time-sensitive, such as e-mail.

Voice QoS and Security

Keeping networks secure is a difficult, ongoing challenge. Security needs to be installed in IP telephony system servers, and in all of the Layer 2 and Layer 3 switches, the routers, and the firewalls. In particular, many IP systems use common protocols. These protocols are wide open in the sense that many hackers know how they work and put a great deal of effort into finding their vulnerabilities.

Organizations use the following to ensure voice quality:

- **QoS solutions**   These solutions mark and prioritize voice and are important to ensure minimal delays for acceptable voice quality. See the upcoming sections "Assessing Network Quality by Using Voice Quality Measurements" and "Prioritizing Voice and Video on a VLAN" for information about voice quality measurements and Virtual LANs (VLANs).

- **Compression**   Compressing and digitizing voice signals impacts quality. For example, the compression algorithm, Adaptive Multi-Rate Wideband (AMR-WB), based on the G.722.2 standard, is able to compress 16,000 samples of voice per second to rates as low as 12.65 kilobits per second. At this rate, each voice session uses only 12.65KB of bandwidth, but provides better audio than earlier compression standards, including G.711, which required more capacity. G.722.2 provides high-definition (HD) voice and is used for some mobile voice traffic.

In addition to the preceding, proxy servers authenticate callers to verify that they are who they say they are before being sent to their destination. *Proxy servers*, located in gateways and firewalls, serve as intermediaries between callers and applications or endpoints, telephones, and other devices connected to the LAN.

Assessing Network Quality by Using Voice Quality Measurements

IT staff members can manage VoIP by using software management tools to assess voice and video quality to analyze the following:

- **Packet loss**   This refers to the packets that are dropped when there is network congestion. Packet loss results in uneven voice quality. Voice conversations "break up" when packet loss is too high.

- **Latency**   This term refers to delays (in milliseconds) that are incurred when voice packets traverse the network. Latency results in long pauses within conversations, and clipped words.

- **Jitter**   This refers to uneven latency and packet loss, which results in noisy calls that contain pops and clicks or crackling sounds.

- **Echo**   This is the annoying effect of hearing your voice repeated, an issue with which so many of us are familiar. It is often caused when voice data is translated from a circuit-switched format to the IP format. This is usually corrected during installation by special echo-canceling software.

Prioritizing Voice and Video on a Virtual Local Area Network

Organizations can program voice telephony as a separate Virtual Local Area Network (VLAN). These "virtual" networks act as separate LANs. IP PBX components use common protocols and control the types of devices that are able to communicate with IP telephones and hold audio and video conferences. See Table 2-3 in the Appendix for additional protocols and VoIP terms.

VLANs perform the following special treatment for IP endpoints:

- 802.1P protocols tag voice and multimedia packets to prioritize them for improved availability with less delay. The tag distinguishes voice and video packets. In addition to multimedia, tagging protocols such as 802.1P are used for conferencing services, as well.

- VLANs shield endpoints from hackers by allowing only certain types of packets through firewalls to reach them. This is accomplished by means of policies for firewall logical ports that are dedicated to voice and video traffic. Logical firewall ports are defined in software rather than actual physical ports.

IP PBX Architecture

Private Branch Exchange (IP PBX) architecture varies somewhat among different manufacturers, but the servers for call processing and gateway functionality are common to all. The gateway converts Voice over Internet Protocol (VoIP) signals to those compatible with the Public Switched Telephone Network (PSTN). These are located in a separate gateway or in a router. In addition, Layer 2 switches transmit calls to other devices connected to the switch and backbone switches.

Connecting IP Telephones to Layer 2 Switches and RJ45 Jacks

Computers and phones often share the same jack and cabling with the Layer 2 switch. In this configuration, the user's personal computer is plugged into a data outlet on the back of the telephone, and the telephone is plugged into the nearest RJ45 data jack. (IP telephones are often referred to as endpoints or nodes, terms for items such as PCs and printers connected to LANs.)

 NOTE RJ45 is the designation for a type of jack into which data devices are plugged to connect to networks.

For greater redundancy and to create a dedicated path to the Layer 2 switch, the PC and telephone can each use a separate RJ45 jack, cabling, and port on the Layer 2 switch. This requires additional hardware in the switch and an extra cable run from the telephone to the switch. In either case, voice, video, and data share the fiber-optic cabling and ports on Layer 3 switches that transmit traffic between floors and buildings. This is the *enterprise backbone*.

Communications Servers and Voice as an Application on the LAN

Communications servers perform call processing, sending instructions on how to set up calls. They send instructions for features such as three-party conferencing, speed dial, and transfer. Communications servers host the software for the system, trunking, and station features. These servers specify the *trunks* over which international, local, and interstate calls should be routed. A trunk is a fiber optical or copper cabling link to broadband or the public switched telephone network (PSTN). The servers have lists of user profiles with extension numbers and permissions. Permissions include specifying who is allowed to use particular features such as video conferencing and placing calls to international locations.

Most IP servers run on UNIX, Linux, or Microsoft's Windows operating systems. These operating systems control basic operations, including how information gets on and off the network, how it's organized in memory, and the administrative interface for staff members to monitor and maintain the system. System administration and programming is performed via a computer logged in to the communications server.

In addition to basic voice features and call processing, some communications servers also hold software for specialized applications, such as audio and video conferencing, speech recognition, contact centers, voicemail, and Unified Communications (UC) systems. In other instances, these applications might be on separate application servers. Whether they reside on separate servers or in the communications server, any device connected to the corporate LAN—even those at remote locations—can be given permission in the communications server to access these applications.

Media Gateways, Protocol Translation, and Signaling

Media gateways contain Digital Signal Processors (DSPs) that compress voice data to make it smaller and more efficient to transmit. DSPs also convert analog voice signals to digital, and vice versa. They then bundle the digital voice signals into packets compatible with LANs. In addition, media gateways include circuit packs with ports for connections to traditional circuit-switched analog and digital trunks.

Media gateways are responsible for managing some security, monitoring call quality, detecting and transmitting off-hook conditions, and handling touch-tone, dial tone, busy signal, and ring-no-answer conditions. Media gateways transmit signals for VoIP such as ringing, call setup, and touch-tone in separate channels from voice calls.

 NOTE In IP telephone systems, the gateways are connected to the public telephone network and the DSPs perform the IP-to-circuit-switched conversions to make IP telephone system calls compatible with the PSTN. This conversion is not required for calls that bypass the public network and are transmitted over data networks such as the Internet.

Central Power Distribution and Backup via Power over Ethernet

Every IP telephone needs its own source of electrical power, unless it's connected to a PC's USB port. To avoid the expense and labor of providing local electricity to each phone at installation, organizations can power them via the Layer 2 switch to which the they are connected. This ensures that all phones are connected to a UPS (Uninterrupted Power Supply) to survive power surges and interruptions. Common power sources and backup also avoid the problem of ensuring that each phone is near an electrical outlet, is plugged in, and has an electrical cord.

To bring power to groups of endpoints, organizations use 802.3af, the IEEE standard known as Power over Ethernet (PoE) that defines how power can be carried from the Layer 2 switch to the IP telephone by using the same cabling that transmits voice and data. Battery backups and generators are deployed in wiring closets where switches support mission-critical telephones or attendant consoles. PoE is also used to power corporate wireless Wi-Fi antennas and base stations. (See Chapter 7 for more information about corporate wireless networks.)

Session Initiation Protocol—Compatible Trunks

Session Initiation Protocol (SIP) signaling is a key protocol for connecting IP networks together. It is also used to connect enterprise locations with data networks for voice calling. Signaling systems used in office phone systems need to be compatible with signals used in a carrier's network if voice calls are to be sent over data links. This is so that the equipment can interpret addressing signals, ringing signals, and busy signals sent by office IP PBXs, and vice versa.

Without this compatibility, organizations with IP telephone systems need to support two different sets of trunks, one set for voice and another set for data. Or they can use a gateway to translate their IP non-SIP calls to SIP. (Trunks are used to carry voice and data on public networks.) Without SIP there are extra costs and long-distance fees for gateways, and voice quality is impaired. The signal's quality is impaired when converting VoIP to formats compatible with SIP data networks when they are sent, and converting them back to VoIP when they are received. Impairment results because compression does not re-create voice in exactly the same format when it's decompressed, and vice versa. Thus, its quality is degraded every time voice data is converted.

Direct Inward Dialing

Direct Inward Dialing (DID) is a feature that routes incoming calls directly to a telephone system extension without operator intervention. DID traffic can be carried on existing digital trunks used for incoming and outgoing voice calls and on SIP-type trunks carrying voice and data traffic.

As Figure 2-9 illustrates, DID service is made up of "software" telephone numbers. Each number is not assigned a specific trunk; rather, a few hundred DID numbers are able to trunk share paths. When DID calls reach a specific slot in the telephone company's switch, the carrier's switching equipment looks at the digits dialed and identifies the call as belonging to a particular organization. The telephone company equipment passes the last three or four digits of the dialed number to the organization's telephone system. The onsite telephone system reads the digits and sends the call directly to the correct telephone.

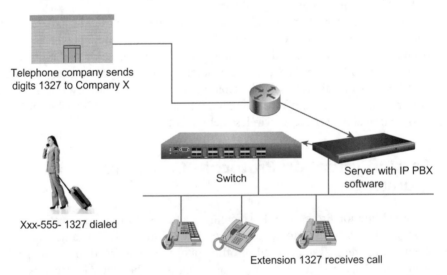

Figure 2-9   *DID soft numbers pointed to an organization's broadband circuits. (Photo by Chun-Tso Lin/123RF)*

UNIFIED COMMUNICATIONS, CONTACT CENTERS, AND VIDEO CONFERENCING ....

Value-added services add functionality to telephone systems. Unified Communications (UC) combines voicemail, e-mail, instant messaging, audio and desktop video conferencing in a single mailbox. Contact centers manage large numbers of incoming and outgoing telephone calls, texts, and e-mail messages. Voice response units (VRUs) enable callers to enter and access computer information. UC applications are available on IP-wired phones as well as mobile devices.

Integrating Conferencing, Instant Messaging, and E-Mail through UC

Unified Communications systems provide the capability to retrieve e-mail and voice-mail messages from a single device such as a PC or a touch-tone telephone. Additionally, they contain presence indicators that show the availability of people in their group.

UC systems enable people who travel to have the convenience of checking only one source for messages and sharing information with others via audio and video conferencing. Retrieving messages from PCs, tablets, and smartphones also affords users the ability to prioritize messages and listen to the most important ones first. It eliminates the need to hear all voicemail messages before getting to the critical ones.

On many Unified Communications systems, when users access messages from a touch-tone phone, text-to-speech software converts e-mail to speech for callers and reads their e-mail messages to them. Employees access messages through e-mail software on their PCs or remotely on their mobile devices. IP PBX providers that supply UC systems provide customers single-source support for their phone and messaging systems. Examples of Unified Communications systems are: 8×8, RingCentral, Mitel, and Vocalocity.

Desktop Video Conferencing

Many UC packages and IP PBXs include desktop video and audio conferencing capabilities. See Figure 2-10 for an example of video conferencing on a personal computer. These require software clients on each personal computer and a server with the software. The conferencing software can be either in the communications server used for the main telephone system, or in a separate server along with other communications applications. Often, as is the case with Microsoft, Mitel and Cisco, the application itself may be hosted in the cloud. Participants in audio conferences with access to collaboration software can also illustrate ideas by using PowerPoint or other types of documents. They can edit as well as view the documents jointly.

VIDEO COLLABORATION

- Web-based interface to video conference application
- High-definition video
- Multiple simultaneous participants
- Screen sharing to collaborate on documents
- Encryption & authentication
- Equipment located in the cloud

Figure 2-10 Desktop video conferencing set-up. (Photos by Andrea De Martin/123RF [top, left]; Mangostar/123RF [top, center]; Dean Drobot/123RF [top, right]; Fizkes/Shutterstock [top, far right; Agenturfotografin/123RF [bottom, left]; Racorn/123RF [bottom, right])

Using video conferencing capabilities such as this, co-workers with video cameras on their devices can work together on a more personal level. Another advantage is that staff members can take advantage of the same communications capability away from the office as they do in their office. If *WebRTC* (Real Time Communications) is embedded in browsers, users with disparate PCs can participate in the same videoconferences.

 WebRTC is a set of IEEE and World Wide Web Consortium (W3C) protocols for software-based codecs in applications and browsers. WebRTC enables real-time voice, video and chat among disparate devices and operating systems.

In addition to the use of licensed video conferencing software, companies now routinely use Skype for audio and video conferencing because of its low cost (or often no cost) and ubiquity. Universal availability is an important feature when attempting to use video conferencing with people outside of your own organization.

Collaboration Software—Productivity Boosts

Collaboration software enables staff in different locations to collaborate on joint projects and documents. Users can look at the same documents on their PC or tablet screens while on an audio conference call or simply speaking together on the telephone. Staff can additionally add comments to documents or edit them. There are also calendaring functions so that people can coordinate dates for meetings. Collaboration applications are generally Internet-based. To improve security, some collaboration services encrypt texts so that data remains private. They may also have strict password and log-on requirements.

One example of collaboration software is Cisco's WebEx collaboration. WebEx can be accessed from desktops, smartphones, and laptops or from specialized video conferencing equipment for meetings. Its screen sharing enables staff to view the same documents while on a videoconference or audio conference or one-to-one telephone call. WebEx provides strong security features such as password management, encryption (the use of algorithms to scramble bits for added privacy and security), and role-based access to limit or widen access to WebEx for designated groups of employees. Many software collaboration tools include the option of purchasing a whiteboard so that a group of remote staff can access documents and add written comments on the white board.

HD video conferencing systems often are integrated with collaboration software. They make it easier to integrate collaboration capabilities that include enabling people meetings at different locations to view and edit the same documents.

Collaboration sessions can be held in real time or people can log in at different times to add comments, send text messages, coordinate calendars, or edit documents. Other companies in addition to Cisco that provide collaboration software are Amazon, Asana, Atlassian, Citrix, IBM, Google Drive, Masergy, Microsoft Teams, Oracle, Slack, Trello, and Unify. There are many others, most of them free.

Video Conferencing

Because of the ready availability and consumers' positive experiences with desktop video conferencing services offered by Google, Amazon, and Skype, staff expect conferencing to be readily available at work. When employees travel with laptops, smartphones, or tablet computers, they often take advantage of formerly residential video offerings to stay in contact with colleagues and customers. These alternative ways to conduct business with distant customers and offices have enhanced collaboration between staff at diverse locations worldwide.

Skype for Business conferencing service and Cisco's web-based WebEx audio and video conferencing can be integrated with Microsoft Office 365 applications on users' desktops.

Video Conferencing Powered by the Cloud

Organizations including Amazon and Google offer video conferencing based in the cloud. Customers who use these services avoid purchasing and maintaining video conferencing equipment. Some of these services offer add-on features such as Unified Communications, and screen sharing where participants can all view the same document. Some of these services are Cisco's WebEx, Citrix's GoTo Meeting, West Corporation's Intercall, and PGI (Owned by Siris Capital Group).

Immersive HD Video Conferencing

The terms "immersive" and HD video refer to group video conferencing systems that transmit high-definition video signals. Rooms designed specifically for immersive video conferencing contain a conference table and have specially configured lighting to enhance the video experience for users. Seating at the conference table might be arranged so that all of the chairs face the video screens.

In addition, rather than just containing one video monitor, these rooms have a wall of either three large, flat-panel monitors or, less often, an entire wall-size monitor. Viewing life-size images of remote co-workers, customers, or business partners in high resolution imparts the feeling of actually being in the same room with them. Prices for room size video conferencing gear have dropped and new user interfaces have resulted in easier-to-use systems. In most cases, there is no longer a need for specially trained IT staff to run the video conferences.

If the video system is based on a common signaling protocol such as SIP and H.323, they can hold conferences with organizations outside of their own company, and with colleagues who might be using another manufacturer's system. Manufacturers of immersive systems include Polycom, Inc., Tandberg (part of Cisco Systems), and Vidyo, Inc.

Communications Platform as a Service (CPaaS) vs. Hosted IP PBXs

As its name suggests, hosted IP PBX services relieve an organization of the burden of maintaining hardware and software for a phone system and adjunct services including contact centers. CPaaS systems, in addition to providing IP voice features, add customized solutions to complex communications issues between companies and their customers.

Hosted IP PBXs—Providers Managing Software and Gateways

Hosted systems have the same features as on-site IP PBXs, but the server software and gateway equipment are hosted at a provider's site. This is an increasingly popular method of maintaining telephone systems. Rather than use capital to pay for a telephone system, organizations pay ongoing subscription fees based on the number of employees and the addition of value-added applications. With hosting, vendors easily add new features to their server without customers needing to call their supplier to reprogram their server software.

Customers do have an administrative screen where they can add and delete staff names and specify classes of service—restrictions on where staff can call or services they have permission to access. Customers that use a hosted IP PBX service are connected to their system via high-speed broadband connections. These network connections also transmit busy signals and ring tones between the provider and the customer's handset.

Hosted VoIP systems are attractive to smaller and medium-sized companies that might not have in-house expertise to manage IP telephony and applications such as collaboration, contact centers, or unified communications. These companies might also be uncertain about their future growth. In addition, hosted systems provide disaster recovery and portability. If the customer loses electricity or their LAN crashes, they can access their telephony functions remotely.

Large companies with specialized needs, such as hospitals and financial organizations, may not choose to use a hosted solution, as it might not fit their special requirements for high-level security and privacy or other specialized features. Hosted systems are designed to provide the same features to all customers. Most do encrypt broadband data on the links between the host and the customer.

VoIP hosting providers include the manufacturers of IP PBXs listed above, as well as telephone companies and cable providers such as AT&T, Verizon, and Comcast Business.

Communications Platform as a Service—Solutions for Communications Problems

CPaaS companies develop software solutions related to voice telephony to often-complex communications issues. For example, Twilio, a communications software developer located in San Francisco, developed communications software that ride-hailing provider Uber uses for messaging and calls between its drivers and people that need rides. It additionally developed the messaging software used by Facebook's WhatsApp.

Most CPaaS solutions are located in the cloud. Genband, Mitel, SAP, and Vonage with its acquisition of Nexmo are other CPaaS providers.

Contact Centers—Efficiencies for Incoming and Outgoing Communications

Contact centers are groups of agents that handle incoming customer service calls, text messages, chat, web queries, and outgoing sales, credit, and collections calls. Contact centers consist of software that is used to manage incoming and outgoing communications with agents, particularly when there are more calls, text messages, chat sessions, and e-mail than there are people to always respond to them immediately. Importantly, contact centers provide statistics on utilization of agents, telecommunications lines, and numbers of e-mail, text, and chat sessions.

The main theory behind grouping agents into "pools" is that large groups of agents can handle more calls than the same number of agents organized into small groups, without overflow of calls between groups. This is analogous to the practice by the United States Post Office of using one long line for postal clerks rather than an individual line for each clerk. With one line for all postal workers, a clerk will be available more quickly from the pool and the same number of clerks will help more people within a given amount of time than by forming separate lines for each clerk.

Contact centers route incoming traffic to the agent that has been idle the longest within the appropriate agent group, based on the telephone number dialed or by the customer's account or telephone number. If all agents are busy, the contact center shunts the call to a queue, routes the call to an alternate group of agents, or gives the caller the option to leave a voicemail message. Sophisticated call centers additionally route calls to groups of multilingual staff or staff with knowledge about particular products or technologies.

Callers to contact centers can recognize when they reach one if they hear a message such as the following:

Please hold, and the next available agent will take your call.

Virtual and Dispersed Contact Centers

Agents using the same contact center software can be located in other cities or countries. The software distributes calls based on criteria such as time of day or level of traffic. In addition, agents can work from home via their broadband connection and remotely log in to the contact center system, which then routes calls and messages to them. These are called *virtual call centers*. Many firms establish virtual call centers to save on real estate, furniture, and utility expenses.

Contact center systems are offered by almost all VoIP manufacturers as well as providers such as software developer Aspect, which offers it independently of the telephone system.

Contact Center Staffing—Do-it-Yourself Transactions

Contact centers are under increasing pressure to increase staff productivity, justify the number of agents hired, and improve the quality of customer service to attract and retain customers. Various companies in the United States and Europe outsource their centers to India, the Philippines, and other countries with lower labor rates, many people with multilingual abilities, and the availability of high-bandwidth networks.

Alternatively, organizations may move contact centers to parts of their own country with lower salaries and office rents.

To respond to more customers without adding more staff in the existing center, companies are deploying technologies such as automatic and written responses to e-mail, speech recognition, web-based sales, online forums, and chats. The practice of customers completing transactions without speaking with an agent is referred to as *self-service.* Some companies operate their sales function almost entirely on the Web. And, of course, Amazon built its entire business models around the Web.

Many of these web-based businesses are well regarded for their customer service, even though they don't actually involve any human contact. Moreover, many consumers prefer self-service on the Web over listening to long, automated menus and waiting in phone queues.

Contact Center Statistics

Reports on the real-time status of calls and electronic messages are the lifeblood of a contact center and are closely monitored by management. Management then uses these statistics to plan network design and analyze staffing requirements. Statistics are also used as an aid in improving web site design by alerting organizations to the most frequently asked questions. These issues can then be more fully clarified on the web site or via automated e-mail messages designed to explain common procedures for fixing or analyzing software issues.

Statistics are organized into reports that provide real-time and historical data on incoming and outgoing calls and agents' usage on individual trunks so that managers will know if they have the correct number of broadband trunks. Reports also indicate the number of calls and web hits associated with each toll-free number and web advertisement so that response rates generated by ad campaigns can be analyzed. They additionally alert supervisors to unusually high or low call volumes so that staffing can be adjusted accordingly.

E-mail Response Management Software

E-mail response management software is another tool for increasing self-service. It can be used independently or as part of call center software. E-mail response management software installed on an organization's server routes e-mail messages to agents by topic, subject, and content. If appropriate, the software can automatically respond to the e-mail. Natural language software for written language is capable of interpreting and extracting concepts in e-mail messages. It can link phrases in a meaningful way. E-mail response management systems also create reports based on the number of messages received, by message subject, date, and content. This provides management with information on which web sections need to be improved.

E-mail response management software pulls out messages to managed mail-boxes such as those addressed to generic functions such as info@company.com, techsupport@company.com, and sales@company.com. They route them to groups of agents or respond to them with an automatic reply, based on subject, message, and content.

Automatic Links to Customer Relationship Management

Customer relationship management (CRM) is a customer-centric strategy that aims to make information such as customers' transaction histories accessible across the entire organization. CRM can comprise many elements including sales automation with automated proposals and brochures available to representatives. CRM also includes marketing tools that track the impact of direct mail, e-mail, and Internet-based campaigns. In addition, customer service with links to billing, payment status, purchase histories, open issues, and universal queues are considered part of CRM. The largest providers of CRM software are Oracle, SAP, and Siebel Systems.

Telephone systems such as Ring Central automatically link agents handling incoming calls to the CRM information about callers so that agents have ordering and other information to more quickly answer and resolve customers' issues. The caller ID with the called party's telephone number automatically links call center agents to the appropriate CRM data.

Voice Response Units—Routing and Accessing Information via Touch-Tone or Speech

Voice Response Units (VRUs) provide information to callers based on touch-tone signals or spoken commands. Customers can call their bank or credit card company to ascertain their balance or learn if a payment has been received. They enter their account number and PIN when prompted by an electronic voice. The VRU repeats the requested information, in spoken word.

Companies justify the expense of speech recognition and VRUs because they need fewer people to speak with live agents.

The following are examples of Voice Response Unit applications:

- Newspapers subscribers can use it to stop and start delivery before and after vacations, or report missed delivery of newspapers.

- Airlines can link to flight information.

- Prescription drug benefit programs enable people to order drug refills.

- Companies use VRUs as adjuncts to or in some cases substitutes for company operators. The voice response unit is programmed to answer and route:

  - All calls

  - Calls to particular telephone extensions or departments

  - After-hours calls

- Here is a classic example:

  Thank you for calling ABC Company. If you know your party's extension, you may dial it now. For sales, press 1. For customer service, press 2.

Poorly scripted, confusing, and overly long scripts tend to be a source of frustration for callers. Another source is the inability in some organizations to speak with a live operator. In some instances, pressing 0 does nothing except trigger the initial confusing menu to be replayed.

Using Speech Recognition to Expand Self-Service

Many call centers add speech recognition to their integrated voice response platforms to make them more user-friendly and faster for callers to navigate. Toll-free directory services ask callers to speak the name of the company for which they require a toll-free number without operator assistance. Local telephone companies use speech recognition so that customers can easily obtain billing information without speaking with a billing representative. Making speech recognition and IVR user friendly is an important factor in ensuring callers' acceptance of the service.

How Speech Recognition Works

Speech recognition works by first detecting and then capturing parts of spoken words (utterances). After removing background noise, it converts the captured utterances to a digital representation. Capturing the speech and digitally representing it is done by DSPs on high-speed specialized computer chips. The speech recognition software then breaks the sounds into small chunks and compares various properties of the chunks of sound to large amounts of previously captured data contained in a database.

Speech recognition systems can be either speaker dependent or speaker independent. *Speaker independent systems* such as those used by Amtrak, Apple, and the United States toll free directory are speaker independent. They recognize words spoken by large numbers of people. Originally, speaker independent systems recognized a limited number of words such as yes, no, and numeric digits. However, improved recognition and faster computer chips now enable speaker independent systems to recognize large vocabularies of words.

Speaker dependent systems include Nuance's speech recognition software for consumers. Nuance also offers speech recognition software for specialized professions that use specific vocabularies. This includes radiologists who use speech recognition to dictate reports on results of medical imaging exams such as x-rays and MRIs. Speaker dependent software needs to be "trained" to recognize a particular person's commands. This is accomplished by having the purchaser of the speech recognition software read a few passages of text until the software recognizes the person's speech pattern.

Natural language speech recognition systems are those with the ability to recognize speech where users don't use specific, predefined commands such as "copy the phrase hello Mary", or "cut yours truly" as found in desk-top speech recognition applications. For example, natural language systems recognize "Turn on the Alarm" as well as "Set the alarm." Digital Assistant products such as Amazon's Alexa are capable of recognizing natural language commands. These systems are speaker independent systems.

High-speed computer processors perform the digitization and comparisons in milliseconds. They also take into account gender differences and regional accents. Speech recognition software contains different databases of expected responses based on the application. A corporate directory has a different speech database than one for airline scheduling or lost-luggage applications.

Until recently, Nuance had somewhat of a monopoly on speech recognition software. But, currently machine learning and computer chips with larger memories and faster transistors have led research universities and large companies including Microsoft and IBM to develop speech recognition, particularly for wearable devices such as Hoboken, NJ-based Essence Group's emergency alert devices that enable an incapacitated elderly person to call for help by voice commands without using his or her hands.

Speech recognition is integrated in:

- Home digital assistants
  - Amazon's Echo and Dot
  - Alphabet's Google Home
  - Microsoft's Cortana,
  - Apple's Siri
  - Baidu's Raven
  - Samsung's ViV
- Set-top boxes
  - Apple TV
  - Roku
  - Comcast X1

Speech Recognition in Home Automation Devices

A digital assistant is essentially a computerized home assistant that supplies information in response to spoken questions and requests for information asked by users. Digital assistants are made possible by natural language speech recognition, high-speed computer networks, and machine learning. (See Chapter 1 for "Machine Learning.")

The large amounts of captured speech and information gathered on search engines and computers are key to the development of digital assistants. For example, Google has troves of data with commonly requested search requests. In addition, as digital assistants' databases of known utterances grow, the systems' speech recognition will continue to improve accuracy.

Digital assistants perform data look-ups using owners' Wi-Fi networks and broadband links. The look-ups are microsecond-speed data connections to the Digital Assistant's manufacturer's data centers, and their partners' computers. These computers send responses back to questions such as "Alexa, what is the weather today?" The following is a sampling of requests that digital assistants can respond to:

- What is the time?

- What is the time in China?

- Add eggs to my shopping list.

- What is the solution to this math problem?

- How many miles is Australia from New York?

- Play relaxing music.

- Play music by Mozart.

- Connect me to Spotify.

- Set the alarm for 6:30 AM

Digital Assistant Software Integrated in Other Devices

Digital assistant software is integrated into smartphones, watches, and computers. An app on smartphones is required for these integrations. For example, Amazon's Alexa digital assistant software is integrated in cars, including Ford Motor Company and Tesla automobiles. There are also agreements to include Amazon's Alexa software in refrigerators, ovens ("Alexa, turn on the oven to 350 degrees, heat water for coffee"), thermostats, and lights. All of these integrations are ways that humans can interact with machines using speech as an input technology.

Privacy with Digital Assistants

Privacy is residential customers' most common worry about home automation devices. According to the 2016 research by consulting firm Parks Associates, a U.S. Research and Analysis firm for Internet of Things (IoT), smart home, and connected entertainment technologies, half of consumers stated that privacy is their most pressing concern about home automated devices. Examples of IoT wireless products are drones, monitors, and lights, controlled by software.

The term privacy denotes the ability of people to control which people can see information about them. There have been fears that Amazon's digital assistants (Echo and Dot) store customers' speech. Amazon has stated that it only saves commands directed to its digital assistants, not other random speech spoken in the same room. It further has stated that each user is associated with a particular randomly selected code and that Amazon does not know which user is associated with any code associated with customers' speech.

Possible Long-Term Impact of Digital Assistants

In addition to privacy, concerns about digital assistants revolve around depersonalization resulting from less need for communications between people. As people increasingly turn to computers to get information will they have less of a requirement to speak to each other?

In addition to privacy and depersonalization, there are worries about a possible decrease in children's ability to do math. This is because "asking Alexa" provides children solutions to even complex math problems. It's still early days in the availability of digital assistants to know for certain what its impact will be in the future. In the early days of calculators, many thought children would not learn basic math skills. Each new innovation brings concerns. The answers to these concerns are initially unknown.

APPENDIX ....

Table 2-2 LAN Protocols, Devices, and Terms

Protocol, Service, or Device	Description
Backbone	The wiring running from floor to floor in single buildings and from building to building within a campus. A backbone connects switches in different wiring closets to one another. Backbones support high concentrations of traffic in carrier and enterprise networks.

Protocol, Service, or Device	Description
Blade server	Blade servers are computers packaged on individual boards—blades—that plug into slots in a chassis. A chassis is the metal frame on which components fit, similar to a custom cabinet with slots for specific items. In high density, chassis blades are arranged vertically. In low density, three- or four-blade servers, they are arranged horizontally. Chassis are placed on racks in data centers. Vertical arrangements conserve space and can share power supplies, fans, and cabling. In addition, blades can be easily added.
File server	A specialized computer with a large hard drive. File servers provide users with access to documents and applications in central locations in LANs.
Load balancing	The capability of equipment to balance traffic between networks and devices so that one network or device is not overloaded while others carry little or no traffic.
Local Area Network (LAN)	A group of devices such as computers, printers, and scanners that can communicate with one another within a limited geographic area, such as a floor, department, or small cluster of buildings.
Layer 2 switch (also called a switching hub)	A switch located in a wiring closet that allows multiple simultaneous transmissions within a single LAN. Layer 2 switches provide a dedicated connection during an entire transmission.
Layer 3 switch (also known as a routing switch)	A switch that routes traffic across the LAN backbone based on IP (network) addresses. They are more complex to manage than Layer 2 switches, but they can use alternate paths if one path is out of service. They are located in data centers and link wiring closets and buildings within a campus.
Layer 4 switch (also known as a content switch)	A switch located at hosting sites and corporate and government sites that host their own web pages. Layer 4 switches connect web traffic to the desired web pages by looking at the URL, the web address from which each packet was transferred to the site.
Router	Routers carry traffic between LANs, from enterprises to the Internet, and across the Internet. They are more complex than switches because they have routing tables with addresses and perform other functions. Routers select the best available path over which to send data.

Table 2-2   (Continued)

Protocol, Service, or Device	Description
Server	A centrally located computer with common departmental or organizational files such as personnel records, e-mails, sales data, price lists, student information, and medical records. Servers are connected to Layer 2 or Layer 3 switches. Access to servers can be restricted to authorized users only.
Virtual Local Area Network (VLAN)	A virtual local area network is made up of devices, usually personal computers or VoIP devices, whose addresses are programmed as a group in Layer 2 switches. This segregates them from the rest of the corporate network so that all devices in the same VLAN can be given a higher priority or level of security. They are programmed as a separate LAN but are physically connected to the same switch as other devices.
Wide Area Network (WAN)	A group of data devices, usually LANs, that communicate with one another between multiple cities.

Table 2-3   Protocols and VoIP Terms

Protocols and Terms for VoIP Service	Description
802.1pq	802.1pq is used to tag certain Virtual LAN traffic to indicate that it is part of a special group. It might tag voice packets to segregate them for special treatment and monitoring. It also contains bits that identify the packet's priority level.
CoS	Class of Service provides priority to particular types of traffic. Voice or video can be designated with a higher priority than voicemail.
DoS	Denial-of-Service attacks occur when hackers attempt to disrupt communications by bombarding endpoints or proxies with packets.
G.711	G.711 is used to compress voice signals at 64,000 bits per second plus a 6- to 21-kilobit header for VoIP services. It produces good voice quality but uses more network capacity than other compression techniques. This technique requires 60 milliseconds to process and "look ahead" (check the route).
G.723.1	G.723.1 is a compression protocol that uses small packets with 6.3Kbps compression. Small packets are more efficient than large ones, in terms of bandwidth use. With the header, total bandwidth is about 16Kbps.

Protocols and Terms for VoIP Service	Description
G.729	G.729 is a voice compression standard used in VoIP. It compresses voice signals from 64,000 bits per seconds to 8,000 bits per second. The header brings the total bandwidth to about 18,000 bits per second.
H.323	H.323 is a family of signaling standards for multimedia transmissions over packet networks adopted by the International Telecommunications Union (ITU). Microsoft Corporation and Intel Corporation adopted the standard in 1996 for sending voice over packet networks. H.323 includes standards for compressing calls and for signaling. It has higher overhead than the newer signaling protocol, SIP.
Presence theft	This refers to the impersonation of a legitimate IP telephone or other device by a hacker.
Proxy server	A proxy server screens communications between endpoints to verify that the called and calling parties are who they say they are and that no virus will be sent. A proxy server might sit between a VoIP server and external devices that request an audio conference or videoconference session. This is referred to as intermediating sessions. Proxy servers are also used between IP telephones and the Internet.
QoS	Quality of Service guarantees a particular level of service. To meet these guarantees, service providers or IT staff members allocate bandwidth for certain types of traffic.
RTP	Real-time Transport Protocol is an Internet Engineering Task Force (IETF) standardized protocol for transmitting multimedia in IP networks. RTP is used for the "bearer" channels—the actual voice, video, and image content. SIP is commonly used for the signaling to set up and tear down sessions.
SCCP	Skinny Client Control Protocol is a Cisco proprietary signaling protocol for sending signals between devices in Cisco telephone systems. It is also referred to as "Cisco Skinny."
SIP	Session Initiation Protocol establishes sessions over IP networks, such as those for telephone calls, audio conferencing, click-to-dial from the Web, and instant messaging exchanges between devices. It is also used to link IP telephones from different manufacturers to SIP-compatible IP telephone systems. It is used in landline and mobile networks.

Part II

Industry Overview and Regulations

3 Competition, Industry Structures, and Regulations

In this chapter:

INTRODUCTION ....

The United States is fortunate to have high-capacity broadband networks throughout most of the urban and suburban areas. These networks are capable of transmitting the growing volumes of traffic generated by enterprises and residential customers. For the most part, the wireline broadband and cellular networks are operated by large conglomerates with the resources to invest large amounts of capital in their networks.

Today's broadband, cellular, and cable TV providers have nationwide networks and very few competitors. This has contributed to the fact that broadband rates are higher than those in almost all countries worldwide. There are two reasons for the dearth of competition. It's enormously costly to build network infrastructure and maintain these networks. In addition, large providers have purchased their competitors. Because of the high infrastructure costs and marketing and advertising expenses, the barriers to entry for new network providers are cost prohibitive. There are however, resellers that lease network capacity at a discount and resell these services on the networks they lease.

Cable TV prices have risen in part as a result of the high costs borne by providers for licensing movies, TV shows, and real-time sporting events. Providers have to bear additional expenses if they are creating original movies and television series. Amazon, Facebook, and Microsoft as well as AT&T and Verizon have built huge networks of data centers to support the services they offer. They have each additionally purchased many start-ups and small companies that have developed specialized software for cloud services, advertising networks, mobile applications, and other offerings. These subsidiaries have enabled these companies to offer a larger range of services. Cable TV providers have also invested heavily in these services and have upgraded the broadband lines that connect to their subscribers.

The number of choices that subscribers have for broadband services will decrease further under the AT&T and Warner Bros merger. With the FCC's approval of the AT&T purchase of Warner Bros., AT&T gained the large cache of content that Warner Bros. owns including HBO, Turner classic movies, and CNN.

The same is true due to the purchase of 21st Century Fox by Disney. The Walt Disney Co.'s purchase of 21st Century Fox has resulted in Disney's acquisition of a vast collection of movies. They were required to divest themselves of Fox's regional sports network. As a result of these mergers, less content is available to AT&T and Disney's competitors. In response, streaming companies are now forced to create more of their own costly content. This may ultimately limit consumer choices for streaming providers and make it difficult, if not impossible, for new companies to enter the field.

T-Mobile has offered to purchase Sprint. If the Sprint and T-Mobile merger is approved, the number of mobile networks with nationwide reach will be reduced from four to three. This will further reduce consumers' choices and may result in higher prices. T-Mobile in particular has offered service at prices lower than AT&T and Verizon. They also were the first to offer unlimited cellular service packages. It's possible that a combined T-Mobile and Sprint merger will mean higher prices. In addition, a decrease in competition often results in less impetus to upgrade networks and offer innovative services.

The proliferation of streaming has impacted how people get movies and TV shows and caused cable TV operators to lose thousands of customers. It has additionally resulted in changes in telecommunications, cellular, and cable TV strategies, which have all begun offering their own streaming services. In addition, a large number of movie chains have closed theaters because rather than going out to a movie theater, many people stay at home and watch streaming shows. Netflix is an example of a company that has used streaming to disrupt an entire industry and change the way people get entertainment.

Unfortunately, there have been negative impacts from the vast improvements in technology and the openness of the Internet. Robocalls made by scammers use high-speed automatic dialers programmed to call thousands of telephone numbers in a short period of time. In addition to being annoying, criminals that initiate robocalls bilk trusting people out of millions of dollars by promising them delivery of purchases and services that don't materialize.

Social networks have had many positive effects on teenagers and adults who enjoy the ease of staying in touch and keeping up with distant relatives. However, bad actors in these networks have taken advantage of the huge numbers of people on these social networks to sway public opinion and publish false statements. Some have also created millions of fake subscribers to these networks. Facebook is attempting to create safeguards so that spam posts don't happen in the future, but the damage has already been done.

Millions of people have had their privacy stolen on Facebook by the sale of their information without their consent. While there are laws protecting children's privacy in the United States, there are no laws that protect adults and teenagers. It's not clear that such laws will be enacted in the near future.

Although broadband networks have more capacity than ever before in urban areas, in many rural areas, this is not the case. Many subscribers in rural areas have access to networks that support only low-data rates. However, in some rural towns and agricultural areas, this is starting to change. Government subsidies have enabled providers in some rural locales to upgrade to higher capacity fiber optical networks.

However, federally funded Lifeline subsidies for low-income people that can't afford broadband are shrinking. Many people that live in poverty can't afford the high prices for broadband links that their children need to access their homework, which is frequently posted online. In addition, adults can't search or apply for jobs online without broadband.

The consolidation in broadband, mobile providers, and social networks has led to companies that have the resources to spend millions of dollars each year to lobby Washington for favorable rules. Loose or favorable regulations impact many companies. There may be no incentive to enforce privacy and strengthen the security of data centers and cloud offerings. Regulations impact pricing, tax policies, and billing practices. Regulatory decisions on mergers and acquisitions impact the absence or presence of competition and prices for consumers, government agencies, and enterprises, all of whom purchase telecommunications services.

THE 1984 BREAKUP OF AT&T ....

Prior to the 1984 U.S. Justice Department Divestiture ruling, what are now AT&T, Verizon, and part of CenturyLink were part of the *Bell system*. The Bell system consisted of 22 local Bell telephone companies that were each owned by AT&T Corporation.

As part of the 1984 divestiture ruling, AT&T kept the long-distance portion of its organization, which it viewed as more lucrative than local calling. The goal of divestiture was to encourage competition for long-distance services. The 22 local telephone companies were re-organized into seven Regional Bell Operating Companies (RBOCs).

The Telecommunications Act of 1996

The goal of the Telecommunications Act of 1996 was to spur innovation and competition for local services. The Act allowed incumbent local telephone companies, who previously were allowed to sell services only within their region, to offer out-of-region long-distance services that the 1984 divestiture had barred them from offering.

The Act also decreed that for the first time, cable TV operators, electric utilities, broadcasters, interexchange carriers, and non-traditional competitive local exchange providers would be permitted to sell local calling, toll calling, and related services. This provision allowed the former AT&T, which was then an interexchange carrier, to resume selling local services.

To encourage competition for local services, the Act prescribed rules enabling competitors to connect to the central offices of incumbent phone companies at mandated discounted rates. However, most of these connectivity rules were gradually rescinded when large incumbents such as the former Regional Bell Operating Companies (RBOCs) challenged the rules in court and won. For a list of these rulings, see Table 3-11 in the "Appendix" section at the end of this chapter.

Telecommunications Act of 1996 Mandated Fees

When the Telecommunications Act of 1996 was enacted, the United States Congress felt that it was not economically feasible for rivals of the RBOCs (Regional Bell Operating Companies) to build all their own local facilities directly to customers' premises. It therefore mandated that incumbents such as the then SBC (now AT&T, Inc.) make their local networks available at replacement cost plus a reasonable profit to competitors such as the former MCI (now part of Verizon). The local network assets included the following:

- The local copper loop from the incumbent's equipment to the customer

- High-speed lines between the Competitive Local Exchange Carrier (CLEC) switch and the incumbent's central office

- RBOC local central office switch ports for connections to local loops

- Operator services

- Signaling services to link central offices to systems, including billing

Many competitors including MCI (now part of Verizon) and Sprint leased entire platforms of incumbents' facilities at a discounted rate to offer service without building their own infrastructure. Some competitors built their whole business around the resale of incumbent telephone companies' platforms. Other competitors built their own facilities in areas where they had concentrations of business customers and used an incumbent's entire platforms in other areas.

Court Rulings on Access to an Incumbent's Equipment and Fiber

In a March 2004 ruling, the United States Court of Appeals for the District of Columbia struck down individual states' authority to set discounts for competitors to connect to an incumbent's facilities, such as central office switch ports, local loops, and high-speed voice and data links.

The circuit court's ruling ended most of the deep discounts available to competitors in metropolitan areas under the initial pricing. The FCC spelled out a limited number of conditions under which eliminating these pricing rules impairs competition.

In another blow to competitors, the courts ruled that incumbent telephone companies are not obligated to share fiber facilities built within 500 feet of customers. As a result, where fiber replaces copper or is within 500 feet of customers, local loops are not available to competitors.

As a result of these court decisions, costs for carriers that don't have their own local central office switches, fiber networks, and local lines increased dramatically. The rules essentially made it uneconomical for most competitors to stay in business. They were all either purchased by competitors or went out of business.

The Impact of the Telecommunications Act of 1996

A major impact of the Telecommunications Act is the legitimization of cable TV operators offering telecommunications services and telephone companies selling cable TV services. Although initially AT&T and Verizon suspended their residential cable TV build-outs, they now compete actively with cable TV providers and offer cable TV services themselves in parts of the United States. With their purchase of DirecTV, AT&T now also sells satellite television service.

A second achievement is the mandate that local number portability be implemented. Consumers now take for granted that they can keep their telephone number when they change mobile carriers, drop their home phone service for mobile service, and keep their business number when they move or change providers. However, this was not the case prior to 1996.

Another benefit of the Act is that increased competition and investment in broadband facilities led to dramatic decreases in prices for high-speed Internet access and long-distance services for small and medium-sized businesses. As most competitors were absorbed into larger telephone companies or went out of business, long-distance and broadband rates remained low.

Large enterprises for the most part rely mainly on AT&T, CenturyLink, and Verizon because of their global networks. Many large enterprises use connections to a backup telephone company in the event of a major network outage at their primary carrier. Large organizations are also more likely to use AT&T and Verizon for mobile services because they are the only providers with close to nationwide mobile networks. Regional providers including Windstream and Frontier sell telecommunications and broadband services but in fewer regions than AT&T, CenturyLink, and Verizon.

Costs and Competition for Cable TV Services in the United States

Unfortunately for many consumers, the choice for Internet access is often limited to the local cable TV provider. Per FCC statistics nearly half of U.S. households had only a single choice of high data rate wired broadband provider by June of 2016. However, AT&T, Verizon, and CenturyLink's recent build-outs of broadband facilities do provide options for a second or, less frequently, a third broadband provider in increasing numbers of areas.

The addition of competition has resulted in higher broadband data speeds for consumers in many areas. However, it has not resulted in lower cable TV prices for residential customers. Moreover, broadband prices remain high compared to those in Asia and Europe. Broadband costs are only $10 per month in Russia and less than $40 monthly in China.

According to the March 14, 2018, *Consumer Reports* article by James K. Willcox, "Your Cable Bill Probably Went Up by More Than You Think," cable TV rates have increased by an average of 3 percent to 4 percent annually for the last four years. One factor in higher cable TV bills is the high fees that content providers charge cable TV companies for the rights to content. However, surcharges such as those for sports access add another $6 to $8 monthly. The high cost of cable TV is a factor in subscribers opting for "skinny" packages with fewer channels and is one reason that people are dropping their cable TV for streaming on Netflix, Amazon, and others.

Table 3-1 is a sampling of the number of lost cable TV subscribers at the end of the first quarter of 2018 broadband and provides a comparison of the number to the same period in 2017. Statistics are from cable TV providers' first quarter 2018 revenue reports.

To make up for the lost cable TV revenues, all cable TV providers are upgrading their terrestrial networks to carry additional streaming, cloud, and Internet browsing residential and enterprise traffic.

Table 3-1   Quarterly Residential Subscriber Losses at Cable TV Providers

Cable TV Company	First Quarter of 2017	First Quarter of 2018	Number of Subscribers Lost
AT&T*	24,089,000	23,902,000	187,000
Comcast	21,520,000	21,210,000	93,000
Verizon	4,681,000	4,597,000	84,000

*Includes satellite and U-Verse subscribers

The Rural Divide—Vast Areas without Broadband

Streaming that is carried on broadband "pipes" requires more capacity than any other service. In much of the United States, providers have upgraded their networks and use this capacity for their and competitors' streaming content. According to FCC statistics, there were at least 96.6 million residential broadband subscribers as of December 2016. (The FCC defines broadband as 25Mbps download data rates). Download data rates of 25Mbps were available to 62.2 percent of the total 96.6 million residential broadband subscribers. However, broadband availability is not distributed evenly in the United States.

There are 24 million people in the United States without wired, terrestrial broadband of 25Mpbs. These people are mainly in rural and Native American tribal areas. The scarcity of broadband puts rural employees and students at enormous disadvantages in terms of access to remote work and students' homework assignments. Moreover, it is next to impossible to attract businesses to these areas because of the lack of adequate broadband infrastructure for such considerations as remote workers and access to cloud computing.

Mobile LTE service is also not as prevalent in rural as urban areas. Only 70 percent of rural areas have mobile LTE and only 64 percent of tribal areas have mobile LTE. Mobile LTE speeds are considered 10Mbps from the network to the subscriber and 3 Mbps from a subscriber to the network. This contrasts with urban areas where 92 percent of the population has access to both terrestrial broadband and mobile LTE networks. The urban–rural contrast in mobile and terrestrial broadband availability is also present in other countries such as those in Latin America, mountainous areas in Western China, and villages in India.

Affordability is an additional hindrance for having broadband availability. Families in which parents are unemployed or have jobs that pay minimum hourly rates are also often locked out of high-speed broadband links. They may not be able to afford to purchase computers and pay the high rates for Internet access charged in the United States.

There are subsidies available for families of school-aged children that live in low-cost Housing and Urban Development (HUD) housing or earn below a certain level of income. Some providers offer subsidized broadband at $10 monthly with data rates between 10 and 15 Mbps: Comcast, Verizon, Google, and AT&T each offer discounted services in their coverage areas.

The Transformation of AT&T, CenturyLink, and Verizon into Conglomerates

As a result of the following mergers, by 2011 the seven RBOCs plus CenturyLink had been reorganized into the three largest telecommunications providers in the United States: Verizon Communications, AT&T, Inc., and CenturyLink.

Here are the pre-2011 mergers resulting in consolidations:

- **AT&T:** In 2005 SBC, one of the seven local telephone companies, purchased AT&T for its international and interstate long-distance network. When it purchased AT&T, SBC changed its name to AT&T because of its higher national recognition. SBC purchased the following providers under its own name until 2005 when it made these purchases under the AT&T name:

  – 1997: SBC purchased Pacific Telesis Group, the Regional Bell Operating Company (RBOC) in California and Nevada

  – 1997: SBC purchased Southern New England Telephone, the incumbent telephone company in Connecticut

  – 2005: AT&T purchased RBOC Pacific Telesis in California

  – 2007: AT&T purchased RBOC Ameritech whose territory included Michigan, Indiana, Illinois, Ohio, and Wisconsin

- **Verizon:** In 1997 regional bell operating company Bell Atlantic purchased NYNEX, the former phone company in New England. NYNEX was created from the merger of New York Telephone Company and New England Telephone Company.

  – 2000: Verizon purchased GTE, the largest non-Bell telephone company in the U.S and changed its name from NYNEX to Verizon

  – 2006: Verizon bought MCI, the second largest long-distance company

- **CenturyLink:** CenturyLink purchased EMBARQ in 2009 from Sprint, which at that time offered landline telephone service in the Kansas area and in the Midwest.

- 2011: CenturyLink purchased RBOC Quest Communications. Quest owned telephone service networks in 14 western states, which gave CenturyLink a presence in metropolitan as well as its existing rural locations.

- 2017: CenturyLink purchased the rest of Level 3 Communications for its large interstate network. Prior to 2017, CenturyLink owned primarily local links connecting homes and businesses to interstate networks.

AT&T, Verizon, CenturyLink and Comcast— Recent Acquisitions

AT&T, Verizon, CenturyLink and Comcast are the largest telecommunications and cable TV providers in the United States. The list of their recent acquisitions in Tables 3-2, 3-3, 3-4, and 3-5 illustrate the increasing scope of their businesses. These acquisitions are aimed at providing software tools to manage their movie and TV content, and to give them skills for positioning themselves as a resource to enterprise customers. In addition to the acquisitions in Table 3-2, AT&T has purchased Warner Bros, a media company whose companies include Turner Broadcasting, HBO, CNN, CW, and Cinemax, plus many others including content in Latin America and Europe.

Table 3-2 *AT&T Mergers and Acquisitions*

Number of Wireline Subscribers	Recent Acquisitions
25,369,000	**DirecTV**—Satellite TV provider
Includes 1.2 million DirecTV subscribers	**FiberTower**—High-frequency spectrum
	Vyatta: Software platform with anti-virus and network load balancing software
	Carrier IQ: Diagnostic software embedded in smartphones
	Nextel Mexico: Wireless network in Mexico
	Otter Media: Streaming company that owns digital content including CrunchyRoll and Rooster Teeth.
	Superclick: Analysis of statistics in Wi-Fi hotspots, and LAN Wi-Fi
	Invidi: Platform for advertising campaigns across TV, Satellite and Streaming TV
	Wayport: Wi-Fi hotspots in United States
	Warner Bros.: Entertainment content company that owned HBO, CNN, CW, Cinemax and CW plus many others including content in Latin America and Europe.
	AlienVault: Cyber Security

Table 3-3   CenturyLink Purchases

Number of Subscribers	Companies Purchased
5,662,000	**Tier 3:** Cloud management provider
	ElasticBox: Enterprise cloud management service
	Level 3 Communications: Interstate fiber network
	NextDC: Data Centers in Australia
	SEAL: Consulting on SAP
	Orchestrate: Database as a service

Table 3-4   Comcast Purchases

Number of Subscribers	Company Purchased
23,500,000	**Adelphia and Time Warner Cable:** Cable TV providers
	iControl Networks: Connected home platform for security, remote management and video management.
	OneTwoSee: A technology platform to deliver real time sports
	Contingent Network Services: Manages technology, and IT projects for enterprises
	Watchwith: Advertising platform
	This Technology: IT network
	30% of Hulu
	Sky: A British pay-TV satellite provider, owns sports-media content
	Wilco Electronic Systems: Provides cable TV service
	Stringify: Internet of Things developer
	Visible World: Television advertising to targeted audiences
	PowerCloud System: A way for telephone and cable companies to provide cloud services to subscribers
	NBCUniversal: TV and Universal Studios content

Table 3-5 Verizon Purchases

Number of Subscribers	Company Purchased
12,600,000	**Sensity Systems:** A suite of smart city solutions
	Niddel: Uses machine learning to autonomously detect security threats
	FiberTower: Spectrum and cell site owner
	Straight Path: Wireless spectrum suitable for fifth generation networks
	XO Communications: Fiber network
	Yahoo!: Mail, search, and news. Verizon sold Yahoo!'s photo sharing company Flickr.
	AOL: News, Weather, Entertainment, and Finance. Verizon merged Yahoo! and AOL to form Oath.
	Vessel: Web-video
	Fleetmatics: Mobile fleet tracking, fuel usage, speed, and mileage using GPS
	Telogis: Fleet management
	WideOpenWest (WOW): Fiber-optic network in the Chicago area for 5G implementation. The sixth largest pay-TV company when purchased.

Cable TV Providers—Comcast, Charter, COX Communications, and Altice

Comcast Corporation, Charter, Cox Communications, and Altice USA are the largest, second largest, third and fourth largest cable TV providers in the United States respectively. Charter operates under the Spectrum brand name. The first cable television station was started in 1948 in a mountainous area of rural Pennsylvania where high mountains blocked over the air television signals. Gradually, other providers started creating cable TV networks.

NOTE Gradually, more communities added Community Antenna TV (CATV), as the first systems were known. These systems were made up of large antennas to which heavy coaxial cabling was connected. Because the systems were analog, they were susceptible to rain leaking into their systems and other impairments. Gradually, cable TV systems became digital with clearer signals and increased subscribers who wanted a wider choice of programs than those available on over-the-air broadcast TV. In the early 1950s there were 259 small providers, but by 1961 there were 288 systems in 36 states.

Most of these early cable TV operators were gradually bought by larger operators, and became part of Comcast, Charter, or Altice USA. When Netherlands headquartered Altice, it purchased New York cable TV company Cablevision, and it changed Cablevision's name to Altice USA. Altice sells services in 21 states under the Optimum and SuddenLink brand names.

All four large cable operators are experiencing large losses of cable TV customers due to competition from streaming services offered by Netflix, Hulu, Amazon, Disney, and over a hundred others. The largest cable companies are fighting back by expanding the scope of their offerings and by offering their own streaming services. For example, Comcast is in the process of upgrading its hybrid copper/fiber optical network with more fiber cabling directly to residences and businesses as well as bringing fiber closer in neighborhoods for the ability to offer the gigabit data rates needed to support dramatically increased traffic from access to cloud services and streaming. Infrastructure capable of supporting this is important for marketing and sales to enterprise customers.

Cable TV providers are also participating in a quasi-price war with competitors where each provider offers a low initial rate and then raises the price after the term of subscribers' initial contract expires. Their main competitors are satellite providers and telephone companies. Telephone companies are building out their broadband networks in competition with cable TV providers for the many broadband customers who have dropped both traditional voice service in addition to cable TV, but who do want high-speed broadband service. The following is a quote from Comcast's 2017 annual report discussing what they consider their major competitor—AT&T's DirecTV satellite service.

A quote from Comcast's 2017 Annual Report:

> *Competition for our cable services consists primarily of DBS* providers and phone companies with fiber-based networks that typically offer features, pricing and packaging for services comparable to ours. Some of these competitors are also offering smaller packages of channels at price points lower than our standard packages, both through traditional and online distribution platforms, which could cause us to offer more customized programming packages that may be less profitable. AT&T, our largest phone company competitor, acquired DirecTV, the nation's largest DBS provider in 2015 to create an even larger competitor, and in 2016 announced a proposed merger with Time Warner a media and entertainment company.*

---

*Direct Broadcast Service (DBS) refers to satellite TV providers.

Cable TV Service for Business Clients

All cable TV providers offer broadband services to small business and enterprise customers. In order to be viable competitors to facilities-based providers like AT&T, Verizon, and CenturyLink, cable TV companies have added additional fiber to their networks to enable them to offer gigabit data rate service and cloud computing. In particular, they provide a direct fiber link to enterprise customers' buildings and campuses in areas where they have nearby fiber-optic cabling.

Regional Telecommunications Providers

While the largest telecommunications and cable TV providers dominate the market, there are important regional providers. The largest ones have bought up other smaller companies resulting in regional providers that cover rural as well as metropolitan areas. The two largest regional providers outside of the "big 4" are Windstream and Frontier. There are additionally hundreds of very small companies with only a few hundred subscribers each. The small companies are located in rural parts of the United States and in Guam.

Windstream and Frontier—Tier 2 Providers

Tier 2 providers are regional carriers. Their networks do not cover the entire United States. But they do own core, fiber backbone networks that are connected to peering points where traffic is handed off between providers. These regional providers for the most part sell cable TV and terrestrial copper and fiber network services. Neither Windstream nor Frontier sell cellular services. They both do sell DirecTV and Dish Network satellite television services as authorized agents. Authorized agents contract with an infrastructure provider to sell services and equipment for which they receive a commission.

Windstream and Frontier depend on the Connect America Fund (CAF) subsidies for service to their high cost areas. The Connect America Fund is described below in Government Regulations. They both offer Internet access and security services to business and consumer subscribers. Neither owns a cellular network. However, Windstream offers fixed wireless Internet access in some areas that is enabled by government subsidies. They both reported losses of voice and video subscribers, and both raised their rates to compensate for subscriber losses.

Continued

Windstream Holdings Inc. is headquartered in Little Rock, Alabama. It is the main telephone company (incumbent local exchange carrier) in rural areas in 18 states, where they sell service under the Kinetic brand. They additionally sell wholesale fiber service to carriers outside of the Windstream network on fiber they acquired by their 2017 purchase of EarthLink. They also offer cloud computing and hosting services. Windstream provides 25Mbps service to 55 percent of their subscribers and 50Mbps data rates to 31 percent of their subscribers.

According to their 2017 annual reports, 25 percent of their subscribers do not have cable TV. Windstream sells services in areas outside of their network infrastructure as well as within their own network. In the first quarter of 2018 they reported a total of 1,432,000 customers.

Frontier Communications Corporation, which is headquartered in Norwalk Connecticut, offers services in 29 states. Frontier purchased Verizon's rural wireline properties in California, Florida, and Texas in 2016, which resulted in an additional 3.7 million customers to Frontier's network. This doubled the number of Frontier subscribers to 4.8 million subscribers. Verizon at the time of the sale was concentrating on building out their cellular service.

REGULATORY ISSUES ....

Telecommunications and cable TV are heavily regulated sectors. Companies are subject to local, intrastate, and interstate regulations. Here is a quote from Frontier Communications 2017 Annual Report:

> *The FCC generally exercises jurisdiction over information services, interstate or international telecommunications services...State regulatory commissions in general exercise jurisdiction over intrastate telecommunications services...Certain federal and state agencies, including attorneys general, monitor and exercise oversight related to consumer protection issues. In addition, local governments often regulate the public rights-of-way necessary to install and operate networks and may require services providers to obtain licenses or franchises regulating their use of public rights-of-ways.*

Utility Pole Attachments—Critical for 5G

Attaching fiber optical cables to utility poles is critical for cellular providers upgrading to fifth-generation mobile protocols. Fifth-generation mobile protocols require a huge amount of new fiber because antennas are closer together and need to be connected by fiber to other antennas and to providers' data centers.

> ## Who Owns Utility Poles?
>
> According to the law firm Electrocution PLLC, in a September 8, 2016, article by Jeffrey Feldman, there are an estimated 180 million utility poles in the United States. The highest two or three wires on the poles carry electricity, and the lower wires carry telecommunications and cable TV signals. The majority of poles are owned by local utility companies. However, Verizon jointly owns utility poles with the local utility in many parts of the country where it manages them jointly with the electric utility that owns the poles. Verizon is also in charge of placing new ones and replacing old ones. Verizon charges $6 per pole for each wire a provider attaches to a pole. As part of their management service, if a wire becomes detached from a pole and is hanging down, a Verizon technician will identify the wire owner so that the utility or the correct provider can reattach it to the pole.

One Touch Make Ready to Streamline Pole Attachments

Utility pole placement and replacements are regulated by the FCC. Formerly, a local permit was required to move, replace, or install each pole. The process for adding equipment to, moving, or replacing damaged poles required a separate permit for each pole replaced or moved, and for each piece of equipment or wires added to it. Industry groups lobbied the FCC for streamlined rules on pole attachments and replacements. One Touch Make Ready (OTMR) allowed licensed contractors to replace, install, or attach equipment to multiple poles with a single truck roll. A single truck roll refers to sending out a truck once to work on multiple poles. In 2018 the FCC made this change to its regulations on pole attachments.

The industry groups contended that a single truck roll is necessary to build out fifth generation infrastructure and backhaul fiber facilities without the delays of requesting permission separately to change or move each telephone pole and attachment. Currently, each provider sends its own installer to do the work. The new rules, which allow contractors to do the pole changes, was opposed by the unionized installers retained by telephone companies.

Universal Service and Rate of Return

In 1913, when the former AT&T was given a monopoly in telecommunications service in the United States, it made a commitment to offer reasonably priced universal services everywhere in its territories. In exchange, the government guaranteed that AT&T

could earn a specific rate of return on its telecommunications services. This marked the beginning of the concepts of *universal service* and *rate of return guarantees.*

While rate of return guarantees did not encourage efficient operations, they did enable the company to invest in research and development through its Bell Labs division. AT&T inventions included touch-tone service, integrated circuits, and laser technologies. These innovations were freely available without patent fees, were adopted worldwide, and are one of the reasons that global networks are compatible with one another today.

In the late 1970s, the introduction of competition from lower-cost long-distance providers such as Sprint and MCI (now part of Verizon) made it untenable for AT&T to continue charging high fees for its own long-distance calling. Gradually, AT&T lowered its long-distance fees and increased its local service rates to compensate. To make up for local service subsidies, regulators set fees for carriers to pay one another for connecting calls to one another's customers. These are known as *Intercarrier Compensation (ICC)* fees, and they marked the beginning of the imposition of access charges.

Decreasing ICC Payments for Connecting Traffic—Gradually Being Reduced

- Intercarrier Compensation (ICC) are federally mandated fees for interstate calls and state-mandated fees for intrastate calls. When a college student called his parents who lived in another telephone company's territory, the student's phone company paid an ICC (Intercarrier Compensation) fee to the other telephone company for connecting the call. These fees are gradually being reduced and rural carriers are instead receiving subsidies to build out their infrastructure.

There are two types of access fees: *originating access fees* and *terminating access fees.* They apply to mobile, wireline, and interconnected VoIP traffic. Interconnected VoIP calls are those made to people on the Public Switched Telephone Network (PSTN). The PSTN is an older network architecture for home telephones connected directly to older telephone company switches, not part of data networks.

The following are examples of originating terminating and access fees.

- Originating access fees are paid by phone companies whose customers lease toll-free numbers.

  - A subscriber on a different carrier's network calls a toll-free (800-888) number that belongs to another carrier's subscriber.

  - A person places a VoIP call to a toll-free number connected to someone on the PSTN.

- Terminating access fees.

  - A person whose phone is connected to the PSTN calls someone on another carrier's network.

  - A person places a VoIP call to someone on the PSTN.

Access fees paid to carriers in rural, high-cost areas are set higher than those in urban areas. Moreover, intrastate access fees, which are set by states, are generally higher than interstate access fees. Access fee rates for local calls are minimal.

The FCC's November 2011 Transformation Order laid out a plan for reducing ICC fees. Terminating access fees, at the receiving telephone company, have been reduced dramatically over the last 7 years, from several cents per minute down to $0.007 cents per minute—and even going to zero in most cases by July 2019. To make up for the loss of revenue experienced by many rural carriers, the FCC also revamped the subsidy fund from which rate of return carriers can draw. A *rate of return carrier* is an incumbent telephone company that is allowed to adjust their rates so that they earn a set return, a profit. The rate reductions for originating access fees are the current subject of another FCC project, for which the FCC is still accepting comments from the public and affected organizations.

Alternate Connect America Model

The United States has a long history of subsidizing telephone service through universal service that initially only applied to voice telephone service. The goal of subsidizing telephone service was to enable subscribers in rural areas to have access to the same quality voice and broadband options at rates comparable to subscribers in urban and suburban areas.

Comparable prices and services in rural areas cost more to provide than those urban areas where costs for upgrading to, say, fiber from copper are offset by revenue from having more customers per mile.

The Telecommunications Act of 1996 codified universal service by establishing the Universal Service Fund (USF), which subsidizes costs for Internet access in rural and high-cost (for example, mountainous) areas. In 2016, the FCC introduced Alternative Connect America Model (A-CAM) and changed the Universal Service Fund name to the Alternate Connect America Model. The A-CAM is paid for by contributions from long-distance, paging, and mobile carriers. Contributions are based on a percentage of revenue from these services. Carriers that mix voice and data on transmission lines that carry traffic to the Internet and to long-distance switches also contribute based on revenue from these services.

The four groups eligible for A-CAM subsidies are:

- Lifeline for low-income subscribers and residents of Tribal lands

- The E-rate for schools and libraries

- Subsidies for rural areas where costs for telecommunications facilities are high because there are fewer homes and businesses per mile

- Rural healthcare facilities

The goal is to enable providers in rural and high-cost areas to offer services at reasonably comparable rates for similar services in urban areas. The portion of the A-CAM that applies to schools and libraries is known as the *E-rate*. The E-rate subsidizes Internet access and infrastructure costs needed for high-speed Internet access.

A-CAM Implementations

In February 2016, the FCC issued a Notice of Proposed Rule Making (NPRM) that recommended support for broadband services as well as the existing phone subsidies as a universal service. The proposed rule would gradually eliminate access fees between long-distance and local telephone companies and offer to replace high-cost support with the A-CAM. The FCC gave rural providers a choice of staying with high-cost subsidies or moving to A-CAM payments. The Connect America Fund funds support new projects and maintenance of existing broadband.

Additionally, there are funds for subsidizing broadband for rural healthcare facilities and hospitals. The goal is to bring these costs down to the same level as healthcare facilities in urban areas.

The FCC stated that a guaranteed rate of return removes the incentive to operate efficiently because rate of return guarantees a certain profit regardless of possible operating inefficiencies. The FCC introduced competitive *reverse auctions* for granting money for non-served areas. With reverse auctions, organizations win grants for low bids for subsidies needed to upgrade infrastructure rather than high bids.

Carriers in these rural areas had a choice of remaining on the high-cost subsidies or participating in the A-CAM reverse auctions to obtain funding. Because the A-CAM supports new projects and maintenance of existing projects, most rural providers that had already upgraded their infrastructure to fiber service opted not to sign up for the A-CAM. Rather, they kept their high-cost subsidies. In contrast, rural providers that had not yet upgraded their networks with fiber-optic cabling more suited to broadband data rates, bid in the reverse auction for A-CAM funds.

Recipients that successfully bid for funds to build broadband networks are subject to requirements to build out their broadband facilities within 10 years. They must also make these services available for a defined period of years. The Connect America Fund supports ongoing maintenance and operations of broadband wireline and wireless networks. Moreover, these carriers will no longer receive funding based on rate of return analysis. Rather, price cap systems will be instituted so that carriers will have incentives to operate efficiently rather than have guaranteed revenues. With price caps, carriers agree to impose an upper limit on their rates and keep them at an agreed-upon level for a specific number of years.

As part of the plan, the amount of money collected for A-CAM was capped at the amount collected in 2011. This did not take into account inflation. This is a major issue for rural carriers building out their networks. Although, more money has been allocated to the program, adequate funding is still an issue.

Lifeline Subsidies for Low-Income Residents

In October 2016, the FCC finalized rules to include affordable broadband in universal service for rural, low-income, and other underserved areas. The fund supports wireline and mobile broadband as well as voice. The FCC currently defines broadband as 25Mbps downstream (from the provider to the customer) and 3Mbps upstream (from the customer to the provider). Currently, 18 million households in the United States do not have broadband access. For the most part these are low-income residents and households in rural areas.

The Lifeline program provides a $9.25 monthly subsidy for Internet access and for mobile services to low-income residents, veterans, and people on or near Tribal lands. This covers only a portion of the monthly fixed line or mobile broadband fees. The fund also supplies subsidies to rural healthcare facilities so that their broadband costs are not higher than for those in urban areas.

Cutbacks in Lifeline Funds

The FCC, beginning in 2016, noted that the program had a great deal of waste and abuse. The Government Accounting Office completed a study showing $137 million of benefits went to fake accounts or dead people. Subsidies are paid for by fees on subscribers' phone bills, which telephone companies collect and pay to the FCC. In cutting back on waste, and slimming down the program, by 2018, many people that actually need the benefits were deprived of them.

In addition to cutting back on waste, the FCC narrowed the eligibility requirements for Lifeline. The new rules specified that only facility-based telecommunications, cellular, and broadband providers were permitted to participate in Lifeline subsidies. The rulings eliminated resellers such as TracFone Wireless and Consumer Cellular from the Lifeline program. This is problematic because many facility-based providers such as Verizon and AT&T that own networks backed out of providing Lifeline subsidies. This created rural areas where people formerly on Lifeline lost their subsidies because there were no facility-based fixed line and cellular providers, only resellers. The facility-based providers in their area had stopped providing services because their revenues were so low. This occurred in areas where the only providers left were resellers who don't own network infrastructure. They are not facility-based providers.

E-Rate Subsidies for Schools and Libraries

A portion of the Lifeline Fund is used for libraries and schools. E-rate subsidies are used to make broadband and Wi-Fi more affordable to these institutions. The subsidies include basic maintenance as well as discounts on Wi-Fi equipment and broadband. Discounts range from 20 percent to 90 percent. The higher discounts are available for higher poverty areas and rural schools and libraries.

Eligible schools and libraries submit requests to the Universal Service Administration Company (USAC). USAC posts the requests on its website for its list of preferred vendors to bid on. After completion of the broadband or Wi-Fi project either the vendor or the institution submits a request for reimbursement.

Media Consolidation Issues

Radio and television over-the-air broadcasts are regulated by the FCC because they use spectrum allocated and controlled by the FCC. The FCC issues licenses to broadcasters for specific channels. The FCC has established rules for these broadcasters including providing equal airtime for political candidates. Rules enacted in the 1970s prohibited one company in each local market from owning both a newspaper and a TV station. It also did not allow TV stations in the same market to merge with each other if that would leave fewer than eight independently owned stations in the local market.

 NOTE   As cable TV stations don't use the public airwaves, they are not regulated under the media consolidation rules.

In 2017 the Federal Communications Commission voted to roll back the 1970s restrictions on media ownership. The new rules allow common ownership of newspapers and broadcast stations in the same market. Critics in the United States Senate stated that the order would enable media conglomerates to manage news content and broadcasts. In particular, senators criticized Sinclair's proposal to purchase Tribune Media.

FCC Commissioner Mignon Clyburn also dissented stating:

> *Mark my words, today will go down in history as the day when the FCC abdicated its responsibility to uphold the core values of localism, competition and diversity in broadcasting.*

In response to his critics, FCC Chairman Ajit Pai stated that the changes were necessary to allow media companies to compete with online giants such as Facebook and Google.

Sinclair Broadcast Group owns 173 radio stations in 81 broadcast markets and locations across the United States. It has been accused of promulgating conservative views in these local markets. Moreover, many of the stations repeat the very same broadcasts as all of the rest along with the same conservative commentary on the news.

In August of 2018 the FCC denied Sinclair's request to purchase Tribune Media. Sinclair would have acquired 42 more local television stations. The FCC opted not to waive media ownership rules.

Spam Calls—Robocalls

Robocalls are those dialed by banks of automated dialers that call thousands of households each hour. It's illegal to call phone numbers on the national-do-not-call (DNC) list without explicit permission. According to the Federal Trade Commission (FTC), in 2017 2.4 billion robocalls were placed every month. Not only are these calls annoying, but many telemarketers that place these calls defraud people by impersonating the Internal Revenue Service and asking for a credit card payment to settle a supposed debt to the IRS. Others make false promises for non-existent goods and services. One telemarketer was fined for trying to sell fake auto warranties.

Another issue is that robocall traffic can flood 911 centers to such an extent that legitimate emergency calls are blocked. This occurred in 2017 in large swaths of the United States. The telemarketers' automatic dialers sent thousands of calls to the ten-digit numbers associated with each 911 call center. Because call centers are designed so that calls forward to backup call centers when there are large volumes of calls, the robocalls affected 911 centers nationwide.

The following is a quote from an October 4, 2017, Federal Trade Commission press release, "FTC Testifies Before U.S. Senate Special Committee on Aging on the Continuing Fight to Combat Illegal Robocalls":

> *The FTC's most recent victory in the fight against illegal Robocalls came this past June, when a federal district court in Illinois issued an order imposing the largest civil penalty ever in a DNC* case—\$280 million against satellite television provider Dish Network. The case charged Dish and its telemarketers with making tens of millions of calls—often Robocalls—to consumers on the DNC Registry, as well as continuing to call consumers who had previously asked not to be called again.*

Fighting Back—Authentication and Verification

The telecommunications industry is fighting back against robocalls that clog their networks and result in millions of calls to telephone companies' customer service centers about fraudulent calls. They have formed an industry group, the Robo Strike Force, to

*Do Not Call

develop technology to identify and block illegal calls, launch a consumer education program, and explore legal options to deter telemarketers. The Robo Strike Force is made up of telephone companies and smartphone manufacturers. Currently, individuals and companies that make illegal robocalls are subject to fines. The Robo Strike Force is lobbying the Federal government to make robocall telemarketers subject to criminal penalties, in addition to civil fines.

And, significantly, the Robo Strike Force is developing technology to identify "spam" calls. The technology is called SHAKEN (Signature-based Handling of Asserted Information using toKENs) and STIR (Secure Telephone Identity Revisited). SHAKEN and STIR are designed to authenticate that calls are legitimate and to verify at the receiving provider's network that they are legitimate. SHAKEN and STIR operates by attaching a 15-character encrypted token to legitimate calls at the originating point of the call and sending the encrypted characters along with the call to the receiving telephone company as a verification that the call is legitimate. SHAKEN and STIR only work on VoIP (Voice over Internet Protocol) voice traffic. Encryption uses mathematical algorithms to scramble bits so that only the intended recipients can decode them.

The Do Not Originate Registry Trial

The intent of the Do Not Originate (DNO) Registry is to block numbers that should never originate calls: invalid numbers, valid numbers that are not allocated to a voice service provider, and valid numbers that are allocated but not assigned to a subscriber. With the FCC's permission, the Strike Force performed a trial of this concept. The trial was considered a success by the Strike Force and the FCC, playing a significant role in reducing IRS scam calls by about 90 percent during the September 2016 to February 2017 test run.

Robocalls that Don't Ring—Ringless Calls

Ringless calls are those that are routed straight to voicemail without ringing a telephone. Marketers who use this service have the voicemail message they want to distribute, or a simple survey recorded on a server at a provider's data center that is programmed to go to the server with subscribers' voicemail boxes. As of mid-2018, the FCC has not ruled on whether Ringless voice mail is an example of a robocall and therefore illegal.

Exceptions to the Anti-Robocall Regulations

The FCC ruled that robocall prohibitions don't apply to government contractors' calls, debt collectors, or political campaigns. Contractors who are agents of the government are allowed to make as many calls as they want to. Thus, people can be called by federal contractors that use voice recordings to ask their opinions on surveys or public issues. Debt collectors are also allowed to make robocalls.

Legislation to Protect the Privacy of Minors

Privacy refers to peoples' control over personal information, the ability to make decisions regarding how they want information accessed, and which information they want available. Privacy settings on social networks ostensibly allow users to control what information is available about themselves and about their children.

Prior to 2013, the only legislation in the United States that protected privacy was the 1998 *Children's Online Privacy Protection Act* (COPPA). This law grants parents of children 12 years old and younger the ability to control what information web sites collect about them. It does not apply to adults or teenagers older than 12 but younger than 18. Furthermore, it makes no mention of privacy on mobile networks or online apps (applications).

COPPA updates were enacted in 2013 and 2015, but neither of them includes teenagers between the ages of 13 and 17. Industry organizations opposed the inclusion of teenagers on the grounds that it was unduly onerous. In addition, they stated that it would weaken privacy because web sites would collect information about web surfers' ages. They also argued that it discouraged sites from directing content to teenagers because of the difficulty of complying with the act, thus limiting services to teenagers.

As a result, young people ages 13 to 17, who often don't have the maturity to understand the damage that can be caused by careless web posts, have little legal protection. It's also unclear, if a similar privacy act is passed, whether teenagers would understand the implications of allowing geolocation services to track and keep information about their location.

The COPPA revisions passed in 2013 and 2015 included the following provisions:

- Widens the definition of personal information to cookies that track children's activity on the Web

- Operators of web sites and online services that are directed to children under 13 or have knowledge that they are collecting information about children under 13 must contact parents and receive parental consent before collecting personal information.

- Mobile application owners must also adhere to these rules.

- The FTC maintains a hotline for parents with questions.

- Web sites and mobile phone apps must now obtain permission for parents to collect photos and geolocations of children.

- Web sites and applications may not collect cookies that track behaviors of children nor are they allowed to send ads to children based on their browsing history or demographics.

- If operators of sites or services inadvertently collect data on kids, they must delete it as soon as possible.

Unfortunately, not all mobile apps adhere to COPPA regulations. An April 17, 2018, article in the *Washington Post* by Hamza Shaban stated that researchers found that 6,000 apps available in the Google Play Store violated COPPA by collecting personal information on children. The research was undertaken by the International Computer Science Institute at the University of California at Berkeley.

Lobbying Efforts to Influence Regulations

Because telecommunication policies are heavily regulated, all large mobile, cable TV, and landline providers spend sizeable amounts of money on court cases and on lobbyists to attempt to influence lawmakers and regulatory agencies.

Lobbying to Influence Government Regulators

Telecommunications and wireless companies are heavily regulated at the federal, state and local levels. All providers spend time and money on lobbying efforts to influence these regulations. They contribute to candidates from both the Democratic and Republican Parties and hire lobbyists to communicate their positions directly with government officials. The issues these organizations lobby for include mergers, patents, copyrights, auto safety, self-driving cars, privacy, online advertising, attachments to telephone poles, and permission for installation of cellular antennas and gear.

Government regulations impact all phases of telecommunications, which is why almost all large providers such as AT&T, CenturyLink, Comcast, and Verizon, as well as medium-sized and small providers spend money on lobbyists every year. According to the Federal Election Committee Commission, in the period between January 1, 2017, and April 26, 2018, Comcast spent $23 million dollars on lobbying at the federal level.

Moreover, lobbying expenditures spike when there are issues providers consider critical. For example, when AT&T offered to purchase Time Warner to gain their cache of movies and television content, they lobbied the federal government for permission for the merger. Thus, it's likely that their lobbying expenses spiked.

Lobbying is not confined to telecommunications organizations. Large technology organizations and social networks expend large efforts on lobbying. Facebook and Alphabet's Google, which are both facing the specter of regulations, are spending millions on lobbying. Facebook is under congressional scrutiny due to allegations that millions of fake posts influenced the outcome of the 2016 presidential elections. Google, part of Alphabet, spends increasing amounts of money on lobbying to influence congress on immigration, tax reform, and antitrust issues. It has also faced questions on its treatment of its own company's search rating compared to Google's rivals.

THE STATE OF THE INDUSTRY—CONSOLIDATION VIA MERGERS ....

The telecommunications industry is dominated by organizations that are among the 100 largest companies in the United States. Technological innovations have enabled companies such as Apple, Google, Netflix, and Amazon to encroach on services that were formerly the exclusive domain of traditional telephone and cable TV operators. Mobile operators, cable Multiple System Operators (MSOs), and Internet companies now vie with one another for revenue from mobile, Voice over Internet Protocol (VoIP), cloud, and streaming services.

Competition to Telephone, Mobile, and Cable TV Companies

Telephone and cable TV companies compete with satellite companies for streaming and voice calling; Amazon and Google for household automation; Facebook, Netflix, and Walt Disney for video, and with each other for all of these services. They additionally compete with upgraded 4th generation and new 5th generation cellular networks capable of supporting streaming, Internet access, and cloud computing. In order to stay competitive, they continuously make capital expenditures to upgrade and maintain their networks.

Mobile Operators

AT&T Mobility and Verizon Wireless are the largest mobile operators in the United States; they are also the only ones with nationwide coverage. Verizon Wireless's network covers approximately 322 million people as of 2018 (98 percent of the population). The vast majority of the 325.7 million people in the United States, as of December 2017, have access to mobile networks. However, high capacity coverage for data is uneven in rural and mountainous areas.

Mobile network upgrades require sizable capital investments in equipment, fiber cabling and spectrum to keep up with the growth in traffic. Moreover, upgrades when new generations of service are introduced require new spectrum, hardware, and software. Spectrum is made up of the invisible airwaves that carry wireless signals. See Chapter 7, "Mobile and Wi-Fi Networks," for more information on spectrum and mobile technologies. In addition, mobile providers need to support older generations of mobile networks until most subscribers have handsets compatible with upgraded protocols.

Because fiber or copper is not needed for every mobile subscriber, initial deployments of mobile networks cost less than building out cabled, fixed line networks from scratch. This is why, in developing parts of the world, most people have cell service, but not fixed-line home telephone service.

Decreasing Churn Rates Among Mobile Providers

In recent years AT&T and Verizon and others have had lower churn rates. Churn rates refer to the percentage of customers that change carriers annually. Lower churn rates result in savings on customer service for activating new customers and deactivating former customers' accounts. Lower churn rates are the result of a combination of more costly handsets, improvements in coverage, and service quality in cellular networks.

When smartphones were first available, mobile networks did not have adequate capacity to handle the increased e-mail and data traffic, and customers changed carriers in hopes of better coverage. With the introduction of upgraded 4th generation LTE service and Wi-Fi networks, and the gradual introduction of 5th generation networks, this is changing. Subscribers now routinely stream video and access their cloud accounts and social networks. Each new generation of smartphone does not need to be upgraded as often to increase capacity.

And importantly, providers are no longer subsidizing smartphone purchases. Formerly AT&T, Verizon, Sprint, and T-Mobile promised subscribers, for example, a $600 iPhone for only $200 if they signed a 2-year contract. At the end of the contract term, subscribers could change to a different mobile provider and have a new phone that they were able to pay off in a few years with low equipment charges on their mobile bills. With providers no longer subsidizing new phones, many subscribers keep their phones longer and don't change to a different mobile network.

Consolidation of Mobile Providers

Until mid-2004, there were six major mobile carriers in the United States: AT&T Mobility, Verizon Wireless, Cingular, Sprint, Nextel, and T-Mobile USA. Currently, there are only four major mobile carriers, and if the FCC and the Department of Justice (DOJ) approve the proposed Sprint and T-Mobile USA merger, there will only be three facilities-based mobile carriers. Table 3-6 lists the largest facilities-based mobile carriers.

Industry consolidation that results in near-monopoly conditions has ramifications for customers as well as competitors. For customers, it can mean higher prices and less innovation. This is because monopolies have few incentives to be competitive with regard to prices or developing new features to attract customers.

Smaller mobile competitors suffer the disadvantage of higher operating costs. For example, large carriers have the clout to bargain for discounts on quantity purchases of cell phones and network equipment. These discounts are often unavailable to small carriers. Another disadvantage is that smaller providers don't have the resources to mount large TV and Internet advertising campaigns; thus, it's more difficult to attract new customers.

In addition to the resources to launch broader advertising campaigns, large mobile carriers have the financial strength to lease spectrum needed for additional capacity and fifth-generation data networks.

Table 3-6 The 10 Largest Facilities-Based Cellular Companies in the United States

Cellular Provider	Number of Connections*	Recent Acquisitions
Verizon Wireless	116 million	Purchased Cincinnati Bell mobile network in 2014, which now resells Verizon Wireless service
		Purchased Alltel Corporation and Rural Cellular in 2008
AT&T Mobility	89.3 million	Purchased Centennial in 2008
Sprint	74 million**	Purchased mobile provider Clearwire in 2013
T-Mobile USA	74 million**	Purchased Iowa Wireless Services 4th quarter 2017
US Cellular	4.6 million	Operates in Pacific Northwest, parts of the Midwest, East, and New Hampshire; part of TDS Telecom
C Spire Wireless (formerly named Cellular South Inc.)	1,000,000***	Owned by private company Telapex, Inc. Service in Mississippi, Florida, Tennessee and Alabama

*Source: Company web sites; includes postpaid, prepaid, and wholesale. Connections refer to the number the number of subscribers. However, some customers have more than one account if they have multiple cellular devices.

** Prior to proposed merger of Sprint Wireless and T-Mobile USA

***Figure is approximate due to the fact that C Spire Wireless is a private company.

It's unclear if T-Mobile will raise prices if the merger is approved. Until now, T-Mobile for the most part has had lower rates than Verizon Wireless and AT&T Mobility. In addition, T-Mobile was the first carrier to offer unlimited voice and data plans for a fixed monthly fee. Verizon Wireless and AT&T Mobility followed suit, offering their own unlimited plans, which they have mostly deleted. These unlimited plans are particularly favorable for subscribers that stream video from companies such as Netflix, Amazon, Hulu, and others.

Analyzing the Impact of a Merger on Consumers and Competition

Mergers between large telecommunications companies require approval of the Federal Communications Commission (FCC) and the Department of Justice. The FCC bases its approval or disapproval on the impact the merger would have on customers. It might disapprove a merger if it determines that the merger is not in the interest of consumers.

The Department of Justice evaluates mergers based on the competitive nature of markets and determines if the merger will harm competition. The FCC and the Department of Justice keep one another apprised during the process. They also bring in outside consultants to help them evaluate the impact of the proposed merger and additionally accept comments from the public. As a rule, competitors and other companies such as suppliers that might be impacted by the merger submit comments.

Generally, when large mergers are approved, there are conditions that must be satisfied for approval. This occurred when Verizon Wireless acquired Alltel in 2008 and was required to divest itself of certain assets.

The Merger of AT&T and Time Warner

In 2016, AT&T and Time Warner agreed to merge. The merger agreement was set up with AT&T buying Time Warner. AT&T gained Warner Bros. content including Turner Broadcasting, HBO, CNN, CW, Cinemax and CW plus content in Latin America and Europe. Owning this large cache of TV and movies provides a library of content for AT&T and their DirecTV unit to better enable them to compete in the growing streaming market.

The merged entities of AT&T and Warner Bros., and Comcast, which bought NBC Universal in 2011 resulted in their owning local networks as well as content. They have the ability to block others' content or charge higher prices for access to their local networks of subscribers by streaming customers such as Netflix, Facebook, Amazon, and other streaming providers which don't own network facilities.

Selling Wholesale Network Services

Wholesale telecommunications providers sell to other telecommunications providers. They don't sell their products or services to end-user subscribers. All major mobile and facilities-based operators offer wholesale services to other carriers because no facilities-based network operator has service everywhere. These operators sell wholesale services as a part of their product strategy. There are companies whose major business strategy is selling capacity on fiber-optic cables they own. These include Consolidated Telecommunications Services, and NEF.

An example of a wholesale provider is Level 3 whose main line of business was wholesale services to other telecom companies before it was purchased by Century-Link. It sold capacity on its interstate long-haul network. Tower builder Crown Castle purchased fiber network provider Lightower and started a wholesale division called Crown Castle Fiber to complement its antenna and tower business.

Electric utilities often sell wholesale data network services. Electric utilities own vast fiber networks over which they transmit electrical signals. They also own *dark fiber*, spare fiber that is not "lit" by fiber equipment. When utilities lay fiber, they lay extra fiber to be prepared for surges in electrical usage or maintenance issues on other fiber strands.

Carriers that sell wholesale services save money on marketing, retail stores, billing, and staff. They hope to make up for lower per-user revenues with savings in operating costs and its customers' quantity leases. Depending on the arrangement with each carrier customer, it might also offer handsets and billing platforms to the carrier.

Backhaul Services

Another way that cable TV operators add services to their existing infrastructure is by leasing spare capacity on their backbone networks to mobile operators. Multiple Service Operators (MSOs) use their backbone networks to link their local cable TV facilities to centralized headends that distribute TV and movies and perform functions such as billing and links to the Internet and other networks.

Backhaul services that mobile providers lease link cell sites (towers and antennas) to the data centers that support functions such as security and billing. Large cable TV operators as well as small mobile operators lease backhaul capacity in locations where they don't have their own backhaul infrastructure. See Chapter 7 for more information on backhaul and cell sites.

Other Competitors to Broadband Providers—Overbuilders

Overbuilders were the first facilities-based competitors to cable TV operators in the United States. They began offering service immediately following passage of the Telecommunications Act of 1996, which for the first time allowed competitors to offer services "over" incumbent cable TV operators' equipment. Overbuilders run their cables over incumbent MSOs' cables on telephone poles in residential neighborhoods. However, they reuse the *drop wires* installed by the incumbent cable TV operator. A drop wire is the cable from the telephone pole to an individual residence. RCN and Atlantic Broadband are examples of overbuilders.

Overbuilders offer voice telephone service and Internet access in addition to pay-TV. Some also sell broadband services to business customers in areas where they operate.

However, overbuilders underestimated the cost of building and maintaining these networks. They also overestimated their ability to win customers from incumbent cable television operators. One factor in the difficulty of attracting enough customers to be profitable was their lack of financial heft to mount the widespread TV and print advertising campaigns incumbents mount.

RCN Telecom LLC is the largest overbuilder. It offers service in New York City, eastern Massachusetts, Philadelphia, and Washington, DC. Private equity firm TPG purchased RCN and overbuilder Grande in 2016 and manages both RCN and firm Grande Communications Network LLC. Grande provides cable TV service in Texas. Atlantic Broadband was purchased by Canadian cable TV company Cogeco in 2017.

Agents

Agents act as independent representatives for carriers. Like insurance agents, a carrier's agent receives commissions on services that it sells. AT&T, Comcast, Verizon, and CenturyLink started agent programs as a way to lower the cost of selling services to small businesses. Today many agents sell telephone services as an adjunct to the telephone and networking equipment that they offer. Agents are certified and receive some training from the telephone and cable TV companies they represent. They do not bill customers directly for the voice and data services they sell; rather, customers receive bills directly from the carriers.

Primarily small and medium-sized organizations use agents because they are often easier to reach, and some have the ability to help troubleshoot problems when it is not apparent whether the problem is in the carrier's connections or the onsite equipment. Moreover, carriers often prefer to serve smaller business customers with agents to reduce their own staffing and selling expenses.

Retail outlets such as Best Buy and Staples act as agents for cellular providers and prepaid cellular services as do small retail outlets in shopping districts and malls. Wal-Mart, Target, and Amazon sell TracFone Wireless's prepaid mobile phones and services. TracFone Wireless is a unit of Mexico's TelMex. In addition to large retailers, there are often networks of small retailers that act as agents for larger companies such as Comcast, T-Mobile, Sprint, and Verizon Wireless. The small retailers display the logos of the carriers that they represent in their stores and sell hardware and accessories for mobile phones in addition to service plans.

Resellers—Mobile Virtual Network Operators

Like agents, resellers do not own network infrastructure. Resellers are also referred as Mobile Virtual Network Operators (MVNOs). Unlike agents, however, resellers provide billing and customer service for their customers and market services under their own brand. Resellers sell wireline service such as data (Gigabit Ethernet and other high-speed services), calling cards, Internet access, local calling, long-distance, mobile services, VoIP services, and international calling. Table 3-7 lists a sampling of resellers with the networks on which they resell services.

Resellers purchase services at discounts from facility-based telephone and cable TV providers. They then mark them up, and often offer them below retail cost. Resellers offer services carried on networks owned by AT&T, Sprint, Verizon, T-Mobile, and other carriers worldwide. Sprint's network hosts the most resellers in the United States compared to AT&T and Verizon.

Table 3-7   A Sampling of Resellers on Facility-Based Providers' Networks

Facility-Based Provider	Resellers
AT&T	Consumer Cellular, Cricket Wireless,* H2O Wireless, Net10,** Pix Wireless, TracFone Wireless**
Sprint	Boost Mobile, FreedomPop, Tello, TracFone Wireless,** Virgin Mobile
T-Mobile	MetroPCS, Mint Mobile, Net10,* Project Fi, Red Pocket
Verizon	CenturyLink, Comcast, Credo Mobile, GreatCall, Net10,** Republic Wireless, TracFone Wireless**

Cricket Wireless is owned by AT&T Mobility
**TracFone Wireless and Net10 resell service on multiple networks*

Competitive providers such as Windstream and Frontier resell service in areas outside of their own coverage areas. This provides them a way to offer nationwide service. In their own coverage area, these and other competitive providers have their own networks and switches and last-mile broadband facilities.

Comcast at one time owned rights to spectrum suitable for cellular service. Spectrum is made up of invisible airwaves over which mobile, satellite and other services' signals are transmitted. Comcast sold their spectrum and instead they now resell mobile services on Verizon's cellular network. CenturyLink and Cincinnati Bell also resell mobile services on Verizon's cellular network. This is less costly because it requires less maintenance and capital for building out a cellular network.

Prisoners Call—Families Pay

In prisons within the United States, when prisoners call their families or attorneys, they are required to make collect calls. Collect calls are those for which people receiving the call pay rather than the person making the call. In addition, all prisoners' calls are recorded. Prisons hire outside firms to manage the calls, the charges, and the recordings. The largest prisoner telephony providers are Securus Technologies and Global Tel Link, also known as GTL.

All of these systems place the calls using VoIP technology. Many of these providers charge prisoners' families rates many times higher than those made from home or business telephones. For example, they tack on a surcharge of up to $3.16 for the first minute of the call plus $0.16 for each additional minute. Various organizations have sued these providers on the basis that the rates are exorbitantly high. The most recent suit, a class action suit against county prisons, was filed in May 2018 at the Suffolk Superior Court in Massachusetts on the basis that these charges amounted to kickbacks to the prisons, which were paid commissions for these calls. Prisoners calls in state prisons cost only $0.10 per minute with no surcharge for the first minute. The class action suit is against the county jails, which are paid commissions by these telecommunications companies.

County prison officials justify these rates by claiming that without these extra funds they would not be able to offer drug addiction and educational programs to inmates. However, when asked, prisoners' families responded that they would prefer lower rates even if some programs were deleted or paid for by higher taxes. The other issue, in addition to high costs, are claims by prisoners' families that not infrequently calls are cut off and prisoners must make a second or third call and pay the initial minute fee of $3.16 a second and third time. Because many prisoners' families have low incomes, receiving these calls is a burden for them.

In another lawsuit, the telecommunications companies sued the FCC stating that because VoIP calls are not regulated they can charge whatever fees they deem appropriate. The outcome of this lawsuit is still pending a decision by the judge. In 2015, the FCC had set limits on charges for prisoners' phone calls.

NON-TRADITIONAL COMPETITORS: ALPHABET, APPLE, AMAZON, FACEBOOK, TWITTER, SNAPCHAT, AND MICROSOFT ....

Amazon, Alphabet, Apple, Facebook, Microsoft, and Twitter are multi-billion-dollar conglomerates. They have each built a near monopoly in their specialty. They were each started by innovators with vision, and technology perfectly tuned to their times.

Google—A Search Conglomerate that Morphed into a Multi-Function Software Company

Sergey Brin and Larry Page, the founders of Google Inc., met when they were PhD candidates in the computer science department at Stanford. Page was looking at how sites link to each other and Brin was looking at data mining—what information is available and how to find it. They shared a feeling that web searching needed to be improved and devised a new approach to sorting results. They took their ideas about searching for information to other search companies. However, these companies were focused on expanding into other areas such as adding functions to their portals (the first screen that people saw when they logged into the site).

In contrast, Brin and Page wanted to focus on search, so they founded their own company, Google, in 1998 and sought venture capital funding. When Google was founded, there was competition from other search engines including Microsoft's Bing and Yahoo!. However, Google's site quickly became popular solely by word of mouth with no advertising.

In August 2015, Google's founder Larry Page announced the creation of holding company Alphabet. Alphabet became the vehicle whereby new technologies and startup companies were funded. Google, a subsidiary of Alphabet, is the cash cow of the organization. Its revenue from advertising is the driving force that enables Alphabet to underwrite new ventures such as self-driving cars.

Google has two sources of revenue: licensing its search software to smartphone manufacturers and enterprises, and advertising on its search sites. Please see "Investigations into Google Search Practices" in Chapter 6, "The Internet," for information on the European Union's investigation of Google's privacy practices and page ranking that favored its own sites for such services as travel and retail over those of competitors.

In addition, Google offers cloud hosting to enterprises in the United States and internationally. The international locations include Netherlands, Montreal, Finland, and Hong Kong. Because of their need for capacity for transmitting data between all of these sites, Google has also invested in subsea, or submarine, cables to ensure that capacity is available for the massive amounts of data they transmit between all of their cloud data centers.

In addition to their software, Alphabet purchased former hardware manufacturer Northern Telecom's mobile telephone manufacturing unit. They also acquired the Android mobile operating system from Android Inc. The initial version of Android was developed by Andy Rubin. The Android operating system is installed primarily on Google's Chrome laptops, Google Pixel smartphones, and Samsung smartphones.

Alphabet made over 100 investments using their profits from Google's advertising and software rights between 2001 and 2018. Alphabet had total revenue of $31.15 billion in the first quarter of 2018. Growth in mobile services, YouTube, and primarily Google advertising revenue, is adding to Alphabet's bottom line. Table 3-8 is a partial list of acquired companies and services developed by Alphabet and its subsidiaries. See "Using Search Engines to Unleash Vast Stores of Information" in Chapter 6.

Alphabet has acquired specialty software firms with key patents and software. Google has additionally enhanced its advertising services with billing and automation capabilities. In addition, Alphabet is hoping to build future opportunities for services and products with its culture of fostering new ideas and innovation by allowing employees to form spontaneous groups to develop new applications.

Table 3-8   A sample of Alphabet's Endeavors

Software or Service Offering	Product or Service Capability	Status and Capabilities
Google Fiber	Fiber to the premises in 10 areas for Internet access, and cable TV in the following metropolitan areas: Kansas City, Atlanta, Charlotte and Raleigh-Durham, N.C. and Nashville, Tennessee	Put on hold in 2016 because of higher than expected costs & fewer subscribers; at that time service had 84,232 TV subscribers and 453,000 broadband subscribers
ITA travel service	Airfare search tool	ITA is advertised on the Internet
DoubleClick	Technology that automates placements of display ads for ad agencies and advertisers	Still in use
Admeld	Software that helps large web sites sell and manage advertising on their sites	Blended into its Double-Click service
Google Pay	Ability to pay bills from smartphones; Verizon, AT&T, and T-Mobile pre-installs software on smartphones they sell	A specialized Chrome tablet computer for small retailers or a small device for grocery stores is needed to accept these payments
Keyhole Technologies, Zipdash, Inc., and Where2, LLC	Software from these three organizations was used to develop Google Maps	Still in use
Google Pay Send	Peer-to-peer payments	A way for people to send payments to each other
Project Fi	Wireless services sold to residential subscribers; not available on Apple phones	Google sells wireless service over leased T-Mobile, Sprint, and U.S. Cellular networks
Nest	Automated thermostats to conserve energy	Programmable thermostat with machine learning that adjusts to customers' patterns for automatically controlling lights, heating and cooling

Software or Service Offering	Product or Service Capability	Status and Capabilities
YouTube	Online short form videos posted by subscribers	Also provides long-form streaming videos on YouTube TV
Waymo LLC	Self-driving car software	Aimed at ride-hailing cars, fleet management, and public transportation; currently in road tests

Amazon—From Online Book Sales and Cloud Services to On-Ground Grocery Stores

Jeff Bezos founded Amazon in 1994 and started its online platform in 1995. The first items that Amazon sold on its web site were books. Books are not fragile, are relatively easy to package, and can be mailed at book rates. He additionally discounted books so that they were often less costly than those at brick-and-mortar stores. Bezos recognized that in order to have a large market presence, he would have to offer low prices. He did this for many years, often operating at a loss or at low profit margins.

The success of Amazon's book sales, whose prices undercut brick-and-mortar retailers, resulted in Barnes & Noble closing a number of stores, and Borders going out of business. To prop up sales, Barnes & Noble branched out into toys, games, and music. Many small, independent book stores went out of business because they were unable to match Amazon's prices.

When they first sold merchandise online, Amazon did not charge the 5 percent to 7 percent sales tax on consumers' purchases charged in most states' retail stores. This put brick-and-mortar stores at a price disadvantage. States objected because it meant a loss in tax revenue. This changed, and Amazon now charges sales tax on all purchases.

An innovation at Amazon was the introduction of customer reviews about products they had purchased. Amazon published both positive and negative product reviews. This is an important feature for online customers that cannot see products in person. Reviews are now a standard feature at many online retailers' sites.

Amazon is the largest online retailer in the United States, about the same size as Chinese online retailer Alibaba. In addition, Amazon has a retail cloud presence in 14 countries outside of the United States. Amazon's success is aided by its fast shipping, free returns, and the breadth of its offerings.

Amazon also offers streaming TV, which is free to Amazon's Prime customers that pay $119 annually for free deliveries and returns on Prime goods. In 2018, Amazon modified its prices for streaming and now offers streaming to non-Amazon Prime customers for a flat fee of $9 per month.

It also hosts Marketplace, a service where other retailers list their products on Amazon.com. In addition to charging Marketplace retailers a hosting fee, Amazon earns a commission on all goods these retailers sell on its site. They additionally charge fees for warehousing and delivering packages for these private retailers if they request warehouse and delivery service. In 2006, Bezos began offering cloud and security services to large and small enterprises on its online data centers. It is the largest hosting provider in the United States. See Chapter 2, "Data Centers and LANs, Storage, and IP Private Branch Exchanges," for more information on Amazon's cloud computing.

Amazon—Expansion and Diversification

In addition to its cloud hosting services and the merchandise on its online site, Amazon developed a low-priced e-reader, the Kindle. The Kindle is promoted for downloading books and streaming its music, TV shows, and movies from Amazon's cloud.

As well as web hosting and e-commerce, Amazon has branched out to providing streaming video, smart TVs, and the home automation devices Echo and Alexa. It also sells Fire tablet computers, and over the top streaming set-top box Fire TV. Fire TV is integrated into smart televisions Insignia, Best Buy's branded television, and Toshiba televisions.

Amazon also provides its facial recognition system, Rekognition, to police departments. The system has a database of hundreds of identified images that it uses to compare to videos that capture unidentified perpetrators committing crimes and people in crowds. It is currently only 80 percent accurate.

Advertising

Amazon accepts advertising on its site. However, the ads are clearly marked as sponsored merchandise. In addition to ads on its own site, it also sponsors an ad network that places ads on web sites across the Internet.

Subsidiaries and Purchases

Amazon is continually looking at new products and services to offer and subsidiaries to purchase. The following are some of these subsidiaries:

- **Goodreads:** A site where people review and comment on books they've read.
- **Twitch:** A video game streaming service that includes chat about games and video game competitions. It also offers streaming of select Saturday Night Live shows on which people can comment.
- **Audible.com:** Audio books.
- **Whole Food Market:** 400 supermarkets throughout the U.S. This is Amazon's largest purchase at over $40 billion.
- **Alexa Internet:** Home automation; includes the smaller Echo.

- **Amazon Game Studio:** Online game development.

- **Amazon Studios:** Producer of original online content for streaming.

- **Internet Movie Database (IMDB):** Online movie reviews.

- **Zappos:** Online shoes and clothing retailers.

- **Blink:** Home security camera that can be used with Amazon Key to monitor Amazon deliveries to homes with special locks that can be opened by drivers. Blink cameras will monitor deliveries left inside the home.

- **Ring:** Video doorbells for smart, automated homes.

- **Music:** Streaming music.

- **ComiXology:** An online platform for sales of thousands of comic books.

In addition to the above purchases, Amazon is testing the provision of supplies to hospital chains and individual hospitals. They have also announced Shipping with Amazon, a service in tests in Los Angeles where Amazon vehicles will pick up packages from businesses and deliver them to the end users.

Facebook—An Influential Social Network

Facebook is the largest social network in the United States. Its primary source of revenue is advertising.

Facebook, which was launched in 2004 by Mark Zuckerberg and Eduardo Severin, was in its early years primarily a vehicle for college students to interact with each other. It has morphed into an enormous social network with over two billion users where primarily adults exchange information and update each other with news about themselves.

To attract additional advertising, Facebook has taken steps to attract younger people to its site. Their subsidiary Instagram is a vehicle for people to socialize and exchange photos and short videos. It adopted some of the same features that Snapchat originally implemented. See below for information on Snapchat.

Unfortunately, Facebook is additionally widely used to sway public opinion on political and economic issues. Moreover, between 2014 and 2016 groups of people with political agendas used the site to spread false information. Millions of people opened accounts under pseudonyms. And it is widely believed that the Russian government was actively involved in using Facebook to sway public opinion with false claims made under fake identities.

Facebook's European headquarters is in Dublin, Ireland where it supports the company's growing number of international sites. Facebook is currently working to establish units in the developing world, including sub-Saharan Africa.

In a similar manner to other social networks, Facebook derives its revenue from advertising on its network. Its ad revenue grew to $11.69 billion in the first quarter of 2018 alone.

In its effort to attract younger subscribers, Facebook has purchased companies and developed new services and apps. Many of these are geared to the younger people Facebook is hoping to win back to its sites to increase its advertising revenue. Advertisers pay higher rates for ads aimed at younger age groups. Its subsidiaries and apps include the following:

- **Instagram:** A social networking app with 800 million monthly users where people share videos and photos. Messaging between users enables multiple video and photo posts sequentially. The multiple posts are available for only 24 hours. The site has photo- and video-formatted ads that are labeled as advertising.

- **Messenger:** A chat app that supports mobile voice and texting. Users are not required to have a Facebook account.

- **Oculus VR:** A headset that supports virtual reality. Virtual reality is a technology that supports immersive reality where people playing video games feel as though they are actually participating in the game. Samsung smartphones can be integrated into Oculus VR. A division of Oculus develops video games for Oculus virtual reality headsets.

- **WhatsApp:** A messaging app that supports texting and VoIP calling between international as well as local locations.

- **TBH:** A polling app geared to teens; it's short for "to be honest." TBH has a list of short surveys with 15 questions that are sent to users' Facebook contacts. Respondents select one of four people that fit each of the poll's questions. None of the descriptions describe negative traits.

- **Workplace:** In 2016, Facebook started Workplace, a cloud-based application for large enterprises with networking features such as messaging via VoIP and audio and video calling. Unlike, the majority of Facebook's consumer sites, Workplace charges fees based on the number of employees that log into Workplace monthly. It is not an ad-supported service.

- **Watch:** An ad-supported streaming media service with long form original video content. Short ads are shown prior to the start of each video.

Hacking, Fake Names, and Political Influence

Facebook has lost subscribers, but its revenue increased despite publicity about Cambridge Analytica's 2014 through 2016 theft of 87 million users' personal data. However, it did take steps to prevent another such theft and the proliferation of fake posts. They disabled one billion fake accounts and millions of posts that contained spam, obscene content, and hate speech. They additionally suspended about 200 suspicious apps and reviewed thousands more. These steps were taken using 10,000 staff moderators plus automated moderating software programmed to look for key words and phrases.

Facebook CEO Mark Zuckerberg testified before the United States House of Representatives and the Senate in April of 2018 about the Cambridge Analytica's hacks, where he pledged to do a better job protecting privacy in the future. He is also now issuing biannual transparency reports about Facebook's steps to protect users' privacy and efforts to monitor posts and apps on its site.

The ramifications of these hacks is not over for Facebook. Its privacy practices are being investigated by many states' Attorney Generals. And the Federal Trade Commission is investigating Facebook's violation of a 2011 agreement to protect subscribers' privacy. If the FTC finds it violated their agreement, they may recommend a record high monetary fine. In addition, a number of senators stated that Facebook should be regulated because they are too large to self-regulate themselves.

Facebook additionally testified in May of 2018 before the European Parliament. The hearing was streamed in real time. It's unknown at this time what steps if any the European Parliament will take in response to the hacks and privacy breaches that occurred at Facebook.

Snapchat—A Visual Social Network App

Snapchat is a social network geared to teens. It aims to be more visual than its competitors, with more video and photos posted.

Snapchat, whose corporate owner is Snap, is the social network of choice for many teens. It has over 300 million subscribers that visit at least once per month. Snapchat was founded in 2011 by former Stanford University students Evan Spiegel, Bobby Murphy, and Reggie Brown. Evan Spiegel is the current CEO. Like Facebook, Snap's revenue is derived from advertising on its site. The brief video ads appear mid-stream in the videos and photos that subscribers view. Many of the long form videos are created by Snapchat staff and partners.

Snapchat subscribers post videos and photographs, "snaps," and socialize on Snapchat mainly with students at their school. They post photos of recent get-togethers as well as messages. One feature that appeals to teens is that photos can be posted as soon as they're taken without first saving them to a photo app. Originally, snaps disappeared 10 seconds after they were viewed. Now subscribers are able to designate Snaps that can be saved. Snapchat has filters and lens that subscribers use to add special effects to photos. The filters enable people to modify photos of themselves by adding special effects such as backgrounds and animal ears. Users can also design emojis and communicate feelings using Snapchat's emojis. Emojis are small pictures such as smiley faces that depict emotions (frowns, winks, etc.) and approval, clapping hands, and other visual messages.

Snapchat has three functions that subscribers can click on. These include recent articles about celebrities organized in multiple channels. Another section is for chatting with friends, and a third section is where subscribers can post multiple snaps into a narrative. Posts can include Snapchat emojis and emojis that subscribers customize using tools on Snapchat. The February 20, 2017, article by David Pierce, "The New Snapchat: Less Social, More Fun," in the online *Wall Street Journal* stated that Snapchat is:

> *a place for hanging out with my friends, taking goofy pictures and watching some fun videos.*

Microsoft—Office Productivity, Operating System Software, Cloud Hosting, and Xbox

Microsoft, which sells the lion's share of office productivity software worldwide, owns the largest network of cloud data centers, Azure. Azure data centers are located in 50 regions worldwide. Azure is a platform on which developers customize Office 365 software for enterprise customers. Azure additionally hosts Microsoft's enterprise software such as Dynamics, Enterprise Resource Planning (ERP) for managing enterprise processes, and Customer Resource Management (CRM) software for managing enterprises' interactions with current and potential customers.

Enterprise customers' staff and developers access the software remotely. Microsoft additionally sells high-security cloud services to governments and in particular to 17 U.S. intelligence agencies.

Microsoft also sells Xbox One gaming controllers and video games. They developed the motion detection used in their controllers and those of other gaming controllers. The other hardware Microsoft sells are laptop and desktop computers as well as the operating systems on these computers. Microsoft owns and developed the Bing search engine, which is the most-used search engine behind Google.

Microsoft's two major subsidiaries are LinkedIn and Skype. LinkedIn is a social network designed for businesspeople. Professionals use it to network with others in their field. It is international in scope, with more than half of its members based outside of the United States. LinkedIn was established in 2003 and is a forum for people to offer services such as marketing and training in new technologies. The issues discussed are pertinent to particular fields and technologies. It is not unusual for posts offering opinions on new technologies to attract hundreds of responses. In addition, recruiters post job openings and people explore employment opportunities by using these posts, which are organized by specific careers.

The $8.5 billion purchase of Skype has a number of advantages for Microsoft. The majority of Skype customers prior to the Microsoft purchase were residential subscribers. In 2018, Microsoft changed the name of Skype to "Microsoft Teams" when marketing it to enterprise customers. It additionally added collaboration to the enterprise package. Skype upgraded and promoted its services from solely residential customers to small and medium-sized businesses and kept the designation Skype for these smaller and residential customers. It also provides an onsite server for enterprise customers that integrates with Microsoft Exchange contact management software. In addition, many businesspeople who travel for work use Skype and Microsoft Teams on the road for video and audio conferencing and international telephone calls. Table 3-9 presents a partial list of acquisitions.

Table 3-9   A Partial Listing of Microsoft Acquisitions

Acquired Company: Year Acquired	Description of Purchased Organization's Technologies
Hotmail: 1998	Web e-mail. Microsoft uses the technology to attract traffic to its Bing search and its Office 365 cloud applications.
Visio: 1999	Charting software used for applications such as project management.
Bungee: 2000	Microsoft's successful Halo series of games that operate on the Xbox 360 hardware are based on Bungee software.
TellMe: 2007	Automated telephone directory activated by voice commands. Used by telephone companies for directory assistance and by large corporations such as airlines, which use it for reservation systems.
aQuantive: 2007	Online advertising software.
Skype: 2011	Skype and Microsoft Teams are the most widely used services worldwide for making international voice calls and audio and video conferences.

Twitter

An international specialized social network, Twitter is another form of social networking. People use Twitter to broadcast microblogs, or "tweets," of not more than 280 characters to others who "follow" them. Many celebrities and most businesses have a presence on Twitter. They use it to post timely information about their business and for public relations purposes. Interestingly, Twitter is used more by people older than 25 than by teens, who mainly use Snapchat and sometimes Instagram. Twitter also streams live events including inaugurations and sporting events. It includes a "Moments" section with photos and updates about celebrities and current events. Users tweet comments on the news and celebrity updates in Moments.

Commercial organizations use both Facebook and Twitter to promote their products and to monitor people's reactions to their products and services. In addition to public relations benefits, feedback on social networks enables businesses to react more quickly to complaints or to learn how to improve their products. It also enables non-profits to conduct fund-raising efforts and candidates for public office to gain a following.

Twitter is a public company with 2018 first quarter revenue of $731.6 million. The majority of Twitter's revenue is from advertising on its sites and the rest from licensing fees.

Apple

Apple, Inc., is the world's most valuable company. It develops both the hardware specifications and operating system software on its Apple Watches, Apple TV, smartphones, desktop computers, Home Ped home automation, laptops, tablets, and Wi-Fi routers. To a large extent, it also controls the applications that users download from its App Store. Apple screens every application before it allows developers to sell apps in its online store.

This control is one factor that has enabled Apple to maintain the high quality of its products. Apple is currently the leader in premium, high-end products. Its devices are priced at the high end of their respective market segments. Its high prices are a factor in Apple's enormous profits and market capitalization, the number of shares of stock outstanding multiplied by the current value of each share of stock. As of mid-2018, Apple's market capitalization was $1 trillion, the highest of any other company in the United States.

Apple devices are based on proprietary operating systems and software. They are "closed" systems that require applications and printers that are compatible with Apple's operating systems. Customers who purchase its iPods often use Apple's iTunes store for music downloads. Compatibility between the applications in its App Store and the iTunes web site provides a compelling reason for customers to continue purchasing Apple gear so that generally all-new apps are not needed for new mobile and wired computers.

Apple's major innovation is its user-friendly interfaces, which have been a factor in the company's success since its inception, across all of its product lines. The emphasis on user-friendly interfaces was instituted by Steve Jobs, Apple's founder. Prior to its introduction of the iPad in 2010, only a small number of tablet computers were sold annually. In contrast, Apple sold 14 million iPads worldwide during the first year they were available because of the iPad's innovative, touch-screen interface. This spurred other manufacturers to introduce their own tablet computers and changed the way many people in business and homes use computers and watch video today.

Apple introduced its iCloud music, photo sharing, and video storage service in 2011. Subscribers can access their music and video stored on iCloud from any mobile or wired computer.

The wireless technology, design, and staffing in its retail stores are another example of Apple's innovations. Apple uses wireless service with which its sales associates can accept credit card payments, print receipts, and have e-mail receipts sent to customers, all through handheld devices. The handheld devices include barcode scanners to enter the purchased item and card readers to accept credit card payment. This results in customers not having to wait in line to pay for purchases, thus saving time and retail space. There are also demonstration computers, tablets, and iPods on display for customers to try out. In addition, Apple improved customer service by introducing the Genius Bar in each store. The Genius Bar is staffed by technical employees who provide diagnoses of hardware and software issues for customers. The retail stores have a web-based system for customers to make appointments with the Genius Bar before coming to the Apple store, further alleviating long waits and lines.

Apple owns iTunes where it sells and streams music, TV shows, and movies. It also offers streaming music subscriptions called Apple Music. Apple is spending $1 billion to develop original content for streaming. The streaming service is thought to be available in the spring of 2019.

Like Amazon, Alphabet, and Facebook, Apple acquired expertise for a host of its offerings by buying companies with the technologies needed for new products and services. Table 3-10 presents a partial list of acquisitions.

Table 3-10 *A Partial Listing of Apple's Key Acquisitions*

Acquired Company	Description of Purchased Organization's Technologies
NeXT	Founded by Steve Jobs to develop user-friendly, graphics-capable computers. Became the basis for Apple's Mac computers.
Emagic	Software used by musicians to produce music. Used in Logic and GarageBand applications.
Placebase	The initial basis for Apple Maps
Lala.com	A music cloud storage and streaming service. Used for iCloud and iTunes Match for music storage.
Quattro Wireless	Software for mobile advertising
Siri	Developer of speech recognition software used in iPhones.
IMSense	Developer of software for cameras. Used on iPhones and iPads.
Shazam	Music Identifying App
Emagic	Software used to develop GarageBand for creating digital music
Beats Electronics	Headphones sold at Apple stores and to resellers.
PrimeSense	Motion Detection software used in Microsoft's Xbox game systems

APPENDIX...

Table 3-11   Regulatory Highlights

Landmark Acts and Court Rulings	Summary of Acts and Rulings
The Federal Communications Act of 1934	Congress created the FCC and gave it the authority to regulate interstate telephone, radio, and telegraph companies.
The 1956 Consent Decree	The Justice Department allowed AT&T to keep its monopoly but restricted it to common carrier functions. The Consent Decree mandated that any patents developed by Bell Labs, then AT&T, be licensed to all applicants requesting them. This led to the availability of—among many other things—microwave technology to MCI and the ability of competitive carriers to build fiber-optic–based long-distance networks.
The 1969 MCI Case	The Federal Communications Commission ruled that MCI, then known as Microwave Communications, Inc., could connect its equipment to the public network provided that the network was not harmed. This decision opened the competitive premises equipment (CPE) market to AT&T rivals such as Northern Telecom and Executone. Prior to this, only AT&T was allowed to provide telephones for connection to the Public Switched Telephone Network (PSTN).
The 1982 to 1983 Modified Final Judgment	The Justice Department, in agreement with AT&T and with approval by Judge Harold H. Greene, agreed to a settlement that • Divested the then 22 Bell Operating Companies (BOCs) from AT&T • Prohibited BOCs from inter-LATA long distance, sale of CPE, and manufacturing • Mandated that the local exchange companies provide equal access (dial 1) from end users to all interexchange carriers
The 1984 Divestiture	The terms spelled out in the Modified Final Judgment were implemented on January 1, 1984. The 22 Bell telephone companies were merged into seven Regional Bell Operating Companies (RBOCs). The RBOCs were allowed to sell local and toll calling within the 197 defined local or in-state Local Access And Transport (LATA) areas. They also retained the Yellow Pages. AT&T retained manufacturing and inter-LATA (primarily interstate) and international toll calling.

Part III

Managing Broadband Networks and Broadband Network Services

4 Managing Broadband Networks

In this chapter:

INTRODUCTION ....

Growing dependence on cloud computing, social networking, and in particular video streaming has caused data traffic to increase more rapidly than ever before. According to Cisco, busy hour data traffic increased 32 percent from 2015 to 2016, and 51 percent from 2016 to 2017. This increase in traffic volume presents enormous challenges to carriers. Adding capacity to networks does not solve issues of managing the added video on networks. In addition to adding capacity, telephone and cable TV operators are implementing software to:

- Automatically reroute traffic around congested or failed routes

- Prioritize content on networks

- Streamline the process of implementing new revenue, producing services for residential and enterprise subscribers.

- Automatically reroute traffic around congested or failed routes

- Quickly and cost effectively deploy and back up network gear

- Quickly add new subscriber and enterprise features by enabling subscribers to activate them

- Manage routing to minimize traffic delays

- Provide 99 percent network uptime

Software Defined Networking (SDN) is being implemented in providers' networks to accomplish the above goals via policies defined in SDN software. SDN control software enables automatic network functions, such as rerouting traffic around network outages. SDN is installed on computers in network operations centers where technicians can react to major outages.

Network Function Virtualization (NFV) is a technology that eliminates the need to install network functions on proprietary hardware. Instead, multiple network functions, including routing and switching, are abstracted in software and installed on commodity servers. The power of NFV is that these pieces of abstracted software can be inexpensively duplicated and backed up in spare servers. Importantly, NFV in networks provides the ability for network functions to be upgraded and equipment installed at a faster pace with lower costs.

To accommodate the growing percentage of data traffic, central offices are undergoing a transition that enables them to better manage the data in their networks from centralized locations. Central Office Re-architected as a Data Center (CORD) specifies re-engineering central offices to be more like enterprise data centers. CORD is used by telephone companies to manage their shared, centralized applications and functions in a similar way to data centers in enterprises.

Similarly to carriers' broadband networks, submarine networks that connect continents using fiber-optic cabling must manage growing amounts of data. According to consulting firm TeleGeography, traffic on undersea cables increased 45 percent in 2016. Reflecting the change in international traffic patterns, traffic from carriers no longer represents the major source of traffic on submarine cables. Rather, traffic from content and cloud providers including Facebook, Microsoft, and Google now generate the largest percentage of traffic on submarine networks.

The desire to ensure adequate capacity on submarine cables has led some organizations to take partial ownership of submarine cable routes. Facebook and Google together own one third of the capacity of a cable route between Hong Kong and California. Microsoft and Amazon also own parts of other submarine cables. Modifications to the electronics connected to fiber-optic cabling on submarine cables are done to increase capacity on submarine cables.

Telephone companies transport traffic on core networks between large cities. They additionally carry traffic on middle-mile networks that connect rural areas to on-ramps to the Internet, and on last-mile networks to individual subscribers and enterprises. Upgrading and installing last-mile, edge networks is challenging. Last-mile networks require the most complex cabling, and entail the highest costs. This is because of the large number of individual connections to homes, enterprises, and multi-dwelling buildings.

Keeping networks available and operational during national emergencies is a goal of all countries worldwide. Monitoring and managing networks for sustainability and the ability to communicate during national emergencies is a major challenge. Alternate routes, software management of networks, and continuous monitoring are critical in ensuring that vital networks are available when businesses, governments, and individuals need them in emergencies and for conducting day-to-day business. In ever-increasing numbers, people depend on broadband networks to stay in touch, access applications, get news, and participate in electronic communications during day-to-day activities.

THE PUBLIC NETWORK......................................

All networks including mobile, Wi-Fi and LAN networks have access (edge), metropolitan (backhaul), and backbone sections. Rural areas generally also have middle-mile networks. The structure of public networks can be broken into five categories. The list that follows provides a brief description of each.

1. Last-mile (also referred to as edge, first-mile, or access networks).

2. Metropolitan area networks (MANs) within cities.

3. Middle-mile or backhaul, located between small cities and long-haul networks, connect rural areas to long-haul (core) networks.

4. Regional networks connect cities that range from 200 to 400 miles apart. This includes Boston to New York City, and New York City to Washington DC. These links carry traffic in large cities to cable TV and telephone company switches or routers where traffic is aggregated and connected to backbone or middle-mile networks.

5. Core networks connect cities and continents. Core networks are also referred to as the backbone section of networks.

NOTE Workers in the telecommunications and data-network industry often use different nomenclature for the same equipment or type of network. For example, core networks are also referred to as long-haul and backbone networks. Access or edge broadband network are commonly referred to as last-mile and first-mile, and edge networks. In addition, the terms "providers," "carriers," and "Internet Service Providers" (ISPs) are also used synonymously. They all provide voice, data, mobile service, video, or Internet access.

Sections of Carriers' Broadband Networks

Access or edge networks	Access networks, also referred to as *first-mile* or *last-mile networks* enable customers to access the network and telephone companies to reach customers. For the most part, local telephone companies and cable TV companies own access network cabling and electronics. For wireless companies, their antennas provide links to customers' mobile devices. Access networks also link long-haul providers to customers via last-mile networks. Some access networks use fixed wireless, as well as landlines and cellular antennas to link people's mobile devices and home telephones to the network.
	Because there are so many cable runs to individual residences and local businesses, these are costly to upgrade, and are often the last part of networks to be upgraded from older copper cabling to higher capacity fiber cabling. Access networks include connections from major skyscrapers and office parks to a carrier's equipment.
Metropolitan Area Networks (MANs)	MANs run from a carrier's equipment in towns to Points of Presence (POPs) and *wiring centers*. A wiring center is a location with a local telephone company switch and connections and electronics for outside cabling. A POP is the location where a switch hands off traffic to long-haul and backbone providers, and vice versa.

Middle-mile or backhaul networks	Middle-mile networks link rural areas to core (backbone) networks. They consist of the fiber or wireless links to backhaul carriers' switches. For the most part, they connect rural areas to inter-city networks and to the Internet. *Backhaul* refers to "hauling" traffic from local sources to core, backbone networks.
Core, backbone networks	These links span hundreds of miles and carry traffic between distant cities. In the United States, backbone networks link Los Angeles to New York City, and Boston to Chicago. Undersea cables that span oceans are also examples of long-haul networks. They carry intercontinental traffic between the United States, Europe, Africa, Australia, New Zealand, and Asia via submarine cables.

 NOTE Because no single telephone, cellular, or cable TV company has service everywhere in the United States or the rest of the world, all providers need connections to and from other telephone companies to transmit voice and data traffic between their own customers, the Internet, the cloud, cellular networks, and customers served by other providers. They additionally need connections to carriers in other countries.

CORE NETWORKS—BETWEEN CITIES AND CONTINENTS ....

Core networks, largely based on IP, transmit the highest concentration of traffic in public networks. They transmit packetized voice (VoIP), shrinking amounts of non-VoIP voice traffic, data, and video on high-capacity fiber-optic cabling. Traffic in the core is transmitted across countries, between countries and continents, and under oceans.

At multiple points along the route, the traffic is:

- Dropped off at wiring centers and Points of Presence (POPs) closer to urban and suburban areas.

- Handed off to other long-haul carriers to be transmitted on other routes.

- Transmitted to Metropolitan Area Networks (MANs) located in cities.

- Sent to residential and business customers over last-mile networks by either the long-haul carrier, the local landline telephone company, or a cellular telephone company.

Carriers also transmit data and VoIP traffic between enterprise sites on long-haul networks. Special arrangements are made with these customers for optional services such as security and priority treatment for voice and video conferencing. These networks are considered part of a carrier's *private data networks*. They are separate from the Internet and offer guaranteed speeds and low latency (unnoticeable levels of delay or no delay) on an end-to-end basis. For more on this, see Chapter 5, "Broadband Network Services."

Software Defined Networks to Manage Traffic Surges

Telephone companies are increasingly upgrading sections of their networks, often in anticipation of upgrading fully to SDN to manage the annual doubling of traffic on networks. SDN, as the name implies, controls networks via policies created in software to manage traffic. The growing amounts of traffic in carriers' networks is due mainly to data the increasing amounts of traffic to and from the cloud, and from streaming video from Netflix, Amazon, and others.

Movies and TV shows that formerly were exclusively available on cable TV networks are now streamed 24 hours a day from sources such as Amazon, Netflix, and Hulu. This causes unpredictable spikes in traffic. Increasingly, cable TV and traditional telephone company customers want anytime-anywhere availability of movies and TV shows. They stream content to smartphones, tablet computers, and Internet-connected televisions at any hour of the day or night.

Streaming video needs to be treated differently from e-mail and text messages. Video in the form of movies and conference calls needs to be prioritized so that delays don't cause breaks and pauses in the audio or video. In order to dynamically treat these massive amounts of traffic, traffic flows are prioritized in real time by type of content and often by application as well. For example, e-mail usually has a lower priority than real time streaming video because short delays on e-mail and text messages aren't noticeable. The software control in SDN is able to manage these peaks and prioritize particular types of traffic.

Software Defined Networks have a centralized controller that specifies the treatment of applications and handling of traffic. This is accomplished via policies sent to network nodes in real time, directing the use of particular routes, and priorities for traffic flows. These policies are transmitted on the *control plane*. The controller sends out policies in real time to network nodes (switches and routers) that transmit the actual data. For example, if a route is out of service, the controller will transmit updated policies to nodes so that all traffic is rerouted to a functioning path in the network.

The following are examples of *control plane policies*:

- Redirecting traffic during peaks.

- Opening bandwidth when it is needed during an event such as a presidential inauguration. For example, carriers commonly rate-limit traffic by running a 400Gbps pipe at 10Gbps. When required, the bandwidth can be easily increased to 400Gbps.

- Reconfiguring an optical multiplexer on the fly, automatically, or manually, via remotely entered computer commands.

- Selling web portal access to IT managers so that they can add more bandwidth for a special event without waiting for the carrier to provision more service.

- Decreasing delays and increasing revenue from new services more quickly by speeding up installations such as cable modems and high-speed network access for commercial customers. This means that an installer can make one visit to an enterprise to install gear, and then power up the service remotely through software. Previously, multiple onsite trips were required for setup.

Virtual Networks and Functions

The term virtual refers to functions or networks that have all the features and functions of hardware or network structures that they emulate, but their physical form is different. In the example of Virtual Network Functions, capabilities formerly found in hardware such as routers and switches are represented in software that has the same features and operates the same as hardware-based switches and routers. The network architecture can also be virtualized. This is done in Network Function Virtualization below.

Network Function Virtualization—Architecture

Network Function Virtualization (NFV) is an architecture in which network functions such as storage, routers, and switches are represented in software. These functions no longer need to be installed on dedicated, vendor-specific hardware. It's similar to server virtualization where multiple applications are installed as virtual machines on servers. However, instead of applications being virtualized, with NFV hardware devices (network nodes) are represented as software in servers. NFV specifies the way that these software functions fit together.

Virtual Network Function—Transforming Hardware Nodes into Software Functions

Virtual network function (VNF) refers to each piece of software in virtualized servers that represents a hardware function. These functions, some of which are listed below, can work together, are easily duplicated, and are generally installed on commodity hardware such as X86 and newer type servers with additional processing power. See Figure 4-1 for an example of VNFs in a single server. The equipment in which multiple VNFs are installed is referred to as a *White Box*.

White Box

The term White Box denotes a server with multiple instances of virtual network functions (VNFs) within a single server. Each of the functions listed below were formerly housed in individual, proprietary, vendor-specific hardware "boxes." The NFV architecture enables these capabilities, previously implemented in various pieces of vendor-specific hardware, to exist with other network functions in a single open source commodity server.

The advantage of a White Box is that functions within it can be more easily installed and duplicated than installing hardware and backing up each piece of hardware in the event of failure. Additionally, network functions can be added more quickly, a factor in increasing the speed of upgrading network functions.

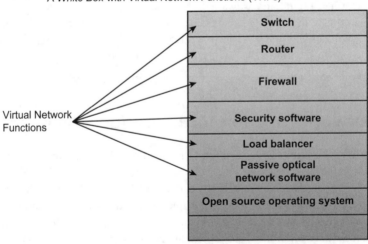

A *White Box* with Virtual Network Functions (VNFs)

VNF Software on a commodity server with an Open Source operating system, e.g. is Linux, Junos etc.
A proprietary operating system can also be used.

Figure 4-1 A White Box with network hardware abstracted in VNF software.

The following are examples of Virtual Network Functions, which can be virtualized as software within servers and White Boxes:

- Routers that route traffic between networks

- Switches that transmit traffic within a network

- Load balancers that balance traffic between multiple broadband circuits so that no single circuit (path) is unduly congested

- Controllers that manage applications and send commands to devices

- Gateways that translate between networks that use different protocols

- Network Address Translation (NAT), which translates between external IP addresses and internal IP addresses for internal devices

- Security software in appliances (appliances are hardware dedicated to a single function)

- Firewalls that screen incoming traffic for viruses and other types of attacks

The key advantages of installing network functions in software are flexibility, agility, and speed of implementation. Functions can be deployed and duplicated easily and quickly using computer commands in software. Instead of programming, purchasing, and managing distinct pieces of hardware, control software can be used to add network functions to the parts of networks where they are needed.

Because these critical functions are all in one server, if the server malfunctions, all of these functions are lost. For greater reliability and sustainability (the ability to be operational during malfunctions), telephone companies often deploy duplicate White Boxes. If one fails the other is able to take over.

Policies defined within Software Defined Networks indicate how to route, prioritize, balance traffic loads, and program firewalls. The policies that control networks are programmed and defined by IT staff at computer screens. They are then invoked automatically as required.

Bringing Up Network Functions—Open Source MANO

Open Source Management and Organization (MANO) is an ETSI ISG standard. ETSI ISG is the European Telecommunications Standards Institute Industry Specification Group. Open source MANO refers to the ability to manage and bring up network functions uniformly by carriers. The goal is to enable networks to interoperate with each other and for telephone companies to be able to purchase commodity hardware. The standard defines operations in wired telephone company networks and cable TV as well as 5G mobile networks. ETSI's Industry Specification Group's goal is to prevent chaos and disorganization when deploying NFV software within SDNs.

Sixty of the largest telephone companies worldwide are members of the MANO (Management and Organization) specification group that defined the MANO standard. The standards are meant to be interoperable with SDN controllers, VFN architecture, and VNF software.

Just as in large data centers where "virtual machine sprawl" can result in unnecessary duplication, organizations can lose control of the location and number of virtualized network functions without standards on how to manage and deploy these functions. MANO is designed to operate in cloud settings as well as onsite data centers. The ETSI NFV MANO standard includes:

- Interfaces to Operations Support System (OSS) to manage installation of carriers' services, and changes

- Ways that carriers' MANO customers are able to remotely program changes to their services. This is particularly relevant to enterprises that want control of their network services

- Interfaces to Billing Support Systems (BSS) to manage telephone companies' billing applications

- The ability to manage elements on Amazon's cloud services including EC2 (elastic cloud) by use of a *plug-in*. A plug-in is a small program that adds capabilities to a parent (larger) program. Plug-ins are also used in browsers

- Control and management of virtualized computing, storage and other network resources

- The ability to use containers. See Chapter 2, "Data Centers and LANs, Storage, and IP Private Branch Exchanges," for containers

- Consistent implementation of open standards across the industry

- Troubleshooting capabilities within networks

> NOTE   The term East–West traffic and North–South traffic is used to refer to traffic within data centers and to data centers. East–West traffic refers to traffic between virtual machines in the same server or between servers in data centers, as in Figure 4-2. North–South traffic refers to traffic from a client where a person types in a request for information from a remote database, storage network, or specialized server. The client can be at a remote location or at the same location.

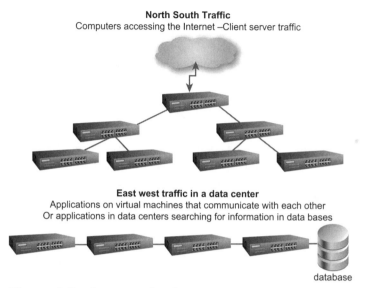

North South Traffic
Computers accessing the Internet –Client server traffic

East west traffic in a data center
Applications on virtual machines that communicate with each other
Or applications in data centers searching for information in data bases

database

Figure 4-2 An example of server-to-server East–West traffic.

Central Office Re-Architected as a Data Center—Streamlined Central Offices

CORD is a set of specifications that lays out a way to design and equip a telephone company's central offices as data centers. The purpose is to implement central offices to be compatible with SDN and NFV so that new services and applications can be delivered more quickly. It specifies open source software and commodity hardware to be used in central offices. ON.Lab, a non-profit industry association based in Berkeley, California developed CORD, in conjunction with large telephone and cable TV companies, and industry manufacturers. Their goal is to define standardized open source communications network standards for central offices.

In contrast to CORD's open source software and commodity hardware, most current and older central offices are made up of large, costly proprietary switches and specialized equipment. These switches are similar to telephone switches used by enterprises. However, they have greater capacity and are "hardened" for greater reliability and sustainability to withstand natural disasters such as hurricanes and tornadoes. Moreover, traditional central offices operate on Direct Current (DC) power. CORD uses Alternate Current (AC) power. Equipping and upgrading traditional central offices is costly and often ties telephone companies into purchasing costly equipment from a single manufacturer in each central office so that all the equipment is compatible and able to interoperate together.

CORD is architected for mobile as well as fixed line networks. There are also versions for telephone and cable TVs' edge networks, which are connected to enterprise and consumer customers. In contrast to today's central offices, Central Office Re-architected as a Data center makes use of Network Functions Virtualization (NFV) to create software copies of network equipment such as servers, switches, and hardware that support and manage access to fiber cabling, cable modems, and mobile networks.

CORD is meant to emulate cloud services that depend on virtualization, can scale up or down easily, and whose features are managed directly by customers. The software in CORD-based central offices can be located in the cloud and managed by manufacturers, or remotely by telephone companies. They may alternately be managed and located at carriers' own data centers.

The goal, in addition to saving money on central offices, is to simplify and importantly, speed up the availability of new applications for enterprise, mobile, and residential landline telephone companies' customers. This is a potential source of new revenue for carriers and may lower telephone companies' total cost of ownership (TCO).

The Central Office Re-architected as a Data center standard includes capabilities that enable enterprise customers to access and download new services and/or change existing features remotely via centrally located consoles. According to the March 22, 2017, LightReading article "CenturyLink Delivers DSL Using CORD Platform," CenturyLink is supplying DSL to enterprise and residential customers from its CORD central offices. In another article published by Fierce Telecom on February 9, 2017, Glen Post, CEO and Chairman of CenturyLink, was quoted as following:

We plan to have 100% of those (POPs) virtualized by the end of 2019.

Enterprise customers have the ability to manage services such as DSL at centrally located consoles from headquarters and branch offices. The modifications and additions can be performed without carriers dispatching technicians to customer sites. This saves telephone companies the expense of "truck rolls," dispatching technicians to customers' locations.

The Pace of Implementation of SDN, NFV, and CORD

Software Defined Networks (SDN), and Network Function virtualization (NFV), are technologies that rely on software to manage functions that previously relied on hardware such as routing and firewalls. Central Office Re-architected as a Data Center (CORD) enables telephone companies and enterprises to more efficiently manage the increasing amounts of data.

Capital Depreciation at Telephone Companies

Changes in telephone central office and network architecture often take years to be implemented. Providers typically depreciate capital expenses such as new central office and networking equipment over 10 years and even 15 years. Thus, the costs for older equipment may still be on their balance sheets.

For publicly traded companies, buying software and hardware while older equipment is on their books lowers their net income. This may result in lower stock prices and shareholder discontent, dampening telecom companies' incentives for costly upgrades.

One strategy that telephone companies use to implement Central Office Re-architected as a Data Center (CORD is to add CORD data center elements within their traditional central office. In this way, the functions in traditional central offices can be gradually transitioned to CORD equipment and virtualized servers.

Telephone companies are additionally merging mobile central office functions (the core in mobile networks) and their landline central office functions in CORD data centers. During the transitions clashes between the two types of staff may occur. However, the end result is lower costs to operate networks.

 NOTE The type of staff required to manage and program SDNs, CORD, and NFV are software engineers able to design, develop, test, and upload software compatible with the cloud environments where CORD offices are located. They additionally are required to understand ways to interface and integrate older network technologies with SDN and NFV via application programming interfaces (APIs).

Staff that monitored network conditions from traditional central offices needed to monitor large telephone networks. In CORD, central offices cloud development (DevOps) skills are required to manage new central offices that are essentially large data centers.

Session Routing—On Virtual Routers

Burlington, Massachusetts start-up 128 Technology was founded in 2014 by staff at former networking company Acme Packet. According to founder Andy Ory, networks have gotten overly complex and costly, and are not suitable for today's traffic patterns. Current networks were designed to connect computers or remote access devices for brief information look-ups, not present-day network transactions, which are predominately session based.

During sessions, people typically access applications in clouds, upload videos, and watch videos. They log onto cloud-based applications such as Microsoft's Office 365 and collaborate with remote colleagues using collaboration software. These sessions are bi-directional with a start, a middle, and an end.

Ory's vision in establishing 128 Technology is to develop software for routers to efficiently and cost effectively route sessions more simply by incorporating additional functions into routers. Per Ory:

> *Routers need to be stateful to keep track of all the parts of sessions that belong together.*

Continued

A stateful device has real-time awareness of packets' identity. Stateful routers have the ability to track and route packets together in a single real time session on the least congested route available.

128 Technology's software simplifies network operations by eliminating the need for "middle boxes," thereby lowering operating costs. Examples of middle boxes are:

- Firewalls that screen traffic to keep malware off internal networks
- Load balancers that balance traffic over multiple circuits
- Network address translation gear
- Deep Packet Inspection (DPI) that inspects packets and blocks malware and spam, and prioritizes specified types of traffic.

The above functions are consolidated into software by 128 Technology, not managed separately in servers. 128 Technology believes that their software can control network routing more efficiently in SDN and other broadband services without layers of abstraction and complexity.

128 Technology's software is installed on commodity hardware, and powered by Intel X86 computer chipsets that eliminate latency (delays) and enable the speed required for real-time, high-speed packet forwarding on commodity hardware. It is additionally able to operate as network virtualization functions on servers.

Security incorporated into the software is zero trust software that assumes the presence of malware. It includes perimeter security that checks packets as they exit the premise to prevent insiders from causing security lapses by falling for phishing attempts, user error, or malicious employee behavior. The zero trust policy looks at the first packet, where it's from (its source), what service is used, and what it is allowed to access. Packets are additionally checked at every point on the route.

In addition, proprietary encryption developed in-house is used to safeguard privacy. Encryption uses complex mathematical formulas to ensure that only authorized devices can "read" user information within packets. Another security precaution 128 Technology takes is the use of Access Control List (ACL) software that filters out packets that are not permitted according to the ACL rules.

128 Technology's software is an alternative method that provides a way to manage networks at lower costs with less operational complexity. It additionally includes security software and the ability to route sessions together on the most optimal routes. 128 Technology's software is at Amazon Web Services and Microsoft Azure web sites where it can be used by customers to manage work flows between cloud suppliers and applications and across data centers.

Submarine Network Systems

Submarine cables connect all of the earth's continents to each other. They connect Asia to the United States, and Africa and Europe to the Americas. Underwater cables are placed directly on the ocean floor. They are connected to land at drop-off points, also known as landing points, on each continent. Figure 4-3 depicts an example of a submarine cable system route across the Pacific Ocean.

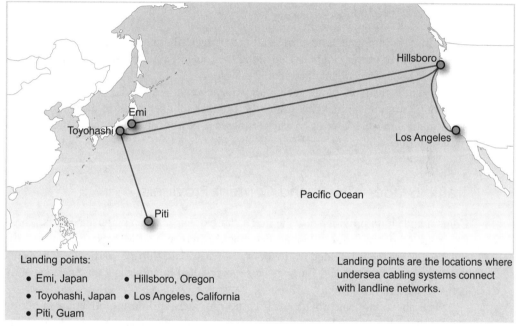

Landing points:

- Emi, Japan
- Toyohashi, Japan
- Piti, Guam
- Hillsboro, Oregon
- Los Angeles, California

Landing points are the locations where undersea cabling systems connect with landline networks.

Figure 4-3 A submarine cable connecting the United States and Japan. (Courtesy of Telegeography)

At landing points, a packet switch or a router delivers traffic to land-based co-location sites where many carriers have a presence. One of these co-location sites is on Eighth Avenue in New York City. At the co-location facility, multiple carriers interconnect their networks and carry one another's traffic to other cities.

Advances in Submarine Cabling Technology

Advances in submarine fiber-optic cable networks took a leap forward between 2012 and 2015. This is when coherent fiber-optic technology enabled already installed fiber-optic cables to be upgraded to carry additional traffic. Coherent optical electronics connected to fiber-optic cables enabled more channels of traffic to be carried with tighter spacing between each channel of data. Without this innovation, the current undersea cables would be out of capacity, and additional cables would have to be laid. According to Telegeography, a consulting firm owned by Primerica and located in Washington DC, by 2020 additional cables will need to be built because of anticipated traffic growth.

Power Limitations

Power must be supplied at the terrestrial end of each fiber bundle. In contrast to terrestrial fiber where power can be added along the route, it's not possible to supply power at various points in each undersea cable bundle.

Currently available power technology at each end of a bundle of fiber cables supports only six fiber pairs. This limits the number of fiber pairs in each route. Various organizations are looking at ways to increase power capabilities so that additional strands of fiber can be supported in each bundle.

Traffic Usage—Cloud and Content Providers

Content and cloud providers use the lion's share of capacity on undersea cables. These hyper-scaled operators are Google, Facebook, Amazon, and Microsoft. Additionally, in recent years there is added traffic between Africa and Europe, particularly between the east coast of Africa and Europe. This has resulted in additional undersea capacity between Europe and Africa.

The above content provider and cloud providers' primary motivation in taking ownership stakes in cable routes is to be assured of adequate capacity. Prior to the enormous growth in cloud and search traffic, carriers such as AT&T and Verizon used the most capacity in submarine cable systems.

Cable Cuts in Submarine Networks

Cable cuts, when they occur, are major problems, disrupting communications between entire countries. Fishing trawlers are responsible for most accidental cable cuts. Due to the specialized equipment needed to repair cables that lie miles deep in oceans, it often takes weeks to repair a cable. See Figure 4-4 for a list of time to repair cable cuts. Repairing undersea cable cuts requires the costly deployment of submersible robots tethered to and controlled by motherships. Large trawling fishing nets are weighted and often snag cabling as they are being dragged across ocean floors. The second most frequent cause of outages results from ship anchors dragged across the ocean floor.

#5 – Route diversity

	Repairs per Year	Outage (days/year)
Philippines- Taiwan	2.7	42.8
Singapore-Hong Kong	2.6	45.5
Hong Kong-Tokyo	2.1	37.8
Mumbai-Singapore	1.0	26.6
Tokyo-Los Angeles	0.5	8.4

Source: Palmer-Felgate, A., and Booi, P., How Resilient is the Global Cable Network?
SubOptic 2016 #OralWE2A-5

Figure 4-4   Submarine cable outages. (Courtesy of SubOptic, first presented by Palmer-Felgate, A and Booi, P [Verizon] at SubOptic 2016)

The following are the reasons for delays in repairing cables:

- There are a limited number of ships equipped to repair submarine cable cuts.

- Nations have concerns that ships in their waters could eavesdrop on communications from ships repairing cables.

- It can take weeks to be granted permission for these ships to be allowed to repair cuts in other countries' waters.

The non-profit International Cable Protection Committee's (ISCPC) goal is to prevent submarine cable cuts. To reach that goal it communicates the criticality of undersea cables internationally, distributes cable maps to marine organizations, and lobbies internationally to reduce nations' reluctance to allow ships to repair damaged cables.

BANDWIDTH CAPABILITIES IN CARRIER NETWORKS...

Carriers mainly use high-capacity 400 Gigabit Ethernet and Terabit (1,000 Gigabit) services to transport IP data, Ethernet, and VoIP traffic on long-haul networks. They additionally carry the decreasing amounts of legacy traffic from analog circuit-switched voice on these networks.

> NOTE *Legacy* is a term used to describe networks and equipment that are based on older technologies such as TDM and analog voice service.

Carrier Gigabit Ethernet

Gigabit Ethernet is used in both Local Area Networks (LANs) and Wide Area Networks (WANs). It operates over fiber-optic cabling. When it is used in telecommunications and cable TV networks, it is sometimes referred to as Carrier Gigabit Ethernet. There are five capacities of Gigabit Ethernet (also referred to as GigE): 1, 2.5, 10, 100, 400, and Terabit. These are used in core, Metropolitan Area Networks (MANs), and access networks. Carrier Gigabit Ethernet is used for VoIP and all IP-packetized traffic. This includes video, data, and graphics traffic that is bundled in packets.

A timing source is included in GigE to make it suitable for switched voice, because it does not natively have timing sources. A timing source provides fixed, guaranteed capacity that circuit-switched voice requires. Without it, circuit-switched voice sounds choppy because of brief, intermittent delays, which are otherwise imperceptible in IP data. An International Telecommunications Union (ITU) 2010 standard called Synchronous Ethernet was developed for chips with timing sources. Timing sources are now standard in most Synchronous GigE switches.

The Drive for Higher-Capacity Carrier Gigabit Ethernet

Large providers such as AT&T and Verizon support 400Gbps capacity in their backbones. The impetus behind 400Gbps Ethernet is the increasing amount of high-definition streaming TV, personal videos uploaded to social networks, network-based storage, cloud based data centers, and mobile broadband backhaul traffic. Backhaul networks "backhaul" traffic from cellular antennas to mobile companies' data centers. Gigabit Ethernet was expressly developed for IP traffic and is less costly to purchase, maintain, and install than SONET.

The wide availability of Gigabit Ethernet switches from many manufacturers has caused Ethernet switch prices to drop. Moreover, because of its standardization by the Institute of Electrical and Electronics Engineers (IEEE), vendors produce compatible Ethernet gear so that providers are not locked into a single vendor's equipment.

Gigabit Ethernet and Ethernet are often used in conjunction with Passive Optical Networks (PONs), discussed later in this chapter. PONs are a lower-cost method of extending fiber to premises and neighborhoods because they enable single strands of fiber to be shared between multiple homes and small businesses.

Circuit-Switched Voice—Unsuitable for Packetized Traffic

After 2012, carriers began carrying most traffic over Gigabit Ethernet both because of its suitability for data and because of decreases in the amount of analog voice and TDM traffic. Prior to 2012, SONET, a North American standard for multiplexing streams of traffic onto fiber-optic cabling was the predominant protocol for transporting traffic at Optical Carrier (OC) speeds. SONET was developed to aggregate (multiplex) and carry TDM (Time Division Multiplexed) and circuit-switched voice traffic from multiple sources. TDM multiplexing saves capacity for voice and data in predictable time slots. However, its top speed of 40Gbps is inadequate for today's long haul traffic. See Table 4-2 in the "Appendix" section at the end of this chapter for SONET speeds.

Using Ring Topology—Greater Reliability and Cost

Carrier Gigabit Ethernet can operate as a straight point-to-point line between sites, in the more fail-safe ring, or in mesh *topologies*.

NOTE Topology refers to the design of how devices are physically connected. It is the "the view from above."

When fiber in a point-to-point arrangement is cut, service is lost. Reliability on fiber is critical because each failure affects potentially hundreds or thousands of customers, particularly if a failure occurs in long-haul networks.

When a medium such as copper carries a conversation or data stream from one telephone subscriber or computer to another, a failure only impacts one customer. Because of the large volumes transmitted by fiber, failures in these networks can put hundreds of businesses, police stations, or hospitals out of service. For this reason, the majority of carriers deploy bidirectional ring topology in long-haul and Metropolitan Area Networks (MANs), where each fiber ring, multiplexer, and power supply is duplicated.

Ring topology is costly because the fiber and the multiplexers are all duplicated, even though this combined capacity is not used on a day-to-day basis when there are no failures. The spare fiber in ring topology is known as the *protect* ring. It reroutes traffic in the other direction, as is illustrated in Figure 4-5. Read the section "Mesh Configuration Backups," later in this chapter, to learn about new, lower-cost mesh technologies that are being deployed.

Control Plane–Enabled Programmable Mesh Network

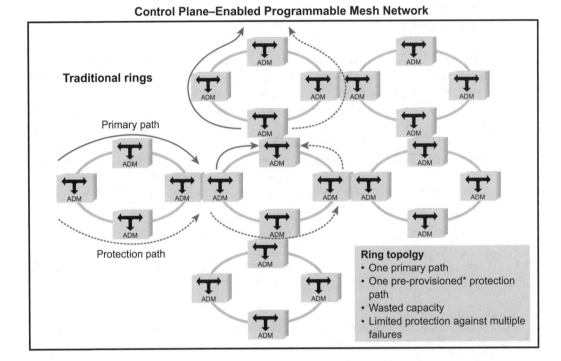

Multilayer Control Plane–Enabled Optical Resilient Mesh

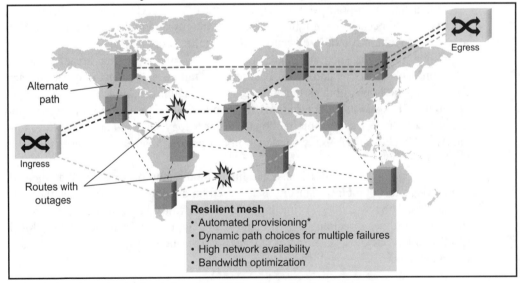

*Provisioning refers to the planning, design, and installation of network equipment and routes.

Figure 4-5 A comparison of ring to mesh topology. (Adapted figure from Ciena Corporation)

OPTICAL TRANSPORT NETWORKS—CARRYING MULTIPLE TYPES OF TRAFFIC.................................

Optical Transport Network (OTN) is an International Telecommunications Union (ITU) G.709 standard for transmitting, monitoring, and managing traffic on fiber-optic cabling. OTN is an OSI (Open Systems Interconnections) Layer 1 service. As described in Chapter 1, "Computing and Enabling Technologies," Layer 1 is the physical and wireless medium over which traffic travels. OTN is used for *asynchronous* protocols such as Gigabit Ethernet as well as *synchronous* protocols such as Synchronous Optical Network (SONET). In asynchronous protocols, traffic is sent at irregular intervals, not at specific intervals. This contrasts with synchronous protocols where bits are sent at evenly spaced, regular intervals according to an internal timing source. The OTN standard provides a framework for transmitting both types of traffic.

In a telephone interview with Dave Parks, former director, Segment Marketing at Ciena Corporation, Parks stated:

> *OTN can be thought of as the freight containers that carry Ethernet, IP, and SONET optical traffic together.*

The OTN standard was created for the efficient operation of providers' multi-protocol metropolitan and global optical networks using interoperable equipment. The standard provides a framework for programming, monitoring, and transmitting the growing amounts of IP packet, Gigabit Ethernet, video, and MPLS (Multi-Protocol Label Service) traffic while preserving its capability to carry legacy traffic on optical networks. All of the services—1 and 10 Gigabit Ethernet, SONET, and video can be on the same line card and are software programmable.

It does so by specifying the encapsulation of legacy SONET/Synchronous Digital Hierarchy (SDH) traffic into OTN frames and its overhead information for addressing and billing on fiber-optic cabling. OTN, which can scale to 400Gbps and Terabit capacities, overcomes SONET's 40 Gigabit per second capacity. See Table 4-2 in the "Appendix" for information on SONET speeds.

OTN equipment has optional modules for connecting to Dense Wavelength Division Multiplexing (DWDM) as well as Reconfigurable Optical Add/Drop Multiplexing (ROADM) so that individual wavelengths can be seamlessly added and dropped off at, for example, carriers' POPs. Both SONET/SDH and IP traffic can be carried on the same wavelength. (DWDM gear splits each pair of fiber cabling into multiple paths called wavelengths.) Manufacturers that offer OTN gear include Calix, Ciena, Cisco, Fujitsu, Infinera, and Nokia.

Today's networks are required to carry a mix of the more efficient gigabit Ethernet as well as traffic using the older SONET and MPLS protocols. Optical Transport Network is an important protocol for transporting both digital Internet Protocol (IP) signals as well older synchronous traffic in a single stream. Gigabit Ethernet supports the massive increases in traffic due mainly to traffic generated by enterprises and consumers accessing the cloud, by consumers streaming TV and movies from Netflix, Amazon, and their competitors, and from applications such as online gaming.

The newer, more efficient Gigabit Ethernet is able to carry many times more bits per second than SONET and MPLS. Gigabit Ethernet is available at data rates of 10, 40, 100, and 400 bits per second. While the amount of traffic generated using Gigabit Ethernet is increasing rapidly, there is still traffic in the SONET and MPLS format. However, the amount of traffic generated in particular by SONET gear is decreasing rapidly. At some point OTN use will not be needed as SONET and MPLS traffic drastically decreases.

Optical Transport Networks and SDN and NFV

Software Defined Networks and Network Function Virtualization traffic are carried over fiber equipped with OTN functionality. SDN and NFV are higher-layer protocols than OTN. SDN's control plane prioritizes and specifies routes on which traffic is to be carried. NFV, as stated above, virtualizes network hardware. SDN and NFV are functionally different than OTN, which manages how traffic is "packaged" or "wrapped" and carried on optical fiber.

Examples of control plane technology functions are available above in the section on SDN.

Mesh Configuration Backups

Mesh backup technology is enabled by signals generated from Control Plane Technology equipment such as is in WA SDNs. The service utilizes a logical rather than a physical design. The physical topology is not designed as an actual mesh, wherein each point on a network is connected to every other node. Rather, as demonstrated in Figure 4-6 above, traffic is backed up in a logical manner with more than one choice of alternate routes. In this way, each carrier and each route do not require duplicated fiber, multiplexing gear, and transmission equipment.

Mesh technology assumes adequate capacity on backup routes. If this capacity is not sufficient, delays will occur. It's a trade-off between flexibility in having multiple backups, idle capacity when the network is operational, cost savings, and possible congestion during emergencies.

ROADMs Interoperability Plus Adding and Dropping Off Traffic

Reconfigurable Optical Add/Drop Multiplexers (ROADMs) enable carriers to:

- Add traffic

- Separate out traffic

- Drop off traffic

ROADM equipment eliminates the extra cost and maintenance for conversion equipment. Conversion equipment converts signals to electrical signals and back to light signals. Prior to the availability of ROADMs, light signals had to be converted to electrical signals before they could be added or dropped off and routed elsewhere.

ROADMs were first deployed in core networks so that, for example, some of the traffic between cities such as New York and Chicago could be more easily routed to Los Angeles. As traffic within metropolitan areas increased, ROADMs began to be used in these areas as well. Dense Wavelength Division Multiplexers (DWDMs) and OTN equipment can be equipped with ROADM cards so fewer pieces of gear need to be maintained.

ROADMs are additionally used to connect long-haul carriers to carriers in metropolitan areas. For example, ROADMs enable AT&T to drop local traffic off to local providers such as Verizon or Comcast. To transmit traffic between different telephone companies, often technicians from each company call each other to make sure their ROADMs can interoperate. The technicians often determine a way to connect via compatible Application Programming Interfaces (APIs). This causes delays in setting up connections.

The Open ROADM Multi-Source Agreement (MSA), which is in tests and limited availability at providers and manufacturers, is a solution to ROADM interoperability. With ROADM MSA, carriers can add and drop single wavelengths to ROADMs manufactured by other vendors. See Figure 4-6 for an example of an open source ROADM. AT&T announced they were able to add and drop single 100 Gigabit wavelengths between Ciena and Fujitsu ROADMs. Legacy ROADMs may not be upgradeable due to older, fixed optical parts that are not programmable for compatibility to the Open ROADM MSA.

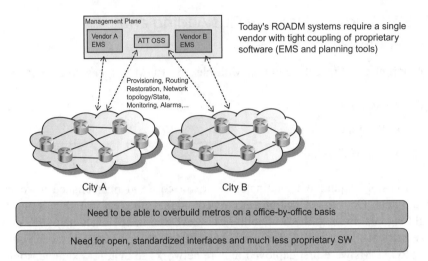

Figure 4-6   An example of carriers connecting using an open sources ROADM. (Courtesy of Open ROADM Multi-Source Agreement [MSA], http://OpenROADM.org)

Akamai—The Largest Content Delivery Network in the United States

People that watch live sporting events, play online games, or stream movies over the Internet expect to stream these events and movies without experiencing delays that interrupt content they're watching. Content delivery networks are an important factor in their ability to seamlessly watch high-quality live and streamed video and sporting events over broadband networks.

As the name implies, content delivery networks deliver content over broadband networks. They route the growing amounts of live-streamed sports events, streaming television and movies, and real time gaming traffic. Content delivery network customers are the content providers that create and film content including large social networks, financial firms, and online gaming companies. Online retailers and large banks also use content delivery network services. The above content providers, online retailers, and financial firms hire content delivery networks to ensure that traffic to their customers is not delayed or interrupted because of congestion resulting in dropped packets.

At Akamai, technicians monitor networks at their Network Operations Centers (NOCs) in Cambridge, MA, Santa Clara, CA, Krakow, Poland, and Bangalore, India. A NOC is a location where network engineers monitor live traffic. Monitoring software used in these NOCs depict live traffic in real time. The software provides engineers information on paths packets travel, congested routes, and

Continued

alternate routes available in the event of outages and congestion. NOC staff reroute traffic in these instances if an alternative path is available.

Akamai developed its own proprietary protocol, FastTCP (Transmission Control Protocol) as a replacement for the 40-year-old TCP, which introduces delays in transmissions. TCP was designed for resiliency, not for today's densely trafficked networks where delays are unacceptable. Delays in TCP are caused by its continual acknowledgments of received packets and negative acknowledgments of dropped packets. Acknowledgments in TCP are known as acks and notice of packets dropped are known as negative acknowledgments, nacks. FastTCP streamlines these processes to prevent delays. FastTCP algorithms are deployed in Akamai edge servers.

According to Eric Buda, Senior Director of Global Platform Operations at Akamai,

> *When streaming, people will start to abandon a website if it takes more than 2 seconds for a video to start. Then every second after that you lose 6 percent of your audience. 80 percent of people abandon a website if their wait for the screen to start to fill is longer than 30 to 40 seconds.*

Akamai also provides a security service for customers. The security software screens packet headers for malware. It doesn't look at the actual payload (user data) in packets. To ensure privacy, payload content is encrypted. When Akamai's security software sees evidence of malware, such as overly long packets or hundreds of percentages of more than the usual amount of traffic, it sends the traffic to Akamai's scrubbing center, which removes the malware and sends the legitimate traffic to the network.

Other content delivery networks in addition to Akamai are Level 3 (part of CenturyLink) and Limelight. Some carriers also operate content delivery networks.

TRANSPORTING MOVIES AND TV IN THE CORE......

Both telephone service providers and cable TV companies have infrastructure in their core networks to receive and transmit entertainment content to customers. They each do this from centralized *headends*.

Using Headends to Receive and Transmit Programming

The term "headend" refers to the site where providers transmit content that they receive from satellites. A group of satellite dishes that receives content is referred to as a satellite farm. Central office switches and Voice over Internet Protocol (VoIP) equipment to support telephone services are also located at headends. Network Operations Centers

(NOCs) capable of monitoring and making programming changes to the network as well as operations support systems can be located here as well. These centers typically serve 7 to 10 towns. Multiple hubs that distribute content are connected to the headend, as shown in Figure 4-7.

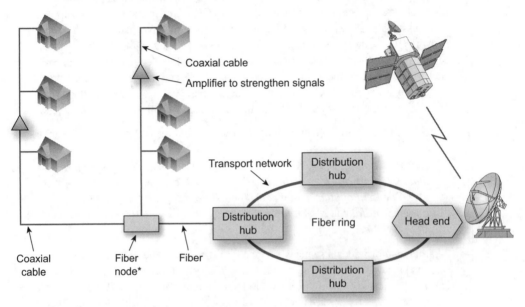

*Fiber nodes convert light signals carried on fiber-optic cabling
to electrical signals for transmission on coaxial cabling, and vice versa.

Figure 4-7 A fiber/coaxial network with transport network linking distribution hubs to the headend.

Hub Sites

Hubs, also referred to as *distribution hubs*, are small buildings that are located closer to customers than headends. Local programming or frequently downloaded content might be located at a hub, which serves between 10,000 and 50,000 residences. In addition, cable modem termination systems, which manage traffic to traditional cable TV customers' modems and to the headend, are located at hubs. For more information, see the section "Using Cable Modem Termination Systems for IP Traffic" later in this chapter. A hub might serve a metropolitan area. Large towns would have two hubs.

Linking Hubs and Headends via Metropolitan Area Networks

Metropolitan Area Network (MANs) are also referred to as *transport networks*, or *regional transport networks*. They link hubs to headends. MANs typically operate over shorter distances than core, backbone networks. They carry a mix of voice, data, and video on demand, as well as television signals. Cable TV Metropolitan networks are made up of hybrid fiber/coaxial cabling with fiber for the core that transmits movies to neighborhoods, and parts of their networks in cities far from the headend. These cities have nodes with wiring center (transmission) equipment.

Older MANs transmit traffic to headends' SONET rings. Cable operators and traditional telephone companies are transitioning parts of their metropolitan networks to all-IP, Gigabit Ethernet. It is complex and costly to upgrade all of a carrier's MANs simultaneously. However, carriers have the option of gradually upgrading a few networks at a time. These upgrades don't involve the immense upgrades as those in core networks. MANs are equipped with either redundant fiber rings or the simpler Optical Transport Network (OTN) option as backup technologies in the event of a fiber cut or equipment failure.

MIDDLE-MILE NETWORKS ....

Middle-mile networks are the sections of networks between the access provider and the connections that carry traffic to the Internet and to national and international core networks. Figure 4-8 shows an example of connections on middle-mile networks. Middle-mile networks can be the source of congestion on both wireless and wireline networks because they transport increasing amounts of Internet, smartphone, and video traffic. This is straining existing infrastructure.

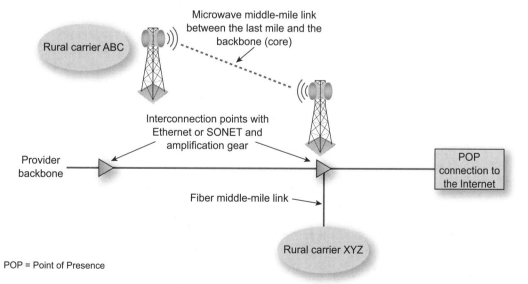

POP = Point of Presence

Figure 4-8 *The middle-mile connection between rural last-mile providers and a core network interconnection point for transport to the Internet.*

Middle-mile networks include the fiber or wireless connections between switches in small cities and the carrier's equipment that transmits traffic to a major carrier's Point of Presence (POP). Within middle-mile networks, the POP serves as the location where a provider's switches and connections for multiple carriers connect to the Internet or to a national or undersea cable. The core switches of large providers are also located at POPs.

Independently operated data centers where data is managed for multiple enterprises are another example of sites that require middle-mile connections. These data centers generate large amounts of traffic for which they require high-speed connections on middle-mile networks to backbone POPs.

Large carriers such as Verizon and AT&T in the United States carry the majority of middle-mile traffic. Level 3 Communications (now part of CenturyLink) is an alternative option in some areas. Level 3 offers to connect rural areas to POPs using spare capacity in its regional and long-haul networks. In the newer networks of these providers, hubs with Gigabit Ethernet switches are able to add and drop off traffic. Connections to Gigabit Ethernet are less costly than those to older SONET facilities. However, they require costly fiber cabling or wireless infrastructure from the rural provider's first-mile network to the middle-mile network switch. Because of the low population densities in rural areas that do not generate adequate revenue, this is not always financially feasible.

The High Cost of Rural Internet Connectivity

High-speed middle-mile connectivity is a major challenge in rural and sparsely populated areas worldwide. Although there are a growing number of fixed-wireless Internet access options, a majority of providers in these areas offer Internet access—predominately on Digital Subscriber Line (DSL) service—with some providing cable modems (see Chapter 5 for a more in-depth description of DSL service). The high costs of laying fiber or high-speed wireless connections to reach a broadband carrier for transport are passed on to customers and result in high end-user prices for cable TV and Internet access.

The National Exchange Carrier Association (NECA) is a nonprofit association of small, rural carriers that was formed by the Federal Communications Commission (FCC) to administer access charges. Access charges are the fees long-distance companies pay to access the networks of the 1,049 small rural local phone companies to complete their long-distance customers' calls. In its publication, *Trends 2015, A Report on Rural Technology*, NECA stated that in the United States, NECA carriers cover 37 percent of the territory, but serve only 3.1 percent of the population. In its report, NECA further commented that the long distances and low population densities in these areas are the primary causes of the high cost of deploying connections to backbone carriers.

Continued

According to Iowa Representative Rod Blum, high cost is the major reason that 39 percent of people in rural areas have no access to broadband compared to 4 percent in urban areas. With fewer customers in their territories, telephone providers must spread out the cost of upgrades over fewer customers. This results in lower profits per customer. Blum's remarks were reported in the June 23, 2017, B&C online journal article, "Small Business Committee has Big Interest in Rural Broadband," by John Eggerton.

The middle-mile costs associated with interconnection to the Internet are passed on to end users in the form of higher Internet access fees. These higher fees are another factor that inhibits many customers from purchasing Internet access in rural areas. Slower speeds that make access to streaming TV videos sluggish and cumbersome are also a factor in lower adoption rates in these areas.

Connections to middle-mile networks by rural providers are a mix of microwave and fiber-optic cabling. According to an anonymous staff person at a long-haul network provider, "The lowest-priced way to reach an *interconnection point* in middle-mile networks is microwave, at $150,000 to $200,000 for the tower and about $40,000 for equipment at the tower." An interconnection point is the equipment cabinet with Gigabit Ethernet or SONET gear, which connects rural providers' networks to middle mile networks, which connect traffic from rural locations to large providers' nationwide, backbone networks.

 NOTE Aerial fiber is less expensive than buried fiber cabling, but more subject to environmental damage such as tornados, snow storms, fallen branches, and so on.

These investments in fiber are too costly for the small rural carriers that NECA reports have an average customer base of only 4,324 access lines. Few of NECA's carriers have more than 10,000 access lines in service, which is the threshold at which these connections become economically viable.

LAST-MILE ACCESS NETWORKS..............................

Last-mile networks are the portions of a carrier's network that connect subscribers directly to the provider's equipment. The large number of connections usually means that the last-mile networks are the last portions of a carrier's network that benefit from upgrades. The terms "access networks," "last-mile networks," and "first-mile networks" are used interchangeably.

Adding Capacity to Access Networks

Upgrading access networks involves numerous devices because service to each telephone company and cable TV customer as well as equipment in neighborhood locations must often be changed. This is a challenge for both traditional telephone companies and cable TV Multiple System Operators (MSOs). However, cable TV providers have newer voice infrastructure than traditional telephone companies because the cable TV providers only started delivering these services around 2004. Thus, their voice switches don't require upgrades at this time. However, upgrading cabling and electronics connected to them for higher capacity is costly and complex.

One driving force behind upgraded access networks is the need to support more channels of high-definition television (HDTV) and video on demand (VOD), so that individuals are able to select from a menu of movies and premium television. In addition, customers are requesting HDTV, which requires more bandwidth and complex electronics than standard definition.

Data traffic is also driving networks to upgrade compression on set-top boxes. Consumers are additionally consuming more bandwidth by streaming video from Netflix and Amazon, and uploading and downloading both short and long form videos to and from YouTube, Instagram and Facebook.

Improved compression and other techniques such as *rate shaping* provide the capability to carry additional video and broadband traffic. Rate shaping adds capacity by using a form of over-subscription. It's analogous to pouring one-and-a-quarter quarts of water into a pail that holds only a single quart. Rate shaping equipment discards bits in real time so that adding 8 megabits of traffic to a 6-megabit channel does not impact quality. This assumes that not everyone will be watching TV at the same time.

Legacy Circuit-Switching Service

Switched services operate on landline and cellular networks that use older mobile protocols. When a person makes a call, the network sets up a path between the caller and the dialed party. Importantly, the path is available exclusively for the duration of the call. The path is not shared. Natural pauses in conversation and data transmission are not used for other voice or data calls. Capacity is reserved in the network for the entire duration of the transmission. This exclusivity causes wasteful utilization of network capacity.

Circuit switching is being gradually phased out in public networks. Carriers increasingly add IP equipment when replacing fully depreciated, older voice switches or when building new infrastructure.

Last-mile access networks use a mix of primarily IP and some circuit switching to carry voice. Traditional telephone companies and cable TV providers are in the process of transitioning to IP in their last-mile networks. When customers select their telephone provider for Internet access and TV services, the provider offers to move the subscriber's voice service to the same broadband infrastructure as that used for data and TV. Most of them provide VoIP over the broadband.

Transitioning Customers to Voice over Internet Protocol and Fiber

Data and video are the largest source of traffic on landline networks, far exceeding the shrinking amounts of voice. Many providers now transmit voice in packets, the same format as data, as a way to use bandwidth efficiently. Providers are additionally adding capacity to last-mile, edge networks by laying fiber in neighborhoods closer to homes or by connecting fiber directly to individual homes.

 NOTE A central office is a centrally located building in which telephone company and cable TV providers locate their switching, battery backup, and transmission equipment. Transmission equipment is in the form of blocks where cabling is connected to, for example, DSL and Ethernet services. Technicians in remote network operating centers (NOCs) monitor signals sent over cabling connected to subscribers and central offices. Because of the need for sustainability during natural disasters, buildings that house central offices don't have windows and are built to withstand flooding, tornadoes, and hurricanes.

Digital Subscriber Line Access Multiplexers

Digital Subscriber Line (DSL) is a service that sends data over the same twisted pair cabling used for voice. DSL is gradually being replaced by fiber to premises, but is still used by residential subscribers and small businesses that don't have fiber. Telephone companies that have not invested in fiber to the premises (FTTP) offer DSL service for Internet access and other data services. It is also used where customers don't have access to cable modem service. (See below for a description of cable TV networks.)

Using Small DSLAMs and Mini-RAMs for Internet Access with Digital Subscriber Line Service

DSL Access Multiplexers (DSLAMs) aggregate traffic from multiple customers' DSL modems and translate electrical signals on copper cabling to light signals before sending traffic to the central office. From the central office Internet Service Providers (ISPs) transmit subscribers' traffic to the Internet or data networks over fiber-optic cabling. DSLAMs are located in a carrier's central office or in remote terminals, which are cabinets placed between the central office and the subscriber. The connection between the DSLAM and an ISP is a potential site for network congestion and delays, if capacity is insufficient between the DSLAM and the central office.

When telecoms move fiber closer to customers in neighborhoods, they often use mini Remote Access Multiplexers (mini-RAMs), which are about the size of pizza boxes, to convert light signals carried on fiber to electrical signals and vice versa. Installing fiber closer to homes results in shorter copper lengths. Shorter copper runs have fewer impairments because electrical signals fade less as they travel over shorter distances. Impairments found on longer copper runs farther from central offices cause DSL speeds to decrease dramatically and often prevent DSL from being viable at even slower speeds. Traffic from mini-RAMs is aggregated in DSLAMs, from where it is transmitted over fiber to central offices and the Internet.

Mini-RAMs can be located on utility poles or in stand-alone boxes on the ground and serve 10 to 24 customers (see Figure 4-9). Local power is not required because it is fed to mini-RAMs through the copper telephone lines either on the pole or underground.

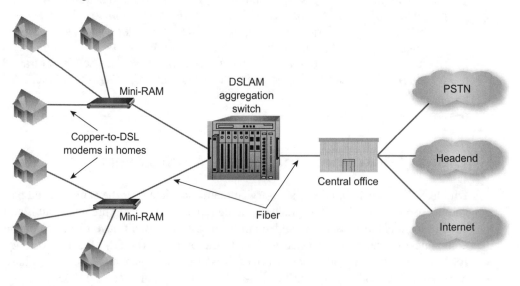

DSLAM = Digital Subscriber Line Access Multiplexer
PSTN = Public Switched Telephone Network

Figure 4-9 Mini Remote Access Multiplexers (mini-RAMs), located in neighborhoods, deliver cable TV and high-speed Internet access.

The Case for Fiber to the Home—More Capacity and Less Maintenance

Cable TV providers and telephone companies in the United States and other countries sell "triple play" services: voice, TV and movies, and Internet access to enterprises, hotels, restaurants, and municipalities as well as residential customers. One way they provide capacity needed to handle all of these services is to add fiber closer to homes and businesses or directly to premises. When carriers transition to fiber to homes, voice signals are sent in digital, voice over Internet (VoIP) packets, rather than as electrical signals on copper cabling. Providers that transition to fiber to homes or even fiber close to homes in neighborhoods, gain these advantages:

- Fiber cabling has more capacity than copper to support the continuing growth in broadband traffic and cloud and streaming media.

- Operating costs are lower because it is more efficient for providers to maintain just one type of cabling and equipment than two types of cabling.

- Central offices only need to be equipped with equipment that supports a single type of cabling rather than both fiber and copper.

- Less network equipment is required because signals on fiber travel further than those on copper cabling before deteriorating. When signals fade, equipment is required to boost signals.

Power Issues—Electricity for Onsite Fiber Gear

Signals carried on copper cabling are electrical pulses that transmit power from the central office along with voice and data signals to homes. This enables central offices to power plain old telephone service (POTS). Plain telephones are not plugged into home electrical outlets, and have limited features.

Power delivered from central offices enable POTS phones to operate during premises' electrical outages. This is because central offices' extensive use of backup generators means for the most part they operate during power outages. Plain phones without LCD screens or most other features are the only home telephones able to function without local power if their service is connected to copper cabling.

Customer premises connected to fiber cabling do lose automatic power backup on all telephones including their plain telephones. This is because the optical network terminals (ONTs) that convert fiber signals to those compatible with the copper wiring inside homes require local power. Signals on fiber cabling don't transmit power signals. They are non-electric light pulses, not the electrical signals carried on copper cabling.

Given the fact that in most homes people have no landline telephone because they rely on mobile service or have "feature" phones that require local power, subscribers are often not concerned or even aware of the switch from copper to fiber cabling.

Battery Backup for Homes Connected to Fiber

The Federal Communications Commission (FCC) requires providers that transition to fiber from copper cabling in neighborhoods to offer in-home battery backup gear. This requirement is meant to ensure that residents such as the disabled or elderly are able to reach 911, police and fire departments, and healthcare facilities during power outages. An example of battery backup equipment for residential customers is containers with 12 D-Cell alkaline batteries. The battery backup devices are connected to optical network terminals. The backup generally provides eight hours of talk time during power outages. The customer is responsible for changing batteries about once a year when they wear down and lose charging ability.

The Economics of Fiber to Large Apartment Buildings and Enterprises

In contrast to the last-mile networks in residential areas, many of which are made up of twisted-pair copper or hybrid fiber/coaxial, cable TV providers and traditional telephone companies lay fiber to their large business customers. This is because the expense of supplying fiber cable to office and apartment buildings with multiple tenants can be spread across many customers. In addition, fiber is required to handle the large amounts of data traffic that enterprise customers generate.

Passive Optical Networks

Telephone companies and cable operators install Passive Optical Networks (PONs) to lower the cost of deploying fiber-optic cabling directly to residential and small business customers. Cost savings are achieved by sharing the capacity of single strands of fiber among multiple homes and small businesses.

Sharing Fiber Capacity—PON Architecture

PON technologies are a less costly way to deploy fiber because the devices, splitters, in the neighborhoods are small and *passive*. They don't require electricity and can be mounted directly on utility poles or in existing equipment cabinets. Fewer cable runs are required from the central office to each neighborhood because the splitter divides the capacity on a single fiber strand among multiple subscribers.

 NOTE Instead of fiber, when cabling is closer to homes, coaxial cabling or unshielded twisted-pair are often used to transmit signals over the last few hundred feet from subscribers.

PONs are used extensively in mobile networks as well where they transmit signals between antennas and carriers' data centers. Data centers in mobile networks are where mobile providers manage their wireless networks, collect usage data for billing, and offer special applications such as voice mail and text messaging.

With PON technology, only one pair of fiber is brought to the neighborhood but multiple pairs are split out from PON interfaces to homes. *Splitters* divide the capacity of the fiber among up to 32 homes and small businesses. Figure 4-10 shows one possible scenario. Splitters are passive in that they don't require electricity and they are small; they're about the size of a smartphone. These are key factors because space in the network is at a premium and electrical costs are soaring. PON equipment at the central office, inside customers' premises, and in cabinets in neighborhoods do require electricity.

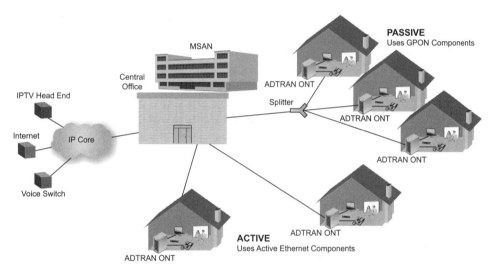

Figure 4-10 *PON splitter in neighborhood; an MSAN (Multi-Service Access node) connects subscribers to the Internet and other networks. (Courtesy of Adtran, Inc.)*

PON Standards—Gigabit Ethernet

In contrast to residential PON services, which have higher capacity for downloads, PON services for business customers have synchronous capacity; equal bandwidth to and from their devices. Business and commercial organizations upload and download applications and data to and from the cloud and the Internet in equal amounts. However, 10Gb XG PONs support 10 Gigabit service downstream and 2.5 Gigabit service upstream. Current standards provide the option of symmetric services directly to business customers as well as the option to virtualize PON gear in CORD-equipped central offices.

See Table 4-1 for ITU-T (International Telecommunications Union Terminals for Telematic Services) PON standards.

Table 4-1   PON Standards

PON Type	Description
GPON (Gigabit PON)	Supports a bandwidth of up to 2.5Gbps
XG PON1 (10 Gigabit Passive Optical Network)	Enables providers to program individual wavelengths for 10Gbps downstream and 2.5Gbps upstream.
XGS PON (10 Gigabit Symmetric Passive Optical Network)	Supports 10 Gigabit capacity on both the upstream (from the customer to the central office) and the downstream (from the central office to the customer) signals.
NG PON2 (40 to 100 Gigabit)	Equipment is programmable via software and supports symmetric streams. Providers can program each wavelength individually on a fiber strand, and dedicate it to a large customer. (A wavelength represents a stream of signals on a particular frequency within a fiber strand.) Wavelengths can also be bonded together. Bonding refers to two paths of a communication circuit operating as a single path. This enables the provider to send extra capacity to high-usage enterprises or commercial sites.

In the newest PON standard, Next Generation Passive Optical Network 2 (NG PON2), wavelengths can be turned on remotely and the lasers connected to the fiber can be modified so that the provider is not required to pay for a "truck roll" to send out a technician to make a change at the splitter. According to PON provider Adtran, the ability to add capacity by programming future-proofs NG PON2 against expected increases in traffic, particularly video streaming and cloud computing. As residents' and businesses' broadband use increases, new hardware is not required. Additional capacity for individual wavelengths can be added via software.

PON service was initially introduced in North America in 2002. Currently, Adtran, Nokia through its purchase of Alcatel Lucent, Tellabs, and Chinese company Huawei manufacturer PON components available in North America. Older PON standards are listed in Table 4-3 in the "Appendix."

PON Components—OLTs and ONTs

OLTs (Optical Line Terminals) are switches with ports on each card. They are located in central offices where they are connected to network nodes in the outside network of cable TV and telephone companies. See Figure 4-11 for an example of an OLT. OLTs place optical signals on the correct fiber optic cable. Each OLT card has from four to eight ports and each port is connected to a specific fiber strand.

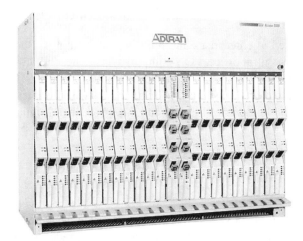

Figure 4-11 *An Optical Line Terminal with ports on cards where fiber is terminated in central offices. (Photo courtesy of Adtran Inc.)*

OLTs for NG PON2s can also be installed in network operators' cloud-based CORD central offices where they are virtual network functions (VNFs) in a White Box on X86 Intel commodity servers. Representing NG PON2s optical line terminals in software makes them less costly to install than separate pieces of hardware.

Optical Network Terminals (*ONTs*) translate between signals on fiber cabling and those on copper cabling as well as between optical signals and wireless signals. ONTs are located wherever fiber optic cabling is connected to other types of cabling and wireless medium where signals need to be translated. This makes them compatible with all types of media.

The following are examples of locations with ONTs:

- Homes

- Enterprises distribution frames where copper cabling is terminated

- Apartment buildings

- Wi-Fi modems if all signals within a building are transmitted on Wi-Fi

- Hospitals

- Cellular backhaul where signals are "backhauled" from cellular data centers to networks

- Wholesale cellular backhaul providers who resell backhaul capacity to facilities-based cellular companies

- Coaxial cabling in cable TV networks where fiber is installed in residential neighborhoods closer to homes

- Nodes in neighborhoods where fiber is terminated closer to, but not directly connected to a residence or small business

Direct Fiber to Enterprises and Multi-Tenant Buildings

Direct fiber is often installed at enterprises and multi-tenant buildings. Because it is directly connected from the central office, PON equipment is not needed. In apartment buildings, data-grade copper carries signals to each apartment unit from the ONT. The ONT converts light signals to electrical signals in the building's wiring center. The data grade twisted-pair copper cabling carries Internet and other broadband signals to each apartment.

Using PONs to Deliver Fiber to the Home in Cities and Sections of Metropolitan Areas

PONs to the home are widely deployed in Asian countries such as Japan and South Korea, and in China, where much of the infrastructure was upgraded or built from scratch. Dense populations are a factor in making it feasible to lay fiber to homes in these countries. The lack of density in the United States compared to other countries makes it costly and challenging to build fiber to homes. Fiber to the home is capable of reaching up to 32 homes from a single splitter. Figure 4-12 presents a list of countries with the most fiber to the home (FTTH).

   Verizon currently has the largest installed base of PON connected fiber. AT&T, CenturyLink, and most cable Multiple System Operators (MSOs) bring fiber deep into

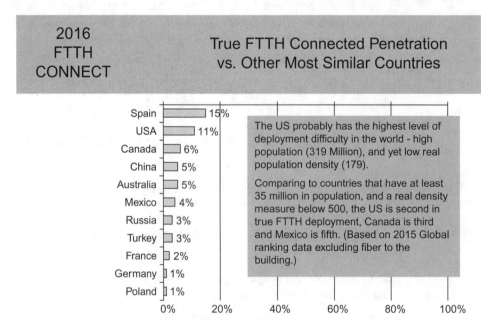

Figure 4-12   Countries with the largest percentage of fiber to the home. (Courtesy of Broadband Association)

neighborhoods and then use twisted-pair or coaxial cabling to serve customers. Some providers bring fiber all the way to curbside pedestals in much of their territory. These implementations serve only 8 to 12 customers per PON device. PON service closer to customers is more expensive per subscriber to deploy but provides higher-speed service because fewer customers share the fiber.

PONs are also used to bring fiber all the way to premises in new "greenfield" developments (new industrial or residential developments). In addition, they are the basis for wireline infrastructure in developing countries. In addition to providing large amounts of capacity, fiber is less costly to maintain than copper cabling. Less equipment is needed to boost signals that fade, there are fewer repair issues, and capacity can be upgraded by changing equipment connected to fiber. Entire new fiber strands are not usually required.

Expanding into New Territories

When telephone and cable TV companies expand into new areas, they are faced with high costs of getting permits from local governments, hanging cables on telephone poles, and digging up streets to lay fiber. Carriers that want to avoid these expenses negotiate 20- to 30-year leases for exclusive rights to spare fiber. These leases are referred to as Indefeasible Rights of Use, IRUs. Examples of organizations with spare fiber are electric utilities and long-haul network providers. Electric utilities have large networks of fiber associated with transmitting power to customers.

According to Google Fiber's head of business operations in Huntsville, Alabama, Caroline de Gantis, "Leasing the infrastructure in Huntsville rather than building from scratch allows us to bring Google Fiber to even more people, faster." De Gratis was quoted in CNBC.com's May 23, 2017, article by Colin Gibbs, "Alphabet's Cost Cutting on Display as Google Fiber Rolls Out In Alabama."

ACCESS NETWORKS IN CABLE OPERATORS' NETWORKS...

Access networks in cable operators' and traditional telephone companies' networks use a different type of customer modem. However, both telephone companies and cable Multiple System Operators (MSOs) face the challenge of upgrading access networks to increase capacity. Access networks are those portions of a network between a provider's equipment in neighborhoods and that of the customer. Per Neilson, cable and satellite TV reception is available to 82 percent of the population in the United States.

NOTE MSOs are large cable TV providers with service areas that extend over many states. They are referred to as MSOs because they grew by purchasing other cable companies and merging operations with these often smaller companies' systems. Comcast Corporation, Cox Cable, and Charter Communication are examples of MSOs in the United States.

Using Cable Modems to Access the Internet

The basic functions of cable modems are to convert digital signals from computers or data networks to those compatible with coaxial cabling and to convert radio frequency (RF) from cable TV networks to digital signals suitable for Internet access and fiber optical cabling. In cable TV, electromagnetic waves carried on coaxial cabling are referred to as RF signals. The cable TV access network is a hybrid fiber/coax (HFC) network.

The Cable Modem "Handshake"

Cable modems perform a "handshake," an exchange of signals before data is transmitted to and from the Cable Modem Termination Systems (CMTSs) located at the cable operator site. (See the following section for information regarding CMTS equipment.) Complex signaling, use of frequencies, the speed at which to transmit, and authentication are agreed on between the two devices. At startup, the network checks the user's login before allowing access to the Web or certain web sites.

Using Set-Top Boxes to Interface to Cable TV

Cable TV set-top boxes are interfaces between televisions, satellite TV, subscription television, and cable TV networks for access to television and other services. At the most basic level, they are tuners that filter out all of the channels except the one selected by the viewer. Because each tuner filters only one channel at a time, set-top boxes used for more than one television simultaneously will require multiple tuners. Personal digital video recorders such as TiVo also have two tuners so that one tuner filters a channel that is being recorded and the other tuner filters the channel currently being viewed. Other tuners in end users' televisions filter signals for interactive services such as programming guides, VOD, and pay-per-view.

Cable operators remotely administer filters and traps in set-top boxes to allow subscribers access to basic cable TV or premium channels. Set-top boxes also have advanced security functions and contain links to billing systems. The security function scrambles and unscrambles TV signals based on the information provided by the billing system as to which channels the subscriber is permitted to receive. Security is higher and TV theft is lower on digital service because of improved scrambling (encryption).

Set-top boxes are becoming more sophisticated. Comcast's X-1 set-top box supports speech recognition on remotes, and access to services including Netflix, Pandora music, photos, and weather. The X-1 is required for the MPEG-4 compression that Comcast is upgrading to on their cable networks. MPEG-4 compresses video signals so that they require less capacity on networks. Software in set-top boxes decompresses the compressed signals so that video resolution is acceptable. See Chapter 1 for information on compression.

The High Capital Cost of Set-Top Box Upgrades

On a cost-per-subscriber basis, when cable TV networks are upgraded, the new set-top boxes required cost more than any other part of the network. This is because upgrades to the headend or core network are amortized over the entire network. By contrast, each set-top box is amortized from payments received from the individual customer. New set-top boxes add up to an enormous amount of money for cable providers with millions of customers. In addition, set-top box upgrades require more administrative time for programming the set-top boxes and answering customer inquiries.

These costs are a major factor in many providers' decision to gradually implement upgrades in their coverage areas. This spreads out the costs over a few years rather than during a single year.

Soft Set-Top Boxes

One way that cable TV providers are saving money is by eliminating set-top boxes on certain Internet-connected televisions. On Samsung, for example, Comcast offers an app with full access to Comcast's program options. Comcast's app is also available on Roku devices. RCN, a regional cable TV provider, offers its program guide on other set-top boxes as well.

USING CABLE MODEM TERMINATION SYSTEMS FOR IP TRAFFIC

Cable Modem Termination Systems (CMTSs) are located at the cable or distribution center (the hub). They *modulate* and *demodulate* (hence, the term "modem") digital voice and data signals and place them on cable infrastructure. Modulation is the technique of making digital signals suitable for radio frequencies (electromagnetic waves) that carry signals on cabling infrastructure. CMTSs demodulate signals received from customers to make them suitable for transmission on a cable company's fiber-optic rings, which connect smaller hubs to headend facilities.

CMTSs monitor the level of traffic at each fiber node so that cable providers are aware when congestion occurs and nodes need to be added to serve fewer homes per node. Moreover, they are responsible for encryption to ensure privacy, security, and *conditional access*. Conditional access is the determination of whether a customer is entitled to certain features. CMTS devices have built-in routers that send traffic to different destinations such as the Internet, long-distance providers, or the cable MSO's VoIP equipment.

CMTSs are similar in function to Digital Subscriber Line Access Multiplexers (DSLAMs) that are used in traditional telephone company networks in that both devices translate between modems at customers' premises and equipment in backbone networks. They both also aggregate traffic from multiple subscribers into a single stream for transmission in the backbone. (See the section "Digital Subscriber Line Access Multiplexers," earlier in this chapter, for a discussion on DSLAMs.)

Supporting More Video via Set-Top Boxes

New modulation technologies enable digital cable to increase capacity two to three times from the former 10 to 12 channels of standard-definition video and two to four channels of HDTV video on each 6MHz channel. Standard-definition TV has lower resolution than high-definition television. Moreover, digital cable results in improved resolution because there is less interference from noise, which creates snow and shadows that appear on the television screen.

Consumers can opt for set-top boxes with hard drives capable of storing content and playing it back at their convenience. Digital cable is the basis for VOD, which allows subscribers to order movies for an extra fee. VOD movies are available for a limited time period of a day or two. Nearly 100 percent of all cable TV subscribers in the United States are located in areas where they can receive digital cable. Pay-TV via cable and satellite are available to 82 percent of households of the population in the United States.

Cable Modem Standards Transition to Higher Speeds

CableLabs, the research and development arm of the North and South American cable TV industry, sets cable TV modem standards. CableLab's standards are intended to provide a technology "road map" for cable MSOs to move toward implementing higher-capacity IP networks used for Internet access. These standards are known as the Data Over Cable System Interface Specifications (DOCSIS). The European Telecommunications Standards Institute (ETSI) and the International Telecommunications Union (ITU) have approved the standards listed in Table 4-4 in the "Appendix" section of this chapter. However, the international versions of DOCSIS vary a little from that used in the United States. The DOCSIS standard in Europe and parts of Latin America is referred to as EuroDOCSIS.

Transitioning from Asymmetric to Symmetric Channels

Until 2016, MSO offerings for residential-consumer Internet access were primarily *asymmetric*, with higher speeds in the downstream channel from the cable provider to the subscriber, and lower speeds upstream from the subscriber to the provider. Splitting the frequencies into different ranges enables the same coaxial cables to be used for both sending and receiving signals. Unlike fiber cabling, for which separate strands of fiber are used for sending and receiving, a separate coaxial cable does not need to be installed for the reverse, upstream channel. With the advent of new cable modem standards (see DOCSIS below), both upstream and downstream capacities are the same. They are symmetric. Upstream and downstream bits use the entire range of frequencies in the cable.

Full Duplex DOCSIS 3.1—Symmetric Speeds

The DOCSIS 3.1 standard specifies support for 10Gbps per 6MHz (6 megahertz) channel. Users on the same node share this capacity. DOCSIS 3.1 is currently the fastest, most advanced cable modem standard. It is compatible with the previous DOCSIS 3.0 that specified bonding to increase capacity on broadband.

Bonding enables support for higher data rates of 173Mbps to 343Mbps downstream to homes, and 123Mbps upstream to the cable operator.

> *Bonding* is the process of combining adjacent channels into one large channel to support higher-speed services. For example, bonding four channels together that each comprise 38 1Mb channels creates a single 152Mb channel. In effect, bonding creates a bigger pipe that is shared by homes connected to the same node.
>
> Bonding increases capacity for Internet access. However, it does so by using channels previously available for video, which of course, decreases the number of available video channels. It does not increase the total amount of capacity on cable networks, many of which had a top capacity of 860MHz. Bonding, rate shaping, and improved compression increase the amount of data (throughput) that the network can handle, but they do not increase overall capacity. For more information on rate shaping, read the section "Adding Capacity to Access Networks," earlier in this chapter.

Fiber-optic cabling supports more capacity than current hybrid fiber/coaxial cabling. For example, Verizon's fiber to the premises (FTTP) cabling enables it to use its entire 860MHz for TV, with additional gigabits available for voice and Internet access. To add capacity on coaxial cable, operators are upgrading their networks using advanced QAM multiplexing techniques.

Because of its support for Quality of Service (QoS), DOCSIS 3.0 supported applications such as voice and video, which are sensitive to delays. An upgrade to DOCSIS 3.0 required a new DOCSIS 3.0–compatible cable modem at the subscriber location and at the CMTS. This made the upgrade a costly endeavor.

Competition from carriers that offer fiber to the premises (FTTP) is one factor that spurred implementation of DOCSIS 3.0 and *full duplex,* sending and receiving on the same cable or channel. DOCSIS 3.1's higher-capacity offerings have capacities from 1 to 10Gbps to support broadband to residential and business customers. MSOs deploy direct fiber to enterprise customers. Unlike offering to residential subscribers, cable TV direct fiber connections to enterprises are not shared with other customers that subscribe to broadband. They are connected directly to cable operators' transport networks.

Capacity on Coaxial Cable

Signals on coaxial cable in cable TV networks are transmitted as electromagnetic waves (radio frequencies [RF]). Capacity on these coaxial cable systems and on TV channels is measured by the amount of frequency. The amount of frequency is determined by the difference between the highest and lowest frequencies on the coaxial cabling.

For example, a 6MHz channel might be within the 60MHz and 54MHz range ($60 - 54 = 6$). Upgrading to gigahertz from megahertz networks adds capacity for additional video channels and higher-speed Internet access for subscribers. See Chapter 7, "Mobile and Wi-Fi Networks," for information on frequencies.

Carrying More Data—Quadrature Amplitude Modulation (QAM)

QAM is a modulation technology specified in DOCSIS standards that increase broadband capacity on hybrid fiber cable (HFC) networks. Modulation standards define how signals are placed on networks and how they are transmitted. Full Duplex 4096 QAM enables cable TV networks to carry two to three times as many high definition (HD) movies as the earlier 256 QAM. However, movies must be transmitted using the IP (Internet Protocol). DOCSIS 3.1 specifies 4096 QAM to deliver 10 Gigabits of symmetric capacity shared by nodes within neighborhoods. Currently most cable operators don't transmit movies using the IP (Internet Protocol).

QAM 4096 is more sensitive to noise and impairments that occur over long distances on coaxial cabling. This is one reason cable TV providers are expanding their fiber footprint closer into neighborhoods. Fiber closer to homes results in shortened coaxial cable lengths. Shorter coaxial cabling runs have less impairment from electrical noise than longer coaxial cable runs.

There is also a DOCSIS 3.1 specification for half duplex, asymmetric service. Asymmetric DOCSIS 3.1 specifies 10 Gigabits downstream and 1 Gigabit upstream from customers to the provider's headend. In these instances, DOCSIS 3.0 spectrum is used for the upstream bits toward the cable TV network and DOCSIS 3.1 spectrum for downstream spectrum to subscribers.

Upgrading to 10GHz adds capacity for Internet browsing as well as movies sent using IP. Unlike bonding, it does not decrease the amount of capacity for video. However, it is costly. Optical transceivers and receivers as well as amplifiers and set-top boxes need to be replaced or upgraded, depending on the age of the existing cabling and electronics. Optical transceivers and receivers convert signals on optical cabling to those compatible with copper cabling, and vice versa. Amplifiers strengthen signals that naturally weaken after traveling over distances, particularly on copper-based coaxial.

 NOTE In symmetric transmissions, which are specified in *Full Duplex* DOCSIS 3.1 implementations, upstream and downstream bits share the same spectrum. This is accomplished by equipment that can listen and transmit at the same time and cancel what the equipment has already "heard." Once the transmitted bits are "heard" they can be cancelled, and only changed bits are transmitted. Symmetric, full duplex transmissions use the HFC spectrum more efficiently than DOCSIS 3.0. They are *spectrally efficient*, enabling both upstream and downstream bits to use the full capacity of the cabling.

Symmetric service is important for business customers that access cloud-based applications where more capacity than previously is needed on the uplink as well as the downlink where data is downloaded from applications such as Salesforce.com located in the cloud. Upstream capacity is also needed for residential subscribers who increasingly upload long-form, high-resolution videos to Facebook, Snapchat, YouTube, and other social networks.

Competition from Streaming TV and Traditional Telephone Companies

Customers that "cut the cord" or that never subscribed to cable TV or satellite TV can opt for *over the air service* television broadcasts beamed from towers. National broadcasters (ABC, NBC, CBS, Fox, and Spanish channels) and their local affiliates broadcast their programs over the air to customers' antennas or from cable TV providers that now offer streaming. Subscribers without cable TV service receive programs over the air via an antenna wired to their TVs. The antenna can be installed on their roof or the outside of their home. Subscribers close enough to broadcasting towers are able to use indoor antennas to receive over the air TV broadcasts.

The escalating subscription fees combined with the many interruptions for commercials on cable TV has motivated many subscribers to "cut the cord" and rely only on *over the top (OTT)* streaming media from Netflix, Amazon, Hulu, and others. According to Nielson, by the first quarter of 2017, 123.6 million people in the United States subscribed to OTT streaming TV from Netflix, Amazon, Hulu, and others. Others subscribe to fewer cable TV stations. They "slim down" their cable TV bundle by subscribing to fewer cable TV stations. These slimmed down cable TV packages are referred to as *skinny bundles.* Many subscribers pay for an OTT subscription in addition to their slimmed down or full cable TV subscriptions.

Traditional telephone companies including AT&T and CenturyLink are encroaching on cable MSOs by offering subscriptions to their movie and TV programming, IP voice telephony, and broadband over their copper or fiber infrastructure. Verizon currently has the most territory in the United States where they offer service bundles over fiber. They carry IP voice, television, and Internet broadband transmissions over their fiber to homes. AT&T and most other telephone companies compete with MSOs by offering triple play services: voice, data, and TV programs. They build out fiber to the closest neighborhood node (equipment cabinet), and use copper for the last few hundred feet in areas where they don't provide fiber directly to homes.

Satellite TV

Satellite TV operators offer bundles with both streaming TV and national broadcast stations. Dish and AT&T's DirecTV are the only satellite TV providers in the United States. Satellite TV is particularly popular in rural areas where fiber to homes is not available. Satellite TV is important in rural areas in the United States, particularly where cable TV is not available because low population density makes it unprofitable to lay cabling directly to homes.

Retransmission Agreements between Pay-TV and Local Broadcasters

All cable TV subscribers, including those with slimmed down, skinny bundles, receive national broadcast programming on their cable TV service. Cable TV, satellite, and traditional telephone companies pay fees to local broadcasters for the right to carry local broadcasts. These agreements are referred to as retransmission agreements. The fees are mandated in the United States 1992 Cable Act.

TELECOMMUNICATIONS SERVICES IN NATIONAL EMERGENCIES ....

During natural disasters, extreme weather conditions, and even armed attacks, the government, military, first responders (hospitals, police, 911 call centers, and firefighters), and ordinary citizens depend on communications to coordinate rescue operations and to stay in contact with family members. Even in the absence of a disaster, the ability to call police, fire departments, and hospitals is critical so that people can report emergencies and assistance can be dispatched as quickly as possible. For these reasons, governments worldwide regulate network reliability and sustainability. Equipment and network *sustainability* refers to the capability to operate continuously during adverse conditions.

In the United States, the Federal Communications Commission (FCC) requires outage reports from the following providers:

- Wireline
- Wireless
- Paging
- Cable TV
- Satellite TV
- Signaling systems

They must further report disruptions that affect the following:

- E-911 facilities affecting 900,000 user-minutes or 30-minute outages in tandem 911 offices connected to long distance networks and other 911 facilities
- Major military installations
- Key government facilities
- Nuclear power plants
- Certain airports

In addition, fiber-optic outages of lines that carry traffic between backbone network switches must be reported. Reports on outages are reviewed quarterly by the Network Reliability Steering Committee (NRSC), which is made up of representatives from nationwide wireline and wireless providers. The committee looks for patterns by type of failure so that they can determine ways to prevent them.

Planning to Insure Reliability and Sustainability

Carrier networks are now largely IP-based, converged networks, wherein a single network infrastructure carries data as well as telephone traffic. Thus, outages cause disruptions to businesses, governments, and consumers. In addition, traffic volume increases significantly in emergencies.

During widespread emergencies, mobile carriers free up capacity for the additional volume required by assigning less frequency to each call. Thus, more calls can be carried, although at lower sound quality. They can also quickly set up portable cell sites and additional generators at towers or mobile switches that lose power. This enables mobile providers to restore service to these areas. In addition, if one part of the country is hit by a natural disaster, other carriers will send staff members and equipment to assist in restoring service.

Carriers plan for emergencies in various ways. For example, they build backup wireless routes between critical switches and public safety answering points (PSAPs) for E-911 calls. They also look at ways to increase security against hackers and terrorists at peering sites where carriers exchange IP traffic. In addition, providers consider methods to avoid user errors. User errors occur most often during network upgrades and programming changes.

FirstNet—A National Public Safety Network

In the days and hours immediately after the 9/11/2001 terrorist attacks on the World Trade Center's Twin Towers in New York City and the Pentagon in Washington DC, firefighters, police, and other first responders found that because of incompatible mobile devices they could not communicate with first responders from other municipalities. This inability to coordinate strategy acted as a heads-up for the need to be able to communicate with other emergency responders during cyber and physical attacks, and natural disasters.

Following 9/11/01, the Federal Communications Commission (FCC) set about making a plan for a nationwide dedicated interoperable wireless network with spectrum (air rights) to be set aside for the exclusive use of the government and first responders. The FCC's plan recommended setting aside a portion of spectrum, the D block, to be used to build a nationwide network. The D block had been freed up when national broadcast television networks transitioned from analog to digital for TV transmissions. Part of the spectrum previously used for analog television was made available for the FirstNet service.

By 2006, the FCC plan was in place, but Congress needed to approve the plan and allocate funds to build the network. At this time the plan faced opposition from some in Congress and from wireless carriers. Members of Congress, federal

Continued

officials, and national public safety organizations held a series of meetings, and by 2007 had ironed out their differences.

By 2012, spectrum had been allocated and Congress authorized the creation of the public-private First Responder Network Authority, known as FirstNet, an independent arm of the Department of Commerce. In 2017, FirstNet awarded AT&T a 25-year contract to build a wireless network dedicated to the use of first responders in emergencies. The U.S. Congress allocated $7 billion for building the network. The money was part of the Middle Class Tax Relief and Job Creation Act of 2012.

Every state in the United States is required to have a compatible wireless network. They can opt in to the AT&T network, which AT&T would build in their state, or build their own first responder network. All states' networks must be compatible with the FirstNet being built by AT&T by December 2017; all 50 states had agreed to join the FirstNet network. In August 2017, Verizon announced that it is also building a national public safety network that will be separate from its commercial network.

First responders in states that have opted into the AT&T offering do have the choice of using Verizon's national public safety network. However, as an added incentive to join their network, AT&T pledged to add cellular infrastructure in areas sparsely equipped for service.

Internet Security and Sustainability

Internet security is a global issue that cannot be isolated within a single country. However, the Federal Communications Commission (FCC) currently has no authority to require that Internet providers report network outages and details about cyber attacks. In its 2009 National Broadband Plan, the FCC recommended looking at ways to ensure sustainable communications over the Internet. It also stated the desirability of expanding international participation and outreach to manage cyber security information. Part and parcel of that, the FCC would like a vehicle for collecting more detailed information about cyber security. The report also expressed concern about how dependent first responders are on Internet communications. The FCC further declared that it is considering asking Congress for the authority to require reporting on these issues.

Because the Internet is classified as an *information service* rather than as a telecommunications service, the FCC has limited authority in regulating it. An information service is defined in the Telecommunications Act of 1996 as a service that adds value to a basic transmission path through functions such as processing information. *Telecommunications* is defined as the basic transmission (delivery) of voice and data. It's essentially the path over which voice is carried as well as the equipment used to send and receive voice and data traffic.

Because of its critical role, the FCC attempted to alter the way the Internet is regulated so that the agency has more oversight of cyber security and sustainability. It attempted to have the Internet classified as a telecommunications entity rather than a value-added service. However, with the changeover of the FCC when Donald Trump was elected president, the FCC has dropped its efforts to classify the transmission component of Internet services as telecommunications. The effort to regulate the Internet did not include monitoring content on web sites or content transmitted to web sites.

SIGNALING ....

Signaling is the process of sending control information over landline and mobile networks to monitor, control, route, and set up sessions between devices. These sessions include video and audio conference calls, data sessions, video calls, and mobile and landline telephone calls. Signaling is also used to set up instant messaging and chat sessions. Signaling is used within public landline and, mobile networks, and the Internet as well as for intercarrier connections and billing.

An Overview of Signaling

Signaling is used to process every call on the Public Switched Telephone Network (PSTN), the Internet, and the public cellular network. When a caller dials a number, he or she can hear progress tones such as dial tone, ringing, busy signals, or reorder tones. These are all signaling tones. In addition to tones, callers might hear digital messages informing them that the number they dialed is not in service or has been changed.

The PSTN (Public Switched Telephone Network) uses Signaling System 7 (SS7); IP networks mainly use variations of Session Initiation Protocol (SIP) as the common platforms for call setup, teardown and activation, and control of advanced features. SIP was originally designed for the Internet, but is now used in private data networks and data networks that carry IP voice as well. A form of SIP is also used for text messages.

Signaling is the basis of interconnection between mobile, global wireless, and multiple providers' networks. When AT&T controlled most of the public network in the United States, it had the necessary control of the public network that enabled it to set a standard (SS7) that was followed across the country and was later adopted, with variations, by the international community. SIP is additionally used in IP PBXs to carry calling identification, and to set up and tear down video and audio conferences.

SIP is an Internet Engineering Task Force (IETF)–approved standard. In both SIP and SS7 protocols, signaling messages are carried separately from user content. In addition, they both provide common functions.

Signaling—The Basis for Billing and Monitoring

Signaling networks monitor traffic on networks around the clock, worldwide. When network problems are detected, alerts are sent over the signaling network to centralized Network Operations Centers (NOCs) where technicians see visual indications of alarms on computer screens. Moreover, sections of carrier networks can be quickly reconfigured from commands sent by centralized network control centers.

When carriers transmit traffic to each other, signaling messages are used to identify each carrier's traffic. This is the method by which carriers bill one another for services that they provide. No carrier has facilities everywhere, so they rely on other providers' networks outside of their coverage area. For example, a provider that sells toll-free service to customers nationwide pays a fee for each call that terminates in another carrier's coverage area. Termination refers to the traffic destination. In the preceding example, a call terminates at the subscriber's location where it is answered.

Incompatibilities between Different SIP Implementations

SIP is an extremely flexible protocol that offers different ways to implement many IP applications. These differing methods are referred to as Requests for Comments (RFCs). RFCs were originally used only to solicit comments when standards are being developed. Once approved by standards bodies, the final versions of standards are then published as RFCs.

SIP has many RFCs, which has been a complicating factor when carriers connect with one another at peering sites and when carriers purchase new IP equipment from manufacturers that use different SIP implementations from the carrier's. In these cases, manufacturers modify their equipment to match the RFC implemented by the carrier for its network. The SIP Forum, a non-profit organization that advances interoperability and hosts interoperability testing, has simplified internetworking between carriers as well as between carriers and enterprises. The forum recommends specific profiles (RFCs) to use when connecting enterprise SIP trunks for VoIP service. Most carriers now use these and other specified profiles.

Interconnecting Carriers and Providing Secure Space for Equipment in Co-Location Facilities

Co-location facilities are sites where network service providers house their switches and routers and connect to one another's networks. Co-location facilities are also referred to as *carrier hotels*.

There are up to 200 carriers located at the very largest co-location sites. Co-location facilities are connected to the Internet, public and private data networks, and the PSTN. Because so many network providers depend on co-location facilities, security and sustainability in the face of natural and human-made disasters are critical. For these reasons, co-location facilities are located in secure buildings with few windows and no company logos to identify them. They are also monitored by security cameras and heavily guarded by security firms. They often additionally duplicate their service in a completely separate facility connected by fiber cabling to their main location.

Carriers rent space in co-location facilities because no provider has outside cabling everywhere. In addition, certain providers have no cabling facilities. Instead, they own switches, which they connect to other carriers' networks. In both of these circumstances, rather than construct their own buildings to house their switches, carriers lease space in carrier hotels. They place their equipment in cages or lease space in equipment cabinets in the carrier hotel. Locked wire cages surround the equipment and access to the equipment is available only to employees of the company that owns the equipment. Carriers also remotely access their servers to monitor and program their equipment. For even more reliability, some co-location facilities place redundant equipment at an additional co-location site.

Leasing space in carrier hotels saves network providers the expense of establishing and maintaining the following:

- Physical security against break-ins
- Access to large amounts of power
- Access to backup power
- Backup generators
- Dual air conditioning systems
- Uninterrupted power supplies
- Backup fiber cabling to the facility
- Fire detection and fire suppression equipment
- Alarms to fire and police departments
- Staff members to plan and maintain the facilities
- Construction of earthquake-resistant facilities

Carriers such as CenturyLink, AT&T, and Verizon have *carrier-owned co-location* facilities. These are generally in the same building as the carrier's Point of Presence (POP). Carriers offer a bundle of services at these facilities, including connections to routes connected to the co-location facility and connections to the carrier's POP, which is often located in the same building as the co-location services. AT&T and Verizon buy services from each other's co-location sites to reach customers whose locations are outside of areas in which they own access networks.

Another type of co-location facility is a carrier-neutral facility. *Neutral co-location facilities* are owned by non-carrier organizations, including Equinix, Markley Group, and Telehouse. Neutral refers to the fact that carriers that use these facilities can send traffic over routes offered by any carrier connected to the same facility. A carrier at a neutral site can lease routes from any other provider at the site, such as Windstream or CenturyLink. Carriers locate gateways, switches, and routers in these facilities to exchange traffic with other providers and to manage their own traffic.

Equinix provides data center services as well as co-location services. It is the largest provider of co-location and data center services worldwide.

Connecting Smaller Providers and Competitors to Customers

Telephone companies and Multiple System Operators (MSOs) rent various portions of their networks to smaller providers and to competitors that might have some of their own switches and/or long-haul networks, but no last-mile connections to customers. They offer access to their networks on a wholesale basis. For example, they offer connections between their POPs and their local central offices. These connections are considered *transport networks*. Smaller providers use these lines to transport traffic between their own switch (which might be located at the POP) and the local telephone company's switch. They also lease last-mile cabling infrastructure to reach each of their customers.

Both large and small providers make these arrangements with one another and with large enterprises. For example, Verizon sells services to large enterprises that have offices throughout the United States and around the world. Often, these enterprises purchase nationwide networking services for all of their locations. Verizon rents transport services from providers such as AT&T in cities where it does not own the local cabling infrastructure. Providers make these types of arrangements with carriers in other countries as well. AT&T, in turn, leases these services for its own large customers' remote offices that are located in areas where AT&T does not have its own last-mile network.

APPENDIX..

Table 4-2 SONET: A North American Standard for Multiplexing Streams of Traffic onto Fiber-Optic Cabling and Transporting It at Optical Carrier (OC) Speeds*

Speed	North American Synchronous Transport Signal (STS) Levels	SONET Channels	European Synchronous Transfer Mode (STM) Levels	Synchronous Digital Hierarchy (SDH) Channels
52Mbps	OC-1	28 DS1s or 1 DS3	STM-0	21 E1s
155Mbps	OC-3	84 DS1s or 3 DS3s	STM-1	63 E1s or 1 E4
622Mbps	OC-12	336 DS1s or 12 DS3s	STM-4	252 E1s or 4 E4s
2,488Mbps	OC-48	1,344 DS1s or 48 DS3s	STM-16	1,008 E1s or 16 E4s
9,953Mbps	OC-192	5,376 DS1s or 192 DS3s	STM-64	4,032 E1s or 64 E4s
39.812Gbps	OC-768	21,504 DS1s or 768 DS3s	STM-256	16,128 E1s or 256 E4s

SONET was developed to aggregate (multiplex) and carry TDM (Time Division Multiplexed) and circuit-switched voice traffic from multiple sources. The international version of SONET is Synchronous Digital Hierarchy (SDH). SONET SDH carries traffic at Synchronous Transfer Mode (STM) rates.

Table 4-3 Older PON Standards

	APON ATM PON	BPON Broadband PON	GPON Gigabit Ethernet PON	10G-EPON Gigabit Ethernet PON
Speed	622Mbps* (OC 12) downstream 155Mbps* (OC 3) upstream	622Mbps* upstream and downstream	2.5Gbps downstream 1.25 Gbps upstream	10 Gbps downstream 1Gbps upstream Or Symmetric 10Gbps upstream and downstream
Comment	Earliest PON standard	A faster version of APON	Efficient for IP traffic	Symmetric suited for commercial customers

Optical carrier

Table 4-4   DOCSIS Standards

Standard	Capabilities
DOCSIS 1.0	Two-way service for Internet access.
	Upstream speed of 5Mbps.
	Uniform specifications so that cable modems can be purchased from retail outlets that are compatible with cable operators' infrastructure.
DOCSIS 1.1	Increases the upstream speed to 10Mbps.
	Improves security and privacy.
	QoS enables operators to provide differentiated quality for VoIP and interactive services such as real time multiplayer games.
	Tier-based services such as higher speeds to heavy users who use more bandwidth or purchase additional data service.
DOCSIS 2.0	Increases upstream capacity to 30Mbps.
	Symmetric services such as those for business customers.
	Peer-to-peer such as VPN with site-to-site connectivity (see Chapter 5 for further information on VPN service).
DOCSIS 3.0	Supports higher capacity of 173Mbps to 343Mbps downstream to homes, 123Mbps upstream to the cable operator, and bonding. DOCSIS 3.0 includes support for IPTV.

5 Broadband Network Services

In this chapter:

INTRODUCTION ....

Today's broadband networks are increasingly made up of high-speed fiber-optic links with the augmented capacity required by the growing reliance on applications located on the Internet and in the cloud. Current workplaces cannot come close to functioning without the reliable, high-capacity broadband links now available. Older broadband technologies with capacity and flexibility limitations have limitations that make them unsuitable for most of today's requirements.

Carrier Gigabit Ethernet and dedicated wavelengths are largely replacing older, inflexible, limited-in-speed, broadband services wherever fiber cabling is available. Gigabit Ethernet is now commonly deployed on fiber cabling at enterprise locations. These links support speeds of up 100Gbps. But large social network companies are deploying 400 Gigabit connections at their data centers. Moreover, telephone companies' core networks that carry traffic between cities, states, and across the country are achieving terabit (thousand gigabit per second) speeds.

Dedicated wavelengths on fiber-optic cabling are a high-capacity alternative to Carrier Gigabit Ethernet. Dedicated wavelengths refer to a portion of the fiber-optic cabling capacity, an individual wavelength, dedicated to a single customer. These often link customers' branch offices, warehouses, and headquarters together.

While increasing capacity on fiberoptic cables is important, it doesn't solve the issues of managing traffic, prioritizing applications and automating functions in broadband networks. Wide Area Software Defined Networks (WA SDNs) are able to prioritize applications and automate routing on broadband networks. They can be programmed to automatically route traffic away from congested routes and parts of networks that are completely out of service.

This flexibility and automation is due to the defining aspect of WA SDN: it is controlled by software. This contrasts with earlier network protocols, which used hardware (routers, switches, and other adjuncts) to control traffic in packet networks. WA SDNs are a layer of software that runs on top of dedicated wavelengths and Gigabit Ethernet.

Multiprotocol Label Service (MPLS), which does prioritize voice and video, is still used by enterprises. However, the routing is rigid and the capacity is limited. It's not uncommon for MPLS and WA SDN to be present in the same enterprise networks with MPLS under the control of WA SDN.

Telephone companies, particularly in urban and suburban areas, are often dropping support for older, slower, inflexible services wherever fiber-optic cabling is available. The older services, mainly T1, T3, and DSL have severely limited capacity and less-flexible configurations than newer broadband. Moreover, it is more costly for telephone companies to support them than the more flexible Carrier Gigabit Ethernet and Dedicated Wavelength services. For these reasons, and because customers are demanding higher capacities, telephone companies are phasing out T1, T3, and DSL wherever fiber cabling is available.

As it's difficult for organizations to accomplish their day-to-day functions when their broadband networks are unavailable, reliability and availability are critical concerns. Many customers take it for granted that because there are few network outages, their broadband networks will be available 7 days a week, 24 hours a day. However, for large financial services companies and medical institutions, this is not adequate. Most of these large institutions have duplicate, backup fiber-optic lines connecting their buildings to broadband links if their primary links fail. Fiber-optic lines cut by a backhoe or a failure in the telephone company's equipment can cause failures.

Managed services are one way that carriers differentiate themselves from regional and smaller competitors, who sell discounted broadband services. Examples of managed services are managing Wi-Fi networks and consulting on data centers. In addition, large carriers distinguish themselves from smaller carriers by promoting their international presence. This is important for enterprises with a global infrastructure. A discount on mobile services is another distinguishing factor that large carriers offer major enterprise customers to lure them away from smaller telephone companies that may offer discounts in smaller regions of the country.

 NOTE The definition of broadband is not limited to signals carried over fiber optics, coaxial cabling, or twisted-pair copper cabling in carrier networks. Broadband capabilities are available in high-capacity mobile networks and satellite networks as well. Broadband networks are able to transmit large amounts of voice, data, and video simultaneously. Increased capacity on broadband networks is the main reason that in many homes, subscribers can watch different Netflix movies on two televisions simultaneously. Wireless broadband services are discussed in Chapter 7, "Mobile and Wi-Fi Networks."

Disagreement within the FCC over the Definition of Broadband

The Telecommunications Act of 1996 requires that the Federal Communications Commission annually:

- Review the definition of broadband

- Determine if advanced telecommunications (broadband) capability is being deployed to all Americans

- Analyze whether advanced telecommunications is deployed in a reasonable and timely fashion

- Define advanced telecommunications capability (data rates)

Defining advanced telecommunications capability means setting the minimum speed that fixed line network operators need to offer subscribers in order for the service to be considered broadband. In 2015 the FCC defined broadband as 25Mbps downstream and 3Mbps upstream. In 2017, the FCC affirmed the 25/3Mbps speeds, and also asked for comments on whether this capacity is adequate for today's needs.

Not everyone agrees with the FCC's definition of broadband. On August 8, 2017, FCC Commissioner Mignon L. Clyburn issued the following statement in response to the FCC's majority opinion keeping the definition of broadband as 25Mbps downstream and 3Mbps upstream. The following are excerpts from Clyburn's statement:

> *We sell consumers short by proposing a speed benchmark that is way too low. The statute defines ... broadband as ... 'capable of originating and receiving high-quality voice, data, graphics and video telecommunications'... the 25/3Mbps standard we propose would not even allow for a single stream of 1080p video conferencing....*

The designation 1080p (1080 pixels) refers to the resolution (number of pixels) on televisions and video conferencing. A pixel can be thought of as a dot or picture element. 1080p is the resolution generally found in high-definition transmissions to televisions.

Broadband Worldwide

A report commissioned by the Broadband Forum and conducted by the market analyst firm Point Topic revealed that there were a total of 871.1 million fixed-broadband subscribers worldwide at the end of the first quarter of 2017. The report covers only broadband access over cabling and fixed, point-to-point wireless services. According to *China Money*'s April 27, 2017, article "China's Fixed-Line Broadband Penetration Rate To Hit 63% This Year" by Pan Yue, China had 310 million broadband subscribers. This is the highest number of broadband subscribers in a single country worldwide. According to statistics company Statista, as of the end of the first quarter of 2017, the United States had 93.9 million broadband subscribers. This is the second-highest number of broadband subscribers worldwide according to Point Topic.

Many people in less-developed parts of the world access the Internet primarily over mobile services. This is because dedicated Internet access over landline networks is frequently either not available or more costly than mobile services in these areas. In addition, electricity is often expensive. In the Philippines, both ISP-delivered dedicated Internet access and electricity are too costly for most citizens. Thus, mobile services are attractive as electricity is only required for charging laptops, tablet computers, and other devices that are equipped with mobile capabilities. Moreover, a single device can be used to make calls and to access sites such as Facebook.

While current mobile networks support broadband services, they're slower than those over most wireline networks. However, new technologies and upgrades to existing standards are vastly improving Internet access on mobile networks and spurring adoption of mobile broadband. See Chapter 7 for information on 5G mobile protocols.

> ### Actual Speeds vs. Advertised Speeds: The Discrepancies Vary
>
> The biggest discrepancies between advertised and achievable, maximum speeds on broadband occur on DSL services. Maximum speeds on DSL are not always reached due to factors such as network congestion, slow-loading web sites, long distances from telephone companies' equipment, and underperforming network equipment. According to the FCC 2016 report "Measuring Broadband America," cable TV providers and Hughes satellite services mostly attained the highest advertised speeds. The same is true for telephone companies that build out fiber to people's homes. However, advertised speeds were not achieved uniformly across the United States. In New York City, for example, on February 1, 2017, New York State's Attorney General, Eric T. Schneiderman, issued a press release announcing that he had filed a lawsuit against Time Warner Cable, part of Spectrum-Time Warner Cable, for advertising misleading Internet speeds. In his press release Schneiderman stated:
>
> > *Wired Internet speeds for the premium plan (100, 200, and 300 Mbps) were up to 70 percent slower than promised.*
>
> Exacerbating subscribers' frustration at the time was the fact that subscribers in many areas of the city had only Time Warner's Internet access as a choice for Internet access.

VOIP CALLING SERVICES OVER BROADBAND.........

When voice is transmitted on broadband networks using Voice over Internet Protocol (VoIP), voice is digitized and bundled into packets to make it compatible with the data packets on broadband networks. Packets are similar to envelopes in that they include headers that specify addressee and sender information (one of the ways that they differ, of course, is that they also provide error correction). Because headers are carried along with data packets, they interface more easily with computer services such as e-mail. Standard computer platforms are used to manage VoIP services.

Residential vs. Enterprise Services

When VoIP services such as Skype were first available, residential customers adopted them before the more cautious enterprises saw their value and began adopting them in large numbers. Additionally, small businesses used VoIP and its related services before large enterprise customers, who were concerned with quality and security lapses. As capacity in broadband networks increased and delays decreased, larger enterprises began using VoIP and its features. Non-profits, businesses, and commercial firms commonly use conference calling, unified communications, and other features available at low costs from VoIP providers over broadband networks. Large telephone and cable TV companies now commonly offer these features as well.

Lower-Priced, Flexible Consumer VoIP Services Adopted by Enterprises

Many consumers and organizations use VoIP for their phone calls. These calls are often carried over their broadband links. Large telephone companies are transitioning their calling services to low-cost VoIP where voice is just another piece of data on the network. VoIP services include features such as voicemail, audio conferences, video conferencing, and unified communications. See Figure 5-1 for transmission of voice on carriers' networks. Because this results in the need to maintain only one type of network—a data network—increasing numbers of enterprise and residential customers' calls are now carried as packets along with video and data traffic. Without VoIP, carriers are required to support both voice and data networks.

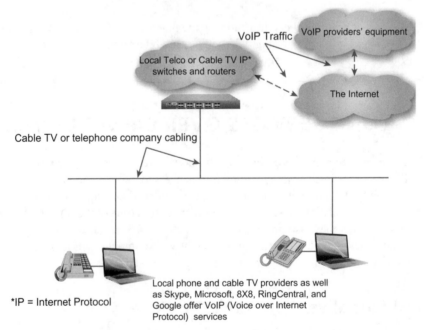

Figure 5-1 *Transmitting Voice over IP traffic (VoIP) on carriers' infrastructure.*

Skype for Enterprises – Microsoft Teams

Consumers embraced VoIP calling because of its low prices and sometimes free service. Examples of VoIP providers include Google, magicJack, RingCentral, Skype, and Vonage. Initially, business customers were leery of using these services both because they weren't sure that the quality was up to their standards and because there wasn't sufficient security protection. However, as employees began using VoIP in their homes, that changed.

Skype was the first VoIP service that enterprises used in large numbers. Their initial rationale for using Skype was the savings on international calling, and low-cost audio and video conferencing. Acceptance accelerated when Microsoft bought Skype as a replacement to its Linc VoIP offering. Microsoft's Skype for Business, renamed Microsoft Teams, includes a server through which all messages between employees within the same building and in buildings connected to the enterprise's network are sent. The server scans packets for malicious transmissions. These servers are now typically located in the cloud.

Because VoIP calls are essentially data within packets, telephone and cable TV providers began rolling out VoIP service to both their enterprise and residential customers. Providers that deploy VoIP in their networks use up less capacity for voice because VoIP packets are transmitted as data along the same part of networks as data traffic. This results in more room for data. In addition, VoIP switches and servers are less costly to purchase and maintain because the software is installed on commodity servers that take up less space than traditional switches used to transmit voice based on time division multiplexing (TDM). TDM uses more capacity than VoIP because capacity is saved in each time slot even when there are pauses in traffic. This wastes capacity. Many providers are eliminating their TDM services both because its capacity is too low and it is not efficient for data traffic. They are replacing TDM with Carrier Ethernet. See below for Carrier Ethernet and the "Appendix" for TDM.

VoIP for Very Small Organizations

Very small organizations and start-ups with fewer than 25 employees often use services from companies such as Google, Skype, and Vonage that have been adapted for business to replace traditional, on-site telephone systems. For example, features might include the ability to transfer calls to another employee in the same facility or in a remote office. The features provided also include a fixed, single phone number for mobile devices, work phones, and home phones, with a single voicemail box for messages from these three types of devices. It can also include audio and video conferencing. Some of these features were previously only available for large organizations with complex, onsite phone systems.

These VoIP services enable organizations to develop a new business or service without purchasing hardware for a telephone system. In addition, the services can be used for businesses in which all or many of their staff members work at home or in remote offices.

Even midsize and large organizations with their own onsite telephone systems often use these network-based VoIP services for certain functions. One of the most common functions is desktop video conferencing from Microsoft Teams or Google. Desktop videoconferences are transmitted over data networks, and they typically require nothing more in terms of equipment than the personal computers or laptops of the participants. In particular, people working from home or traveling can participate in these conferences, incurring minimal or no charges. Consumers and small organizations still use Skype, but large organizations are transition to Microsoft Teams.

The Impact of VoIP and Wi-Fi on Traditional Carriers

Consumers and business people alike use Skype, social media features, and Wi-Fi via cell phones to call home and the office when they travel. The savings are significant when travelers use these low-cost services to call their home or business from international sites. In addition, many immigrants and international students use video and audio calling to stay in touch with family members in their native countries. Using these services for free or low cost video conferences is particularly meaningful as people see facial expressions, and grandparents and close relatives stay in touch with grandchildren with firsthand images of them as they grow.

In addition, social network apps WhatsApp, Weibo, Weixin (WeChat in English), QQ, and Viber provide low-cost or free international calls. Moreover, international calls on certain mobile phones are free if they're made over Wi-Fi networks. Calls over Wi-Fi are particularly cost-effective on international calls.

The Demarcation Point at Which Telephone Companies Wire Trunks

The local telephone company brings telephone lines into buildings and wires them to interfaces. The interface is called a *jack* or a *punch-down block*. Each outside line is punched down (wired) to the connecting block. *RJ11c* jacks connect one line per jack. The RJ stands for *registered jack*. These are the jacks found in most homes. The *RJ21x*, which holds 25 lines, is the interface to which local telephone companies wire multiple, outside lines in businesses. The RJ21x jack is a point from which telephone lines and trunks can be tested. For instance, if there is a question with regard to where a problem lies, the telephone company can test its trunk to the RJ21x jack, and the equipment vendor can test service between the equipment or router and the interface. The RJ21x jack is the demarcation point between the telephone company line and the inside wiring.

The most common data jack is the *RJ48* jacks. Data trunks such as Carrier Gigabit Ethernet terminate on these connectors. Both these jacks are at customer premises, and they are the points at which telephone companies test trunks if there is an outage. The most common type of high-speed trunk for incoming customer contact centers is Carrier Gigabit Ethernet for data. Information on these services is in Chapter 4, "Managing Broadband Networks."

MULTI-PROTOCOL LABEL SWITCHING FOR INTEROFFICE CONNECTIONS ....

Multi-Protocol Label Switching (MPLS) is a Virtual Private Network (VPN) network service that large and midsize organizations deploy to link their domestic and international sites together. MPLS traffic is carried on a provider's core private data network rather than on the Internet. MPLS is suitable for transmitting packetized voice (VoIP), video, and data between sites. MPLS is starting to be replaced by Wide Area Software Defined Networks (WA SDNs) services, which have more capacity and flexible treatment by type of content, as well as flexible, real time routing. An example is Comcast that no longer offers MPLS and is promoting WA SDNs instead for enterprise customers.

MPLS Virtual Private Network—A Managed Service

MPLS provides VPN (Virtual Private Network) features. VPNs have the features and functionality of private networks. However, unlike private lines, which are not shared and are for the exclusive use of a single organization, MPLS operates on network links shared by other customers. The links are virtually private, and offer many of the features found on private lines such as user control and privacy. In addition, they are less costly than private lines to lease and operate.

MPLS has the capability to classify traffic so that voice and video have higher priorities than services such as file transfer and e-mail, which are less sensitive to delay. Because of these and other capabilities managed by providers, MPLS is also referred to as a *managed network service*.

Routes and Security on MPLS

MPLS is inherently more secure than using the Internet for site-to-site traffic and access to other networks because it is transmitted over a carrier's private data network. For added protection from hackers, customers often use separate circuits to access MPLS circuits and the Internet. This is more costly than combining access to both services on the same line, but it isolates MPLS transmissions even further from viruses and attacks sent over the Internet. Figure 5-2 illustrates an example of segregated circuits for Internet access and MPLS service.

MPLS minimizes traffic jams by selecting the shortest, least-congested route for all messages in each transmission. *All packets in every message are sent over the same route.* In contrast, in WA SDN networks, each packet can travel on a different path, depending on congestion or network failures.

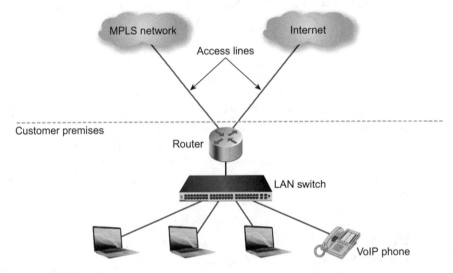

LAN = Local Area Network
VoIP = Voice over Internet Protocol

Figure 5-2 Implementing separate access to the Internet and a Multi-Protocol Label Switching (MPLS) network.

MPLS Implementation

When customers sign up for MPLS service, they give their provider a list of the IP addresses associated with each site that they want included in their MPLS service. Each IP address identifies a specific location on a network. The carrier uses this list to define a closed group of sites that are allowed to communicate with one another over the MPLS network. The list can be amended by notifying carriers of IP addresses to be added or deleted.

In addition to an IP address, each location connected to the MPLS network requires an access line from the customer to the carrier's network. However, a single link from each location can transmit messages to all sites. Each location does not need a separate physical connection to every other site on the MPLS network. The MPLS service is referred to as an *any-to-any* network.

 NOTE MPLS is a Layer 3 protocol that switches traffic between IP addresses rather than Media Access Control (MAC) addresses. MAC addresses are assigned to individual computers and other devices on a network. With MAC addressing the message is received at the customer end, and onsite equipment sends the MPLS content to individual devices. By contrast, IP addresses are assigned to the network or to the Virtual LAN (VLAN). Managing fewer addresses makes routing by using MPLS with its IP addressing less complex to manage. It also enables networks to scale to larger sizes. MPLS is an optional feature in routers.

MPLS for Multinational Locations

Internationally, most large providers have a presence in Europe, the United States, the Middle East, and parts of Asia. However, they have less presence in fewer Latin American cities, and the lowest presence in Africa. The term *presence* means that they have a switch in a local provider's Point of Presence (POP). A POP is the physical building in which a telephone company's switch (central office) is located. The POP is connected to the Internet as well as to other central offices that are located close to customers.

For remote countries in which carriers have a switch, large carriers including Verizon and AT&T have agreements with local providers. These agreements specify the type of circuit (local access line) from the customer to the local provider's network and at what price the local provider will lay cabling from the distant office to the MPLS carrier's switch. MPLS carriers place orders with local providers for access lines to the remote offices of MPLS customers. This creates international MPLS networks.

An issue in designing MPLS networks for international organizations is that rural and sparsely populated areas often don't have MPLS available from the same carrier that installs the service for the rest of the enterprise. (Because of technical and network management incompatibilities, MPLS requires that the same carrier supply end-to-end service for each site on the network.) This is particularly problematic in underdeveloped areas such as parts of Africa and outside of most populated cities in Latin America.

Prioritizing Traffic via Classes of Service

When customers want to differentiate certain traffic for specific treatment, they select from their carrier's list of classes of service. These classes of service are used to define the priority given to traffic for each class. For example, there might be three classes for data, one for voice, and another (the most expensive) for video. Voice and video are generally assigned higher priorities than data. Routers at customer sites add bits to packet headers with Class of Service (CoS) designations. At the MPLS edge router, these designations are added to the MPLS labels, along with addressing data.

Some organizations use the lowest-priced CoS for most data and higher-priced CoS for database lookups. This can vary by industry. Retail organizations that depend on point-of-sale credit card lookups for revenue might assign these applications the highest priority. Carriers apply CoS according to tags attached to packets for each protocol. Routers attach a different type of tag to packets containing e-mail messages from those that contain video. Carriers that don't meet these SLAs generally rebate agreed-upon credits to customers.

MPLS Service Components

In addition to classes of service, customers also specify the following:

- A *port speed* at the provider's POP, often at a lower speed than their access line. The port speed refers to the number of bits per second that can enter the carrier's network.

- Additional managed services including managed security, and the use of the provider's network and staff for operating, setting up, and managing the videoconferences.

- The *speed of the access line*, which is the circuit connecting the customer to the provider's network. Typically, remote offices use slower-speed Gigabit Ethernet; higher-trafficked headquarters use Carrier Gigabit Ethernet at speeds ranging from 100Mbps to 400Gbps. Higher-capacity services cost more than slower services.

IP VIRTUAL PRIVATE NETWORKS OVER THE INTERNET ....

Internet Protocol Virtual Private Networks (IP VPNs) provide the features of private dedicated links, without the cost of leasing dedicated circuits from ISPs or MPLS. Rather, each location leases a line connected to the Internet from the local telephone company. These leased lines use IP VPN technology for site-to-site links, access to the cloud, and for remote access from:

- Branch offices

- Employees' homes to access computer files at headquarters

- Other cities in which employees are traveling

Using IP VPNs between Offices—Less Costly than MPLS

Organizations use IP VPNs to link sites together so that remote offices can share resources such as centrally located e-mail, Internet access, and applications. A particular difference between IP VPN, SDN, and MPLS networks is that organizations that use IP VPNs only pay for Internet access. This is a major cost advantage in favor of IP VPNs. Some companies do pay carriers for security services to screen incoming traffic for viruses. However, IP VPNs do not offer Quality of Service (QoS) or Class of Service (CoS). Thus, voice, video, and remote desktop traffic are treated the same as e-mail messages.

However, IP VPNs do not guarantee quality of service (QoS). If there's congestion, packets are dropped. IP-based networks such as the Internet are *connectionless*. With connectionless networks, each packet is transmitted as a separate entity. Unlike MPLS, a path is not saved in the network for the entire transmission. Rather, every packet can take a different route, and if there is congestion on a particular route, packets are dropped. The router at the receiving end reassembles packets into their original form, minus the dropped packets.

Real time applications such as voice, video, and remote desktop access are more vulnerable to dropped packets than e-mail messages. E-mail messages don't have the urgency of delivery and gaps between delivery of parts of e-mails are not noticeable. However, dropping parts of voice or video streams can result in choppy voice and video with noticeably poor quality. As more long form video traffic is sent over the Internet from mobile devices and landline facilities, the likelihood of congestion and dropped packets increases.

Another issue with IP VPNs is that they are not inherently secure. Thus, organizations add security protocols to IP VPNs, bits at the beginning and end of each packet to hide packet content from snoopers and hackers. The main security protocols used in conjunction with IP VPNs are described below in the section "Adding Security on Traffic Sent Over IP VPNs."

Avoiding Congestion on IP VPNs—Access to the Internet Service Provider

The most common points of congestion in IP VPNs are the access lines connecting organizations to the Internet and points in the Internet where carriers connect their networks together. Organizations can add capacity to their headquarters and branch office access lines, but they have no control over capacity on the Internet itself. If an organization experiences congestion on its access circuits, it has the option of adding access lines or increasing the capacity of its existing access circuits. It can upgrade to Carrier Gigabit Ethernet from slower data rate megabit Ethernet.

In addition to monitoring and upgrading access circuits, where possible, organizations lease Internet access from the same provider at all of their sites to limit the number of carriers from whom they get service. This is not possible in remote and international areas where the primary carrier does not provide coverage.

ADDING SECURITY ON TRAFFIC SENT OVER IP VPNS...

Because the Internet is open to users from all over the world, organizations deploy security software designed to protect information from snoopers. Most security protocols on IP VPNs employ tunneling and encryption. Tunnels surround packets with bits that protect privacy on the packets, and encryption uses complex mathematical algorithms to scramble bits so that only matching protocols at the receiving end of the transmission can unscramble (decrypt) the bits into readable formats. Virtual Private Networks have many of the features of private lines dedicated to single organizations, but they are not dedicated to single enterprises in a carrier's private network. They are sent over the Internet where they share capacity other data sent over the Internet.

Security Protocols on Access to IP VPNs

Security protocols designed for IP VPNs all create a *tunnel* for their transmission. Tunnels are special bits at the beginning and end of each packet. In essence, the tunnel encapsulates messages so that others cannot see what is being transmitted.

Tunneling protocols establish a secure connection between the corporate Local Area Network (LAN) and the remote user by encrypting and tunneling the bits and hiding the IP header in each packet. This ensures privacy. Tunneling prevents hackers from learning corporate LAN IP addresses. Specific protocols encrypt packets to further protect their privacy. *Encryption* is the use of a complex mathematical algorithm to reorder bits so that only the receiving end with matching encryption is able to decipher and read them.

To access the corporate network, customers with broadband services log on to the public Internet. From there, traffic is routed to the Internet and then to the megabit or gigabit dedicated access line connected to their remote place of business. For organizations that allow remote access to headquarters applications and files, remote users are routed via the Internet to the organization's headquarters, as indicated in Figure 5-3.

The most common security protocols on access networks are the following:

- **Internet Protocol Security (IPsec)**   This is an older security protocol that requires software to be installed in every computer that accesses the network remotely.

- **Layer 2 Tunneling Protocol (L2TP)**   This protocol evolved from an earlier protocol Point-to-Point Tunneling Protocol (PPTP) developed by Microsoft; it has stronger authentication security for screening devices that access the network. L2TP is also used with IPsec.

- **Transport Layer Security (TLS)**   This is a newer access method that does not require client software. The earlier version was Secure Socket Layer.

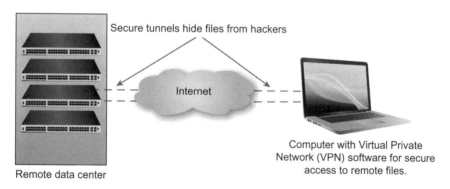

Figure 5-3   *Secure access to headquarters' files over an IP VPN with tunneling protocol to protect data transmitted over the Internet.*

The Complexities of Using VPNs with IPsec

Internet Protocal Security (IPsec) is a protocol that requires users to install IPSec software on their devices. IT staff members distribute software to each person's computer. (They also handle calls from employees who are having trouble logging on to the VPN or who have lost their laptop or smartphone.) Employees can only access their e-mail and other applications from their own computer or supported mobile smartphone, such as an Android or iPhone.

Users work with IPsec *client software* installed on their computers launch the remote access client. Client software enables access to applications located on other computers or servers, usually in data centers or the cloud. It is supplied and licensed by the organization that develops the IPsec software. The client software is a special program written to interact with security software located in the data center and cloud.

Layer 2 Tunneling Protocol

Layer 2 Tunneling Protocol (L2TP) initial versions from Microsoft do not provide encryption and are often replaced by up-to-date versions. There is a new version of L2TP that has improved its tunneling. Like PPTP, it is also used with IPsec for encryption. In addition, IPsec has stronger authentication than L2TP.

Secure Sockets Layer/ Transport Layer Security

Secure Sockets Layer (SSL)/Transport Layer Security (TLS) is a newer VPN protocol than IPsec. SSL/TLS is a clientless protocol; that is, it does not require the installation of client software on each computer that's used for remote access. Rather, SSL/TLS works from within standard browsers on computers and smartphones. This makes VPNs easier to use and requires less administrative support from IT personnel. The simplified login results in fewer user errors. Recent releases of SSL are referred to as *Transport Layer Security* (TLS). For added security, SSL is frequently used with tunneling protocols.

Because it is a higher-level security protocol, SSL installed on *appliances* can enable access to particular applications based on privileges granted to classes of employees. An appliance is a specialized computer that is dedicated to a particular application.

It's possible for remote computers to pass viruses to corporate networks, so some SSL appliances have the capability to scan remote computers for antivirus software and automatically download patches to computers that don't have the latest security updates. Other appliances have the capability to remotely wipe out passwords and corporate data from shared computers in public areas such as libraries and airports. This eliminates the possibility of computers in locations such as kiosks to store and pass on private information and passwords.

Adding Additional Layers of Protection with Two- and Three-Factor Authentication

Most remote access requires *two-* and sometimes *three-factor authentication*. Two-factor authentication requires a password plus a way to identify that the user is who he or she claims to be. Two-factor security is a safeguard that prevents unauthorized users from using stolen passwords, social security numbers, or birthdays to log into files. Three-factor authentication might require a token ID in addition to a password plus biologic identification. A hacker with a stolen password would most likely not have the means to be authenticated. Authentication refers to the requirement that users prove to computer systems that they are who they claim to be and are authorized to log on to the network.

Security software at the user's organization issues prompts for usernames, passwords, and a form or multiple forms of authentication such as:

- A token ID (identification), which is a small dongle with a screen, which can be attached to a key chain. Random numbers that change about every 60 seconds appear on the token's screen and are typed into the users' screen for access to the cloud, a secure area such as a lab, or particular files.

- A security app from iPhone, Amazon, or Google requesting a user ID and password plus a code sent by Apple, Amazon, or Google.

- A text message with a code sent to a user's phone that the user types in to gain access.

- Biologic authentication such as a fingerprint, iris, or facial recognition scan.

To prevent remote users from passing viruses from the Internet to corporate networks, the client software will often not function if there is an open connection to the Internet while the user is logged on remotely.

Deploying Firewalls to Protect against Malicious Attacks

A firewall is a device, software application, or set of devices at carriers, enterprises, and homes that screens incoming and internal traffic to prevent hackers from accessing files. Firewalls deny hackers access by allowing only designated users to access networks. In an organization's network, firewall software is installed on routers and appliances. For additional protection, organizations that use their carrier's firewall protection have onsite firewall protection, as well.

Firewalls provide networks partial protection against Distributed Denial-of-Service (DDoS) attacks and intrusion. They use various techniques including *address filtering*, which looks at a user's IP address and accepts or rejects messages based on that address. Important applications might contain their own firewalls for extra protection. Communications can also be restricted to certain addresses. Firewalls contain hundreds of ports and can filter on a port-by-port basis. In addition, they can be programmed to recognize applications and content and pass them through the firewall using a specific port. However, even with these filtering capabilities, DDoS attacks can congest access to the organization's files.

Firewall ports can be virtual as well as associated with physical equipment within the firewall. A virtual port is programmed to allow certain traffic such as VoIP calls to pass through the firewall to its destination. A virtual port is represented in software.

Because employees use their laptops at home to surf the Web and then bring them into work, corporations monitor internal transmissions as well as communications from the Internet. Many organizations program employees' remote computers to reach only locations on the Internet deemed secure to avoid contamination from Internet locations that have viruses that can spread to the corporate LAN.

Firewalls don't protect against, for example, new (*black day*) viruses and all e-mail spam. Corporations often subscribe to security services that keep them posted about new software attacks. The security software monitors their networks for unusual amounts or types of traffic and downloads software patches for protection against new types of attacks.

Firewalls as a Service—FaaS

Instead of supporting on-site firewalls, organizations have the option of using a cloud provider's firewall service. For example, a multisite enterprise may choose to contract for Firewall as a Service rather than installing and maintaining a firewall at each of their branch offices and warehouses. In these instances a service provider's staff maintains the firewall and keeps it updated to protect from new viruses and new security threats.

All traffic flows through the cloud provider's firewall rather than through onsite firewalls. Because of their greater capacity, FaaS may be better able to protect organizations from Distributed Denial of Service attacks because of their firewalls' greater capacities and speed than many customers' onsite firewalls.

Safeguarding Privacy and Intellectual Property by Employing Property Data Loss Management

Organizations are legally obligated to protect the privacy of their employees. There are privacy statutes that prohibit enterprises from sharing employee and customer personal information such as Social Security numbers, license numbers, credit card data, and data collected by human resources. In addition, companies need to protect their strategic plans, medicine formularies, and product designs from leaking. These assets are considered *intellectual property*.

To accomplish these goals, organizations use property data loss management software to scan outgoing e-mail. The software is programmed to flag specific words relating to their products or services as well as key phrases or formats which indicate that credit card data, social security numbers, or license numbers are included in a message. Flagged messages can be manually scrutinized. To protect privacy, enterprises and universities may have policies limiting which computers store private information such as social security numbers.

MANAGED SERVICES...

Managed services are add-on consulting, cloud-based, or software services that carriers offer customers. These offerings are intended to supplement carriers' long distance and local calling service revenues. But an important goal is to make it more difficult and complex for customers to change providers. Managed services are considered "sticky." The more managed services that customers use, the more dependent they are on carriers, and the more complex it is for these customers to change providers.

Managed Services Rather than Dumb Pipe Providers

Many carriers view broadband offerings such as private data lines, MPLS, and Gigabit Ethernet (GigE) as commodities available from other providers. To avoid being organizations whose only offerings are characterized as dumb pipes with commodity services, carriers often distinguish themselves from competing carriers by offering specialized and managed services. Without distinguishing features, customers can shop around for the lowest price on, for example, Gigabit Ethernet.

Managed services are one way that carriers differentiate themselves from smaller competitors. Moreover, managed services provide an additional monthly revenue stream for carriers and help to cement the relationship between themselves and their customers. This is because it is complex and potentially disruptive for international enterprises to change both their network and their security provider or data center service across all of their sites. Thus, supplying this wider range of services creates a "stickier" relationship with customers, and a sticky customer is one that is less likely to change vendors.

In addition, carriers such as Verizon, Sprint, and AT&T have the resources to build international data centers and hosting facilities as well as hire consultants with specialized skills in developing applications for vertical markets such as healthcare, transportation, and insurance.

Managed Services—For a Variety of Functions

Carriers have long offered managed services in conjunction with the networking devices connected to broadband services. In addition to managing servers, routers, and modems, they now offer to manage the NFV (Network Function Virtualization) hardware containing routers, firewalls, and security applications represented as software in off-the-shelf servers. The NFV server is connected to a customer's broadband circuits. Carriers additionally offer more complex, varied services in the hope that customers will be attracted to the possibility of one provider managing their wide area, mobile, Wi-Fi, and computer networks. These offerings include the following:

- Hosting applications in carrier data centers
- Storing and backing up files remotely
- Developing software applications to be run in carrier data centers
- Operating room type video conferences
- Security consulting
- GPS tracking solutions for fleet management
- Consulting on call center services
- Managing outsourced data centers at carrier facilities
- Providing and designing interactive voice response services with menus such as:
  - Press 1 for Sales
  - Press 2 for Marketing
- Offering security services that protect against Distributed Denial of Service attacks and viruses
- Connecting to cloud computing sites
- Storing data in the cloud
- Managing employee mobile devices

In conjunction with managed services, carriers have personnel who have expertise in particular managed services for wireline as well as mobile networks. These include experts in enterprise mobile devices, video conferencing, security, data centers, contact centers, and wireless LANs (Wi-Fi networks).

Many carriers that own mobile and landline networks recognize the potential of mobile services. Their sales staff who were previously dedicated to only landline or only mobile products and services now sell products and services for both mobile and landline networks. They actively promote mobile managed services that improve productivity such as developing applications for service organizations that dispatch technicians to homes or businesses. When a carrier's account staff determines that there might be a mobile application to increase productivity, it brings in experts to meet with its customer. After learning about the customer's needs, these experts propose a consulting service to develop a software application to address those needs.

DIGITAL SUBSCRIBER LINE—DISTANCE LIMITATIONS; OPERATES ON COPPER CABLING......

Local telephone companies introduced Digital Subscriber Line (DSL) technology in 1989. The telephone companies saw the advantage of using existing copper cabling to combine voice and data on the same copper cabling that was ubiquitous in developed countries. However, DSL has capacity and distance limitations that make it less suitable than transmissions now available over fiber cabling. Higher capacity broadband technologies are replacing DSL in areas with fiber-optic cabling.

How DSL Technology Works

DSL operates over the same copper cabling used for voice in last-mile networks close to homes and small businesses. Very-High-Data-Rate DSL (VDSL2) gear supports high-definition TV, voice, and Internet access over short lengths of copper cabling. The most advanced DSL service, VDSL2, supports 200Mbps on cable lengths up to 1,000 feet. The copper cabling transmits these signals between a user's premises and a provider's fiber-optic cabling in cabinets or neighborhood nodes. (See Table 5-4 in the "Appendix" section at the end of this chapter for information on the types of DSL.)

DSL Limitations

On copper cabling, background noise intrudes, or "leaks," from adjacent copper wires (crosstalk) or a nearby electric motor (electromagnetic interference). To prevent transmission degradation and speed loss, equipment on advanced DSL services constantly monitor the line for noise. Monitoring is complex because noise can change over time.

DSL services over higher frequencies carry more bits in shorter time spans than lower frequencies. Think of it in terms of a commuter subway system:

- If the trains don't come very often (low frequencies), fewer people are moved in a given span of time;
- If the trains arrive more often (higher frequencies), more people will be moved through the system in the same time period.

Both copper cabling used for DSL and wireless services carry signals that are made up of wavelengths (frequencies). Low frequencies have longer wavelengths that can carry signals over greater distances. High frequencies have shorter wavelengths that do not travel as far, but they can squeeze more bits into each transmission.

To achieve greater capacity, DSL must use high frequencies. However, the shorter wavelengths render high-frequency signals more vulnerable to damage from environmental sources such as magnetic interference. At the same time, vulnerability to attenuation (weakening and fading) means that high speeds are supported only on short lengths of copper cabling. Some carriers use bonding to increase the capacity on DSL. Bonding also has the advantage of increasing the length of cable over which high frequency DSL signals can travel before they fade.

> **NOTE** Bonding is the use of equipment called inverse multiplexers to increase bandwidth by combining two or more circuits or pairs of copper cabling such that they act as a single circuit. Providers that don't have fiber in an area may double the speed of DSL service by bonding two DSL circuits together using an inverse multiplexer. See Figure 5-4 for an example of bonding on DSL. Bonding is also used to add capacity on direct interconnections to providers' clouds. See the section "Direct Dedicated Interconnections to the Cloud" later in this chapter for information on Dedicated Interconnections.

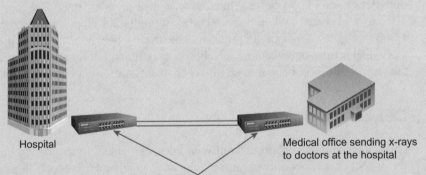

Hospital

Medical office sending x-rays to doctors at the hospital

Inverse multiplexers bonding two lines together to double the capacity

Figure 5-4 An example of bonding two DSL circuits together to double its capacity.

Replacing DSL with Higher-Capacity Fiber and Wireless

Carriers are replacing DSL because of its lower capacity and because enterprises and residential subscribers require higher broadband capacity to access cloud-based applications, stream video, make purchases, and access social networks. Carriers are replacing DSL with Gigabit Ethernet wherever increasing amounts of fiber cabling are available. In rural areas they are replacing DSL with fixed wireless to reach customers.

IP Addressing and Symmetric Speeds for Business Customers

IP addresses use a numerical format such as 193.555.46.329 that is translated into words such as ABCcompany.com. IP addresses can be either static or dynamic.

Dynamic IP addressing refers to the fact that carriers don't assign permanent IP addresses to particular customers or devices such as routers. Rather, carriers assign IP addresses on the fly from a pool of addresses as they are transmitted. Dynamic IP addresses can be reused after being idle for a specified period.

In this way, they don't use up as many scarce IP addresses. Residential customers that publish unique e-mail addresses, e.g. johnsmith@localcompany.com, obtain their e-mail address from non-telephone companies such as Google. They specify forwarding for their e-mail messages at their telephone company that provides their broadband service. Their broadband provider forwards all e-mail from johnsmith@localcompany.com using a dynamic IP address.

Static IP addressing is for the most part used by business customers who buy the rights to use the address. With static IP, customers select their own unique fixed-IP address using their domain name (such as J.smith@ABCcompany) for their e-mail address. Enterprises pay an extra fee for every static IP address that they have.

CARRIER GIGABIT ETHERNET ....

Carrier Gigabit Ethernet (GigE) is a site-to-site and Internet access high-speed service. Gigabit Ethernet uses the Ethernet protocol to reach Gigabit capacity on broadband networks. It operates over fiber-optic cabling. GigE transmits data, video, images, and packetized voice (VoIP). It is the most commonly used broadband technology for enterprises.

Carrier GigE was first introduced in the late 1990s. At that time, it was not widely available, both because it required fiber-optic cabling to the customer and because the central offices of providers were not widely equipped with GigE switches. In contrast, carriers now offer GigE services to small and medium-sized organizations as well as large ones. GigE is now more widely available because more central offices have been equipped to support it and fiber is more widely deployed to business customers. These services start at speeds of 10Mbps and currently scale up to 100Gbps. Capacity is expected to increase to 400Gbps in the future. Facebook and Google are experimenting with 400 Gigabit Ethernet in the WAN.

Bandwidth demand by all types of organizations has created the impetus for carriers to invest in gear that meets this demand. Customers that previously used T3 service now have either Megabit or Gigabit Ethernet. Smaller organizations can order the slower Ethernet service of 20, 30, or 60 megabits with the option to easily upgrade later. Moreover, most carriers including Windstream, Verizon, and AT&T have retired all non-Ethernet services including T1 and T3 services.

Carrier Gigabit Ethernet Flexibility and Scalable Speeds

Gigabit Ethernet is offered by carriers for accessing the Internet, MPLS networks, and connections to other sites within cities. When used for accessing these networks, enterprises might use GigE at their headquarters. At remote sites, depending on the level of traffic at each site, slower data rates might be adequate. See Figure 5-5 for an example of Carrier Gig-E at a multi-site organization. Importantly, once Carrier GigE is installed, enterprise customers can request that their telephone company provider increase or decrease the capacity of their service remotely. This is done by modifying data rates remotely at the central office. Cabling does not have to be changed and most customers' Carrier Ethernet switches can be programmed for added capacity. Because there are few requirements for technicians onsite to make changes, GigE is less costly to support than the older T1 and T3 services.

Organizations with many buildings within cities also use GigE for point-to-point private lines within the metropolitan area. See Figure 5-5 for Ethernet links between buildings in a campus. These organizations include large hospitals, universities, and government offices that use GigE to transfer large files between sites. One example is the connection between hospitals and the facilities where patient records and imaging files are stored. It is also used for connections to storage area networks (SANs) that hold backup files. Access to the backup files is via either the Internet or private lines. Finally, higher level services such as WA SDN services are carried on Carrier Gigabit networks. For an over view of broadband network services see Table 5-2 in the "Appendix."

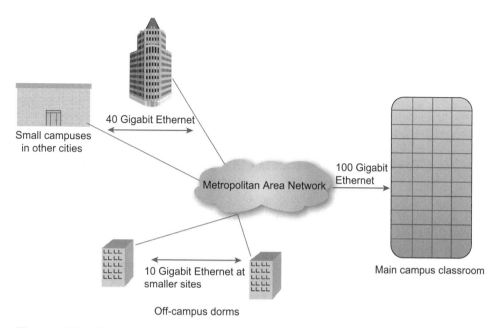

Figure 5-5   *Carrier Ethernet in between buildings on a campus.*

Dedicated Wavelengths

Organizations with high-capacity requirements often lease an entire wavelength on fiber optical cabling. The entire bandwidth of a dedicated wavelength is reserved for a customer. It is not shared with other organizations. Dedicated wavelengths may be used for connections to cloud services, between companies' offices, at large data centers, carrier hotels, and long-haul networks that run between cities and between countries. Passive optical network service NG PON2 supports dedicated wavelength service. For information on NG PON, see Table 4-1, "PON Standards," in the "Appendix" of Chapter 4. Dedicated wavelengths support gigabit and terabit speeds. A terabit is equal to 1,000 gigabits. Dedicated wavelengths are used in 5G cellular networks to connect small antennas to each other. See Chapter 7 for information on 5G cellular service.

T1 and T3: Services Largely Replaced by Higher-Capacity Broadband

T1 service is a digital broadband technology that utilizes a multiplexing scheme, which enables one circuit to carry 24 voice, video, or data channels. The entire circuit runs at 1.54Mbps. T3 is also able to carry a variety of traffic types but operates at 44Mbps. E1 and E3 are the multiplexed services used in Europe. Ethernet, where it's available, is largely replacing T1 and T3 because it provides a more scalable solution and is not limited to 44Mbps.

In the United States, AT&T and Verizon no longer support T1 and T3. They are gradually replacing them with Carrier Gigabit Ethernet, which is not limited to 44Mbps and has more flexible speeds, and is less costly for telephone companies to support.

TDM Shortcomings—Wasted Capacity, Higher-Support Costs

Each device that communicates over a T1 or T3 line is assigned a time slot. If there are eight telephones or computers contending for any of the above channels, a time slot is saved for each telephone and computer for the duration of the particular telephone call or data session. Telephone or computer device 1 might be assigned time slot A; telephone or computer 2, time slot B; and so forth. During pauses in voice conversations, the slot is not assigned to another computer. The assigned time slot is transmitted without any information. These idle time slots result in wasted capacity. For this reason and because TDM capacity is limited to 44Mbps, TDM is not efficient for the higher capacities required for cloud and broadband services. In a network with millions of time slots, empty time slots result in many idle time slots and wasted bandwidth.

T1 and T3 – Costly to Support and Install

In addition to its lack of flexibility and capacity, T1/T3 service is costly for telephone companies to support. This is mainly due to the cost of equipment in the central office required for timing and the interfaces at customers, which providers support. These issues increase costs for space at the telephone company central offices, as well as installation, repair, and maintenance expenses. For details on T1 and T3 Digital Signal Levels See Table 5-3 in the "Appendix."

NETWORK TOPOLOGY ON DEDICATED, PRIVATE LINES ....

As the name implies, private lines are those dedicated to a single institution; not shared by various organizations. In contrast to IP VPNs, the transmissions are not sent over the Internet. Private lines are used by organizations such as financial institutions, armed forces, weapons suppliers to armed forces, and government agencies that require the highest levels of security on transmissions to other sites. Other than these institutions, private lines dedicated to individual organizations have been largely replaced by newer, less costly and easier-to-maintain and configure MPLS, VPN, and WA SDN offerings. Network topology refers to how devices and sites are connected to one another in networks. It is essentially the "view from the top." Topologies include straight lines, hub-and-spoke designs, and mesh designs.

Dedicated Private Lines—For Greater Security

Dedicated services, also known as private lines, are circuits leased by enterprises for their exclusive use. Private lines are expensive, and the number of them used by commercial organizations has decreased dramatically. For all but the largest organizations, MPLS, WA SDN, and IP VPNs have largely replaced private lines. These are less costly to maintain and boast lower monthly lease rates. However, large enterprises, utilities, armed forces, weapons suppliers to governments, and financial services organizations still use high-speed private lines for applications such as money transfers because they are the most secure method of transmitting data. Most of these organizations have the expertise for the initial design and sizing of the dedicated network, ongoing maintenance, and redesign for new applications.

Dedicated Services in Wide Area and Metropolitan Area Networks

Dedicated, private lines are available for the exclusive use of the customer that leases them from a network service provider. Large organizations such as the Department of Defense, large cloud computing organizations, and pharmaceutical companies connect their multistate sites via circuits running at 100 gigabit and greater data rates.

Metropolitan Area Networks (MANs), which are a type of Wide Area Network (WAN), consist of private lines that connect buildings within a city or metropolitan region. Large hospitals transmit customer records, research files, and radiology images over MANs; major universities also use them.

Private lines have the following characteristics.

- **Fixed monthly fees**   Private, dedicated links are priced at flat monthly fees. The fees are not based on minutes used or the amount of data transmitted.

- **Fixed, inflexible routes**   Dedicated lines are not flexible. Calls and data can only be sent between the fixed points to which the lines are connected. Thus, communication with a site that is not on the network is not possible.

- **Exclusive use**   Only the organization that leases private lines can use them. For example, companies with dedicated connections to video conferencing equipment can only hold video calls with organizations that are a part of their private network.

- **Voice, video, and data**   Dedicated lines are suitable for transmission of video, voice, and data. These services can share the same dedicated services or they can use completely different dedicated lines.

- **Fixed capacity**   Dedicated services are leased or built from carriers such as AT&T, Verizon, or CenturyLink with a fixed capacity or bandwidth. These speeds range from a low 10Gbps to higher Gigabit Ethernet speeds.

- **Security**   GigE is used in large, private networks operated by entities such as financial firms and the military for data communications between sites. Some organizations feel that the extra fees and maintenance are justified. Private networks are more secure than even MPLS networks for transmitting sensitive military information and financial transactions.

An important factor when deciding to use dedicated services is the desire for secure transmissions. Some firms believe that network services such as MPLS are too public or prone to hacking for confidential applications such as funds transfer. They want to control their own networks and have staff members available to monitor transmissions over these facilities. Additionally, encryption is used to further ensure privacy and security.

Local and Inter-Exchange Channels

Rates for private lines are based on distance and speed. Higher-speed lines that run over longer distances cost more than slower circuits that run over shorter distances. A 10 Gigabit line is less expensive than a 100 Gigabit line.

Pricing for dedicated, private lines consists of two items:

- **Local channels**   Local channels run from a customer's premises to the carrier's equipment. One local channel is required at each end of the private line in a point-to-point circuit. Local channels are also referred to as *local loops*. The incumbent telephone company often supplies local channels. Because of limited competition for this service, pricing on these short links is often close to the same as that for the longer inter-exchange circuit. Local channel fees are also charged for circuits used to access the Internet, SDN networks, and MPLS networks.

- **Inter-exchange miles**   Inter-exchange mileage is the portion of the circuit located within a carrier's network. The mileage runs from the access point, where it enters the carrier's network, to the egress point, where it leaves the carrier's switch.

Organizations that lease T1 circuits for Internet access also pay for the local loop that connects their site to their carrier. The local loop is a private, dedicated service from the customer to the local provider. When traffic reaches the Internet, it is carried over a shared network. The same is true for access lines to VPNs.

Network Topologies—The View from Above

Topology refers to the way nodes or circuits in a network are connected together. For example, are all the locations or computers connected in a straight line? Are all devices or locations connected to a central headquarters? Can every location reach every other location without going through a central site?

Topology is a consideration in designing private lines in the following:

- Carriers design of networks

- Organizations design of internal networks

- Large enterprises leasing or building their own private, dedicated line networks

The shape of the network (the configuration in which lines are connected to one another), impacts cost, the ability to scale (add or delete sites), reliability, and access to the lines.

Consider the multipoint configuration in Figure 5-6. An application for multipoint design is one used by utilities for communications to monitor the control equipment in their plants. They run fiber-optic cabling on their existing rights of way, over which signals are sent. If the link to one of the large sites is out of service, the other sites cannot reach the main location. However, in the mesh configuration presented in Figure 5-8, if one link is out of service, traffic can be rerouted over other links. There is a trade-off between designing and constructing the more reliable mesh networks that are more costly and simply using a less reliable multipoint configuration.

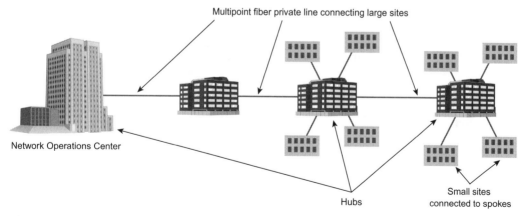

Figure 5-6 Multipoint private lines connecting large sites.

The following are common network configurations.

- **Point-to-point**   One line connects two locations. An example is a hospital with a private line to a medical office where hospital doctors see patients.

- **Multipoint**   One line connects more than two sites together. This is also referred to as *multidrop*.

- **Star (hub-and-spoke)**   All locations connect to, or "hub into," a central site. Data switches in Local Area Networks (LANs) are configured in star topologies. Another example is a corporation with centralized e-mail, financial, and sales applications. If the central site, the switch, or headquarters crashes, all sites connected to it are also out of service. This is illustrated in Figure 5-7 with the sites connected by Carrier Gigabit Ethernet.

- **Secondary hub-and-spoke**   A secondary "hub" is wired to a central site and connects to a cluster of smaller locations. The secondary hub sends traffic from the small locations to the backup central site.

- **Mesh design**   All points on the network nodes connect to one another in a flat or non-hierarchical manner. Peer-to-peer networks for music sharing are examples of mesh networks. Carriers often design their core, backbone networks in a mesh configured with multiple failover routes. Mesh networks are the most expensive because they require the most links. See Figure 5-8 for mesh topology.

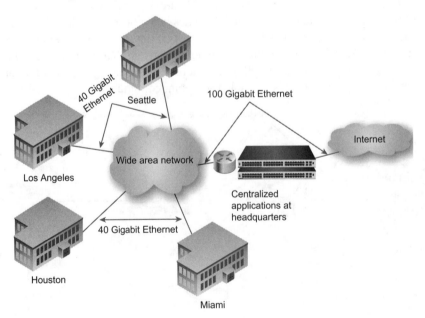

Figure 5-7   A hub-and-spoke design for centralized applications such as e-mail. The disadvantage here is that if e-mail or another application at the central site crashes, all sites lose access to it.

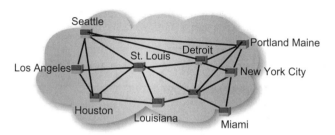

Each site can connect directly with every other site

Figure 5-8   A mesh network connecting all sites together.

Direct Dedicated Interconnections to the Cloud

Customers have a choice of accessing the cloud from the Internet or via a dedicated connection. To access the cloud via the Internet, residential and business customers log in via their same broadband connections from which they access the Internet. These connections are sometimes slower and can cause delays if there is congestion in the Internet. They additionally are not as secure as direct dedicated connections.

Large organizations with critical applications in the cloud often directly connect their locations to their servers and applications on the cloud. These direct interconnections can have capacity of 10 to 100 Gbps. The fact that the data is in the cloud or at a hosting center is seamless to end users because there are minimal delays. In this way they emulate connections within the building to internal data centers in the same organization. To ensure low latency, close to continuous uptime, and low mean time to repair problems, many companies sign a Service Level Agreement (SLA) with commitments from their interconnection provider, specifying the percent of uptime, mean time to repair, and the amount of latency in accessing the cloud. If the SLA conditions are not met, the customer has the option of discontinuing the service without a monetary penalty.

An additional option on dedicated interconnections is to bond multiple Gigabit Ethernet trunks together to double or triple the connection capacity. For example, Google supports bonding of up to eight connections to reach its services.

Amazon Web Services, Microsoft Azure, Oracle, and, Equinix all support direct, private interconnections to organizations' cloud-based applications on their hosting and cloud data centers. Equinix and Coresite provide a service whereby multi-location enterprises connect to Equinix or Coresite from their main location. They both in turn connect enterprises to each of the cloud sites at which their applications are located. See Figure 5-9 for an example of direct interconnection to multiple clouds. This obviates the requirement for a separate connection directly to each provider's site. In addition to minimizing latency (delays in getting responses to queries), direct dedicated connections provide more security and privacy than do Internet connections to cloud and hosting sites.

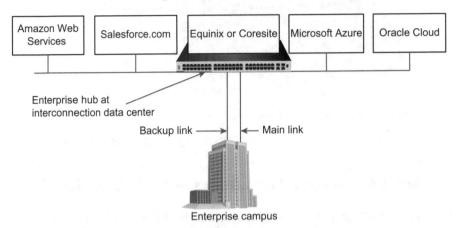

Figure 5-9 A direct connection to multiple cloud providers from corporate hub sites.

Session Initiation Protocol—Out-of-Band Signaling

SIP signaling is used for connections between telephone companies in:

- IP networks
- Telephones connected to internal telephone systems
- Trunks that carry traffic into enterprise locations.

Using SIP Trunks for Caller Identification in Call Centers

Session Initiation Protocol (SIP) signaling is an IETF (Internet Engineering Task Force). It is used in broadband networks for connections between carriers and in on-premises telephone systems. Because SIP trunks carry signaling bits including those with the calling party's names and telephone numbers, most call centers' incoming calls are carried on SIP trunks. The telephone system captures the caller information and sends it to display-equipped telephones. Figure 5-10 illustrates a SIP trunk for transporting caller ID. Employees who receive heavy volumes of calls from vendors or who prefer to only take calls from certain callers use caller information on SIP trunks to screen calls. Unanswered calls are automatically forwarded into voice mail.

Large call centers that use SIP trunks have an additional benefit—the caller ID data can be treated differently than the call itself. This is significant because it enables the telephone system to access information differently from the call. It can send the telephone number to a database that matches the telephone number to the customer account number. The data network sends the account number to the agent's terminal to which the call is sent, which saves agents time by eliminating the need to key in account numbers.

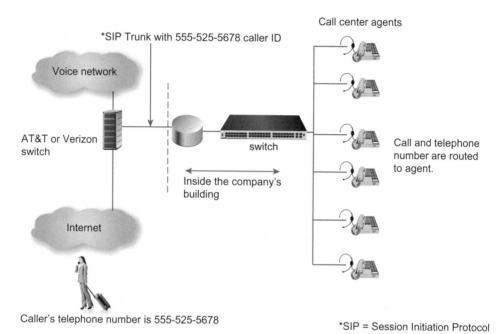

Figure 5-10   SIP trunks used in an organization to identify callers' names and phone numbers. (Stock photo by Chun-Tso Lin/123RF)

Wide Area Software Defined Networks for Enterprises

In earlier generation networks, hardware—routers and switches—were key factors in operating local area and wide area networks. They were programmed to perform specific routing tasks such as routing packets to other networks. In software designed wide area networks (WA SDNs), software external to router and switching functions control the routing, switching, and other functions in the network. See Figure 5-11 for an overview of routing on WA SDNs. A controller is programmed with rules that are applied under specified conditions. For example, alternate routes are set up so that if there is congestion or a malfunctioning section, traffic is automatically sent over an alternate route. WA SDN is used to manage traffic at branch offices, headquarters, and data centers as well as in carriers' core networks.

Network Controller at telephone company with script for
alternate routes if there's congestion on the main route

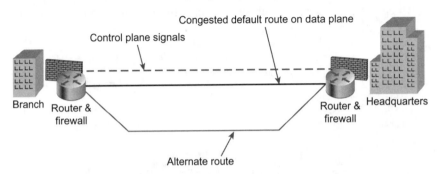

Figure 5-11   An overview of routing on Wide Area Software Defined
Networks.

SDN software can be located in the cloud, or at the telephone company's data center—within their CORD. CORD is short for Central Office Re-architected as a Data Center. For information on CORD, see the section "Central Office Re-architected as a Data Center (CORD)—Streamlined Central Offices" in Chapter 4, "Managing Broadband Networks." Or, large enterprises may use WA SDN to manage traffic within their own broadband networks.

WA SDNs are used to invoke commonly used operations under specified conditions. For example, configurations for branch offices can also be defined and tested centrally before being downloaded to each location. In large organizations with many branch or warehouse locations, network configurations can be downloaded sequentially to each location once there are circuits installed at the locations.

An *Application Program Interface* (API) is used as an interface between external software and each device on the network that is configured for SDN. The API translates between external software on controllers and each device or service on the NFV server. NFV is a key element of WA SDNs.

The APIs used in WA SDNs are *Open APIs*. Open APIs are those which can be used by the public. They enable customers to access features in SDN from enterprises' third-party applications. Private APIs give certain users access to only specified applications. Private APIs are most often deployed in enterprises to give access to particular parts of their network to contractors or employees. For information on NFV see the section "Network Function Virtualization (NFV)—Architecture" in Chapter 4.

Companies that supply hardware and software for SDNs include: ADVA, Advantech, Cisco, Ciena, Citrix, Dell, Riverbed Technology, VeloCloud, Versa Networks, and Viptela.

Control Plane vs. Data Plane Signals

All networks need to transmit both control plane and data plane signals. Control plane signals include addressing, routing, and billing signals. The data plane carries actual applications or user data such as cash register receipts to retailers' headquarters, database look-up requests, applications, and PowerPoint presentations. In newer networks, data and control signals are sent separately so that the network can route them individually as needed to servers for billing and other functions.

In SDN networks addressing, billing, and other overhead bits are transmitted in the control plane and applications and user data on the data plane. Control plane signals and data plane signals are transmitted within both wireline and mobile networks. In SDNs, the controller transmits control plane bits identifying billing and network identification. The actual data and configuration updates and changes are transmitted on the data plane. On SIP trunks, control and data plane signals are also treated separately. Although control and data plane signals are treated individually, both are carried on the same cables. Older networks transmit control and data plane signals within the same channel.

Orchestration and Automation

Orchestration and Automation are features within WA SDNs.

Automation is the use of software to control specific functions within the network. Scripts written in software are used to perform particular tasks. Examples are use of a script for routing traffic to alternate routes in networks if there is congestion on the main route. Or it may define when traffic should overflow to a private line from an Internet-connected IP VPN. Another example is when telephone companies automate turning on ports in optical equipment in response to traffic levels in broadband networks. For instance, a large bank used the same configuration at each of its 50 branch offices. A configuration might include policies on routing critical applications, videos, and the Internet. For the bank, a telephone company contact person first tested a configuration at one branch location. Once the test was completed, the same configuration was downloaded to each branch via access circuits at the branch. Note that a working circuit was already in place at each of the 50 branches.

Orchestration refers to the ability to use automation to control many functions within open source software on SD WANs. It may, for example, send instructions to configure all branch office locations within an organization uniformly. Orchestration is intended to automate on-demand services across multiple providers.

Automation and orchestration are challenging to implement for customers and telephone companies with hardware and software from multiple vendors. This greatly increases the complexity of implementing WA SDN. WA SDNs operate best and are least complex to implement and manage for customers and telephone companies with open hardware and servers with open source software.

The Hybrid Wide Area Network—MPLS and WA SDN

Many organizations keep their Multi-Protocol Label Switching (MPLS) service at some locations and deploy WA SDN at headquarters. MPLS's primary advantage is that it prioritizes voice and video using bits in the MPLS label. Its disadvantage is the long lead time needed to configure and implement the service. However, once it's in place, MPLS does have advantages in that it prioritizes voice and video. WA SDNs are able to control which traffic goes over the MPLS service so that MPLS links are integrated via control plane signaling into the SDN network. See Table 5-1 for a comparison of broadband services.

Implementing WA SDN—Staff Buy in a Challenge

A major challenge in implementing WA SDN service at enterprises is IT employee resistance due to fears of being laid off because some operations are automated.

There is additionally often a lack of expertise to manage WA SDN service. This is because once automation is operational, fewer employees may be required to implement changes that are now automated. Additionally, some organizations hire their telephone company to implement and manage some or all of WA SDN's functions. Moreover, SDN is new and requires new skills to program scripts for automation and knowledge of orchestration.

Another issue is that employees that manage the service might not have the authority to implement needed, more costly features. This creates delays and confusion.

Table 5-1   A Comparison of Broadband Services*

	SD WAN	MPLS	IP VPN	Gigabit Ethernet	Dedicated Wavelength
A managed service	Carriers manage traffic	Carriers manage network	Managed by customer	No	No
Layer 2** broadband	No	No	No	Yes	Yes
Why used	To prioritize and route traffic	To prioritize voice and video between offices	To secure site-to-site & remote access over the Internet	To attain high speeds of 100 to 400 Gigabits	To guarantee speeds up to a 1,000 Gigabits (1 TB)
Factors	Complex to install; routes applications	Costly, limited capacity	Speed not guaranteed, low cost	Can carry SDN traffic	Can carry SDN traffic

*For additional broadband services, see Table 5-2 in the "Appendix."
**Layer 2—Data layer of the Open System Interconnection (OSI)—The protocol of transferring data between networks.

Network Backups—Protection from Outages

Cellular services are a lower-cost backup to their fiber-optic–based broadband links than DSL because cabling is not required. Small organizations and even some medium-sized companies use cellular as a backup. It may have less capacity than DSL, but the costs are lower, the fiber services rarely fail, and it's possible to designate only to allow key staff to use the backup service.

DSL as a Backup Option for Business Customers

Medium-sized and large commercial and business customers lease DSL services primarily as a low-cost backup service in the event that their primary Internet access circuits fail. Many of these primary circuits are installed on fiber-optic cabling. The large volume of revenue generated by enterprise customers makes a carrier's investment in fiber-optic cabling for business customers viable.

Fiber cabling supports higher speeds than the copper cabling used for DSL and requires less maintenance by providers than copper cabling. For these reasons, major telephone companies are adding more fiber to networks, eliminating DSL, and replacing it with Gigabit Ethernet circuits over newly installed fiber cabling. However, organizations may keep DSL for backup in case service on the fiber crashes or the fiber cable is cut.

Cellular Backups for Small and Medium-Sized Organizations—Outgoing Calls

Cellular backups are lower-cost options than adding duplicate fiber or DSL. However, in an outage the organization loses incoming calls. In these cases, customers can request that during an outage, their telephone company forward calls to their cellular service. Alternatively, onsite routers capable of load balancing traffic between cellular and fiber-optic lines may be able to automatically fail over to cellular service.

Employees generally have cell phones and can make outgoing calls even when there is a fiber cut and service to their building is lost. Cellular service is particularly suited to temporary locations such as pop-up stores, construction trailers, and other temporary locations. Cellular service is also faster to install than wired connections that require telephone company technicians onsite and remote programming.

Deploying Duplicate Fiber Cabling—Costly but High Capacity

Alternate fiber runs are the most costly option for backing up voice and data traffic to buildings. With fiber backups, organizations provision one set of fiber to, say, the left corner of their building and the other fibers at the right-hand corner. In this way, a backhaul digging up the earth that inadvertently slices fiber on one side would not cut the fibers on the other side of the building.

However, if the organization's telephone company equipment malfunctions, service will be lost unless each set of fibers is routed to a different provider. Large financial institutions, large pharmaceuticals, and cloud data centers often provision fiber with different telephone companies as a precaution in case one provider has a service outage. Another commonly used option is to use cable TV providers as a backup option.

Emergency Call Reporting—911 in the U.S., the Philippines, and Canada

Almost all countries provide a way for residents to report dangerous situations and request help in emergencies in the event of fires, natural disasters, accidents and health crises. Per Trey Fogerty of the National Emergency Number Association, there are more than 240 million 911 calls answered each year by PSAP (Public Safety Answering Point) operators in the United States. A PSAP is a call center staffed with personnel that answer 911 calls. This statistic was published in a San Antonio publication, KTSA, on June 3, 2017, in an article titled, "911 Convention in S.A. This Week." According to the article, which paraphrased Fogerty:

> Soon, 9-1-1 systems will be able to accept text messages, photos and videos.... Some communities just don't have the money needed to make the upgrades.

The main goal of emergency management staff is to quickly respond to calls or texts by contacting the appropriate emergency responders. If someone is choking, a delay of 60 seconds can make the difference between life and death. During a rapidly spreading fire or an armed robbery in progress delays can result in death and extensive property damage. These types of crises demand rapid responses.

Security, Financial and Technical Hurdles

In the United States, emergency call centers face a number of challenges:

- Adequate funding to purchase up-to-date technology. 911 call centers receive money from fees tacked onto landline and mobile telephone bills. These fees are not always adequate to meet the needs of PSAPs with fewer customers from which to collect fees.

- Sustainability to keep their equipment up and running during natural disasters. 911 centers have duplicate cabling to their facilities in case one is disabled or cut. In addition, telephone companies prioritize repairs and outages at PSAPs. In an outage caused by, for example, hurricane damage, PSAPs forward all of their calls to another center.

- Security to protect their operations from hackers. Hackers sending massive amounts of calls to PSAPs with denial of service attacks have caused outages at 911 centers.

- Identification of callers' locations when they reach 911 agents via text, VoIP telephone, enterprise telephone system, TTY (Teletypewriter), and mobile phones.

When 911 was established in 1968, all people reached 911 call centers from their wired, home telephone. Signaling on these calls transmitted callers' telephone numbers, which were matched up with the address for each telephone number in databases. Thus, dispatchers were able to quickly notify ambulance, firefighters, or police and let them know the location of the problem.

With the advent of mobile phones, the location of the nearest cell tower is transmitted to 911 agents. In locations where cell towers are far from each other, it's difficult to precisely locate the caller. The issue of location identification is challenging when people contact 911 via text messaging and VoIP telephones as well. All of these types of messaging are not necessarily associated with a fixed address. However, text messages are important in situations such as when a victim is hiding and does not want to be overheard. The FCC and wireless service providers are working together to resolve these issues. The 5G cellular protocol specifies cells with antennas close to each other, narrowing down the location identification.

NOTE | 911 is not universally assigned for calls to emergency providers. Most of Europe reaches Public Safety Answering Points by dialing 112, and in China people dial 120 for an ambulance, 119 for firefighters, and 110 for police. In Japan people dial 119 for medical and fire emergencies, but 110 to reach the police.

APPENDIX..

Table 5-2   An Overview of Broadband Network Services

Network Service	Places Typically Used	How Used
30 to 60 Megabit services T1: 24 voice or data channels 1.54Mbps E1: 30 voice or data channels, 2Mbps plus one channel for signaling and one for framing and remote maintenance	Commercial organizations Being replaced by Gigabit Ethernet	Internet access, connections to long-distance and local telephone companies for voice and data, private lines between company sites. Each channel = 64Kbps. E1 is the European version of T1.
T3: 672 voice or data channels, equivalent to 28 T1s E3: 480 voice or data channels	Large and medium-sized organizations Being replaced by Gigabit Ethernet	Access to long-distance companies, Internet access, high-speed private lines between company sites. This is the European version of T3.
BRI ISDN: Two voice or data channels and one signaling channel	Organizations	Video conferencing; but new systems mainly use IP; supplanted by other technologies.
PRI ISDN: 23 voice/data channels and one signaling channel in the United States 30 voice/data channels and one signaling channel in Europe	Business and commercial customers	Call centers, videoconferencing; PRI ISDN has different speeds in the United States and Europe.
Digital Subscriber Line (DSL): 128Kbps to 44Mbps	Residential consumers, small and mid-size businesses where fiber to premises not available	Internet access, television.
	Telecommuters	Remote access to corporate files and e-mail.

Network Service	Places Typically Used	How Used
Carrier Gigabit Ethernet 1Mbps to 10Gbps over fiber	Mid-size to large commercial customers	Access to the Internet, connections to storage area networks, and LAN-to-LAN connections; data only.
	Carrier networks and cable TV core and metropolitan networks	To aggregate traffic in metropolitan networks and send it as a single stream to central offices or cable headends.
Asynchronous Transfer Mode (ATM): Up to 2.5Gbps	Telephone companies	Not suited to today's capacity requirements. Transmits voice, video, and data traffic. Rarely used because ATM switches are required.

Table 5-3 Digital Signal Levels—These Services are Being Replaced by Higher-Capacity Carrier Ethernet

Level	North America		Japan		Europe	
	User Chan.	Speed	User Chan.	Speed	User Chan.	Speed
DS-0	1	64Kbps	1	64Kbps	1	64Kbps
T1 (DS-1)	24	1.544Mbps	24	1.544Mbps	24	2.048Mbps
T2 (DS-2)	96	6.312Mbps	96	6.312Mbps	120	8.448Mbps
T3 (DS-3)	672	44.7Mbps	480	32.06Mbps	672	34.368Mbps

Table 5-4 Digital Subscriber Line Standards

Digital Subscriber Line Service	Upstream Top Data Rate	Downstream Top Data Rate	Voice	Comments
ADSL (Asymmetric DSL)	800Kbps	7Mbps	Yes	Offered to residential customers. Uses one pair of wires.
ADSL2	1Mbps	8Mbps	Yes	Most common standard worldwide for Internet access.

Table 5-4   (Continued)

Digital Subscriber Line Service	Upstream Top Data Rate	Downstream Top Data Rate	Voice	Comments
ADSL2+	1Mbps	24Mbps	Yes	Supports video on demand on short cable runs.
ADSL2— Reach extended	1Mbps	8Mbps	Yes	Increases reach of ADSL2+.
SHDSL— Symmetric High-Data Rate	5.6Mbps	5.6Mbps	Yes	Single or two pair. Two pair speeds higher than single pair.
VDSL (Very-High-Bit-Rate DSL)	1.5Mbps 2.3Mbps	13Mbps 52Mbps	Yes	
VDSL2—12MHz	30Mbps	55Mbps	Voice	Requires short cable length; TV/data/voice.
VDSL2—30MHz	100Mbps	100Mbps	Yes	Requires short cable length; TV/data/voice.

Part IV

The Internet and Cellular Networks

6 The Internet

In this chapter:

INTRODUCTION ....

The Internet is the single most important innovation of the 21st century. It's a ubiquitous network available in much of the world, and a disruptive technology that has displaced many traditional retail businesses and services. It has created the perception that the world is smaller and changed how we communicate, shop, and spend leisure time. It has upended numerous industries, shrunk distances, led to new industries, and enabled improved communications across countries, between countries, and between continents. According to an international university student from China:

> *I am my parent's only child, and the ability to make free video calls over the Internet to them weekly is the thing that most helps me stay in touch with them and share my experiences. Knowing that I will chat with them every week makes my parents and myself less lonely.*

Technologies used in the Internet are radically changing the ways consumers access and view movies and television shows and negatively affected movie theater attendance. People can now view high-definition movies and television on their widescreen TVs in the comfort of their living rooms. Many additionally have high-end audio systems to supplement their viewing experience. Increases in the number of people using streaming, the high video and audio quality, and improvements in actual content have all precipitated large decreases in the numbers of adults that go to movie theaters and lower profits for movie theaters. Attendance at movie theaters has dropped steadily since 2016 and is expected to continue dropping as more people adopt streaming.

The Internet has radically changed how companies conduct commerce. The Internet is the main vehicle by which businesses contact customers, handle customer service, and interact with internal staff. The Internet is particularly attractive to young people, many of whom grew up with the Internet as a part of their daily lives. Web sites that are well designed and make it easy for customers to find what they need and to check out, lessen customers' desire to actually speak with or e-mail a customer service rep. A well-designed, easy-to-use web site, an extranet, saves costs for businesses. Extranets are online e-commerce sites where consultants, partners, and customers access particular databases and services.

The Internet is not a single entity. It is made up of multiple large networks connected to each other by routers and switches and with growing amounts of capacity enabled by the following advancements: fiber-optic cabling, and more powerful servers and computer chips, all of which have resulted in higher-capacity broadband fiber-optic networks.

Streaming is a major disrupter of home entertainment and pay-TV. It has been enabled by both the Internet and home Wi-Fi. The number of people using streaming services has grown every year since Netflix first offered it in 2007 and many analysts expressed skepticism over its future. Streaming is widely available worldwide in developed countries in Asia, Europe, the Americas, and some countries in Africa. The rise of streaming has caused the bankruptcy of Blockbuster and other DVD retailers, and decreased the number of people subscribing to cable TV packages. Importantly, it's changed the way people get their home entertainment.

Because of its acceptance, pay-TV providers now offer their own streaming services with content they create, own, or lease. For example, Verizon owns Yahoo!, and AOL, which they merged into their Oath unit, and AT&T, which owns DirecTV, purchased Time Warner, the owner of HBO. Furthermore, Comcast owns NBC and Universal, with its cache of movies and television shows. Thus, the three largest broadband providers own and create content through their subsidiaries. This results in competition between content providers Amazon, Netflix, and other streaming content companies including Facebook, and large telephone, cable TV, and satellite companies over which Amazon, Netflix, and others stream movies to homes and apartments. This often creates a situation where pay TV providers compete with the very organizations that stream movies and TV shows over their networks.

To prevent large telecoms from slowing down or blocking competitors' content, the Obama era FCC instituted *network neutrality*. Under network neutrality rules, owners of broadband (pay-TV providers) are not allowed to slow down or block competitors' content. Cable TV providers, however, lobbied for the elimination of network neutrality, stating that they should be compensated for carrying streaming traffic. The Federal Communications Commission eliminated network neutrality in 2017. However, their ruling is being adjudicated in courts and in legislatures in the United States.

Worldwide connectivity has led to the challenges of keeping networks secure and information private. Organizations, individual subscribers, and governments grapple with keeping information secure and employees' and customers' personal data private. Hackers know how internal networks are architected and where to look for vulnerabilities. Furthermore, malicious employees and staff errors add another layer of complexity in maintaining secure networks. Keeping enterprises 100 percent secure is almost impossible. Hacking is profitable and not often punished. Thus, hackers have a huge incentive to steal information they sell, or otherwise profit from illegal tampering with businesses' computer data and networks. It's an ongoing race between hackers finding new and novel ways to interrupt and steal information and to damage and hijack networks, vs. enterprises and governments keeping networks safe.

WHAT IS THE INTERNET? ....

The term Internet is derived from *inter* and *network*. It's a vast network of globally interconnected networks. If one part of the Internet is down, routers send traffic on alternate routes. It's a survivable, robust network with parts of it able to function during natural disasters and attacks. The United States Department of Defense funded the original Internet with the intention of having a robust network able to survive an attack or national disaster. They awarded money to the University of California at Santa Barbara for the purpose of developing a resilient network. In addition, faculty in the IT department at the University of Michigan collaborated on new protocols to be used in the Internet.

At that time, 1969 until the mid-1990s, researchers at universities and government agencies were the main users of the Internet. They used it to collaborate on research. Additionally, staff at universities used the Internet to access early forms of electronic mail (e-mail) using arcane commands such as k to display the previous message and n to display the next message. Logging into the Internet and using e-mail acquired a user-friendly interface when Tim Burners Lee developed the Nexus *browser* in 1989. Examples of browsers include Chrome, Internet Explorer, and Safari. Mosaic and Netscape were early browsers. Easily accessible, user-friendly browsers are a large part of the reason that the Internet was widely adopted.

Features of the Internet

The following are some of the most prominent features of the Internet:

- It uses a common set of IP protocols
- It is a packet network
- Routers send packets on the least congested routes
- Routers send packets around disabled, broken links
- It has defined protocols, such as IPv4 and IPv6 for addressing
- It can grow to keep up with growing amounts of traffic
- The backbone is made up of fiber-optical cabling connected to electronics in which capacity can be increased, often using software at remote data centers
- The United States federal government does not regulate the Internet
- Because of the simplicity of its protocols, IP, TCP, and HTML markup language, the entire world can communicate over the Internet
- Voice, video, and data are transmitted on the Internet
- Carriers exchange traffic at peering points

Protocols Used on the Internet

The single most important factor in the worldwide spread of the Internet is the standard, easily implemented protocols used on the Internet. Worldwide, all countries use the same IP protocols to transmit data across their sections of the Internet. This means that people access broadband in a uniform way regardless of their location. When the Internet was designed, simplicity was purposely kept in mind so that the networks could be uniformly and easily duplicated. The fact that these designs are accepted worldwide has been a critical factor in adoption.

The following are examples of the Internet protocols:

- **Internet Protocol:** IP is a "best effort" protocol. When a message is sent over the Internet, it is broken up into packets. Each packet is sent on a different route and reassembled at the receiving end in the correct order. If there is congestion the router drops packets. The dropped packets are not resent. This is why IP is known as a best effort transmission protocol.

- **HTTP:** HyperText Transport Protocol links are the standard way documents are moved around the Internet.

- **HTML:** HyperText Markup Language is used to compose web pages. It is not, strictly speaking, a protocol.

- **TCP:** Transmission Control Protocol provides error checking on messages sent over the Internet. It is a connection-oriented protocol. Messages are sent between sending and receiving computers on the Internet that communicate whether the message was received or whether errors occurred. If there are errors, bits are retransmitted.

- **IPv4** and **IPv6:** Internet Protocol v4 and v6 define the numeric structure of Internet addresses. The newer IPv6 was launched in 2012. It specifies longer addresses and is being implemented by Internet providers and telephone companies. It has capacity for more IP addresses than the shorter IPv4 structure.

The Impact of Capacity—The Availability of Broadband Networks

An important factor in the wide use of the Internet in everyday life and business is the availability of high-capacity broadband and cellular services. This availability exists in Western Europe, North America, much of Asia, parts of Africa, and in the Middle East. The capacity and availability of the networks that make up the Internet are enabled by technologies such as fiber-optic cabling and the supporting electronics connected to it: lower-cost, smaller graphical processor chips in wireless handsets and laptops; faster computers; and improved compression to support multimedia video streaming and high-capacity content downloads. These improvements, along with search engines, enhance the user experience for consumers and businesses alike, as do improvements in web site designs.

The Public Network Prior to the Internet

At the time the Internet was developed and through the 1990s, the public switched telephone network, which carried only voice, was made up of large central offices called *tandem offices*. Smaller central offices were connected in a hub-and-spoke design to each tandem office. If the tandem office crashed, all the local central offices were also out of service. The designers of the Internet wanted to avoid this centralized control where an outage at a central or tandem office disabled large swaths of the public telephone network.

The Internet—A Distributed Network with No Central Control

The Internet is a distributed network with no single ISP (Internet Service Provider) or other entity controlling it. It's a distributed network in which multiple carriers manage particular parts of the network. If a router crashes, other routers send traffic along alternate paths in the Internet's backbone. The backbone is the part of the Internet that carries traffic across the country between cities and states, and between countries.

Although the Internet was designed to function when any route crashes, if the central databases that hold IP addresses are disabled, the Internet won't function. See the section "The Criticality of Root Servers" below for information on root servers.

Largest Carriers Worldwide—Backbone Providers

The telephone companies with the largest Internet backbones in the United States are Sprint, Verizon, CenturyLink (through its purchase of Level3), and AT&T. There are a number of local carriers (ISPs) that connect users to the Internet because no single provider has service everywhere.

According to the May 24, 2017, article by Antoine Gara in the *Forbes* online article, "The World's Largest Telecom Companies: AT&T & Verizon Top China Telecom," the following are the largest telephone companies by total revenue worldwide. The list includes their headquarters locations. However, most of them have services in other countries as well:

- AT&T—U.S.

- Verizon—U.S.

- China Mobile—Hong Kong, China

- Nippon Telegraph & Telecom—Japan

- Softbank—Japan

- Deutshe Telekom—Germany

- Telefonica—Spain

- KDDI—Japan

- China Telecom—China

Using Search Engines to Unleash Vast Stores of Information

The introduction of sophisticated search engines by organizations such as Google, Microsoft, and Yahoo! (part of Verizon) made browsing the Internet convenient by organizing the enormous amounts of information available on the Internet. Search engines from Google and Baidu in China and others including DuckDuck Go Search, Bing (part of Microsoft), Dogpile Search, Yippy Search, and Webopedia Search earn revenue from advertising on their sites and from ranking companies that pay fees for higher placements (rankings) in search results.

Page ranking refers to the placement on a web page of search results. Ranking a product or service higher places it closer to the top of search results, with a higher likelihood of people clicking on the link. In addition to paying for higher ranks, ranking is done by analyzing the number of other sites that link to a particular site. For example, if someone searches for Greek restaurants in San Francisco, the Google engine looks at and ranks the restaurants partially on how many sites link to particular Greek restaurants in San Francisco and the type of sites linking to it.

Google not only earns the highest search-engine-based advertising revenue in the United States, but because of its many acquisitions, it has the potential to skew results of searches in favor of its own sites. When search results are returned, search engines such as Google can rank their own sites higher than those of competitors. Google's search engines are located in hundreds of countries worldwide in addition to its presence in the United States.

Over the years, Google's owner Alphabet acquired many software companies, including the following:

- Zagat (restaurant and hotel reviews)

- Android operating system software for smartphones

- Adsense (Google's network for advertising sales)

- DoubleClick (advertising network used to target ads to particular classes of people)

- Google Maps (GPS plus local guides and advertising)

- Keyhole Technologies, Zipdash Inc., and Where2 LL2 (software that forms the basis of Google Maps)

- ITA (airline flight aggregation information)

- Motorola Mobility (mobile devices; patents for mobile services)

- YouTube (online videos and streaming TV)

- Waze GPS (global positioning service)

- Zipdash (now part of Google's location services)

In addition to possibly skewing search results toward their own sites, search engines have implications for privacy. Marketers can determine the following based on terms people search on:

- Gender

- Income Range

- Health

- Type of computer (Mac or Microsoft Windows)

- Location

This information may be shared with advertisers who target ads at particular demographics based on search history. For example, they might show pop-up and sidebar ads on the Internet based on people's purchasing history. See the section "Privacy" below.

Search Engines—Mathematical Algorithms and Page Ranking

Google, a unit of Alphabet, attracts the most search engine traffic worldwide. Baidu in China is second and Microsoft's Bing and Verizon's Yahoo! are third and fourth respectively. Search software uses mathematical algorithms and page ranking to determine search results. Proprietary mathematical algorithms analyze keywords, titles, site structures, and descriptions to determine which sites fit the search terms specified by Internet users. They look at headlines, bolding, and the proximity of words to each other for relevance of textual data on the page.

Search engines have massive indexes (lists) in databases of past searches and URLs, or locations of web sites. They additionally have the ability to find and add new web sites and discover sites that are removed. This is done by *spiders*, software that continuously and automatically crawl through the Internet looking for new and updated sites.

Search Revenue—Advertising, Page Ranking, and Software Licensing

Google has the largest revenue from search worldwide, primarily from advertising on its sites. As reported by its parent company, Alphabet, it had $26 billion in total sales for the quarter ending June 30, 2017. Of that total, $25.8 billion was from search: advertising, software licensing, and page ranking.

Search companies earn revenue by a combination of ads, favorable ranking of web sites in search results, and licensing software to other search companies and to enterprises. Large enterprises deploy the licensed search software to assist staff in finding information on health and retirement benefits, information about departments, and directories of employee addresses and telephone numbers.

Investigations into Google Search Practices

In June 2017, the European Union fined Google $5 billion for favoring its own companies in search results. The European Union judged that Google demoted rivals' links in favor of its own company's links and search results. This is important because the top 10 ranked search results receive about 90 percent of all clicks. The EU's investigation was prompted by complaints from EU companies, that search results were skewed in Google's favor and that EU companies' results were demoted to lower rankings on search result pages. For example, Google might rank its own flight information service higher than a competitive flight information service. The EU complaint stated in part that Google was using anti-competitive tactics to take advantage of its 90 percent market share in searches.

As a result of the EU fine and agreement, Google stated that it would let companies bid for the top placement in search, rather than ranking search results by links to products retailers who had paid Google to rank high in searches. Google further agreed to make some changes in its search shopping methodologies, and to stop promoting its own shopping services while demoting rivals' comparison sites.

The EU left it up to Google to create its own solutions to these issues. Per EU competition commissioner Margrethe Vestager, if the EU is not satisfied with Google's changes made within 90 days of the fine, the EU will fine Google up to 5 percent of its total global search revenue each day. The EU hired accounting firm KPMG and search engine optimization marketing company Mavens to monitor Google's search results for compliance with the EU agreement. Despite this agreement, Google has stated that it will continue to challenge the fine in the courts.

In addition to the EU's investigation into Google's search practices, in 2016 the EU filed anti-trust charges against Google over its dominant position in search on Android operating system mobile phones and tablet computers. The complaint alleged that Google is monopolistic in requiring that Android phone manufacturers pre-load the Google Chrome browser and Google Search on phones. The charges are further based on Google's practice of offering financial incentives to carriers and manufacturers to make Google's search services the only pre-loaded search on mobile phones. In 2016, Russia filed a similar anti-trust complaint against Google's policies on mobile phones and tablet computers. In 2017, Google and Russia reached a settlement where Google agreed to pay Russia $7.8 million to settle the claim.

Internet2—A Non-Commercial Outgrowth of the Internet

Internet2 is the predecessor of the Internet. In contrast to the public Internet, it is a non-profit private network. Internet2 was established as a way for university and research professionals to collaborate over a private connected network. Internet2 is the largest private network in the world. The scope of Internet2 has grown from university and research organizations to include corporations, and private and governmental national research entities in over 100 countries.

A core group of Internet2 technology staff maintain and upgrade the network to include high data rate services including SDN and Gigabit Ethernet. In addition to the local data centers at members' locations, Internet2 maintains a central data center at Indiana University. An important focus of operations at the data center is maintaining the security and privacy of information transmitted over Internet2 links.

In the United States, Internet2 drops are located in metropolitan areas on the east and west coasts, as well as throughout populated areas along the southern coast. There are fewer Internet2 locations in less densely populated cities in the midwest.

Collaboration and research data transmitted over Internet2 includes cooperation between branches of large universities. For example, many universities now have branches throughout urban and rural areas, as well as in distant cities of large countries. Internet2 also links university sites in distant continents. Scientists and researchers are able to partner with distant colleagues on designing new drugs and other innovative technologies using Internet2 links.

STREAMING—A DISRUPTIVE TECHNOLOGY ....

Streaming media, also called Over-the-Top (OTT), refers to television, movies, and music streamed directly to people's homes and apartments from the Internet. OTT streaming has had and is continuing to have a direct impact on decreased cable TV and broadcast TV revenues and is a leading cause in the decline of movie theater attendance as more people abandon cable TV and move to Netflix, Amazon, and YouTube TV for movies and TV shows.

Growth in Streaming

Streaming entertainment from the Web to televisions is a key application that is growing year after year and causing losses for pay-TV (cable TV, telephone companies, and satellite TV) providers. However, not all subscribers that stream have "cut the cord" on all pay-TV. According to an October 27, 2017, article by Wayne Friedman in *TELEVISIONNewsDaily*, "53% of U.S broadband homes subscribe to pay TV as well as to OTT streaming." But streaming hours grew 100 percent from 2016 to 2017, according to the article, "Streaming Hours Up Over 100% in 2017, Study Says," by Alex Weprin. The article cited Conviva for the statistics and for the statement that live sports were an important driver of the increase.

However, in increasing numbers, subscribers are canceling their pay-TV service. According to a September 13, 2017, *Variety* article by Todd Spangler, "Cord-Cutting Explodes: 22 Million U.S. Adults Will Have Canceled Cable, Satellite TV by End of 2017," the 22 million people that have canceled their pay service is a cumulative total of subscribers that rely entirely on streaming options. These statistics were credited to eMarketer. Added to these losses is the fact that growing numbers of children and young adults are growing up assuming that they can access all their television shows and movies on their mobile devices and computers via streaming. To wit, a September 15, 2017, *USA Today* article cited statistics from Videology that 9 percent of Millennials plan to cancel their cable TV subscriptions in 2017. This does not include the young adults, college students, and children who already rely entirely on streaming.

Additional studies have tracked the rise of streaming and the decline in pay-TV usage:

- A 2017 survey conducted by Hub Entertainment Research found that 52 percent of respondents watched their favorite shows online rather than through their cable TV set-top box. This causes lower revenue for cable TV as subscribers sign up for lower cost, less inclusive pay-TV packages. This statistic was published in *DigitalNews* in an article published on November 9, 2017, by Alex Weprin, "Study OTT Overtakes Set-Top Box as Source for Favorite Shows."

- A survey done by Videology found that only one third of Millennial males intend to subscribe to pay-TV in 2017. Adam Levy cited these statistics in a September 15, 2017, article in *USA Today* titled, "Cost Is Not Why More Millennials Than Ever Are Cutting the Cord."

Easier Set-Up and Increased Internet Uptake

When over-the-top streaming was first available in 2007, accessing it from traditional televisions was complicated because at that time most televisions did not have the HDMI (High Definition Multimedia Interface) ports needed for set-top boxes such as Apple TVs and Roku. With the universal availability of HDMI ports on new televisions, this requirement is no longer a major impediment to the adoption of streaming. In addition, increased capacity in broadband networks and growth in broadband adoption are factors in the growth of streaming. According to Netflix, Inc. CFO David B. Wells on their October 16, 2017, third-quarter earnings call:

> *I think, in general, it is the continued adoption of Internet entertainment that is driving our growth.*

Accessing Streaming—Connected TVs, Game Consoles, and Mobile Devices

Subscribers access streaming media on mobile devices as well as on flat-panel televisions. Streaming movies and TV shows to tablet computers and smartphones is particularly useful when traveling. In addition, university students who may not have television in their dorms often stream to laptop computers, smartphones, and tablet computers. An additional option for connecting to streaming service is via game consoles connected to televisions. Subscribers to streaming can easily log into their streaming service from game consoles such as the Sony Wii and the PlayStation Vue. Two examples of services compatible with game consoles are Netflix and Hulu movies and TV shows, which have been made compatible with game consoles so that they can be streamed directly to them.

Another way streaming is becoming more widely available is via Internet-connected televisions, also referred to as smart TVs. Internet-connected televisions have menu-driven screens for surfing the Internet and selecting programming. New smart TVs also have Roku software integrated. This eliminates the requirement for an HDMI cable and a physical set-top box because Roku features are built into the TV. Consumers can use the televisions' remote controls to click on icons from sites such as Netflix, Amazon, and Hulu to stream movies and television shows to their TV. These televisions connect to the Internet via home wireless networks or by connecting Ethernet cabling to the Ethernet port on their television. The cable is then plugged into to their Wi-Fi router and their cable TV or broadband modem.

Set-Top Boxes for OTT Streams

Apple TV, Roku, Google Chrome, and Amazon Fire are examples of set-top boxes made expressly for over-the-top streaming. Each of these devices has software with options for accessing content from a specific list of providers. The set-top boxes plug into the HDMI (High Definition Multimedia Interface) port on flat screen televisions. Streaming content is sent to subscribers' set-top boxes via their Wi-Fi networks.

Roku's Business Model

Roku set-top boxes were first available in 2007 when Roku was a unit of Netflix. Netflix sold it in 2009 because they were concerned that owning a streaming device might put them in conflict with hardware providers such as Apple. Netflix traffic accounts for a third of content streamed over Roku set-top boxes. And Roku leases space in Netflix's headquarters location in Los Gatos California.

While Roku sells the most streaming devices in the United States, ahead of Amazon, Google, and Apple, the majority of its annual revenue is not from hardware sales. Rather, Roku makes the bulk of its revenue from platform sales. Platform sales consist of advertising, sales of its partners' content sold through Roku's software, and subscriptions on its hardware. It additionally has its own streaming service from which customers can stream movies and TV shows.

In addition to streaming on connected TVs and its set-top boxes, Roku has put its name on co-branded televisions manufactured by Insignia, Sharp, TCL, and others. These televisions have Roku software pre-installed, which enables consumers to use Roku without adding an external set-top box. Televisions with embedded Roku software display the Roku menu at start-up. Embedding software in televisions is a way to keep customers tied to Roku.

Another way that Roku makes content available is by formatting a selection of movies and TV for mobile operating systems. Customers that stream to mobile smartphone and tablet computers download a Roku app (a small application) to their mobile device. Movies and TV shows streamed to smartphones and tablets are formatted to appear on the particular device and operating system used on the device to which the movie, TV shows or music are streamed.

In addition to the United States, Roku streaming players and software are sold under the Roku brand in Canada, Mexico, the United Kingdom, France, and the Republic of Ireland.

Keeping and Attracting Subscribers—The Criticality of Content

Quality content that appeals to a wide range of people is an important strategy in attracting and keeping subscribers. The number of over-the-top providers in the United States competing for subscribers is on the rise. Whereas in the early days of streaming, Netflix was able to license content from studios including Disney and Universal, as these contracts expired, many studios stopped licensing content to Netflix and others in favor of streaming their own offerings.

Both Amazon and Netflix are building up their collections of original content as well as attempting to license rights to content from other studios. Netflix announced plans at their October 2017 third quarter investor conference to spend up to $8 billion in 2017 for original content. This is riskier than purchasing existing known hits, but with less licensed content available, it is a necessary strategy.

Disney, with whom Netflix previously had a contract, opted to not renew its licensing agreement with Netflix in 2017. Disney has instead started its own streaming service with content from its movies, TV shows, and its ESPN sports division. In 2017, Disney purchased the studio library of 21st Century Fox. The content that Disney gained includes Fox's movies (*Star Wars*, *Avatar*, and *X-Men*), television (*The Simpsons*, *This is Us* and *Modern Family*). Importantly, the Fox acquisition strengthens Disney's international presence in India and other non-European countries. In a similar strategy, Comcast purchased Universal Studios in 2011 for their NBC television and Universal Studios' libraries of movies. They recognized the importance of content to round out their offerings of cable TV service.

The issue of content is also complicated by the fact that some cable TV providers also own rights to movies and TV series and/or national broadcasters. In January 2011, Comcast received approval from United States regulators to purchase a controlling stake (51 percent) in NBC Universal, which owns Universal Media Studios and Universal Pictures' Focus Features; the NBC broadcast network; and cable networks USA, Bravo, and CNBC. It is part owner of the Weather Channel and majority owner of MSNBC.

Major content providers and a partial list of what they own include the following.

- Time Warner owned the most content in the United States and Canada. Some of its properties were HBO Films, CNN, New Line Cinema, 10 percent of Hulu, TBS, Turner Entertainment, and Warner Bros. Animation. It owns CW Television Network jointly with CBS Corporation. AT&T purchased Time Warner in 2018.

- Comcast with its NBCUniversal division owns NBC, MSNBC, NBCSN, E! CNBC, Telemundo, Bravo, USA Network, DreamWorks Animation, The Weather Channel, 30 percent of Hulu, and Universal Studios along with their parks and resorts. It is the largest broadcasting and cable television conglomerate by revenue in the world. In 2018 it purchased Sky, a pay-TV service available throughout Europe.

- See below for Walt Disney Company's purchase of 21st Century Fox's library of films and television content.

- Viacom is an international cable TV and content company. It owns Comedy Central, MTV, Spike, Nickelodeon, VIVA, Paramount Pictures, BET, and VH1, as well as others. Privately owned National Amusements, Inc. owns a majority of Class A common stock in Viacom. National Amusements is controlled by the Sumner Redstone family, which also owns movie theater companies.

- CBS mainly produces commercial television and radio shows. It owns CW Television Network jointly with Warner Brothers, CBS films, Smithsonian Network, UPN, Infinity Broadcasting, Viacom Outdoor, Showtime Networks, Simon and Schuster Publishing, and Paramount's television studio. National Amusements is a parent company of CBS as well as Viacom.

- Sony Pictures Entertainment is a wholly owned subsidiary of Tokyo based Sony Corporation through its Sony Pictures Entertainment Division. It owns Columbia Pictures, TriStar Pictures, Sony Classic Pictures, Dutch production company 2waytraffic N.V., and Sony Pictures Animation. Sony also manufactures Bravia TVs, Blu-ray players, and the PlayStation game console. It is offers its content through its Internet-connected televisions, Blu-ray players, and home entertainment systems.

- The Walt Disney Company owns the ABC broadcast network, ESPN, The Disney Channel, A&E Network, Touchstone Pictures, Lucasfilm, Maker Studios, Marvel Entertainment, and Pixar. It is part owner of Lifetime Entertainment, the History Channel, A&E Networks, and Freeform, 60 percent of Hulu, and 14 theme parks worldwide. In 2018 Disney purchased 21st Century Fox which included part ownership of National Geographic Partners. Blue Sky which produces and distributes motion pictures worldwide, its film libraries, and Fox Home Entertainment. The purchase did not include Fox's TV or sports stations. The Walt Disney Company is the second biggest conglomerate by revenue in the world.

 NOTE A large part of the reason subscribers enjoy streaming is the absence of commercials in most offerings. Traditional network, cable TV, and satellite TV programs have 20 minutes of commercials in every hour of non-premium programs. The exceptions are pay-TV premium channels such as HBO and Starz for which subscribers pay extra fees.

A Snapshot of Companies that Offer Streaming

Although, it has the largest customer base of streaming customers worldwide, Netflix does have competition. According to market research group Parks Associates, there are over 200 streaming services in the United States alone. This statistic was published in the December 19, 2017, *Wall Street Journal* article by Sarah Rabil, "Streaming's Goldrush Upends TV." According to audience measurement firm CommScore as published in the April 10, 2017, TechCrunch.com article by Sarah Perez, "Netflix Reaches 75% of Streaming Users, but YouTube is Catching Up," Netflix currently has 75 percent of customers that stream in the United States. The article further stated that of the Wi-Fi–equipped homes in the United States, 53 percent of them use streaming services. As more homes are equipped with Wi-Fi, the number of people streaming content will continue to grow.

And competitive streaming providers are gaining market share:

- Amazon offers free streaming for its Prime customers. Prime customers pay $100 annually for no-fee fast deliveries, plus other privileges including free downloads to Amazon's Kindle e-reader.

- Facebook Watch offers sports videos, short form videos of 5 to 10 minutes in length, and its own original content of 20- to 30-minute videos.

- Hulu offerings include content from broadcasters and access to live sporting and other events.

- HBO Now is free to people that subscribe to their pay HBO pay-TV offerings.

- Sling TV includes content from live broadcasts plus many pay-TV channels, and streaming sporting events.

- The Walt Disney Company has announced its intent to offer streaming channels with its own content including ESPN and 20th Century Fox's original content, which it is purchasing from 21st Century Fox.

- Google's YouTube TV includes broadcast stations and pay-TV channels such as ESPN and the Disney Channel.

Ad Revenue on Streaming Services

OTT streaming is available with subscription fees without commercials, or free but with commercials. Social network giant Facebook has announced its intention to offer longer form streaming video supported by advertising. Hulu, majority-owned by the Walt Disney Company and Comcast with minority ownership by AT&T, offers options for low-cost subscriptions that include ads or higher-cost subscriptions with limited, brief ads. Hulu has access to premium and broadcast TV content through its broadcast and studio owners' libraries of content.

Streaming Worldwide

Streaming services are available in most regions worldwide, including Europe, India, China, North and South America, and parts of Africa. Netflix alone offers service in 190 countries worldwide. In developing countries such as India and where its available in Africa, coding techniques used in streaming media enable users with slow-speed mobile and wired broadband connections to receive television shows and movies of adequate resolution. Coding techniques that use compression to shrink the number of bits enable many subscribers that would otherwise not have access to receive an acceptable quality of streaming. According to Netflix Chief Product Officer, Gregory K. Peters:

> *Encodes we're using are super-efficient so that we can provide a really, really, high-quality video experience, and with lesser and less bits.*

Netflix is a global entity with over-the-top streaming available worldwide. Its online streaming service is compatible with more than 100 formats on devices such as the Apple iPad and iPod, mobile handheld devices, Roku devices, and game consoles such as the Microsoft Xbox, Nintendo Wii, and Sony PlayStation.

Ease of Use and Technological Enablers

It is no longer necessary to connect laptops to high-definition televisions to stream movies from the Internet to the TV. Dedicated set-top devices such as the Roku and Apple TV are easily linked to flat-panel televisions via the High-Definition Multimedia Interface (HDMI) video interface and audio cable.

Significant technological improvements have occurred that enable multimedia streaming on the Internet in homes and consumer equipment that simplifies streaming to mobile devices and TVs. These innovations include the following:

- Dedicated electronic devices, such as set-top boxes from Apple TV and Roku that connect directly to televisions for streaming TV shows and movies from the Internet.

- Adaptive bit rate streaming software on content providers' and cloud servers that dynamically alter the speed of video streams to match consumer devices and bandwidth. This provides a more consistent video stream with fewer disruptions.

- Improvements with respect to in-home wireless Wi-Fi networks.

- The availability of Internet-connected televisions with icons on the start-up screen for Netflix, YouTube, Hulu, Amazon, Roku, and others that negate the requirement for a set-top box dedicated to streaming.

- The attractiveness, sound quality, and lower prices in home entertainment sound systems with the capability for high-definition images on large flat-screen televisions that make home viewing attractive.

- Over-the-top streaming directly to portable, wireless devices including tablet computers and smartphones with enhanced resolution.

Cable providers and telephone companies that own local broadband facilities now compete with companies such as Netflix with its 100 million subscribers worldwide and Amazon Prime. Netflix and its competitors have an advantage in not needing to build broadband infrastructure to support their services. This eliminates the significant capital investment required to build a network, and lowers the barriers to entry into the market. Competitors such as these are referred to as *over-the-top* (OTT) providers. See Figure 6-1 for a diagram of OTT streaming. It is one impetus for people to opt for high-speed Internet access. In a quote from Netflix CFO David B. Wells at the Netflix 2017 third-quarter investor's conference, he says:

> *When we try to explain the quarter-to-quarter perturbations or some of the lumpiness in our net additions, we tend to use explanations that sort of focus on the incremental, which could be content slate or a particular title that had some notable strength. But I think, in general, it is the continued adoption of Internet entertainment that is driving our growth,*

Time Warner's HBO GO.com division makes no-fee HBO content available online to cable TV subscribers of HBO. Subscribers that pay for HBO can watch any HBO Go content streamed on the Internet. Comcast and other cable companies now embrace TV over the Internet as a strategy to retain profits and subscribers for their pay-TV services in the face of competition from OTT providers.

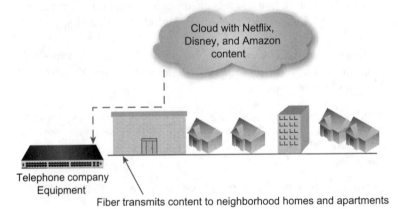

Figure 6-1   Over-the-top streaming between the content provider and residential locations.

Specialized set-top boxes for streaming make it convenient for customers to receive streamed video from the Internet. Set-top devices have interfaces that enable communications between homes' Wi-Fi networks and televisions. The set-top boxes interface wirelessly to home Wi-Fi networks as well televisions. The set-top box connects to the television's HDMI port. These set-top boxes commonly also have an Ethernet interface to connect the TV to a residential network's Ethernet cabling if it's available. Blu-ray players with Wi-Fi and Ethernet interfaces can also be used to stream content from the Internet, as can Internet-connected TVs.

Pay-TV—Skinny Bundles Plus Streaming on Set-Top Boxes

Pay-TV providers (cable and satellite TV) companies have a two-pronged strategy to retain customers that are increasingly moving to OTT streaming to save money on high pay-TV prices and to watch the appealing and more flexible viewing options available by streaming. Pay-TV companies now offer options for lower-cost, pared-down bundles plus streaming services such as Netflix included on their set-top boxes.

To lower prices, and retain customers, they are offering subscribers "skinny" packages that include just the broadcast stations; ABC, NBC, CBS, Fox, The CW, Telemundo, Univision, and the non-commercial PBS, plus HBO or another premium station. Previously, subscribers had to pay for an entire tier of cable channels in order to have the option to subscribe to commercial-free premium stations HBO or Starz.

Technical Challenges

Chris O'Brien, founder of Motionbox (now part of Snapfish, a Hewlett-Packard company) and SoftCom (now part of Interactive Video Technologies), stated in a telephone interview that

> the challenge today is keeping up with the incredible diversity of tablets, mobile phones, and other devices. All of these different devices are creating an enormous challenge for video publishers, which convert the video into formats compatible with all the different screens and display capabilities.

This is complicated by the fact that there is no single format that can be displayed on devices from different manufacturers. Tablets from companies such as Apple, Samsung, and Dell all use a different format, as do mobile devices that use different operating systems and are connected to mobile networks based on differing protocols.

Even using the same type of compression is no guarantee of compatibility. If otherwise compatible audio and video codecs are stored in a different container (file) format, the video cannot be played. A container is a server with multiple small programs that share an operating system. See the section "Containers: A Newer Form of Server Virtualization" in Chapter 1, "Computing and Enabling Technologies," for a description of containers. Desktop computers with the same type of audio and video compression as iPods won't be able to play the same video if the container format in which the compression is stored is different.

There are a number of audio/video container formats (QuickTime, Windows Media Video [WMV], ASF, AVI, and more), and each of these can contain a variety of different audio and video codecs. So, for example, H.264 video with AAC audio in an MPEG4 container might play on your desktop player but not on your iPod, even though they both support H.264 video with AAC audio. Again, this is because they are stored in different containers.

Conversion and Distribution Engines to Process Video

Because of challenges in distributing video content to match the many formats used worldwide, specialized companies such as Brightcove and Ooyala manage the conversion and distribution of video for many online video distributors, including cable TV operators. Other examples are media companies such as online newspapers and magazines, pay-TV operators, and broadcasters.

Authentication and Reporting

Video processing engines perform other tasks associated with distributing video. When cable subscribers watch programs from televisions connected to broadband, the authentication software built into a set-top box automatically sends messages to the cable provider's networks verifying that this is a legitimate customer with a subscription for particular services such as video-on-demand (VOD).

Authentication is more complex when subscribers attempt to view content from other devices such as a tablet computer. The authentication software needs to determine if this device belongs to a legitimate subscriber. Authenticating a set-top box associated with a particular subscriber is simpler because it involves only a single set-top box, at a fixed location.

THE STRUCTURE OF THE INTERNET ....

The Internet is made up of edge and backbone routers that direct traffic based on addresses contained within the headers of data packets. In an effort to reduce delays, Content Delivery Networks (CDNs) install servers at their own locations and that of the carrier's site at the Internet's edges, thus placing content closer to the end users that request it.

Edge Routers

Edge routers are located at the edge of a carrier's network where they connect to customers and to other routers. They are often located at Points of Presence (POPs) where multiple providers connect to the Internet.

The edge of a network needs to support complex applications, protocols, and video. Edge routers must support multiple protocols, including Internet Protocol version 6 and version 4 (IPv6 and IPv4), Multi-Protocol Label Switching (MPLS), Wide Area Software Defined Networking (WA SDNs), and complex accounting software to track packet usage per customer. On MPLS networks, edge routers attach labels as described in Chapter 5, "Broadband Network Services," that include information regarding addresses, protocol, and Quality of Service (QoS). For more information about IPv4 and IPv6 addressing protocols, see the section "Address Structures" later in this chapter.

In addition, edge routers commonly handle aggregated Digital Subscriber Line Access Multiplexer (DSLAM) traffic in various formats; therefore, routers need to support both newer and older variations of IP and Wide Area Software Defined Networking (WA SDN). See Chapter 5 for a discussion of WA SDN.

Edge routers also use addressing information to determine how to handle the data. See Figure 6-2 for an example of a router.

Figure 6-2 An edge router programmed with the features listed above. These features are not present in backbone routers. (Courtesy of Cisco Systems, Inc. Unauthorized use not permitted.)

Services on edge routers include the following (if a router is used in the core, it does not require the extensive services listed here):

- Authentication that verifies the sender is indeed who he identifies himself to be when he logs on to networks.

- Protected session setup that confirms that each multimedia session conforms to the features and QoS allowed to the computer making the request. This protects against fraud and ensures accurate billing.

- Network Address Translation (NAT) addressing that translates external IP addresses to internal IP addresses, and vice versa.

- Support for IPv4 and IPv6 addressing. IPv6 is designed to replace IPv4; it supports many more IP addresses than IPv4's 4.3 billion addresses.

- Layer 2 switching for creating Virtual Private Networks (VPNs) to communicate directly with databases and applications in data centers. (See Chapter 5 for a description of VPNs.)

- Firewall software that protects networks from hackers.

- Accounting to track subscriber packet usage in the event that carriers charge for usage.

- QoS per application and per user for VoIP and video.

In addition to more intelligence, there are requirements for greater capacity in routers. This is caused by increasing use of video conferencing, greater demand for video streaming by residential customers, access to cloud-based services, and growth in mobile smartphone Internet browsing. Router ports now commonly support multiple 10Gbps as well as 100Gbps services. Total capacity of edge routers ranges from 1 to 3 terabits per second (Tbps). A terabit is the equivalent of 1,000 gigabits.

Aggregation Routers in Core Networks

Core routers carry the highest concentration of traffic. A single core router connects to multiple edge routers, aggregates traffic from these edge routers, and then sends it to distant cities and countries. If a single router doesn't have the capacity to handle this aggregated traffic, multiple routers can be networked together. When this is done, the networked routers function as a single entity with a single management interface. This simplifies the carrier's operations, upgrades, and remote diagnostics.

Networking routers together is commonly done through virtualization. (See the section "Virtual Network Function [VNF]—Transforming Hardware Nodes into Software Functions" in Chapter 4, "Managing Broadband Networks" for information on virtualization.) Virtualization enables multiple functions including routers to appear as individual pieces of hardware on servers that can be networked together. In addition, traffic is balanced among all the networked routers. If one router fails, the others absorb its traffic.

Ensuring Reliability in the Core and Edge

Routers sold to carriers and to large web sites such as Google and Amazon are designed for "*five 9s*" of reliability. This means that they offer 99.999 percent uptime. They are sold with *hot-swappable cards* that connect to other services and networks. If a card fails, it can be replaced without taking the router out of service. They are also offered with options for duplicate processor cards and often come standard with dual power supplies. Power supplies connect to sources of electricity. It's also common for carriers to install duplicate routers that can be seamlessly brought online in the event of a failure. Duplicate routers are crucial at the edge, where if the router fails, all other networks and customers connected to it lose service.

Enhancing Internet Performance by Using Content Delivery Networks

Content Delivery Networks (CDNs) provide a number of services at the edge of the Internet that alleviate congestion on the Internet's backbone. In its simplest form, a CDN reduces congestion by decreasing the distance that the traffic must travel. One way they accomplish this is by storing frequently requested web pages at their servers, nearer to the end users, often in a service provider's location. This is referred to as *caching*. Many enterprises with large web sites use CDNs to replicate their web content at many edge locations to prevent delays at their web or e-commerce sites. For traffic that traverses the Internet backbone, CDNs use mathematical algorithms to map out the best paths for traffic to take.

Exchanging Data at Peering Points

Large multinational carriers are referred to as Tier 1 carriers. Tier 1 carriers own the majority of the high-speed lines that make up the Internet backbone. These carriers, all of whose networks are international, include Nippon Telegraph and Telephone Corporation (NTT) in Japan; Telefónica in Spain and Latin America; Deutsche Telekom in Germany; France Telecom in France; and AT&T, Sprint, and Verizon in the United States.

Regional carriers—which are referred to as Tier 2 carriers—also own core, backbone facilities. Comcast and Charter are considered Tier 2 carriers because their networks do not cover the entire country and they purchase backbone capacity from Tier 1 carriers. These Tier 1 and Tier 2 carriers interconnect with other carriers in places where they do not have coverage. These interconnections are referred to as peering points.

Network service providers transfer Internet Protocol (IP) traffic among one another at peering sites. Peering sites are also referred to as Internet exchanges and Network Access Points (NAPs). ISPs lease ports on the routers of other providers as a means of transferring IP traffic between networks. This enables carriers to send traffic that originated from their own customers to areas where they do not have network facilities, as demonstrated in Figure 6-3.

Peering Site with Connections between Carriers' Routers

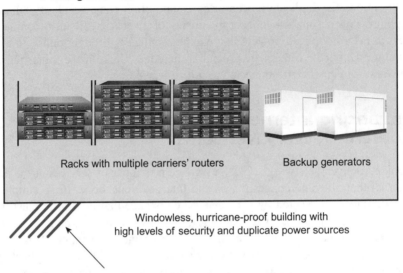

Racks with multiple carriers' routers   Backup generators

Windowless, hurricane-proof building with
high levels of security and duplicate power sources

Fiber-optic cables to carriers and power sources

Figure 6-3   Traffic at peering points is routed between the facilities of
multiple network operators.

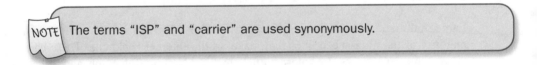

NOTE   The terms "ISP" and "carrier" are used synonymously.

     Carriers that own peering points charge other carriers for connections to ports on their routers. However, traffic at these peering centers has the potential to create delays in the Internet if carriers lease too few ports from one another in an attempt to save money. If carriers exchange about the same amount of traffic, they often don't charge one another under this arrangement. Security, routing, traffic policing, and Network Address Translation (NAT) take place at peering points.

Address Structures

Two universal addressing schemes, IPv4 and IPv6, are used to transmit messages from computers, smartphones, and tablet computers worldwide. The system of routing messages based on IP addresses is managed by 12 organizations that administer 13 clusters of servers, called *root servers*.

The Criticality of Root Servers

The root name server system was implemented in the 1990s. The Internet cannot function without root servers, which route messages to the correct organization. Root servers are critical for the sustainability, capacity, and survivability of the Internet. To lessen the system's vulnerability to malicious actions such as Denial-of-Service (DoS) attacks, wherein millions of fake messages bombard a site, root servers balance incoming messages among multiple servers within each root. If one server within the root is brought down, other servers within the root handle the traffic. Ensuring protection against hackers is an ongoing endeavor.

The 13 Root Servers Worldwide

The *Domain Name System* (DNS) is the umbrella name of the Internet's capability to translate alpha characters to numeric IP addresses within root servers. Carriers and organizations send traffic addressed to locations outside their networks to one of the 13 sets of root servers, usually the one nearest to them, to determine where to route these messages. The root servers, which are massive databases, translate alphabetic hostnames (gmail.com) into numeric IP addresses (193.22.1.126), and vice versa. Root servers are connected to peering exchanges where large carriers exchange traffic with each other. Each of the 12 organizations that operate the root servers has root servers located in multiple cities or countries. They each operate between 2 and 196 locations.

Examples of organizations that operate the 13 root servers are:

- Each of the following organizations operates two sets of root servers:
  - Information Sciences Institute manages root servers U.S. Army Research Lab, which operates root servers in Los Angeles U.S.A. and in Miami U.S.A.
  - U.S. Army Research Lab manages root servers in Aberdeen Proving Ground, U.S. and San Diego, U.S.
- WIDE operates 196 root servers, the most of any operator

Tracking and Managing Top-Level Domains

The Internet Corporation for Assigned Names and Numbers (ICANN) is the organization responsible for managing the technical aspects of the databases of domain names in root servers. It in effect manages the Internet's address book. In a web or e-mail address such as name@companyname.com, the .com portion is the *top-level domain name*, and *companyname* is the domain name, which is also referred to as the *secondary-level domain name*. Every country has a top-level domain name. For example, for China, it's .cn; for Russia, it's .ru. In the United States, some top-level domain names include .edu and .mil for educational and military institutions, and.gov for the government.

Voting ICANN board members were appointed by the United States Department of Commerce until 2009 when the Department of Commerce had sole responsibility for these policies. However, increasing criticism by other countries regarding what they felt to be too much control by the United States of major aspects of the Internet has led to the establishment of international review and policy determination.

Two years after 2013 when Edward Snowden revealed multiple instances of United States government surveillance of other countries and their leaders, the international community began organizing increased efforts for representatives from additional countries to manage ICANN. After years of negotiations, technical leaders from multiple countries agreed on a framework where control of top level domains would be managed by an international group of technical people, governments, and representatives from private companies. A group made up of these representatives now controls ICANN.

The Inclusion of Non-Western Domain Names

Initially, addressing systems used only the Roman alphabet character set (A–Z, a–z, the digits 0–9, and the hyphen). However, pressure from countries that use other character systems eventually led to the inclusion of other alphabets for addresses. These non-Roman alphabets include Arabic, Persian, Chinese, Russian, Japanese, and Korean. China, South Korea, and Arabic-speaking nations had already started assigning non-Roman domain names. These addresses introduced the possibility of duplicate domain names because they were outside of the root system. This created pressure for ICANN to alter their addressing requirements and make the technical changes in the root system that translations from other alphabets require.

Transitioning to IPv6

The main addressing scheme used on the Internet was initially IPv4. IPv4 was developed in the 1970s and addresses are only 32 bits long. On January 31, 2011, the Internet Assigned Numbers Authority (IANA), which managed the central supply of Internet addresses at that time, gave out the last of their IPv4 addresses to each of the five regional Internet registries. By April 2011, the Asia Pacific region had given out all of their addresses, and the remaining four registries distributed all of their addresses within the next few years, Capacity is being depleted by the addition of new Internet-enabled wireless devices and the growing number of Internet users, particularly in Asia.

To ensure that they will be able to get new IP addresses, most organizations are now transitioning to the newer 128-bit IPv6 protocol, which is capable of accommodating billions of additional addresses. Most carriers have transitioned to IPv6. The IPv6 IEEE standard was published in 1998.

Most new routers, web browsers, and computers are compatible with both IPv4 and IPv6. The transition to IPv6 can be complex because it means assigning new addresses to every device with an IP address, including routers, firewalls, network management software, and all servers, including e-mail servers. In addition, it's not a simple matter to determine which applications and devices are compatible with IPv6. Enterprises that transition to IPv6 often need to be able to handle messages that are still in the older IPv4 scheme. Encapsulating IPv6 addresses within IPv4 can address this problem. There are also software packages that support both protocols.

SECURITY: CONNECTED, UBIQUITOUS NETWORKS—VULNERABLE TO MALICIOUS HACKERS ....

Hackers exploit the inherent openness of the Internet and common protocols to steal personal and corporate information, earning billions of dollars from selling information they steal. Hacking into networks and selling information is not only lucrative, it's comparatively punishment free. Hackers are rarely caught and jailed for stealing personally identifiable information such as Social Security numbers, birthdays, and intellectual property from businesses. For one thing, it's not always easy to trace IP addresses back to their origin; secondly, many countries from which hackers launch attacks don't have extradition treaties with Europe and the United States. Without a treaty, attacked countries are not able to extradite hackers and bring them to trial. This prevents hackers from countries such as Russia, China, and Iran from being brought to trial in countries such as the United States and many in Europe in which hacking attacks occurred.

NOTE Extradition treaties are agreements between countries whereby a country in which a crime took place can receive permission to bring criminals back to trial in the country of their suspected crime.

Methods Hackers Use to Attack and Infiltrate Networks

The following are the most common ways that hackers attack networks:

- Phishing emails

- Stolen passwords

- Weak Wi-Fi security

- Incorrectly configured software

- Unpatched software applications with known vulnerabilities

- Ransomware that encrypts organizations' computer files, making these files unreadable

- Distributed Denial of Service where massive amounts of hacker traffic block legitimate users' access

The Five Rs of Information Security

Managing security in government agencies, enterprises and commercial organizations requires 24-hour-a-day scrutiny. Organizations must put in place the tools to *resist* multiple types of attacks. They need the capability to *recognize* when they've been attacked. Viruses have been known to hide in corporate software undetected for months and even years. Additionally, companies need to *respond* to, and *recover* from attacks. Many also seek legal *redress* by attempting to identify attack perpetrators and initiate legal proceedings against them.

Resistance to Hacking

Resistance to hacking is an important way to safeguard private information about personnel, customers, and intellectual property containing product and software designs crucial to organizations' business success. Firewalls are one way organizations screen incoming traffic for known viruses. Firewalls are software- or hardware-programmed to block incoming known viruses and malware. In addition to firewalls, organizations typically have specialized appliances with security software that identifies and blocks malware.

Because of the criticality of security, large and medium-sized organizations hire Chief Security Officers and specialized security staff that monitor incoming and outgoing traffic to keep information secure. The jobs of Chief Security Officers and their staff are increasingly complex due to the fact that employees now access organizations' data stored on the cloud, at hosting centers, and branch offices, as well as at company servers and computers. Staff access this data from mobile as well as landline devices and from remote locations as well as from headquarters. There are multiple places where viruses can infect internal networks. To protect data stored in the cloud, organizations use a combination of, for example, Amazon cloud security software and/or security software designed to operate in the cloud. Security software can additionally be located on servers to protect particular applications and at remote branch offices.

Specialized Security Software

Specialty security software is also available for e-mail and other applications. In addition to security software, firms hire outside organizations to conduct security audits to identify weaknesses that leave the organization vulnerable to attacks. Auditors might identify out-of-date software that needs to be patched, or they might find unauthorized wireless devices without the requisite security software.

As security programs become more sophisticated, hackers find new ways to get around them by creating increasingly sophisticated malware. It is an ongoing challenge to respond to every new type of security breach with improved defenses. This is a particularly difficult challenge because there is generally a lag between when a new software bug or worm is discovered and a software patch is created to guard against it. It's also time-consuming to add patches to not only software security but also application programs such as browsers that might introduce security vulnerabilities. One advantage of Software as a Service (applications in the cloud) is that the cloud provider adds patches to these applications, thus eliminating breaches caused by software with known vulnerabilities.

Intentional and Inadvertent Security Breaches by Insiders

Employees who have been fired or those who feel entitled to access information are frequent causes of these incidents. An employee with high-level authorization to sensitive data can copy it or corrupt it in some way. The employee might then provide the sensitive data to competitors or cyber criminals.

Employees who change jobs are often in the position to copy entire files and use them in their new positions. They might use information such as lists of customers to help them succeed in their new job. They additionally may sell inside information or use it to start a competing company.

In other instances, employees inadvertently open infected e-mail attachments. They might unknowingly insert infected portable storage devices such as USB flash drives into network-connected computers. These viruses can then spread through a corporate network. To prevent this from happening, organizations often purchase security software that automatically screens e-mail attachments, laptops, and external devices for known malware. They can also install software that prevents USB devices from being inserted into LAN-connected computers.

Other inadvertent security lapses caused by insiders include lost laptops, smartphones, tablet computers, backup disks, or flash drives containing files with medical and demographic patient data or other private or strategic information.

User training is an important strategy toward preventing inadvertent security breaches and in gaining the cooperation of employees in adhering to corporate practices. If employees understand the crucial nature of lost data, they might take extra precautions to protect it. This can include measures as simple as not taking strategic information out of the organization, reporting losses immediately, and not leaving passwords on sticky notes under keyboards. They will also be more careful in not allowing unauthorized outsiders entry into the organization. This can be something as fundamental as not allowing people without badges to walk into secure areas behind them. Another point that should be stressed is not leaving unattended computers active so that other users have access to strategic information and e-mail messages. To prevent this, some organizations configure their computers to time out and enter a password-protected standby mode if they are inactive for a specified amount of time, or they institute rules that all employees must shut down their computers at night.

Training Employees on Security Best Practices

Because employee actions can seriously impair security, training all personnel on the importance of security including strong passwords, ways to recognize to phishing, safeguarding passwords, and the importance of using encryption on company data stored on smartphones or tablets. Depending on the industry, there may be legal requirements on managing personal employee and customer information. For example, certain industries such as the medical and financial fields are required to keep client data stored on their computers private. Training on steps to protect this data is critical. According to a Chief Security Officer at a large credit union:

User education is required by financial service regulations and is most effective. Training is the single most important way to prevent phishing attacks. We conduct security training every single month—with a new module monthly on some aspect of security. It's cloud-based education software that takes 5 to 10 minutes to complete. It has a small quiz 2 weeks after the security module has been made available. Staff with a perfect score on the quiz have an opportunity to be in a pool for a gift card drawing. People really like it and it keeps security fresh in their head. New employees are required to attend a classroom when they start at the company. We try to keep them engaged so they retain the security information. The quizzes and prizes keep staff engaged so they retain the information.

Recognition of a Hacking Attack—Tactics for New Types of Viruses

Just knowing when an organization has been infected with rogue, malignant data is one of the most difficult aspects of security management. Malware can lurk in company networks undetected for years. This occurred in the 2017 Equifax and the 2016 Yahoo! attacks. Publicity about customers whose private information has been compromised can cost companies millions of dollars in damages and legal fees responding to law-suits, and from harm to a company's reputation.

In past years, organizations have screened traffic for known viruses. This is no lon-ger as effective as other strategies because of the tens of thousands of known viruses. Newer security software is able to differentiate a list of applications and bitstreams from new, unrecognized data streams. The security software quarantines unrecognized traffic until security staff determines whether the streams contain viruses or are permit-ted traffic. Never-before-seen attacks are known as *zero day attacks*. As extra protec-tion, large organizations often have their broadband provider screen known (zero list) viruses and the enterprises inspect and quarantine the whitelist of unrecognized bit patterns that may contain viruses.

Responding to an Attack

To limit damage from malware, organizations use security software to monitor all incoming and outgoing traffic. Security software is able to issue alerts to specified telephone or mobile numbers, or send e-mails to security staff. Once alerted, staff can take action against the attack. For example, infected computers and servers can be taken offline until the malware is erased from all hard drives and disks connected to it.

Many organizations use Intrusion Detection System (IDS) software or devices to monitor traffic and attempt to block Distributed Denial of Service attacks of millions messages meant to block legitimate incoming traffic. These systems monitor packets for malware and report them. Intrusion Detection and Intrusion Prevention Systems (IDPSs) attempt to stop these attacks as well as identify and report them. Often these types of software can divert the attacking bits to a part of the LAN separated from legitimate servers and computers. However, this is one of the most difficult breaches to protect against as automated bots, short for robots, are programmed to send millions of simultaneous strings of data to enterprises. This makes the network unavailable to legitimate incoming and outgoing traffic.

Security Software

Security software can be embedded in virtualized servers and containers with other applications or in a standalone appliance (a computer with a dedicated application).

There is a trend to embed security in multifunctional devices. Routers are often equipped with firewalls, and Local Area Network (LAN) switches also contain optional security software.

There is also specialty security for e-mail and other applications. Security software can be used to encrypt files containing passwords to protect the files from snoopers and employees not authorized to view sensitive files with personal information or intellectual property. This is important because many employees, contractors, and business partners now access files remotely and are allowed access only to particular applications and files.

In addition to all of these practices, firms hire outside organizations to conduct a security audit to identify weaknesses that leave the organization vulnerable to attacks. Auditors might identify out-of-date software that needs to be patched, or they might find unauthorized wireless devices.

Most security software and hardware products and services offer software that generates audit trails. Software records display indications of security breaches. Paying attention to them is an aid to identifying network weaknesses. In IT departments with large workloads, this does not always happen.

 Encryption is the use of mathematical algorithms to make files unreadable except to users who have the software, the key, necessary to decrypt the files. Encryption is also used on files transmitted between corporate sites and between remote staff and their offices.

Block Chain

Block Chain is new a security protocol now being tested to manage data, track assets, and process financial transactions between banks. It is a distributed protocol without a central entity managing the interactions between nodes (computers). All data transmitted is encrypted when it is sent and decrypted at each node through which the data passes. All nodes along the transmission path must verify the data is not spam or fake in any way. Block Chain is made up of three main components: a network of computers, a protocol, and a way to reach consensus.

Block Chain is envisioned for tracking assets and shipments, and for money transfers between banks. It is also the basis for digital cryptocurrencies. In tests of financial transactions between clearing houses, transactions that formerly took 3 days to complete, were done in just seconds.

Continued

Other applications for Block Chain include tracking assets within organizations and payments between people and institutions; all can be completed without a central clearinghouse. Block Chain transactions and tracking are done through the use of a ledger, which has copies of all transactions and merchandise tracking steps. Each node (computer) in the chain of communications has a copy of the entire ledger and takes part in verifying each transaction.

One challenge in implementing Block Chain is that all of the nodes in each transaction need to be based on compatible network operating systems, network protocols, and back-office systems. Cryptocurrency tokens that are used for financial transactions include Bitcoin, Zeash, Monero, Ripple, and Ether.

Block Chain is architected in a mesh configuration with all nodes and institutions able to communicate with each other without a central entity managing the interactions. Each node verifies and authenticates the data as it is transmitted through networks. Platforms that use Block Chain operates on include Ethereum, Cardano, and Shuttle Fund.

It's likely that there will be additional applications for Block Chain, which is a security protocol. It's not known what the future of cryptocurrencies is.

Mounting Defenses via Firewalls

Firewalls are used to screen incoming messages for known viruses, worms, and *Trojan horses*. Trojan horses are computer programs that appear to have useful functions but actually contain malicious code. A video sent from Facebook can have a Trojan horse embedded within it. Some firewalls can also detect anomalies that are indicative of an attack, including packets that are too short. Firewalls can be in the form of software located at the ISP, the cloud, or at enterprise locations.

Protection from Internal Sabotage

The human factor is the weakest link in securing networks. Current technology is unable to prevent humans from acting in opposition to policy. Many human errors that result in security lapses are inadvertent. However, there are malicious employees who purposely steal or copy intellectual property or insert malware into computer files. An important safeguard against malicious employees is careful screening and reference checks before hiring staff.

An additional way to guard corporate data is a need to know policy that allows employees to access only applications that they need for their job. Other strategies include setting up rules such as not allowing the use of thumb drives in USB ports on computers, and building in alerts if a thumb drive is inserted into a staff person's computer. In addition, security staff can revoke all passwords and access to files as soon as a person's employment is terminated. Some organizations have security personnel walk fired staff or staff that quit their job out the door to ensure that they don't take company computers and/or files with them when they leave.

Recovery from Ransomware and Other Hacks

Recovery from attacks containing malware requires organizations to rid their network of corrupted files and computers that have viruses and other malware that enables hackers to spy on computer files. If duplicate files are stored offsite, the damaged disks containing viruses can be wiped clean or removed and replaced with the back-up files.

Ransomware attacks occur when a user clicks on a phishing link in their email that sends her to a malicious web site. The web site then automatically downloads encryption software to the user's computer and to other computers connected to the same LAN segment. The encrypted files are unusable because in most instances only the hacker has the software key that can *decrypt* (unlock) the files. Hackers behind ransomware attacks demand a payment in return for decrypting files to make them readable. This is a common ploy used against mostly small but also large organizations.

Small organizations are likely to pay the ransom to get use of their files back. Larger companies are more likely to have backups to the encrypted files, thus making them more immune to ransomware. An exception is Uber, which secretly paid a $100,000 ransom to a hacker in 2016 and only disclosed the breach in November of 2017. Uber is now facing five lawsuits because of its delay in reporting the breach.

In a minority of attacks, hacked companies have access to the decryption keys that can unlock the particular encryption used on their files. This is because they belong to a ransom security organization that stores decryption keys for a limited number of encryption codes. No More Ransom is an example of an organization specializing in decryption and protection against ransomware.

Redress—Taking Legal Action Against Hackers

Redress is the ability to take legal action against hackers and bring them to trial. One challenge in taking legal action against people responsible for hacking is the lack of extradition treaties between many western countries with China, Iran,

North Korea, and Russia. Thus the hackers originating attacks from these countries don't necessarily face trials and legal actions for their crimes of hacking into organizations in Europe and the Americas. Many of the hackers in these countries have the blessing of their government to steal data useful in manufacturing or weapons development.

When a hacker is brought to trial, building an airtight case is challenging. Hard drives containing viruses must be preserved exactly as they were following the attack. Computer forensics, evidence on computers, and storage systems must be conserved and presented in court. Any evidence of tampering with the evidence can invalidate the court proceeding.

Cyber Terrorism between Countries

In the past, countries engaged in spying and sabotage by planting agents in other countries. They hoped to learn strategic information about their enemies and potential enemies through networks of spies who often disguised themselves as friendly citizens. Some spies went beyond gaining information to planning acts of sabotage that damaged property, such as roads, bridges, and factories. These same countries also used networks of agents to ferret out spies trying to infiltrate their own institutions. All of these strategies still exist, but they are supplemented by cyber terrorism. Most cyber terrorism is conducted via the Internet.

Acts of cyber terrorism can also be implemented by using *sneaker attacks*, whereby inside employees are co-opted by foreign governments or terrorist groups to learn government secrets, plant software bugs in computer-controlled weapons systems, or copy strategic information inside the organization. This strategy is used to circumvent security measures whereby strategic departments such as armed forces or defense departments attempt to shield themselves by bypassing the Internet for all data communications. Entities such as these communicate to other locations on private lines that they lease or build. These networks only connect to other trusted departments or perhaps suppliers.

Cyber terrorism attacks not only cause computers systems to malfunction; they can also disable computer-controlled weapons systems. This is what occurred when North Korea launched its WannaCry worm that infiltrated computers networks worldwide. A *worm* is a software bug programmed to be activated at a later time. Worms are also referred to as bots. However, bots are more complex than worms and can do more damage. The May 2017 WannaCry attack was so sophisticated that many security experts thought a government, not an individual, planned it. WannaCry attacked hospitals, banks, and over 300 computers in hundreds of countries worldwide. Microsoft had issued a patch, which it classified as critical. However, it was ignored by many organizations, highlighting the criticality of keeping patches up-to-date.

PRIVACY...

Privacy is the ability of people to control who sees information about them. It includes the ability to not share private information such as social security numbers, birthdates, job applications, and medical information. Privacy often conflicts with merchants' desire to use personal data for business purposes.

For example, information about consumer buying habits is a source of valuable information for advertisers who purchase ad space on the Internet. However, it can also create issues for people concerned about privacy. Software used by marketers is able to add small software files to browsers. These software files track which sites an individual visits. For example, if a user clicks an ad containing a video that uses Adobe's Flash or HTML5, the advertiser can compile a list of sites that he visits after clicking the ad. With this information, it can display ads based on what these habits suggest about his interests. For instance, advertisers might display ads about sporting events to people who visit sports-oriented sites.

When a shopper purchases, say, a skirt online or even browses for skirts, advertising networks can automatically display ads about these types of clothing to the purchaser when they visit other sites. In addition, information gathered in this manner from social networks is a powerful way to attract advertisers. In turn, advertising networks that use bots, small programs programmed to automatically collect information, place ads at many different sites and help amass large databases of demographic information about users' browsing and purchasing habits.

Another way that marketers collect information about users is from online games on social networks such as Facebook. Every time a Facebook member downloads a game application, the game developer acquires information about the game player. Developers track the user's data, compile it into lists along with information about other users, and then sell the data to marketers.

Web Site Tracking, Connected Devices, and Free Search Engines

The growth in numbers of computerized connected devices such as home thermostats connected to the Internet are sources where providers can collect information that can be sold to marketers. Toys are an example of Internet-connected items that have the potential to compromise children's privacy. Toy company Genesis manufactures an Internet-connected doll that answers questions children ask it. The questions are transmitted via the Internet to Nuance, a speech recognition company. Nuance sends back answers to their Genesis dolls.

A lack of enforcement in search engines, social networking applications, and e-commerce sites can compromise privacy. Advertising on search sites and social networks is a large percentage of web sites' business. According to Google owner Alphabet's annual report, Google earned 84 percent of its $34 billion revenue from advertising in the first quarter of 2018.

Merchants that advertise on these venues gain information about consumer behavior often in exchange for providing free services to consumers. These services include free online games, flight information, and travel advice. Information on consumer behavior is compiled in massive databases and sold to advertising partners.

Additional connected devices collect information about consumers. Web sites sell this information to marketing companies that use data analytics to spot trends in user behavior that they use to target specific groups of individuals for marketing and to develop new services. The following are examples of where personal data is collected and organizations that amass data:

- Connected TVs that send data on Internet links on which viewers click. In 2017, the U.S. Federal Trade Commission (FTC) fined television manufacturer Vizio $2.2 million for collecting information about customers' viewing habits without first getting their permission.

- Overhead drones are able to collect data using sophisticated long range cameras.

- Credit bureaus have massive amounts of information about people. In the Equifax security breach made public in 2017, 143 million personally identifiable Social Security numbers were stolen.

- Automated toll scanners have the ability to track where cars have traveled by scanning license plate numbers.

- Late model cars with diagnostic software are able to track cars' routes and owners' driving habits.

In addition to the above, Verizon's Oath as well as other companies provide free e-mail. They state that they do not actually read the content in these messages. However, many do track user data. France's privacy watchdog fined Google $165,516 in 2017, claiming Google amassed large amounts of user data for advertising purposes without getting users' permission to collect the data. The privacy watchdog also accused Google of collecting data on sites users visited on the Internet. Subscribers to Verizon Wireless's Up reward program receive credit for every $300 they spend on Verizon Wireless services. The credits can be used for free concert tickets, movie premieres and phone upgrades. Verizon uses the data they collect in the Up ptrogram for the advertising businesses they acquired from Yahoo! and AOL.

THE IMPACT OF E-COMMERCE ....

E-commerce is a major factor, but not the only factor, in the drop in numbers of shoppers actually going to brick-and-mortar retail stores. Retailers that sell clothing, electronic devices, groceries, and pharmaceuticals are all suffering a loss in the amount of foot traffic. According to market research firm Statista, Retail e-commerce accounted for 10 percent of total retail sales in the third quarter of 2017. Providers of non-Internet outlets including travel agencies, book stores, and many magazines and newspaper subscriptions have been losing business to e-commerce since the early 2000s.

In addition to its impact on retail sales, e-commerce has affected how people of all ages find dating partners through web sites such as Match.com and Tinder. Additional drivers of e-commerce are massively multiplayer online games, online gambling, and pornography.

Combining Online Services with On-Site Stores

Online services provide convenience. People can access them at any time of day and from anywhere they have a broadband wireless or wireline Internet connection. Web site owners can also enhance their sites with photographs, video, and links to other locations. However, there are advantages of having both online and physical stores.

Amazon is a high-profile example of a business that initially started as an online-only business that has morphed into a combination of online and on-site retail stores. They purchased Whole Foods in 2017 as one way to establish a foothold in brick-and-mortar retailing. One of the advantages of this combination is the availability of a place where customers can pick-up packages ordered online. The ability to pick up packages at brick-and-mortar stores avoids the problem of stolen packages. Families where both people work often don't have anyone at home during daytime hours when merchandise is dropped off and left outside. This is an issue for people that live in apartment buildings as well.

Amazon is using its own retail outlets as well as its Whole Foods division, as drop-off points for deliveries. Customers are notified when a package is available at a Whole Foods location or an Amazon Go store near them for pick-up. An individual locker at stores avoids the issue of lost and stolen packages. As a rule these orders do not incur delivery fees.

Amazon, which until recently has had an online-only presence, is now opening Amazon Go brick-and-mortar convenience stores with automation that does away with the necessity of cashiers and checkout lines. Rather, people make purchases simply by taking merchandise off shelves after scanning their smartphones into a reader to enter the store. Facial recognition is used to match individual shoppers with their credit card data on their mobile phone. In contrast, Wal-Mart has closed stores, built up its e-commerce web site, and purchased Jet.com, presumably as a vehicle for distributing products ordered online in the United States. In 2018 they acquired Flipkart Pvt Ltd, the largest online commerce site in India and an Amazon competitor there.

Currently, the Amazon Go store is not available to people without a smartphone with a credit card associated with it. Roughly 67 percent of the population had smartphones by early of 2018 according to consulting firm Statista. But, per Statista only 23.16 percent of retail sales were paid for using mobile payments.

FOSTERING CIVIC PARTICIPATION AND ENGAGEMENT—ONLINE FORUMS ....

Not all web activity is designed with a profit motive. Many blogs and mailing lists are started to further social causes or provide support and information to communities. Numerous online forums are non-profits: They generate no profit to people that start and support them; they simply disseminate information on topics of interest. For example, new mothers living in Brooklyn, New York, organized a neighborhood mailing list using the Google Group application to set up the mailing list and invite people to join. The list quickly grew to 120 mothers who all had babies around the same time and who lived in the same neighborhood of mostly townhouses and a few apartment buildings.

Town E-Mail Lists to Keep Communities Informed

Other examples of e-mail lists that provide a community forum are those organized around city and local services. One New England city, Framingham, Massachusetts, uses E-Democracy software to support citizen discussions. E-Democracy forums now host 50 forums in 17 locations across three countries: the United States, New Zealand, and the United Kingdom. The first one, a forum with information about elections, was started in 1994 in Minneapolis.

The city of Framingham has three E-Democracy e-mail forums: Framgov (Framingham government), Frambors (short for Framingham Neighbors), and Nobscot Neighbors to which residents can subscribe.

- Framgov is a forum in which people express opinions about upcoming votes by City officials, including taxes and recent government decisions. It is additionally a forum in which news and announcements about local government and schools as well as opinions about ordinances up for a vote are posted.

- Frambors is a forum for subscribers to ask for recommendations for service providers such as plumbers, contractors, electricians, beauty shops, and nearby restaurants. It provides a place to post opinions about services with which locals are happy as well as those they feel are unsatisfactory. Service providers often respond on Frambors to these comments. Frambors has more than 1,700 subscribers.

- Nobscot Neighbors is a forum at which people that live in the Nobscot section of North Framingham discuss zoning, new building permits, and traffic in their neighborhood.

The following is a quote from the moderator, Linda Dunbrack, who established the Frambors, Framgov, and Nobscot Neighbors online forums after the founder of the original forum died. At that point maintaining the forum founder's server was no longer feasible. The statement was written when the forums were established.

> *After Founder Steve Orr's unexpected death, we wanted to find a way to carry on the legacy of his community email list Frambors. After considering a variety of options, we decided to move the list to a non-profit host called E-Democracy.org.*
>
> *Steve Clift, Executive Director and Founder of E-Democracy, was a huge support as we made the transition, and helped us to make the transition as smooth and as painless as possible. According to the E-Democracy web site, "It is an organization dedicated to promoting civic engagement." It seemed to be a perfect fit, and comes with software and support that is customized to the needs of local issues forums.*

Creating the policies that govern it are critical. On Frambors, Framcom, and Nobscot Neighbors, the policy is that posts may not make personal slurs about another person that has posted a comment. Another example of such a policy decision is that all messages must be signed in the body of the message. This is different from the comment sections of newspaper articles where virtually all messages are anonymous and people feel free to say anything that's on their minds, often with little consideration. On the one hand, signing can inhibit those people who are uncomfortable with the loss of their anonymity, resulting in lowered written participation. On the other hand, signing messages has resulted in changing the whole tone of the conversation; civility, care in detail, and a number of other subtle characteristics all contribute to a marked degree of integrity in the list as a whole. The moderator of each forum first warns, and then disallows people from a list in which they post disparaging remarks about a specific person.

NETWORK NEUTRALITY ....

Network neutrality is the concept of broadband providers treating all traffic equally. It applies to people's ability to access the content they choose from wired as well as mobile devices. The following are the basic tenets of network neutrality:

- Treat all users' traffic in an equal manner.
- Prohibit slowing down traffic to particular web sites.
- Prohibit blocking lawful content from any provider.
- Prohibit blocking access to lawful content or service.
- Network operators are required to publicly disclose actual attainable speeds on their networks as well as reasonable network-management practices and terms of service.
- Landline network operators are not allowed to block lawful content, applications, or services, subject to reasonable network management. Operators of wireless networks are not allowed to block access to lawful web sites, subject to reasonable network management. Wireless operators are additionally not allowed to block applications that compete with their own voice or video telephony services.
- Providers of fixed broadband are not allowed to discriminate in transmitting lawful network traffic over a consumer's broadband access service.

During the Obama presidency, the primarily Democratic United States Federal Communications Commission (FCC) enacted the above network neutrality rules for wireline and mobile companies.

The Issues Surrounding Network Neutrality

However, in 2018, the Republican majority in the FCC rescinded network neutrality rules specifying that ISPs (Internet Service Providers) that provide access to the Internet (essentially telephone companies) must notify customers of their network policies. They additionally changed the classification of the Internet from telecommunications provider to information service. This is significant because the FCC regulates telecommunications services and not information services. The FCC order was titled "Restoring Internet Freedom Order." In overturning network neutrality on July 17, 2017, Ajit Pai, the chair of the FCC, stated:

> *Today, we take a much-needed first step toward returning to the successful bipartisan framework that created the free and open Internet and, for*

almost 20 years, saw it flourished. By proposing to end the utility-style regulatory approach that gives government control of the Internet, we aim to restore the market-based policies necessary to preserve the future Internet Freedom, and to reverse the decline in infrastructure investment, innovation, and options for consumers put into motion by the FCC in 2015.

The two main issues around network neutrality are that some large ISPs such as AT&T, Comcast, and Verizon control networks throughout the USA and sell movies and television content. Comcast acquired content through its partial ownership of Hulu, and its 2011 purchase of NBC Universal. Comcast and AT&T transmit Netflix, Amazon, and Roku's content. These companies are competitors with whom these and other ISPs compete to attract streaming customers. Moreover, the merger between AT&T and Warner Brothers means that AT&T owns content including HBO and HBO NOW. Thus, they too will compete with streaming companies.

Network Neutrality Rationale—Compensation for Adding Network Capacity

Carriers that provide broadband and/or mobile network infrastructure have lobbied the federal government to overturn the Obama-era network neutrality rules. ISPs' public statements are that they should be compensated for investing in new equipment to carry the added traffic created by streaming services. The number of streaming providers and its percentage of streaming traffic are both growing. Thus, ISPs want to be paid for carrying this additional streaming traffic to homes in neighborhoods and over cellular networks. Below is a December 14, 2017, statement by CEO Jonathan Spalter of the USTelecom, a trade association made up mainly of broadband service providers, made the day after the FCC overturned network neutrality and classified the Internet as an information service, not a telecommunications service. The FCC is empowered to regulate only telecommunications services, not information services. The Federal agency referenced below is the FTC (Federal Trade Commission):

> *Today, the future of our open, thriving internet has been secured. The nation's top consumer protection agency now has jurisdiction over fairness and neutrality across the Internet; ensuring consistent rules apply to all players, including the most powerful online companies. And America's broadband providers—who have long supported net neutrality protections and have been committed to continuing to do so—will have renewed confidence to make the investments required to strengthen the nation's networks and close the digital divide, especially in rural communities. It's a great day for consumers and our innovation economy.*

The major carriers are in favor of eliminating network neutrality. They want to be compensated for upgrades to their networks to accommodate increased traffic. Currently, most wireline access in the United States offer tiered unlimited plans for residential customers. Thus, most of these customers have no incentive to cut back on streaming because they pay a flat fee for broadband capacity however much capacity they use.

Pro Network Neutrality Proponents Against Fees and Throttling

Network neutrality proponents are concerned that network service providers have a monopoly or near monopoly on infrastructure and might slow down (throttle) or even block competitors' traffic in favor of their own services without concerns that subscribers will move to a different ISP. This puts competitive services at a disadvantage against the services offered by broadband providers and might lock consumers out of new, possibly lower-cost, offerings. This could be a problem for streaming providers because they are likely to pass on some of these costs to their customers. It will additionally increase consumer and enterprise costs for broadband connections because ISPs will have the option to charge content providers for not slowing down their traffic. This, essentially, creates a fast lane in networks for large content providers that are able to pay these fees.

Web site owners such as Zappos and content providers such as Netflix, Amazon, and Facebook profit from services they sell over the Internet. They pay for connections from their site to the Internet via local carriers. When these carriers transfer traffic to other networks needed to reach customers, neither the other network owners nor the carrier connected to the subscriber are compensated. See Figure 6-1 in the section "Streaming—A Disruptive Technology" in this chapter, which illustrates Netflix and others' streaming traffic connections to telephone companies' equipment.

Zero Rating

Zero rating is the process whereby ISPs and cellular providers exempt consumers from data fees and data caps for certain services, including unlimited video streaming. Carriers sometimes exclude their own content from data caps limits or fees for data. This is what AT&T instituted when it eliminated data caps from its DirecTV service. In a similar vein, Comcast eliminated data caps for its Stream TV service.

Another instance of zero rating is AT&T Mobility's 2012 announcement of a plan to shift some of its data network costs to developers whose customers generate the traffic. Under the plan, developers will have the option of paying fees to AT&T Mobility for cellular traffic generated by their applications. The applications for which developers pay usage fees will not count toward customers' data plans. Critics of the plan charge that it favors established developers that can afford the fees, which results in free usage for their customers.

The Have's vs. the Have Nots: First Class and Everyone Else

Many consumer watchdog organizations feel that creating exceptions for certain possibly lucrative applications will in effect create two different Internet classes of network services. They fear that the part of the network providing priority "first class" treatment for new applications will take increasing amounts of capacity away from ordinary applications and bog them down. This is because without network neutrality, carriers are free to charge content providers extra for not throttling the movies and TV shows carried over the Internet to subscribers.

Content providers such as Netflix and Amazon may pass on these fees they incur to customers. For many ISPs, competition for their wired broadband services has been non-existent or in a minority of locations; they have one competitor or at the most two competitors. This means they can demand concessions from Netflix and Amazon and their competitors without losing broadband customers. This makes it easy for them to make whichever policies are advantageous to them and to block content from providers that won't pay a premium for faster transmission. Customers in these locations have no or limited options for ISPs to use.

Prioritizing certain applications over others has the potential to increase congestion and slow down traffic that is not prioritized. It additionally has raises the possibility of a slowdown innovation and competition by making it costly for start-ups to pay for specialized treatment for the traffic they generate. Owners of smaller web sites as well as start-ups may not have the money to pay broadband networks for not slowing down their traffic.

Attempts to Overturn the Repeal of Network Neutrality

Opponents of the FCC's cancellation of network neutrality are currently pursuing two options for overturning this ruling. A coalition of 21 states' Attorney Generals plus Washington DC are suing the FCC over its cancellation of network neutrality. In addition to the states' efforts, Internet activists have also initiated suits to overturn the FCC's ruling. These include Mozilla Corp. (the producer of Firefox), the Open Technology Institute (part of the New America Foundation), Public Knowledge, the Free Press, and The Internet Association whose members include Google, Facebook, and Amazon.

There are additionally legislative efforts in the Senate to overturn the FCC's cancellation of network neutrality. However, even if the Senate succeeds, there is the hurdle of passing the bill in the House of Representatives. And, the president has the power to veto the legislation if it passes both houses.

Most ISPs agree that both wireless and wireline carriers should adhere to rules on transparency and that transparency should apply to network management and disclosure in understandable language about conditions and characteristics of their networks. Network management refers to a carrier's efforts to handle congestion and security threats. However, transparency means that ISPs will disclose throttling. It does not mean that they will not throttle or block certain traffic.

THE DIGITAL DIVIDE: BANDWIDTH, SKILLS, AND COMPUTERS ....

Most middle- and high-income residents in urban and suburban areas have Internet access with adequate capacity. This is not always the case with residents in rural areas where, if broadband services are available, they are often costly and slow compared to service in more developed regions. The slow speeds discourage users from signing up for these services because services such as video depend on a higher capacity to work well.

For low-income groups, costs for computers and broadband can be prohibitive, given their limited resources. These circumstances contribute to what has been termed the *digital divide*, by which segments of populations do not have equal access to Internet and computer services. These populations are essentially locked out of online educational services, the ability to apply for and look for jobs online, and other services such as instructional materials and electronic training for their children.

While the digital divide between wealthy and poor residents is decreasing, as of January 2018, FCC member Jessica Rosenworcel stated that there are still over 24 million Americans and 12 million children with no broadband services. Government policies and allocation of resources have a major impact on bandwidth availability. Countries can provide free computer training for the unemployed to open up new opportunities for them. Training can enable the unemployed to apply online, which opens additional opportunities.

The digital divide is more than the simple measurement of whether or not Internet access is available. The digital divide is further measured by the following:

- **The amount of available bandwidth**   This is the network capacity in terms of bits per second and cost per kilobit or per megabit compared to urban sections of a country. In 2018, the FCC in defined broadband bandwidth as 25/3—25 megabits downstream to subscribers and 3 megabits upstream to the Internet.

- **The quality of computer equipment available to users**   Is it compatible with the latest browsers and is it capable of handling video?

- **The availability of training**   Do users know how to navigate the Internet to accomplish their goals?

The digital divide in the United States is decreasing in part because of the use of fixed wireless technologies in rural areas. AT&T, CenturyLink, Verizon, and Frontier all have stated their intention to increase broadband capacity in rural areas using new, higher capacity fixed wireless. See Chapter 7, "Mobile and Wi-Fi Networks," for information on fixed wireless technologies. However, according to Pew Research Center's 2016 surveys, the digital divide in the United States is most pronounced in:

- Minority populations

- Groups with lower incomes

- Residents in rural areas

- People with disabilities including those with low vision, hearing loss, and physical limitations

- Seniors—particularly lower-income, less-educated seniors

Economic policies make a difference in the availability of broadband. Tax credits for new networks encourage carriers to upgrade equipment and infrastructure. Outright subsidies are a more direct option for improving networks. Countries such as Australia, China, and Japan have underwritten the cost of building fiber-optic or advanced mobile networks in rural areas. Improved broadband is one step in bringing remote areas into the online economy.

Community resources can bridge some of the gaps in the digital divide. In the United States, public libraries provide free Internet access, computers, and often training in how to use them. This is particularly critical in areas where residents do not have up-to-date computers or the expertise to access the Internet. In an effort dubbed "The Library of Things," some libraries lend technology gear to families to promote computer literacy and Internet access. For example, they lend portable Wi-Fi hot spots so that people without Wi-Fi can access the Internet from a computer and Roku set-top boxes so people can try out streaming.

Internet Pricing and Competition

The cost of Internet access is a factor in increasing or lessening the digital divide. In 2017 the United States had the 12th highest average Internet speed worldwide according to speed monitoring company Ookla in the December 17, 2017, article at *recode*, "Global Internet Speeds Got 30% Faster in 2017," by Rani Molla. In contrast, the average cost in the United States—$66.17—was 114th highest in the world out of a total of 196 countries surveyed. Iran and the Russian Federation were among the 113 countries with lower-cost Internet access. This statistic was published in the *Forbes* November 22, 2017, article, "The Most and Least Expensive Countries for Broadband," by Niall McCarthy. The source for the statistic was consulting firm Statista.

Because people in many areas of the United States have few or no choices for an ISP, there is little incentive for carriers to lower their prices so that it is more affordable for lower-income people. Another factor on higher prices in rural areas is the higher cost to cable rural areas. These steep costs result from the fact that there are fewer customers per square mile in sparsely populated areas so ISPs don't earn enough revenue from the few customers to make it worthwhile to lay fiber and charge lower prices in these areas.

INTRANETS AND EXTRANETS ....

An *intranet* is the use of web technology for the sole, dedicated use of single site and multisite organizations. Intranets are a way to collaborate, distribute information, software, and other services within an organization using web-like software tools.

Extranets extend the reach of intranets from internal-only communications to sharing documents, fixing software bugs, and providing information for business-to-business transactions. Online banking is an example of an extranet.

Intranets

When they were first developed, intranets, which are based on web technology, served as repositories of centralized information. Intranets are still a single source of an organization's information. However, they are now as a whole better organized so that employees can find what they are looking for faster. Clear organization of information is an important area where intranets can excel. In large organizations this is not always the case, as some departments do not always update intranets with the latest information. Having management to which the intranet is important creates a culture where departments update their intranet when needed. Examples of intranet software include Facebook's Workplace collaboration and networking software, Microsoft's Teams, Axero, Jostle, MyHub, and Intranet Connections.

Collaboration where people in distant offices can work jointly on projects and reports is an important way to improve productivity. Some additional intranet functions include:

- Staff reading documents and agreeing on or modifying parts

- Commenting on sections of documents by employees who work at different physical locations to foster working together on joint projects

- Discussion forums

- Content approval flows by appropriate staff

- Calendaring for setting up meetings

Intranet functions that support employee functions include:

- Online training that users can complete on the intranet

- Posting internal job openings

- Providing company-recommended software and updates that employees can download to their computers

- Checking whether user applications need updating and that all security patches are in place when employees log on to the intranet

- Managing human resources functions such as accessing pay stubs and appraisals, making changes to tax forms, changing user addresses, and selecting benefits

- Enabling the ability to submit time cards and expense reports on the intranet

- Making available corporate documents, such as organizational practices, required documents, templates for résumés and sales proposals, technical magazines, and corporate directories

- Establishing wikis with information about particular technologies or work-related information

In addition, intranets at global organizations often mimic web functions by providing social networking functions. The directory might have fields in which people can list special interests such as trekking or music. Employees can form groups around these interests.

Firewall and other security software control staff members' access to corporate information on intranets. Restrictions can be applied to prevent employees from accessing inappropriate databases and applications. Not everyone has access to all files. Rather, employees can be placed in groups based on the applications to which they are allowed access.

Potential Issues with Intranets

The most common complaints about intranets are the difficulties in keeping them updated. Time and attention devoted to organizing information often depends on whether top management buy into the intranet as a priority. If the information on the intranet is out of date, the intranet loses much of its value. Organizations without either management support or tools to support automated or simple maintenance and implementation might have intranets do little to enhance employee productivity.

In some organizations, every department posts their own updates. If updates are cumbersome and time-consuming to make, they might not be posted in a timely fashion. To make it easier to update intranets, organizations can deploy software packages such as Adobe Dreamweaver, Microsoft SharePoint Designer, and Expression Web, all of which have user-friendly interfaces that make it easier to update intranets and extranets. Often, a centralized IT organization manages the intranet and sets technical standards for it. Having a single-password, single-sign-on procedure for a uniform intranet saves time on calls from users who forgot their passwords.

Extranets—Saving Money on Customer Service

Extranets use a web interface for secure access by customers, business partners, and temporary employees. Organizations typically limit access to applications more so than intranets because they are used with outside individuals and organizations. Individual vendors or partners have access only to specific applications. Access to extranets is generally password-protected or password-plus-token. A token is a small device about the size of a large house key that generates random numbers at predefined intervals. Users key in the number displayed on their token plus their password to access applications.

Online banking is an example of an extranet service that saves staffing costs. Customers transfer money between accounts, pay bills, and gain instant, graphical interfaces to the status of their accounts. This is highly advantageous to banks because it saves money on financial transactions as well as staffing costs. Moreover, banks' extranets are a way to solicit business. They offer customers services such as loans, home mortgages, and other financial instruments. Banks and other organizations also offer customers online bank statements and electronic bills through their extranets. These electronic services save mailing expenses and printing costs.

The following is a quote from an employee on the benefits of their extranet, which is used for business to business transactions:

> *In my company, each of the customers is given a special identification number and access to a specific application. The customer can use his identification number and log bugs and issues that he sees in our product. The customer can specify the importance of the bug and keep track of the progress made on its resolution.*

Because of security concerns, many extranets are located at web hosting sites. The hosting company's customer has his own computer at the hosting company. High-speed Carrier Gigabit Ethernet capacity lines connect the hosting company to the Internet backbone. Companies often remotely upload or download information to their host-located computer via Carrier Gigabit Ethernet. Online learning is an example of an extranet service. It provides web-like access to educational material for school staffs and students. This is an advantage to schools that offer it because it enables them to offer their courses to students that are not within commuting distance of the college or university. In addition to supplying extranet software, online-learning companies offer to host the application at their own site.

7 Mobile and Wi-Fi Networks

In this chapter:

INTRODUCTION ....

Mobile devices are a central part of many people's lives. This is especially true of young people. When graduate students at a university were asked if they agree with the following statements, the majority of them agreed.

- You wake up in the middle of the night to check your phone.

- You check your smartphone within 10 minutes of going to sleep at night.

- You check your smartphone within 10 minutes of waking up every day.

- You study at cafes, and check your WeChat or Instagram accounts there too.

- You play games on your phone at the subway.

- You check for messages while walking to class.

Some students stated that they check their phones 15 and more times every hour. Young people and not-so-young people use their phones for online gaming, video streaming, and social networks. It's an integral part of their day. High usage is not confined to teenagers and twenty-somethings. It's an important part of everyday life for much of the population.

Growing capacity, availability, and ease of use enable adults as well as twenty-somethings to use cellular networks for an increasing number of functions. People use these networks to stay in contact with friends and family, receive email and text messages, and keep up-to-date on news. While waiting for an appointment in a doctor's or dentist's office, most people use their device to make the time pass faster. And people that travel often bring tablet computers on airplanes and train trips to watch downloaded videos.

The increased use of smartphones and tablet computers has created pressure on mobile carriers to add capacity by upgrading their networks to protocols that enable them to pack more traffic on the airwaves that carry wireless voice and data.

In essence, mobile networks are becoming densified, meaning cell sites with antennas and adjunct equipment are spaced closer together with each supporting higher data rates. Densification requires adding new cell sites to support gigabit data rates achievable with upgraded Long Term Evolution 4th generation (LTE) networks and new 5th generation mobile protocols. Densified wireless networks are architected with fiber-optic cables that connect heterogeneous networks (HetNets) together. The name HetNets is derived from the fact that HetNets are made up of cell sites with various amounts of coverage and antenna sizes.

There is additionally more usage over Wi-Fi networks inside homes, cafes, and buildings as people increasingly use smartphones and tablet computers for video streaming, reading newspapers, and accessing social networks within buildings. There are new and emerging protocols that support gigabit data rates and improved security in Wi-Fi networks. The same phenomenon of large increases in wireless usage is occurring inside buildings and homes as in cellular networks in wider outdoor areas. In many residences, it's not unusual for each person to have multiple devices with many in use simultaneously.

Satellites along with ground-based wireless networks are being designed and upgraded to support broadband services in areas with sparse availability of high-capacity cellular networks and broadband networks. In particular, low earth orbiting satellites (LEOs) that orbit closer to the earth than traditional satellites are being deployed. LEOs are made up of smaller, less costly satellites than traditional satellites. Because they are lower in the sky, more LEO satellites are required to cover the entire earth. However, even at the lower price, it takes a group of investors to raise additional funding to build these high-cost satellite networks.

The requirement for new satellite networks, 5th generation mobile network infrastructure, and upgrades to LTE mobile networks require ongoing investments. The same is true of infrastructure and protocol development in Wi-Fi networks. Moreover, the challenge of operating these complex networks is sparking an interest on the part of providers to use cloud-based services to manage the large numbers of dense network components.

SPECTRUM FOR WIRELESS NETWORKS—A CRITICAL ASSET...

In wireless networks, spectrum consists of the invisible electromagnetic energy used to transmit signals. The spectrum over which signals are carried is a critical asset that carriers require to operate their mobile networks. All governments regulate the allocation of spectrum. This is to prevent multiple transmissions from different mobile providers from interfering with each other. Mobile networks are critical for communications in national defense and public emergencies, particularly when landline networks may not be available.

Cellular Structures—The Foundation of Mobile Networks

Cellular service was first put into operation in 1984. It uses spectrum more efficiently than earlier, non-cellular systems by enabling networks to reuse the same frequencies in non-adjacent cells within cities and towns. The reuse of frequencies within non-adjacent cells was a creative innovation that added capacity to cellular networks. AT&T's Bell Laboratories (now part of Nokia) created this first generation of cellular service. At that time, Bell Labs was owned by AT&T, which in turn owned all of the local telephone companies in the United States. Bell Labs provided the research and development for all the AT&T-owned telephone companies at that time. See the section "The Breakup of AT&T" in Chapter 3.

The Division of Airwaves into Frequencies

All wireless services operate over spectrum. Spectrum is divided into and allocated by frequencies. A *frequency* is the number of times per second that a radio wave completes a cycle. A cycle can be imagined as a letter *S* lying on its back, such that it appears similar to looking at a cross-section of an ocean swell. A cycle is complete when energy passes through an entire radio wave from the highest to the lowest portions of the wave. For a visual depiction of a complete wavelength cycle, see Figure 7-1. Frequency is measured in *hertz*, which refers to the number of complete cycles per second. Thus, for a frequency of 30 million hertz—or *megahertz* (MHz), as it is called— energy passes through 30 million resting *S*'s in one second.

Radio Wavelengths

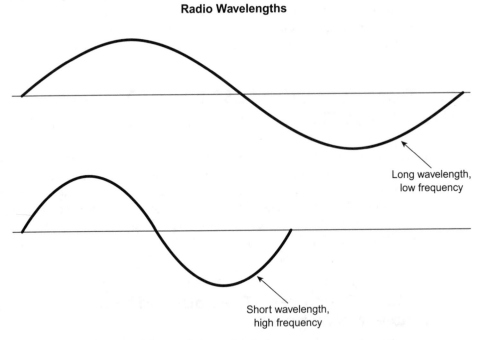

Long wavelength, low frequency

Short wavelength, high frequency

Figure 7-1   A comparison of short, high-frequency wavelengths and long, low-frequency wavelengths.

The Characteristics of Short and Long Wavelengths

Spectrum is divided into frequency ranges from low ranges of frequencies of about 30MHz to 300MHz allocated to government agencies, local police, highway, and state police to high frequencies such as 24 to 50 gigahertz (GHz) for fixed, point-to-point wireless service and for 5G networks. Each range of frequencies is measured by the wavelength in the range. Wavelengths in low frequencies, such as AM radio at 100Khz, measure 9,000 feet (3,000 meters) long. Higher-frequency 10Ghz wavelengths measure 1.78 inches (3 centimeters).

Because of their longer wavelengths, low-frequency signals travel farther than high-frequency signals. Their longer lengths allow them to better withstand physical barriers such as rain and other solid materials. Thus, low frequencies can penetrate walls, buildings, and similar obstacles better than high frequencies. For these reasons, broadcast services such as those for traditional TV and for TV broadcasts designed for mobile devices typically use lower frequencies.

High-speed mobile data networks operate over a variety of spectrum, such as 600MHz, 700MHz, 2.1GHz, 2.6GHz and 39GHz. Higher frequencies require more closely spaced antennas because these signals fade over shorter distances. New 5th generation mobile services will be based on high-gigahertz frequencies such as 39GHz spectrum. For the most part, cells in urban areas cover a smaller area, resulting in many small cells with small antennas rather than large towers. Smaller, closely spaced cells are needed to support dense amounts of high-data-rate mobile traffic in metropolitan areas with high-pedestrian traffic.

Spectrum Blocks

Governments allocate spectrum in chunks of frequency bands that are measured in ranges of, for example, 12-, 15-, 22-, and 30MHz. The size of the spectrum band is determined by subtracting the lowest frequency of the range from the highest frequency (highest frequency minus lowest frequency). For example, if an organization is granted the rights to use the spectrum band from 785MHz to 800MHz, it has the right to a 15MHz band (800 − 785 = 15).

Spectrum bands, which are set aside for specific services, are divided into blocks designated by letters of the alphabet. For example, within the 700MHz band (between 700MHz and 799MHz), the A block refers to a different block or range of frequencies within this larger range of frequencies than the B Block. The A Block might be allocated to one carrier in a region and the B Block to a different carrier for competing services in the same region. As new technologies are developed, certain spectrum bands are used for *shared spectrum*. With shared spectrum, sophisticated protocols in antennas send signals around signals from other traffic.

Using Numeric Designations for Roaming Compatibility

In addition to alphabetic designations for blocks of spectrum, numeric ranges are designated for particular portions of spectrum within blocks. Standards bodies designate the numeric bands of spectrum for *uplink* and *downlink* transmissions. These bands are specified by numerals. For example, the 3rd Generation Partnership Project (3GPP) designated band 13 spectrum of the 777–787MHz range for uplink transmissions.

- Uplink (UL) transmissions are those from subscribers to carriers' antennas, and

- Downlink (DL) transmissions are those from the carrier to the subscriber.

The goal is to enable equipment compatibility so that customers can more easily use their mobile devices on other networks. Mobile devices have preset designations for which frequencies are used for uplink and which are used for downlink communications. Thus, they only work on networks that use the same bands within frequencies.

The 3GPP specifies other bands, such as 12 and 17, for either uplink or downlink transmissions. Not all technologies require separate frequencies for uplink and downlink communications. In these instances, numeric designations are not required.

Using Auctions to Allocate Spectrum

Because it is finite and critical to industry, security, and emergency preparedness, all governments allocate spectrum for particular uses. Portions of the public airwaves and frequencies are allocated for satellite, broadcast TV, Wi-Fi, 4th generation, and 5th generation mobile service as well as other services.

Governments often provide spectrum at no charge when they believe it is in the national interest to foster development of new services. This happened in Asian countries such as Japan and others where the government felt it was in the national interest to foster construction of higher-capacity wireless networks. Japan's allocation of spectrum was based on the government's evaluation of organizations' ability to build and manage a cellular network. These were dubbed *beauty contests*.

Strategies to Gain Rights to Spectrum

Rules about spectrum allocations are set by the FCC and by Congress. The rights to these blocks are strategic assets that enable carriers to offer new, competitive services. Mobile carriers and governments use the following strategies to gain new spectrum:

- Purchase rights to it at government auctions

- Discontinue the use of their older cellular services and *refarm* this spectrum for more advanced protocols. Currently, mobile carriers are building LTE Advanced and 5G networks on spectrum formerly used for 2nd and 3rd generation networks. (See below for *refarming*.)

- Purchase entire companies for their spectrum

- Purchase non-cellular companies' unused spectrum (See the feature "Acquiring Spectrum by Buying Companies that Own Spectrum Suitable for 5G" later in this chapter.)

In order to free up spectrum for high-capacity mobile networks or other national needs, organizations and government agencies already using these bands must be moved to other bands.

Using Incentive Auctions to Speed Up Spectrum Availability

In February 2012, Congress allocated $7 billion for the build-out of a nationwide public safety network and authorized the use of an *incentive auction* for that purpose. In an incentive auction, entities selling spectrum to the government keep lowering their prices until the FCC determines the amount of money they collect from the auction is adequate to pay for needed spectrum from the entities giving it up.

The FCC held the first incentive auction in 2016 and announced the results in 2017. It offered the D Block of 700Mhz spectrum that analog TV stations ceded in return for spectrum for digital television. The auction raised $19.8 billion, $10.8 billion to pay for the broadcasters' spectrum and more than $7 billion that was deposited in the U.S. Treasury. AT&T won the bid in the auction held on March 29, 2016, and is in the process of building out the FirstNet network for first responders from diverse communities to communicate with each other to coordinate strategy in natural disasters and national emergencies.

This first-ever incentive auction resulted in refarming spectrum from use for analog TV channels to a national public safety network. As a result of the auction, over-the-air broadcasters changed from analog to digital TV using the spectrum given to them by the FCC. Digital airwaves have capacity for two channels in the same amount of spectrum needed for one analog channel. In addition to spectrum for the public safety network, cellular providers won spectrum for new mobile wireless licenses needed to add capacity to their cellular networks.

Auctions Held between 1998 and 2017

- In 1998, the FCC auctioned PCS 1.9GHz spectrum to open mobile services to new providers. The goal was to increase competition, thus lowering per minute prices so that more users could afford cellular service. Prior to this there were only two providers in each part of the United States: the incumbent telephone company and a single competitor.

- The FCC auctioned a 700MHz block in 2008 to a variety of carriers for higher-capacity, higher-data-rate services. Verizon Wireless won regional licenses to spectrum in the A and B blocks, and AT&T Mobility won rights in the B and C blocks. AT&T's B blocks are in a different region from Verizon's. None of the licenses cover the entire country. The auction raised $19 billion for the federal government. All of the auction winners were required to use this spectrum to build networks capable of supporting higher-speed data on next-generation LTE networks.

- In 2014 an AWS (Advanced Wireless Services) auction of 1.755 to 1.78GHz and 2.15 and 2.18GHz spectrum bands was held. Results were announced in 2015. The winners were, in decreasing order of the amount of spectrum won,

AT&T Mobility, Verizon Wireless, Dish Network, T-Mobile, U.S. Cellular, and a mix of five private companies including American Movil, a cellular company owned by Mexican mogul Carlos Slim and his family. The American Movil spectrum is used in Puerto Rico.

- In 2017, the FCC held a reverse auction of 600Mhz spectrum. T-Mobile won the largest percentage of this spectrum. AT&T and Dish Network won lesser amounts. AT&T subsequently began selling the spectrum it won because it purchased FirstNet for its nationwide spectrum. Other winners included U.S. Cellular and Comcast. Verizon did not bid, possibly because it is concentrating on building out a network of small cells using GHz spectrum able to carry large amounts of data.

Enhancing Spectral Efficiency to Increase Capacity

The ability to carry more traffic within a given amount of spectrum is crucial to keeping up with the growing amounts of mobile data traffic. Carrying more traffic using the same amount of spectrum is called *spectral efficiency*. Each successive generation of wireless protocols is more spectrally efficient than the previous one. For example, 4th generation (4G) wireless technologies are capable of carrying more high-speed wireless data and video than third-generation (3G) technologies and 5G is expected to be more spectrally efficient than 4G.

The successive spectral efficiency in newer generations of mobile services is gained by building more efficient antennas, faster chips in radios located at cell sites and in users' mobile devices.

Profits from Unused Spectrum on the Secondary Market

In addition to obtaining spectrum at auctions, carriers purchase spectrum on the secondary market from organizations that purchased it at earlier auctions but either did not build a network on it or were unsuccessful in their service offerings. For example, beginning in 2011, Dell computer owner, Michael Dell bought up TV and radio stations for the value of their spectrum, which he sold in the 2016 incentive auction for billions of dollars.

Taxpayers currently receive no revenue from the sale of unused spectrum by non-governmental organizations. In 2011, cable TV providers Comcast, Time Warner Cable, and Bright House Networks agreed to sell the spectrum that they purchased through at an auction to their joint venture, SpectrumCo, to Verizon Wireless for $3.6 billion. The cable companies earned a windfall of $1.4 billion on their $2.2 billion spectrum purchase. They subsequently built out a nationwide network of Wi-Fi sites over which cable TV subscribers reach the Internet from Wi-Fi–enabled cafes and public spots. None of this profit went to taxpayers.

To ensure that entities that purchase spectrum use it for actual mobile networks, the FCC has ruled that carriers and other winners of spectrum must use their spectrum within 12 years. If it's not used within this time frame, the FCC can reclaim the idle spectrum. This has not stopped spectrum owners from selling their spectrum at huge profits to cellular networks before the 12-year deadline.

In fact, the FCC did require that FiberTower return all of its 24GHz that it won, but on which it did not build infrastructure. It allowed FiberTower to keep its other spectrum. See below for information on AT&T's purchase of FiberTower.

 NOTE Fixed Wireless to the Home (WTTH) is the use of cellular service at homes for broadband service. Fixed wireless requires dishes at subscribers' homes and equipment on telephone poles for access to the Internet. It also requires a small converter box to convert the cellular signals to those compatible with the residence's Wi-Fi signals.

Acquiring Spectrum by Buying Companies that Own Spectrum Suitable for 5G

In addition to leasing spectrum from governments, large mobile carriers purchase companies that already have underutilized or unused spectrum. In recent years Verizon Wireless and AT&T Mobility purchased companies for their high-frequency spectrum. High frequencies are suitable for building thousands of the small cells needed for 5G services in heavily trafficked downtown areas.

In early 2018, AT&T acquired FiberTower, which owned 24GHz and 39GHz spectrum. However, they only got a portion of its 39GHz spectrum and none of its 24GHz spectrum. The FCC seized the 24GHz spectrum because FiberTower hadn't utilized this spectrum. But AT&T did acquire FiberTower's 188 billion points of presence, which are used to backhaul data from cell sites to mobile network switches and core networks. AT&T also purchased Straight Path Communications in 2017 for its 29GHz and 39GHz spectrum.

Verizon bought fixed wireless company XO Communications in 2017. Its XO purchase included the rights to lease XO affiliate NextLink's 28GHz spectrum, which is located in and around large cities in the United States. These high-frequency spectrum bands are desired for 5G mobile networks. The FCC must approve these purchases of spectrum before the spectrum transfers are finalized. The Competitive Carrier Association (CCA) objected to this spectrum transfer because it had not been offered at an auction so that smaller mobile carriers would have an opportunity to bid on this valuable spectrum.

Continued

> The CCA was quoted in a FierceWireless article on January 19, 2018, by Mike Dano, titled "AT&T to lose hundreds of 5G millimeter wave licenses as part of FCC/FiberTower settlement." The CCA stated "If the pending transaction [between AT&T and FiberTower] is approved, the terms of the settlement agreement will afford FiberTower a financial windfall for sitting on unconstructed licenses for years and AT&T a windfall to acquire valuable 5G spectrum." The FCC approved AT&T's purchase of FiberTower on February 12, 2018.

Synchronizing Spectrum Internationally

Spectrum allocation is administered on both an international and a national level. The International Telecommunications Union-Radiocommunication Sector (ITU-R) manages the allocation of spectrum for services such as satellite and television that cross national borders. It also acts as the umbrella for other services such as determining spectrum bands for 3rd, 4th, and 5th generation services. These functions have become more critical as subscribers worldwide depend on their mobile devices when they travel for business and leisure.

In the United States, the International Bureau of the FCC, the National Telecommunications and Information Association (NTIA), part of the Commerce Department, and the State Department work with the ITU-R. Generally, working groups comprising representatives from many countries hash out particular issues under the auspices of the ITU. Decisions on spectrum and new 4th and 5th generation protocols are made at the ITU's World Radiocommunication Conferences (WRC), held every 5 years.

Geographic Licensing Schemes

Because of its large size, and mountainous, sparsely populated areas, no single carrier's network provides complete geographic coverage across the entire United States.

There are six regional groupings in the contiguous United States and others for regional groupings such as Alaska and Hawaii. The Gulf of Mexico also retains its own grouping.

Verizon Wireless and AT&T Mobility cover almost all of the metropolitan areas in the United States, but not all of the rural areas. No other carrier has such extensive coverage or the financial wherewithal to purchase spectrum to cover these large areas. In the 2016 auction, T-Mobile was the major bidder. They scooped up almost the entire spectrum in the 600MHz range. This spectrum is particularly suited to fixed wireless in rural areas because of its ability to travel distances without fading.

Fixed wireless is important in rural areas where it's not cost effective to lay fiber to homes miles apart from each other. See Figure 7-2 for an example of fixed wireless service. Deploying fixed wireless from telephone poles to homes is many times less costly than laying fiber in rural areas. There are fewer residences in rural areas from which mobile companies can recoup the cost of constructing fiber networks to homes.

Homes in a rural area with wireless broadband for Internet access. Each home is connected directly to the mobile telephone company's antenna.

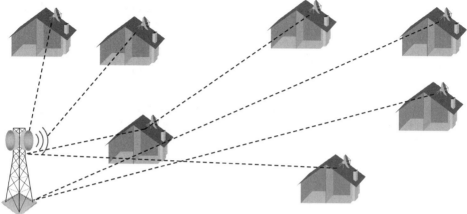

Figure 7-2   Fixed wireless in rural areas.

Mitigating Interference

When transmissions use the same frequencies in the same locations or even next to one another, they can interfere with one another. For example, if people install Wi-Fi wireless equipment such as cordless telephones as well as microwave ovens that operate at 2.4GHz near each other, they may experience operability problems. These problems are caused by interference. Newer wireless protocols have the ability to hop between channels when they sense that other signals are in the same channel.

Concerns about interference often lead to political conflicts between factions. This can occur when new uses for spectrum or new technologies are proposed. This occurred, as illustrated in the next section, when it was first proposed that white-space spectrum be allocated for other uses and also when LTE U was proposed. See Table 7-2, "LTE Types."

Unlicensed Spectrum for "Super" Wi-Fi

Governments specify portions of the spectrum for unlicensed services such as Wi-Fi and *Bluetooth*. Bluetooth is a wireless standard for communications between short distances such as wireless mouse or headsets linked to PCs and smartphones. Unlicensed spectrum is available free to companies that do not have to apply for a license to use it. This significantly lowers the cost of deploying service, but it doesn't mean the government does not regulate unlicensed spectrum. Every cellular and wireless device must be registered with the FCC and adhere to regulations on the amount of power emitted.

Devices that emit high power may interfere with nearby devices. Moreover, the government can designate bands of spectrum as unlicensed for public benefit.

In 2010, the FCC designated licensed spectrum formerly used in conjunction with analog TV as unlicensed spectrum to lower the cost of bringing new broadband services to rural areas. When broadcasters changed from analog to digital television broadcasts, The FCC auctioned off most of the 6MHz of that spectrum formerly used as *guard bands* for analog TV and still used for wireless microphones.

Guard bands, also called *white spaces*, are unused bands of frequencies surrounding each channel that prevent wireless signals from adjacent analog channels from interfering with one another. Wireless signals are not enclosed in cabling, and thus can leak or spread into adjacent spectrum. Analog signals leak more than digital signals. For this reason, when the FCC originally allocated spectrum for analog television, it set aside 6MHz of spectrum as guard bands between all adjacent TV channels.

When the FCC announced its desire to make these white spaces available for Long Term Evolution (LTE) because they were no longer used as guard bands, broadcasters and Broadway theater producers objected. They were concerned that new services in the spectrum might interfere with microphones and other equipment used at public events such as those in stadiums, concerts, and even churches. After extensive testing, including an experimental license granted in a small rural town, the FCC ruled that the former white spaces could be used as unlicensed spectrum. It ruled that it could be used for "super" Wi-Fi, a Wi-Fi standard whose signals can travel over longer distances than traditional Wi-Fi signals. "Super" Wi-Fi is the informal name for the 802.22 IEEE standard.

The FCC hoped that this spectrum would be used to bring high-speed Internet access to rural areas. Making the spectrum unlicensed further supported the goal of lowering the total cost to bring Internet access to rural areas. Because this spectrum is in the 700MHz range, which is a low frequency, the signals can travel the distances required in rural areas. Using wireless obviates the need to lay fiber-optic cabling and install costly electronic equipment near customers or directly to premises.

Power-Level Specification for Unlicensed Spectrum

Because of the potential for wireless spectrum to cause interference, governments establish rules regarding issues such as signal spreading and power limitation to protect adjacent licensed spectrum bands against egregious interference emanating from unlicensed spectrum transmissions. All equipment used in licensed and unlicensed wireless networks must meet government specifications to receive certifications. That is why even a Bluetooth mouse is certified and assigned an FCC ID number.

Roaming—Using Mobile Devices in Other Networks

Roaming is the ability to use the same mobile devices when traveling in other carriers' networks. These other networks may be within the United States or in international locations where a subscriber's mobile provider does not offer service. Roaming is important because no single carrier has coverage everywhere. Roaming is a profitable source of revenue in many parts of the world. Exceptions to this include within European Union countries, most cellular providers for traffic within India, and depending on each customer's plan, traffic within the United States.

In June of 2017, the European Union eliminated roaming surcharges for residents of the EU that travel within EU countries. Another example of no-cost roaming is T-Mobile, which offers customers on certain plans no-fee texts, voice, and data usage when they roam in 140 countries internationally.

Agreements among carriers are required for every region in which roaming is enabled. Roaming agreements spell out costs, billing, and payment terms. To illustrate the complexity of roaming arrangements, most carriers have agreements with 200 to 250 other carriers. Some carriers use brokers that already have agreements worldwide and share revenue with the broker. Thus, calls made and received while roaming are more expensive than those in the subscriber's home territory; with the additional costs covering the fees imposed by the other network.

Once the agreement has been signed and the service tested, roaming is activated. Carriers lease high-speed links to other providers such as AT&T, France Telecom, and Belgacom (in Belgium), all of which have an international presence. These links carry the actual voice and data traffic. Signaling links are also established to perform functions such as the *handshake* between the handset and the user's home carrier. The handshake verifies that users are legitimate customers of the originating network and have roaming privileges. Gateways are used to translate signaling between handshakes that use incompatible types of Session Initiation Protocol (SIP) links over which the handshake is done.

Roaming revenues are shrinking because many customers use Wi-Fi in cafes and hotels when they travel internationally. For more on Wi-Fi international networks see the section "Wi-Fi for Roaming" later in this chapter.

MORE EFFICIENT 4TH GENERATION DIGITAL NETWORKS ....

Mobile protocols define how data and voice are carried on cellular networks. For example, 3rd generation (3G) networks carry data and voice separately. However, 4th generation (4G) networks specify that voice and data are to be transmitted on the same spectrum streams. They essentially treat voice as data and transmit it in IP packets. This is a significant improvement in spectral efficiency that eliminated the need to set aside separate spectrum for voice calls.

All 3rd generation and newer cellular services are digital. This improves privacy as eavesdropping on digital transmissions is more difficult because the digital bits are encrypted (encryption uses mathematical algorithms to reorder bits, making them unreadable to unauthorized people) before they are transmitted over the open air between handsets and an operator's equipment. See Table 7-1 for a list of the main mobile protocols along with the various implementations within each generation.

Unlike 3rd generation protocols, which used different technologies in Europe and parts of the United States, 4G LTE is for the most part is implemented uniformly throughout the United States and Europe, as well as in Asia and parts of Africa.

 NOTE All current mobile services including 2G (second-generation) services are digital. Digital mobile protocols use codecs to code analog voice into digital bits and decode them to analog at the receiving user device. Digital transmissions enable features such as caller ID, speed dialing, and voicemail message notifications. Signals for these features are carried separately in the signaling channel.

3G standards had various releases or revisions, which improved upon and increased capacity and suitability for mobile networks capable of carrying voice, video, and data. However, even in these revisions, voice is transmitted using the less-efficient circuit switching where spectrum that could be shared with data is set aside for voice. More information on 3G and 3G standards are in Table 7-6 and Table 7-7 in the "Appendix." In 4G networks, voice is carried in Internet Protocol (VoIP) packets on the same spectrum as data.

3G protocols are still available in even advanced networks because there are still older phones that are compatible with only 3G and not 4G protocols. Once mobile providers find that a large majority of subscribers have phones compatible with newer protocols, 3G spectrum will be refarmed (repurposed) for 4th and 5th generation cellular services. *Refarming* refers to using spectrum previously used to carry older generations of traffic to use with 4th and 5th generation protocols.

Table 7-1 Main 3rd, 4th, and 5th Generation Cellular Service

Generation	Variations	Where Used	Characteristic	Transmission
3G**	CDMA (Code Division Multiple Access)	Implemented by Sprint and Verizon in U.S. and in South Korea & other Asian countries	Data carried as digital bits	Voice transmitted on separate spectrum
	WCDMA (Wideband Code Division Multiple Access)	Implemented in Europe and most of the rest of the world	Data carried as digital bits	Voice transmitted on separate spectrum

Generation	Variations	Where Used	Characteristic	Transmission
	HSPA+ (High Speed Packet Access Plus)	Upgrade from WCDMA	Higher for data capacity than WCDMA	Voice transmitted on separate spectrum
4G	LTE* (Long-Term Evolution)	Implemented worldwide	Evolved to support 100Mbps of data downlink	Voice and data transmitted together in data packets
5G	5GNR (New Radio)	WTTH (Wireless to the Home) is the first 5G service implemented	A replacement for low-capacity copper links in rural areas	Less-costly broadband option; not as fast as fiber.

Additional varieties of LTE are in Table 7-2, "LTE Types."

**More details on 2G protocols and mobile services worldwide are listed in Table 7-5 in the "Appendix."*

3G Technologies—Incompatible Standards

The International Telecommunications Union (ITU) defined IMT-2000 (International Mobile Telephone) digital standards for 3rd generation voice and data on cellular networks. Unfortunately, the ITU subcommittees endorsed several different, interoperable 3G techniques due to political pressure from operators and manufacturers who wanted standards to more closely match the equipment they produced and used in their networks.

The two main standards organizations, 3rd Generation Partnership Program (3GPP) and 3rd Generation Partnership Project 2 (3GPP2), specified non-interoperable protocols and architectures (the way devices are connected together and interoperate). 3GPP (3rd Generation Partnership Project) is a collaboration agreement formed by European, Asian, and North American telecommunications standards for cellular protocols.

See Table 7-6 in the "Appendix" for more details on 3G networks.

Early LTE Implementations

The earliest version of LTE was a pre-4G service. The capacity on these early LTE implementations reached ranges between 2Mbps and 25Mbps, not the 100Mbps defined in the 4G LTE specifications. LTE's use of Multiple-Input Multiple-Output (MIMO) antennas is a key factor in increased capacities.

LTE—THE FIRST TRUE 4TH GENERATION CELLULAR PROTOCOL ....

Long-Term Evolution (LTE) is the first protocol to use spectrum more efficiently by transmitting both voice and data as IP packets over the same spectrum bands. It is no longer necessary to set aside spectrum exclusively for voice on different spectrum than that for data. LTE is additionally the first mobile protocol suitable for video and high-capacity data transmissions.

Initially, LTE protocols did not support the full 4G rates defined by standards bodies; the ITU-R specified that 4G technologies support 100Mbps downlink transmissions from the network to the user. Criteria for 4G protocols are set by the ITU-R. The ITU-R defines the capabilities required for protocols to be considered 4G, but the 3GPP (Third Generation Partnership Program), does the actual development work of how these recommendations will be implemented.

According to the ITU-R definition, which was published in November 2010, all 4G technologies must meet certain capabilities. The key 4G criteria are as follows:

- Data rates of 100Mbps downlink (from the network to the user device) for mobile devices such as those in cars or trains, and 1Gbps downlink speeds for low-mobility devices. Low mobility refers to devices used in fixed locations or portable only within a building.

- Internetworking with services based on international mobile telecommunications (IMT), earlier 3G protocols, and with services transmitted on fixed, landline networks.

- An all-IP packet infrastructure.

- Internet Protocol version 6 (IPv6) addressing, which has more addresses than IPv4. See Chapter 6, "The Internet," for information on IP addressing. See the section "Addressing Protocols" in Chapter 6 for information on IPv6 and IPv4.

- The ability to support mobile TV.

- Efficient use of spectrum.

- Worldwide roaming compatibility between mobile 4G devices.

Internetworking refers to the fact that 4G devices can seamlessly be handed over between cell sites that use 3G and 4G protocols without transmission interruptions. See Figure 7-3 for an example of a handover between 3G and 4G networks. Handovers are the process that occurs when subscribers travel between networks that support different protocols.

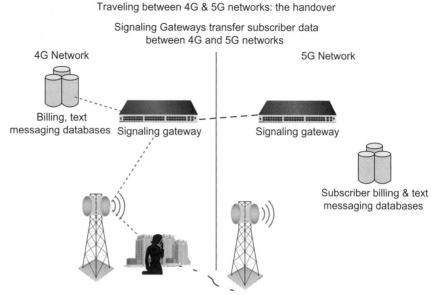

Traveling between 4G & 5G networks: the handover

Signaling Gateways transfer subscriber data between 4G and 5G networks

Smartphone transmits device ID data as subscriber moves to 5G network.

Figure 7-3 The handover between 3G and 4G networks.

A number of manufacturers compete with one another to supply 4G and 5G network software and hardware. These include Ericsson, Huawei, Nokia, Samsung, Xiaomi, and ZTE.

4G LTE—Designed to Transmit Data and Voice in IP Packets

4G technology was developed with the goal of supporting high-speed broadband and video transmissions. It is the first mobile protocol designed primarily to transmit data. It supports voice, but only as IP within data packets. LTE has improved antennas, and faster chips in handsets and in radios in the network. The mobile core is the mobile carrier's data center. It is equipped with servers containing databases and software to control and monitor the network as well as providing connections to other networks.

LTE is the 4G protocol adopted by carriers worldwide. Manufacturers produce a wide choice of devices for networks that use these air interfaces, because these networks represent a large pool of potential customers. Handset prices also tend to be lower because there are more choices and more competitive pressure.

LTE Capacity

LTE (Long Term Evolution) supports web surfing, mobile broadband, and Quality of Service (QoS) for video streaming. QoS saves a path in the network for each video transmission for the entire duration of the video. This provides the consistent service required for video. True IMT-Advanced, 4G LTE, based on Release 11, supports 100Mbps downloads, and is available in much of the world.

  LTE is not a one-flavor protocol. It has evolved into a true 4th Generation protocol with variations. These variations are listed in Table 7-2, "LTE Types." Each variation operates on specific spectrum bands and is suited for particular applications such as low-speed Internet of Things (IoT). Another LTE variation is suitable for fixed WTTH in areas with no fiber or high-speed Internet access to homes.

 IoT is the ability of equipment and machines to communicate with each other and with central servers for monitoring and collecting information. Monitoring automobile traffic is an example of an IOT application. Collecting subway fees and parking meter credit card transactions remotely are other IOT applications.

Mobile Service in Sub-Saharan Africa

Mobile broadband is particularly significant in developing areas such as countries in sub-Saharan Africa, where high-capacity fixed broadband is not widely available. Much of the population in sub-Saharan Africa that live in cities own mobile phones, but the capabilities are limited in large part to 2G and 3G services. Exceptions are major cities in Democratic Republic of Congo, Ethiopia, Nigeria, South Africa, and Tanzania. This is starting to change as mobile operators have announced plans to build out LTE capabilities. Cell phone ownership in sub-Saharan Africa is lowest among women and children under 16.

LTE Cell Sites' Additional Functionality

An LTE cell site consists of antennas, amplifiers to adjust power levels, and a single piece of equipment, the evolved NodeB (eNodeB). The eNodeB allocates radio frequency (wireless spectrum) to users' devices and passes calls off to other cell sites and to the mobile carrier's core IP network. Importantly, the eNodeB manages Multiple-Input Multiple-Output (MIMO) antenna functions and Orthogonal Frequency-Division Multiplexing (OFDM) signaling. See the section "The LTE Orthogonal Frequency-Division Multiplexing Air Interface" later in this chapter.

Coaxial cabling connects the eNodeB to the cell site's antenna. The eNodeB contains a blade with a software-defined radio containing the air interfaces tuned to the applicable spectrum. A blade is a densely packed, horizontally placed circuit board with many ports. The modem in the software-defined radio translates radio frequency signals into those compatible with landline networks, and vice versa for outgoing traffic.

The eNodeB is also referred to as the *base station*. Together with the antennas, amplifiers, and spectrum, it is used to access the mobile network. In combination, this equipment and spectrum make up the Radio Access Network (RAN). The eNodeB manages the RAN.

LTE architecture is streamlined in terms of the amount of equipment and protocols required compared to earlier generations of mobile networks. Figure 7-4 presents a diagram of LTE architecture. This streamlining and distribution of functions at fewer servers results in data stream transmissions that use fewer protocols and equipment hops. This decreases latency (delays).

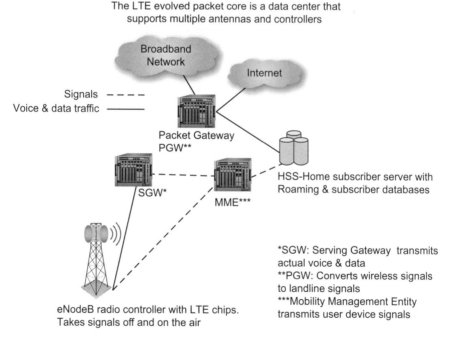

Figure 7-4 Fourth-generation (4G) Long-Term Evolution (LTE) architecture in the Radio Access Network (RAN) and the evolved packet core.

Backhaul—Connecting Cell Sites and Core Networks

In addition to managing vast amounts of cellular traffic, carriers operate large landline networks between their cell sites and their IP core. The links between cell sites and equipment in their core are referred to as *backhaul*. Backhaul is also referred to as the *transport network*. Traffic from many sites is backhauled to a central location—the operator's core network. This network transports signals between base stations and core networks. Transport networks consist of links to mobile switches and other networks. From the core, traffic is sent to the operator's mobile central office switch, the Internet, or another public data network. See Figure 7-5 for an example of backhaul links. Depending on the amount of traffic, backhaul networks use the following:

- Microwave (a Wireless Transmission Service at 44Mbps/34.4Mbps) or wireless Carrier Ethernet at speeds up to 40Gbps

- Fiber-optic cabling transmitting Gigabit Ethernet traffic

- Gigabit Ethernet and Multi-Protocol Label Switching (MPLS) (multiple 100Gbps streams with MPLS-enabled QoS capabilities) on fiber-optic cabling

A backhaul network is made up of traffic from cell sites that is aggregated and transmitted to the core.

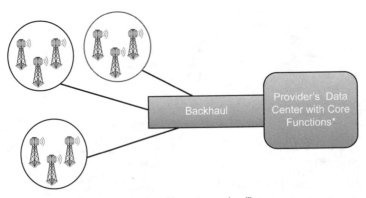

*Billing, tracking devices, tracking outages, signalling

Figure 7-5 The aggregation backhaul network consolidates traffic from multiple cells and sends it to the core.

In the United States, most providers have upgraded much of their backhaul network to fiber. In areas of the country and worldwide where fiber is not already installed, backhaul traffic is carried by microwave and other higher-capacity wireless technologies. The higher costs for fiber are viable because more traffic is carried on these links. Fiber is likely to be more readily available in aggregation networks where carriers have previously laid fiber that often has spare capacity.

In many instances, the landline divisions of mobile carriers build these networks. When Verizon Wireless upgraded its backhaul network to fiber, it used the wholesale division of Verizon Communications to build it out. Verizon's wholesale division offers backhaul services on a wholesale basis to other providers in addition to Verizon Wireless. Cable Multiple System Operators (MSOs), AT&T, and other long-haul network carriers also provide backhaul links to mobile carriers. The traffic is transported on the same fiber that transmits traffic from landline carriers.

The Functions of Radios and Modems in Mobile Networks

Every wireless device contains a radio. Radios in mobile networks extract radio frequency signals from the air and convert them into small bits of frequency compatible with the devices. The radios then hand off slices of bits of data to modems within devices. At the transmitting end, radios convert signals to the frequencies used in the cellular network, and then transmit these wireless signals over the air.

At the receiving end, modems remove noise caused by interference and decode the radio frequency data signals into those compatible with the landline network. If the amount of noise is so great that the signal can't be decoded, the modem requests that the base station retransmit the signals. Removing the noise from signals is the most complex function in modems. At the transmitting end, modems encode (modulate) the signals to make them compatible with the radio frequency wireless network. Modems also add encryption at the transmission end for protection from eavesdroppers.

Elements of LTE Infrastructure

LTE has a simplified infrastructure and cell sites with fewer pieces of equipment to manage than early generations of mobile protocols. Moreover, LTE software and hardware can be installed on standard computer platforms so that carriers can choose from a wide range of equipment manufacturers. LTE cell sites also support more users per cell site than 3G technologies because the air interface is more flexible and uses spectrum more efficiently. See Figure 7-6 for LTE architecture.

The elements of LTE Networks are:

- The RAN is the only wireless part of mobile networks. This is the link between the user device and the antenna or tower. A base station located adjacent to the tower or antenna is dubbed an e-NodeB.

- The backhaul "hauls" traffic to the core from the RAN and vice versa. It is made up of fiber-optic cabling or high-capacity microwave.

- Fronthaul is the fiber link between antennas in Heterogeneous Networks (HetNets) LTE and 5G architecture in which small cell sites are linked to larger macro cells with fiber. The fronthaul is the fiber linking the small cells to the macro cell within the same area. These cells are controlled by base stations at the macro cell site. See the section "Heterogeneous Networks—Architectures for Densely Trafficked Areas" later in this chapter for information on HetNets.

- The evolved packet core is the mobile providers' data center with routers and software for signaling systems to manage mobile traffic and identify cell phones' owners

- Transmitting traffic to the other networks

- Converting mobile traffic to be compatible with wired networks

- Billing and tracking

- Tracking roaming by users

- Tracking and identifying applications using Deep Packet Inspection, which identifies bits inside packets

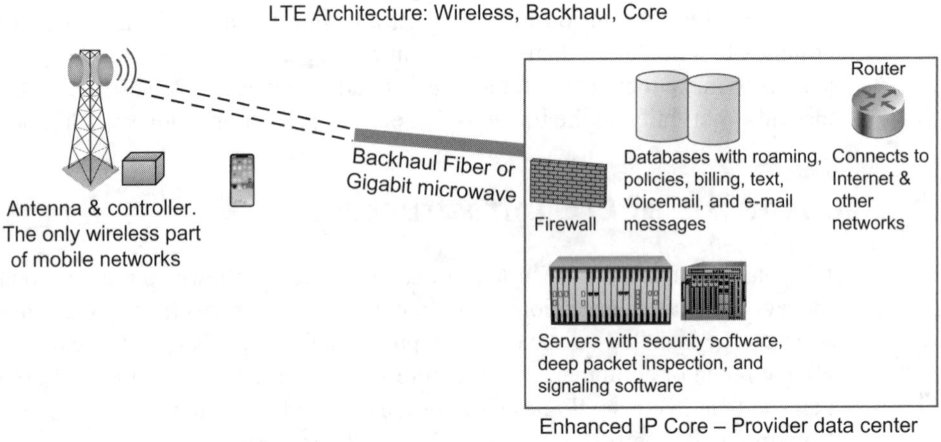

LTE Architecture: Wireless, Backhaul, Core

Antenna & controller. The only wireless part of mobile networks

Backhaul Fiber or Gigabit microwave

Firewall

Databases with roaming, policies, billing, text, voicemail, and e-mail messages

Router

Connects to Internet & other networks

Servers with security software, deep packet inspection, and signaling software

Enhanced IP Core – Provider data center

Figure 7-6   LTE architecture.

Location Indicators—Signals between Handsets and Mobile Switches

A mobile handset is essentially a radio that can be tuned to particular spectrum bands (frequencies). In order to operate in a particular area, mobile devices must have radios capable of being automatically tuned to the same spectrum as that of the radios in cell sites' base stations. In addition, each carrier must authorize every mobile handset before it's allowed on the network.

Mobile devices constantly send out signals to the nearest mobile company's switch, essentially notifying the switch of their location. For example, Verizon has five major switches in the New England states that receive signals from Verizon mobile devices. Fiber-optic cabling connects each of these switches to cell sites at the mobile carrier's towers, which tracks cell sites. The signals carried over this fiber cabling indicates each mobile handset's cell site and tower location. Moreover, each new tower is tested before it is "turned up" to ensure that the nearest 911 call center can be reached when users dial 911 when they are within range of the cell site.

NOTE | Mobile switches and the large amounts of fiber-optic cabling are critical parts of all mobile networks and they all depend on power to operate. Mobile networks are not immune to power outages caused by storms and natural disasters. Lightning strikes and snow emergencies are particular challenges because they can knock out electricity to switches and cell sites. Outages can occur at cell sites not equipped with a back-up generator. Not all carriers have adequate backup. Some have battery backup for momentary power glitches and short outages lasting only a few hours. Adequate backup is a growing challenge because of the increased number of small cells and natural disasters.

The Three Elemental Functions of the LTE IP Core

The LTE IP Core functions as mobile providers' data centers. Traffic from hundreds of cell sites passes through a mobile carrier's core network. Signaling gateways that translate protocols for 3G networks are located in the core along with 4G equipment. The LTE core network, also referred to as the *evolved packet core*, routes this traffic to data networks, the Internet, other mobile carriers, and other cell sites within the carrier's mobile network. Equipment and software located in the core also perform signaling and tracking calls for billing purposes.

A key factor in improved functioning is LTE networks' flexibility in handling voice and data is the fact that signaling messages are carried separately from user data and IP voice. Signaling messages are used to keep track of usage, perform security functions (to keep the network free from hackers and malware), authenticate users, setting up a session (voice, data, or video) and enforce policies. Policies include rules on the number of bits included in various data plans. Signaling enables carriers to monitor this volume so that a message can be sent to the user's device, notifying him that he has used up his planned quota and will be charged extra for additional transmissions.

Functions within the LTE evolved core network are divided into three functional elements. The evolved packet core contains servers for managing these elements. Two elements, the *Serving Gateway* and the *Packet Data Network Gateway*, are generally located in the same router. The functional elements making up the LTE's IP core are as follows:

- **Mobility Management Entity (MME)**   This performs the signaling functions in the IP core. It sends and receives signaling information needed to set up, bill, and address calls to the eNodeB and to the Serving Gateway. In addition, the MME contains the security protocols for authentication and authorization.

- **Serving Gateway (SGW)**   The SGW forwards the data and voice packets on bearer paths between the eNodeB at the cell site and the Packet Data Network Gateway. Bearer paths carry the actual user IP data. The SGW handles the protocol conversions between LTE devices and 3G systems and relays this traffic to and from the Packet Data Network Gateway and earlier- or later-generation gateways.

- **Packet Data Network Gateway (PGW)**   This interfaces with the public data network (the Internet and carrier private data networks). It additionally allocates IP addresses to user devices and is responsible for policy enforcement. It can classify packets as requiring Quality of Service (QoS). It also generates usage records that it sends to the carrier's billing system, indicating levels of customer voice and data usage. The PGW has links to the roaming database for functions related to roaming and billing roaming traffic.

The PGW and SGW transmit mobile traffic to the Internet and other data networks. 3G traffic is handed off to these LTE gateways by earlier-generation controllers and signaling gateways. Note that Voice over LTE is outside of the evolved packet core.

Databases in the LTE Evolved Packet Core

Gateways in core networks connect to a variety of databases that support roaming, billing functions, voice messaging, and text messaging services. The following is a listing of key Evolved Packet Core databases in core 4G networks:

- Home Subscriber Services (HSSs)—Keep track of roamers' locations and temporary records of roaming subscribers' devices. Store telephone identities and authentication codes for digital phones. Perform security functions including authenticating that users are subscribers.

- Messaging center databases and processors—Handle text messages. Also store multimedia messages including voicemail, facsimile, and e-mail.

- Policy and Charging Rule Function (PCRF)—Contains QoS parameters and details of each subscriber's plan. A Traffic Detection Function enforces these Policy and Charging policies. The PCRF sends information to the Packet Data Network Gateway, which then forwards traffic to the Internet and broadband networks.

- Billing databases—Contain specific information on contract terms for each subscriber. The Packet Data Network (PDN) transmits usage records to the PCRF, which is connected to billing software.

In addition to above databases and functions, there are security applications in the evolved packet core. This may include firewalls that screen traffic for malware. The firewall may be located in the cloud.

Voice over LTE—Packetized Voice

Voice over LTE (VoLTE) is an international standard for transmitting voice over LTE. VoLTE codecs digitize voice and put it into packets to be transmitted along with data and video. When LTE was first available, voice was carried separately on spectrum used for older protocols.

The 3GPP developed VoLTE as a standard way to transmit VoIP. The VoLTE protocol is tightly specified so that roaming and interoperability with earlier-generation networks are possible. VoLTE is designed to interoperate with Internet Protocol Multimedia Subsystems (IMS). IMS enables applications for voice, video, and online games to be stored, billed for, and accessed on a common IP platform. See below for IMS.

Advantages of VoLTE include:

- Higher-voice quality equal to that of calls made from landline phones

- High-quality video calls

- Efficient use of the same spectrum for voice, data, and video

- A standard way of handling voice

- Faster call connection times

- Support for E-911 calls

- Spectrum previously set aside for voice can be re-used for other services

Simultaneous Voice and Data

The VoLTE protocol specifies that the same device can be used for voice and Internet access simultaneously. Prior to the advent of VoLTE, when a user received a voice call, her data connection was dropped. With VoLTE, someone using her device to browse the Internet, can answer a phone call without dropping her data connection. This is also true when a subscriber is on his phone and he looks up the weather forecast or checks his phone's calendar without dropping his voice call.

Using High-Definition Voice to Improve Quality

Voice quality on LTE has dramatically improved from that of previous mobile generations. This is due to improved codecs that compress and decompress analog voice for transmission on digital data networks. The VoLTE standard specifies improved noise cancellation. Noise cancellation distinguishes between voice and background noise and removes the noise so that voice is clearer. Matching codecs are required in the handset and in the network.

High definition voice supports higher and lower frequencies than previous mobile protocols. See Figure 7-7 for voice frequencies on VoLTE. High frequencies up to 7000Hz (think sopranos) are not cut off, and neither are lower frequencies down to 50Mz (think bass sounds). This results in clearer sounds in noisy locations. In short, users in noisy locations can hold clearer conversations on their LTE and 5G smartphones.

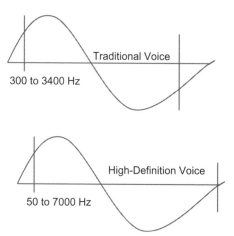

High Definition Voice:
High and low frequencies are not cut-off
Noise cancellation strips out background sounds.

Figure 7-7 Voice frequencies on VoLTE (high-definition voice) compared to those without VoLTE.

Accessing Applications and VoLTE—The IP Multimedia Subsystem

IP Multimedia Subsystem (IMS) is a 3GPP open-standards architecture made up of multiple protocols and standards by which customers can access applications from many types of mobile devices. These applications include unified messaging and multiplayer games that are installed in a provider's network-connected platform. The signaling and control of IMS services are built around session initiation protocol (SIP), which is the signaling protocol used on IP networks such as the Internet for transferring traffic between carriers and for linking enterprise sites to IP networks. SIP signaling is used for functions such as setting up a video session (a call), tearing down the session, carrying numbers dialed and mobile devices' identity. For information about SIP, see the section "Session Initiation Protocol—Out-of-band Signaling" in Chapter 6.

VoLTE is based on the IMS, IP Multimedia Subsystem standard. IP IMS is access independent. See Figure 7-8 for IP Multimedia System. Access independence refers to the fact that subscribers, for example, on Gigabit Ethernet, any mobile protocol, Wi-Fi, or cable modems can access IP-based applications such as video calling or chat services on the IMS network. In contrast to IMS's goal of universal access, specialized services such as WhatsApp and Tencent's Chinese Weixin—We chat in English—IMS is meant to be globally interoperable on carriers' networks and not part of a closed network.

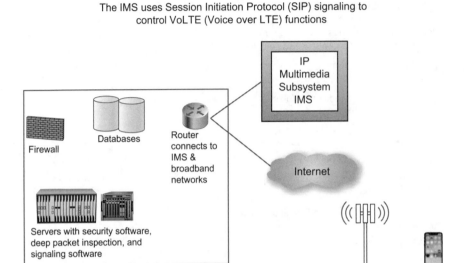

Figure 7-8 IP Multimedia Subsystem (IMS) for mobile subscribers. A Session Border Controller converts signals from the mobile network to those compatible with VoIP equipment.

IMS is based on IP protocols. Interoperability and control of sessions in interactive online games, conference calls, instant messages, and so on are managed in Session Border Controller (SBCs) and signaling gateways. SBCs are located at sites where carriers connect their IP networks to one another. These controllers have functions such as security, session management, policy control, and address translation. Policy control refers to the ability to prioritize certain traffic based on agreements between carriers.

The following is a sampling of applications that users can access from both mobile and landline devices:

- Presence so that subscribers are able to determine if friends and colleagues are available online

- Advertising that works across wired and wireless platforms

- Gaming so that users can participate in online games together

- Text messaging

- Video calling

Connections to Customers and Mobile Networks via the Cell Site, Towers, and Mobile Switches

A cell site is the physical area in which a set of frequencies is used. The link between users' devices and towers or antennas is the only part of mobile networks that is always wireless. The increase in data traffic in shopping malls and downtown areas with heavy pedestrian traffic areas requires dense arrays of cell sites.

The air interface between mobile handsets and equipment at antennas and towers are the only parts of mobile network that are wireless. The air interface is the wireless link between the user device and the equipment at the cell site's tower or antenna. The base station at the tower or antenna contains a radio that receives and transmits mobile traffic and amplifies (strengthens) signals. It also transmits traffic to other antennas and performs the conversion of signals between over-the-air radio frequency formats such as LTE to those compatible with landline networks, and vice-versa on the traffic between the backhaul and the base station.

REITs—A Way to Finance New Antennas and Towers

Companies such as Crown Castle and American Tower specialize in building towers and antennas. They don't offer cellular service; they lease space on their towers to mobile carriers who use the land around the towers for cell site equipment. Instead of each mobile carrier owning their own tower, these third-party companies build towers and lease shared space on them. For example, a large operator might lease space on a tall water tower for its antenna and land surrounding the tower for ancillary equipment. Carriers often share space on these towers to save costs.

Crown Castle and American Tower are structured as real estate investment firms (REITs). With REITS, outside investors underwrite tower construction by purchasing the land on which the towers and cell sites are located and leasing the space back to American Tower and Crown Castle. In return, Crown Castle and American Tower provide investors a stream of payments from their subsequent profits providing shared space on their towers to mobile carriers. Some mobile carriers including Verizon build their own towers or hire contractors to build them.

NOTE Cell sites are the costliest part of mobile networks because there are large numbers of cell sites in 4G and especially in 5G networks. These steep costs make it challenging for all but the largest mobile providers to build out their networks for use with new generations of mobile protocols that require many more cell sites because of their use of high-frequency, gigahertz spectrum bands and the increases in the amount of data and video traffic.

In addition to the high costs of operating cell sites, mobile providers manage huge wired networks made up principally of fiber-optical cabling and some microwave links. These links connect RAN traffic to:

- Backhaul between the evolved packet core, which is a mobile carrier's data center, and cell sites

- Other cells in the mobile network

- Other mobile networks

- The Internet

- Enterprise broadband networks

Heterogeneous Networks—Architecture for Densely Trafficked Areas

Heterogeneous Networks (HetNets) is a 3GPP architecture that defines the way small cells connected to each other support mobile networks in areas with dense pockets of traffic. It is a network made up of a mix of different types of base stations and antennas, thus the term heterogeneous networks. Often these are in downtown areas in cities with large numbers of pedestrians, office buildings and apartments. HetNets are suited to handle the increasingly bandwidth-intensive traffic such as streaming video and online games. HetNets were developed to add capacity for the growth in data and video usage, not to expand coverage. HetNets are used in both LTE and 5G networks.

Capacity is important at the edge of cells where performance may degrade as traffic is handed off between cells. The main issue at the cell edge are delays when calls are handed over to adjacent cells. HetNets are additionally suited to the increasing use of high-frequency gigahertz spectrum used because gigabit spectrum is capable of handling increased traffic. However, gigabit frequencies only travel short distances before fading, thus more small, low-powered cell sites are needed to support traffic over gigahertz spectrum.

Characteristics of HetNets

HetNets are made up of large numbers of small cells controlled by larger *macro cells* to which they are connected wirelessly or by fiber-optic cabling. HetNets' low-powered cells have smaller antennas, and fewer macro cell sites with towers. The architecture includes larger macro cells that each control small cells as required by locations of dense traffic. See Figures 7-9 and 7-10 for examples of HetNets architecture.

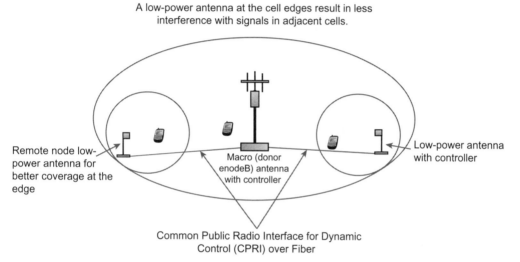

Figure 7-9 An example of HetNet architecture.

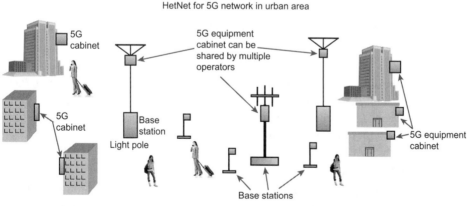

Figure 7-10 HetNet architecture for 5G networks. (Stock photo by Chun-Tso Lin/123RF [center] and Thomas Northcut/Getty Images [left, right])

Equipment in HetNets—Small Low-Powered Base Stations

HetNets are made up of small low-power cells. Low power results in decreased areas of coverage at each cell. Low power is important in HetNets because it is less likely to cause interference with frequencies in nearby cells. Low-power signals are not carried as far as those at higher powered cell sites. In HetNets, the macro evolved NodeB (eNodeB) provides the radio in a large cell while a low-powered macro eNodeB is in a small cell.

The following are low-powered base stations used with existing *macro* evolved NodeBs. Macro cells cover larger areas and can be connected to towers, rather than the smaller antennas seen at low-powered small cells. Macro and small cells are connected to each other either by fiber-optical cabling or mobile frequencies.

- Remote Radio Heads (RRHs) are small antennas and base stations located on outdoor furniture such as thin light poles, telephone poles, and the side of buildings.

- Micro Evolved eNodeBs (eNBs) are smaller eNBs controlled by macro eNBs

- Home eNodeBs (HeNBs) are small cells used for coverage indoors in a closed service group within, for example, office buildings. HeNBs are also termed Femtocells.

- RNs (Relay Nodes) cells are Pico cells that serve smaller groups than femtocells. These are also in a closed service group within buildings.

In addition to the above base stations, HetNets are made up of:

- *Macro cells* control traffic to small, remote cells

- Fiber connections between the small cells and to macro cells over the *CPRI* (*Common Public Radio Interface*). CPRI is a specification for carrying traffic between small cells and to macro cells. It was developed by the following consortium of mobile equipment manufacturers: Ericsson, NEC, Alcatel Lucent (now part of Nokia), and Nokia. It was intended as a replacement for coaxial cabling.

- *Backhaul* fiber-optic cabling where aggregated traffic from multiple macro cells is transmitted to the mobile core. Backhaul traffic may also be carried on high-capacity wireless radios. Higher capacity radios are available that support full duplex Gigabit Ethernet at 10 Gbps. In duplex services, sending and receiving signals are sent simultaneously over the same channels.

A Deeper Dive into HetNets—Pico and Femtocells

Pico and femtocells are small cell sites installed in residences, enterprises, arenas, and outdoor areas within buildings to improve cellular reception. Femtocells cover larger areas and can handle more users (about 100). Pico cells are used in smaller sites such as homes with fewer users than femtocells (five or six users). Both technologies provide relatively low-cost ways to add coverage inside buildings and outdoors. Building owners rely on carriers to provide pico and femtocells because only carriers have rights to spectrum used for mobile services. Femtocells can cover about 5,000 square feet and pico cells about 2,000 square feet. Like traditional base stations, pico cells support multiple standards LTE and 5G networks as well as multiple frequencies.

New buildings that require coverage often use Wi-Fi rather than pico or femtocells within office buildings. The Wi-Fi service is connected to the LAN, which links Wi-Fi traffic to the external broadband network. This eliminates the need to coordinate installation with a mobile carrier to access their spectrum. Staff with cell phones can now enable voice over Wi-Fi to use their smartphones for voice calls as well as data.

Mobile providers and tower companies install pico cells that are used for outdoor coverage. They can be attached to telephone poles, thin poles, and multistory buildings in densely populated areas with high concentrations of mobile traffic. This solution is an inexpensive way to gain capacity by reusing a carrier's spectrum within a smaller area than that covered by larger *macrocells*. A macrocell site is a cell site with a larger antenna and a controller that covers a larger area and can handle more traffic. Pico cells require local electricity and connections back to the mobile carrier's equipment.

Femtocells and Pico Cell Gateways

Femtocell traffic within buildings is routed within secure, encrypted software tunnels over a customer's broadband connections to a carrier's data center. At the data center, femtocell traffic is routed to a gateway. The gateway removes the surrounding bits in the tunnel and sends the femtocell traffic to the carrier's core network. The gateway transmits traffic from thousands of femtocells either to the Internet or, for voice calls, to the mobile switching center.

A key enabling technology that makes femtocells and pico cells feasible are the software algorithms that detect signals from macrocells. Traffic at the edge of the cell has the potential to interfere with frequencies in macrocells because signals can "bleed" into surrounding areas. Improved software algorithms in femtocells and pico cells have the capability to sense both the frequencies and the power levels in the microcell and adjust them as required so that the femtocell signals don't interfere with the macrocell traffic.

Femtocells and pico cells can sense the radio conditions in adjacent cell sites before they start transmitting. This so-called "Network Listen" scan enables the femtocell to, for example, raise its power if the signal from the surrounding macrocell is strong, or conversely, reduce its power if the signal from the macrocell site is weak.

This decreases interference and improves voice quality and data speeds for mobile users in the vicinity—both those served by the femtocells as well as those in the surrounding macro network.

Cellular on Wheels—Short-Term Coverage for Sporting Events, Concerts and Natural Disasters

During a sporting event or concert that attracts thousands of people, mobile carriers often bring in temporary service in the form of Cellular Service on Wheels (COWs). COWs are also deployed during natural disasters such as earthquakes, or hurricanes that may knock out cellular service. COWs are trucks equipped with antennas and base stations that can be quickly deployed.

However, for COWs to be effective, roads must be passable for the truck with the COW to reach hard-hit areas. This is a problem during natural disasters when roads may be washed out or made impassable, as occurred in the aftermath of the 2018 hurricane in the Florida panhandle and Gulf Coast areas. Many sections of the fiber network connecting cell towers to the core cell network were also damaged. Repairing and laying new fiber is a time-consuming endeavor.

Using Distributed Antenna Systems for In-Building and Subway Coverage

Distributed Antenna Systems (DAS) are an alternative for coverage within buildings. DASs consist of *repeaters* connected to coaxial or fiber-optic cabling in buildings. A repeater amplifies cellular signals transmitted throughout buildings, subways, or stadiums by equipment that the cellular carrier supplies. Repeaters are located throughout the building and transmit Radio Frequency (RF) signals to the macrocell. Unlike super femto cells, they don't actually offload traffic from the larger cellular network because they are not capable of reusing spectrum. They are connected to building broadband services to offload traffic from carriers' backhaul networks.

DASs are also located in subway systems where traditional cell sites don't generally reach or provide adequate coverage. Municipalities negotiate contracts for carriers to install the cabling over which the repeaters are connected and the signals travel. The carrier installs antennas that provide the cellular signals. In some of these systems, particularly public spaces such as subways and airports, multiple carriers are connected to the DAS. This enables travelers and multiple mobile carriers' subscribers to use their mobile devices in these locations. An example of a DAS is the one installed at the Kinnick Stadium in the University of Iowa. In this DAS, fiber is used between repeaters, and coaxial cable is installed for the final 30 to 40 feet to antennas and base stations.

Building Out Mobile Networks without the Challenge of getting Permissions from Municipalities

Prior to 2018, arranging permission from municipalities to run fiber and place antennas needed for the thousands of new small cells carriers are building for HetNets in LTE and 5G networks was the biggest challenges in upgrading mobile networks. Rights of way for the increased fiber needed to connect small cells to macro cells were one issue. Another was zoning regulations and other permissions that often cause major delays in building infrastructure. Officials in cities with historic buildings were reluctant to have equipment mounted on them. In residential areas, neighbors don't want antennas near their homes because of fears that the radiation from antennas may be harmful. It took years to negotiate these issues with municipalities.

Running fiber required permission from cities to use their rights of way. In cities with fiber already running in conduits under the ground, mobile providers negotiate the monthly fees that municipalities charge in return for space to lay fiber within these conduits. In an effort to speed up the process, telecom and cellular firms lobbied the FCC to issue rules that restrict local municipalities from oversight of 5G gear. In 2018 the FCC issued rules that eliminate the majority of these delays in getting permission to place 5G gear by restrictions on local cities and towns efforts to impose fees and zoning rules on 5G infrastructure.

Frequency- and Time-Division Air Interfaces in LTE

The 3GPP standards group has defined two different *air interfaces* for LTE. An air interface is the way signals are transmitted between cell sites and user equipment. The most common air interfaces are Frequency Division Multiplexing and Time Division Multiplexing.

Frequency-Division Multiplexing (FD-LTE) is the most commonly implemented air interface. FD-LTE uses one frequency band for down-link from the cell site to the user device and another set of frequencies on the uplink from the user device to the network.

Frequency-Division Multiplexing (FDM) requires paired frequencies, which means that one spectrum band is used for the downlink and another band is used for the uplink. See Figure 7-11 for an example of FDM and TDM. When mobile carriers that use FD-LTE acquire new spectrum, they obtain one band specified by the government for uplink service and a different band specified for downlink service. Most of the rest of the world, including AT&T and Verizon, have implemented FD-LTE.

Frequency Division Multiplexing

Time Division Multiplexing

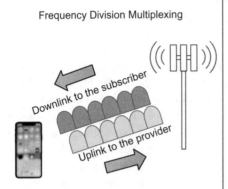
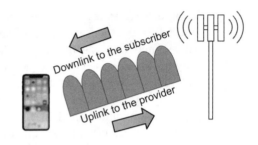

Two separate bands of spectrum

A single-stream spectrum for the uplink and downlink

Figure 7-11   Frequency Division-LTE compared to the Time Division air interface.

In contrast to Frequency Division Multiplexing, TD-LTE uses the same set of frequencies for uplink and downlink transmissions. Time-Division Multiplexing (TD-LTE) is also referred to as Time-Division Duplex (TDD). TD-LTE does not require paired spectrum, and unlike FD-LTE, it is asymmetric; a different amount of spectrum can be used in the downlink and in the uplink. This is more spectrally efficient and flexible. For example, more spectrum can be allocated to the downlink than the uplink. China Mobile, the largest mobile carrier in the world, and some carriers in the rest of Asia use TD-LTE.

Core networks are the same for both types of LTE. The same network core and backhaul support both Frequency Division and Time Division air interfaces. However, radios in users' devices must have chips to match the type of air interface for their devices to access the cell sites. Chip designers have integrated both TD and FDD into their platforms so that carriers are able to support both types of LTE. Carriers able to support both FDD and TD-LTE support roaming for users with either type of handset.

4G Multiple-Input Multiple-Output Antennas

LTE is designed to operate with Multiple-Input Multiple-Output (MIMO) antennas in base stations. MIMO antennas benefit by having more than one antenna and multiple receive/send channels. Thus, they can carry as many separate streams of voice or data as they have input/output channels. Each stream of traffic is carried on a separate frequency. An 8×8 antenna has eight antennas and handsets communicating with it also have eight antennas. This is analogous to multilane highways with eight lanes in each direction.

MIMO antennas are available in 2×2, 4×4 and 8×8 send/receive channels. The 8×8 antenna is specified for LTE Advanced, the 100Mbps, true-4G air interface. As antennas become more powerful, with additional antennas, it is technically challenging to equip handsets with multiple antennas because space is required between them to avoid signal interference. See Massive MIMO below for information on antennas suitable for 5th generation (5G) networks' high-frequency bands.

The LTE Orthogonal Frequency-Division Multiplexing Air Interface

Orthogonal Frequency-Division Multiplexing (OFDM) is the air interface used in LTE mobile broadband protocols. It is not used in earlier protocols and is an important factor in increasing capacity in mobile networks. OFDM increases spectral efficiency by sending several multiplexed streams of data over separate, narrow bands of spectrum simultaneously in orthogonal streams. Orthogonal streams are those that are transmitted at right angles to one another. Figure 7-12 illustrates an example of orthogonal streams in OFDM.

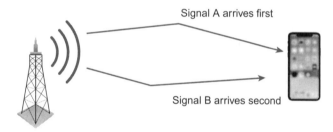

- Multiple streams of data at slightly different frequencies arrive at their destination at different times
- Receiver decodes signal A and then signal B

Figure 7-12 *Streams of bits sent by using the Orthogonal Frequency-Division Multiplexing (OFDM) protocol.*

In addition, guard bands between each stream of data are not required, which is an important factor underpinning the spectral efficiency of OFDM. Guard bands are unused channels of spectrum that provide a buffer between streams to protect data from interference. Guard bands carry no data. This narrowband, efficient use of spectrum is the main reason why LTE supports many more users in each cell site than the 3G technologies.

NOTE Throughout this book, the term "carrier" has been used almost exclusively in relation to network service providers. However, as it applies to telecommunications, the term actually has two meanings. Thus, in addition to describing a network service provider, it can also refer to slices of spectrum as it does in Orthogonal Frequency-Division air interfaces.

A Variety of LTE Flavors

The evolution of LTE includes technical standards approved and developed by the 3GPP 3rd Generation Partnership Project, a worldwide technical standards group made up of representative of telephone companies from all over the world. See Table 7-2 for LTE types. Some are being implemented on shared Wi-Fi spectrum and others are based on high-frequency Gigahertz spectrum. Data on Gigahertz spectrum is able to travel only short distances before fading. However, it supports higher data rates.

Table 7-2 LTE Types

Name of LTE	Use of LTE	Spectrum Type	Other info
LTE A (Advanced)	Aggregates multiple spectrum streams into a single high-capacity stream	Most spectrum bands	Combining (aggregating) multiple streams of data to achieve more capacity in the air interface.
LTE LAA (License Assisted Access)	In tests to use 5 GHz unlicensed spectrum bands	5GHz	Used in small cells to increase LTE availability.
LTE U (Unlicensed)	LTE used in unlicensed spectrum In tests for this spectrum for added capacity	1.710–1.755 and 2.110–2.155GHz 5 GHz	Wi-Fi providers are concerned about interference from Wi-Fi networks in the same spectrum.
CBRS Citizens Band Radio Service	5G Fixed Wireless service for rural broadband access	3.5GHz	Uses different spectrum from 27MHz used by truckers to communicate with each other.
LTE Cat-MI & M2	Computer chips for enhanced machine to machine* communications	Various spectrum bands previously used in 2G networks	For low-power, low-bandwidth applications where batteries last 5 to 10 years. May be replaced by NB-LTE. In tests for Internet of Things applications.

Name of LTE	Use of LTE	Spectrum Type	Other info
LTE–NB LTE Narrow Band	May replace LTE Cat-M1 and M2	Spectrum previously used in 2G Networks	Internet of Things, e.g. remote meter reading.
LTE C-RAN Cloud Radio Area Network**	The core is managed from the cloud. LTE is at the cell site.	2.3GHz, 2.5/2.6GHz, and 3.5GHz, Verizon testing CRAN in 28GHz and 39GHz bands	Remote management at telecoms' cloud-based data centers. Billing and other functions in cloud.
VoLTE Voice Over LTE	A way to transmit voice in the same format as data, in IP packets	Uses the same spectrum as the LTE network on which it's transmitted	Depends on a type of SIP signaling in each carrier's IP IMS

Machine-to-machine services include monitoring of automobile and truck fleets, alarms, and electric meters.

**Can also refer to centralized Radio Access Network in heterogeneous networks. See above for HetNets.*

5G MOBILE NETWORKS—SMALL CELLS; ADDITIONAL CAPACITY ....

Fifth Generation protocols support gigabit data rates that are key to carrying the massive amounts of future streaming, gaming, and Internet traffic from mobile devices. Most mobile providers are now testing 5G networks, which will be available in a limited number of areas in 2019 with predictions of wide availability in 2020.

Massive MIMO Antennas for 5G Networks

The 5G specification includes *Massive MIMO* antennas, each with 16×16 send/receive channels. In addition to more send/receive antennas, massive MIMO antennas can handle traffic in a 360-degree pattern: a full circumference of the antenna. Thus, in addition to handling 16 send and 16 receive streams of traffic, massive MIMO antennas provide service to traffic in all directions of the antenna, in 360 degrees.

5G New Radio Service and 5G Applications

Fifth Generation NR (New Radio) will be one of the first types of 5G service available. 5G NR will be used over high frequency 28GHz and 39GHz spectrum capable of transmitting gigabit data rates. These high data rates are made possible by aggregating carriers (channels) together. AT&T and others are now testing applications on 5G NR. One future use is for controlling applications within cities to manage operations, including traffic congestion. Other applications envisioned on 5G are self-driving cars and trucks, the Internet of Things, and monitoring healthcare patients wearing wirelessly connected devices including blood pressure monitors.

C-RAN Centralized or Cloud-Based Radio Access Networks in 5G Networks

C-RAN in 5G networks refers to the management of the radio access network's antenna, and controller centrally. C-RAN management is already occurring where mobile network providers manage multiple HetNets and traditional cell sites from within their data center. The signals that enable centralized management are transmitted over fiber-optic links from macrocells. These signals are monitored by engineers at computer screens at data centers. Cloud C-RANs are in the early stages of implementation and are planned for the future as a way to manage the complex 5G infrastructure. Because there is no agreed-upon standard, equipment from different vendors might not be able to interoperate. Cloud RANs will additionally use virtualized components for ease of replacement and space conservation. The radio access networks will consume less space because they will be represented in software, not hardware.

Interoperability and Fall Back on 5G Mobile Networks

A major concern around 5G networks is that different telecom companies' implementations may differ in small ways. This can result in non-interoperability between their networks. Thus, data and voice traffic might not be seamlessly transferred between providers without dropping calls or causing delays in data sessions.

Another feature that needs to be compatible between mobile networks is fall back. Fall back is the ability to transition to earlier generations of service as subscribers move from cell site to cell site. A subscriber that starts a call in a part of the network already using 5G service needs to be able to continue the data session, voice call, or Internet browsing when they walk or ride to an area with LTE service. All of these and other facets of compatibility are in the process of being ironed out. But, earlier network implementations may hit some bumps.

Device Compatibility—A Multi-Year Gap

A major issue in upgrading from LTE to 5G is when 5G-compatible smartphones, tablet computers, and laptops with 5G radios on chips in the device will be available.

Without 5G chips in mobile devices, they aren't able to achieve gigabit data rates or any other features available in 5G networks.

This is the reason that cellular providers continue to support older mobile protocols when new ones become available. It can take 5 years for the majority of subscribers to upgrade to new generations of cellular service.

Killing Lost or Stolen Portable Computers Using GPS

A majority of security lapses can be attributed to the loss or theft of corporate laptops and smartphones. Confidential corporate information and private e-mail messages are often stored on these devices. Currently, mobile carriers have the ability to remotely disable and determine the location of mobile handsets, laptops with cellular chips, and tablets when corporations report them lost.

Global Positioning System (GPS) chips within these devices enable organizations to locate them so that data can be deleted, or the device can be locked. For the carrier to locate a device, it must be turned on and within the carrier's coverage area. Thus, if a device is turned off, it cannot be located.

Killing and locating lost devices is enabled in all current mobile networks. These networks depend on GPS to synchronize the timing in their networks so that signals arrive at their destination only once for functions that require precise timing. GPS-equipped mobile networks can be used to provide location information, as well. Location-based applications that use GPS include applications that give parents the ability to track their children's locations and to find friends who are in the area.

Pedestrian Injuries While Walking, Talking, and Texting

Walking while using mobile devices is a serious safety issue. The National Highway Traffic Safety Administration (NHTSA) estimates that 5,000 people were killed and 76,000 pedestrians were injured in 2016 while using mobile devices. Another problem with using mobile phones while walking is that distracted drivers using cell phones or even changing a radio station might miss a stop sign or just not see a pedestrian in a crosswalk. Injuries from distracted walking included bumping into someone else, tripping, sprains, broken bones, concussions, and spinal cord injuries.

A study published in Safety Science on February 2016 found that talking on mobile phones resulted in the most injuries. Texting and viewing content on mobile phones resulted in fewer injuries and listening to music had the least impact on walkers. To combat distracted walking, Honolulu imposes fines of up to $99 on pedestrians that text while crossing intersections. In Boston and New York legislators are studying the issue.

THE INTERNET OF THINGS (IOT)

Wireless networks have progressed from enabling people to speak together without being tethered to wires, to transmitting data at broadband rates, and now to machines autonomously communicating with each other via the Internet of Things. According to Verizon in their January 1, 2017, *Data Breach Digest,*

> *IoT, "the Internet of Things" [is] a term that describes a network of physical objects connected to the Internet. These may be discrete items like building automation solutions. Embedded in each device are electronics capable of network conductivity along with sensors or other features.*

Most IOT devices have embedded batteries on chips that operate over LTE–NB (narrowband) standard. Early implementations of IoT used LTE–M1 or M2, which required a gateway to translate between the network and the devices. The fact that LTE–NB does not require a gateway makes it less costly to manage and implement because there is one less piece of equipment to install and monitor.

Embedded software in IoT devices can be updated and monitored by centralized servers. Remotely monitored devices include automobiles, drones, parking meters, gas and electric meters, municipal traffic signals, water towers, and soil conditions and farms. A list of IOT applications are included in Table 7-3.

Table 7-3　Examples of IoT Applications

IoT Applications	Purpose	Comments
Self-driving cars, battery powered cars	Decrease congestion on city roads and air pollution	Improved batteries and Graphical Processing chips (GPUs) on which developers apply machine learning so that GPUs "recognize" road conditions, obstructions, and traffic signals. Nvidia computer chips have these capabilities.
Hybrid battery, Electric self-driving cars	Decrease air pollution; if battery not available car runs on gasoline	Graphical processing chips as described above.
Self-driving, battery powered trucks	Save costs on hiring drivers; fewer accidents	Trucks can travel for more hours because driver fatigue is not an issue.

IoT Applications	Purpose	Comments
Drones (unmanned aircraft)	Track wildfires and mudslides; Monitor soil conditions, and livestock on farms, military surveillance	An improved way to manage natural disasters and agricultural productivity; used to automate armies for attacks and reconnaissance.
Parking meters	Automate collection of parking meter fees	Save municipalities' expense of manually collecting coins in meters.
Industrial robots	Control manufacturing systems; speed up warehouse functions	Industrial robots are used in automotive plants and other manufacturing systems to speed up processes and save money on salaries
Subway fare collection	Transit passengers use payment software in smartphones to access subway trains	Diminish delays at subway entrances; lessen fraud; require less staff. Enabled by Near Field Communications (NFC), a low-power, short-range communications protocol.
Industry	Automate lighting and heating control systems; monitor manufacturing systems	Save costs on utilities and manage manufacturing quality.
Highway toll collection	Eliminate toll booths and traffic delays caused by manually collecting tolls	All cars need transponders that identify their license plate number for billing purposes.
Smart cities	Monitor traffic, water, and safety, elevated trams and underground high-speed transportation systems	Future projects aimed at making cities more livable with new types of off-road transportation to lessen traffic gridlock
Medical devices in hospitals	Automate data collection and inventory of equipment for more accurate data	Sensors on equipment identify each wheelchair and other equipment. Heart and blood pressure monitors send data and alarms to central computers and nurse stations.

Information and Privacy on IoT Services

With the millions of devices connected to the Internet using IoT LTE–NB in the future, major challenges will be keeping these networks secure and private.

Security in IoT Networks

There is no easy answer for securing Internet-connected IoT networks. Devices connected to the Internet are open and inherently vulnerable. The first step in ensuring security is to encrypt IoT information as it's transmitted. This ensures privacy. However, it doesn't mean that hackers can't disrupt services. Many organizations including major telecom providers such as Verizon Wireless are developing security protocols for Internet of Things networks.

Privacy on Connected Devices

In addition to security, IoT devices that collect data with identifiable information have the potential for companies to store vast amounts of private information about people using IoT equipment and other equipment that collects information about customers. Computers in cars are a prime example of equipment with the ability to collect information about where people drive.

This information and more like it provide data about consumers' buying habits as well as the routes they take. This information can help companies choose locations for billboards and retail operations.

Marketing companies sell this information and give a share of the revenue to car manufacturers: a lucrative opportunity for marketers and car manufacturers, a loss of privacy for consumers.

Unmanned Aircraft; Drones—Military and Commercial Applications

Drones are unmanned aircraft equipped with cameras and remotely controlled from the ground. Commercial drones can do more than deliver packages, which they are not suited for because most packages are too heavy for the lightweight, 55-pound drones. Drones are used in commercial and military applications. Some of these include monitoring combat zones for threats and enemies, and surveying natural disasters such as wildfires, mudslides, earthquakes, and hurricanes. In 2017's Hurricane Harvey in Puerto Rico, drones provided cell service. The drones were tethered to antennas and radios for temporary cell service and communications. The drones additionally captured images of oil damage and electrical outages. Movie directors and journalists use drones to record overhead views and difficult to reach high-altitude locations.

In the future it is likely that cameras within drones will transmit information to public safety officials. Thus, drones will track criminals so that helicopters won't be needed. Often helicopters crash during pursuits of criminals, killing or severely injuring pilots or even people on the ground. One of the security precautions being developed will track drones in restricted airspace such as military bases and commercial airports where saboteurs might launch drones to compromise safety in these areas.

Battery Life

Inadequate battery life is a major issue with smartphone and tablet computer owners, self-driving car and truck developers, and myriad other services that depend on battery life. Battery technology has not kept up with users' dependence on mobile services and development of new, automated technologies. People are more dependent on portable devices for their voice and text communications as well as social networking, music, and increasingly, for video. They also use these devices on Wi-Fi networks and for video conferences.

Data applications require more power from the device. Bandwidth-heavy applications such as Internet access, video, and e-mail drain batteries more quickly than voice calls. This is because voice requires fewer bits than data when transmitted. In addition, large color displays drain batteries more quickly than the less-sophisticated screens on earlier devices. Thus, as people become increasingly dependent on mobile devices for more functions, it is important to find ways to extend battery life.

A current focus is on ways to design mobile handsets that use power more efficiently. One such technology extinguishes screen backlighting when it is not required. The technology senses ambient lighting to determine when backlighting is needed. It maintains color by creating brighter color pixels so that mobile devices don't draw current from backlights in daylight.

Another way that manufacturers design handsets to improve power management is by including automatic sensing circuitry that shuts down memory, processors, and peripherals when a handset is not transmitting. For example, if the user is not in a Wi-Fi zone, the Wi-Fi circuitry is disabled so that it does not draw power when it can't even be used. Most smartphones and tablet computers include this form of power management. Other manufacturers are developing new screen technologies that consume less power.

More Convenient Way to Charge Batteries

Electronics companies have developed more convenient ways to charge smartphones. There are wireless charging devices on the market able to charge phones placed on top of them. So, instead of tossing a phone in a kitchen drawer or on a dresser in the evening before going to bed, users are able to simply place it on a small charging device and have a fully charged tablet or smartphone waiting for them in the morning. The charging device itself must be plugged into an electrical outlet.

Charging mobile devices gradually wears down the battery and shortens its life. Over time, batteries hold charges for shorter amounts of time. This is because every charge deposits chemicals on the device's contacts. These chemicals corrode the contacts creating resistance to the charge. A lithium-ion (Li-ion) battery experiences corrosion in a different manner, but it, too, becomes resistant to charges. Thus, less voltage reaches the circuitry that carries the current to the battery. Voltage refers to the "pressure" of the electricity flowing through the handset's circuits. Low "pressure" or voltage means that less electricity is reaching the battery.

People that need more battery power than that built into the phone purchase battery packs that clip onto their mobile devices or mobile phone cases already equipped with battery packs.

APPLICATIONS AND SERVICES.................................

Applications on mobile devices attract customers, generate revenue, and are a tool for retaining customers.

Mobile Payments

Mobile handsets can be utilized for mobile banking, financial transactions, contactless payments at retail outlets, and instead of cash at subways and toll roads. These mobile payment options include the following:

- **Payments for mass transit**   Users can pass their smartphone near a reader to pay for subway, bus, and train transportation instead of using tokens or purchasing monthly passes. Apps on mobile phones can take advantage of a short-range wireless technology called Near Field Communications (NFC) to interact with the reader. The user simply needs to pass her phone within 1.56 inches (4 cm) of the payment reader.

- **Check deposits**   Smartphone apps use the device's camera to take a picture of the check and then transmit the image to the user's bank for deposit.

- **Money transfers directly to a mobile phone in a developing country**   When a relative or friend sends money to a person in a developing country via Western Union, the electronic cash is sent directly to the receiver's handset. MoreMagic, a Massachusetts software developer, created this application.

- **Online payments**   People surfing the Internet on their smartphone can make online purchases through PayPal rather than having to type in their credit card number along with their name, postal address, and e-mail address.

All of these transactions require some type of software platform that sits between credit card processing companies or banks and the mobile network. The platform must have integrated security protocols and the ability to communicate with the financial institutions that process payments. They also need to communicate with servers at merchants' sites and devices that act as "readers" of the mobile device making the transaction.

Each mobile handset and reader requires chips with NFC capability or special software. The cost of these readers is often a stumbling block for retailers because they need to place one at every cash register. Alternatively, readers can be embedded in portable devices that sales associates use to process credit card sales. Another challenge for retailers is that there is no agreed-upon standard software platform. Thus, different chips and software are required for Apple OS and Android operating systems because different carriers and mobile operating systems adopt different software.

Machine-to-Machine Communications between Devices with Embedded Radios

Machine-to-machine (M2M) mobile services refer to services that automatically monitor the status of other systems or send software updates to devices. An example of an M2M service is a central system that monitors vending machines remotely to determine inventory levels and diagnose possible problems. Another example of M2M traffic is automatic monitoring of residential electric meters.

Both of these applications require software platforms and radios at customer data centers as well as software and radios in the device to be updated or managed. Software is required in the vending machines and meters that are able to connect to a mobile network. However, these upgrades might require large investments. This is true when new software is added to a utility's meters. There is a potential to save on operational costs by eliminating the need for technicians to manually read the meters. It also has the potential to enable utilities to use energy more efficiently by monitoring the grid and adjusting power distribution accordingly.

These transmissions are carried over a mobile carrier's second-generation network. Many of the current applications do not transmit enormous amounts of data. M2M applications represent a revenue opportunity for mobile carriers. One reason is that there are many more machines than there are end users, and many machines now include software that can be upgraded for over-the-air diagnosis and updates.

Automobiles are examples of systems that contain more and more software, including in-car entertainment systems that require automatic over-the-air updates. Many new cars include options for touch screens on dashboards to activate various networked functions and entertainment systems. These include in-car Wi-Fi hotspots for passengers, outside sensors, rear-view cameras to assist in parking, and embedded GPSs.

Another advantage to carriers of M2M service is the ease of support. Currently, carriers operate large customer service centers for responding to questions about billing and technical issues. Customer service for M2M service is lower than that for handsets because inquiries and customer service requests are only required for the centralized staff members who manage these applications for customers.

Using Prepaid Mobile Services

Prepaid wireless services are those for which customers pay in advance for mobile voice and/or data services. Prepaid service is most widely offered to customers who do not have credit and who pay cash for service. They "top up" their service, making additional payments when they need more minutes.

This contrasts with the postpaid cellular model by which customers are billed for and pay for services *after* the end of the monthly billing period. In the prepaid model customers give providers a credit card number that is billed every month. Most mobile providers in the United States rely on postpaid customers for the bulk of their revenue, but many offer prepaid as a way to round out their offerings.

With postpaid plans, customers receive monthly bills and often sign one- or two-year contracts for their service. The consumption of prepaid service is particularly high in developing countries such as India, Bangladesh, and many African countries. Prepaid is important in areas where most people don't have credit cards or bank accounts.

The advantages of prepaid for carriers are mainly the elimination of the costs associated with issuing bills and collecting overdue payments. For some carriers, it's a way to attract lower-income or immigrant customers who don't have credit. In countries where mobile penetration is high and most people already have existing postpaid service, prepaid is another way to add customers.

Whether purchasing prepaid directly through a carrier or through a reseller, customers are connected to a prepaid platform, which authenticates their device and tracks usage to determine either whether to charge a credit card or if the subscriber's amount of time or usage has been used up. The prepaid platform is connected to the carrier's core mobile network. Wal-Mart sells prepaid services using Straight Talk's prepaid platform.

WI-FI STANDARDS, ARCHITECTURE, AND THEIR USE IN CELLULAR NETWORKS ....

Residential consumers and enterprise staff expect the same level of mobility within homes and work environments as they experience in mobile cellular networks such as those operated by Verizon Wireless and AT&T Mobility. Wi-Fi provides short-range wireless service within these locations. Wi-Fi networks are widely deployed in cafes, libraries, and municipalities as a service to customers and city and town residents.

The 802.11 Wi-Fi Standard

The designation 802.11 refers to the family of Institute of Electrical and Electronics Engineers (IEEE) standards around which most Wireless Local Area Networks are built. Wi-Fi, short for wireless fidelity, is widely accepted worldwide with small variations. Table 7-4 lists the earliest commonly installed 802.11 network protocols.

Table 7-4 802.11 Wireless Local Area Network (Wi-Fi) Standards

Standard	Top Speed	Achievable Speed	Number of Channels*	Frequency Band
802.11a	54Mbps	25Mbps	24	5GHz
802.11b	11Mbps	5Mbps	3	2.4GHz
802.11g	54Mbps	12- to 25Mbps	3	2.4GHz

The number of channels varies internationally.

A Deeper Dive into Wi-Fi Standards

The standards presented in Table 7-3 refer to the frequencies, speeds, and number of channels in each Wi-Fi standard. Other 802.11 standards that specify capabilities such as security, Quality of Service (QoS), and internetworking with cellular networks are listed in Table 7-8 in the "Appendix" section at the end of this chapter. Wi-Fi networks in enterprises commonly support all three of the standards plus additional standards that specify higher data rates.

The frequency of a signal impacts its range (how far it is able to travel). Signals in lower-frequency bands travel farther than those in higher bands because these waves are longer (refer to Figure 7-1). The 802.11b and 802.11g standards cover a range of about 100 to 150 feet; 802.11a covers only about 75 feet. Because they cover smaller areas, networks that utilize 802.11a antennas require more antennas. Equipment that supports both standards is referred to as dual-band equipment. As its name implies, dual-band equipment supports two frequency bands. Tri-band support is now common as well.

The higher speeds achieved by 802.11a and 802.11g are possible because both are based on Orthogonal Frequency-Division Multiplexing (OFDM). This is because OFDM sends multiple streams of bits simultaneously. See the section "The LTE Orthogonal Frequency-Division Multiplexing Air Interface" earlier in this chapter to read more about OFDM in LTE networks.

NOTE In order for user smartphones and other devices to access any Wi-Fi standard, the user device must contain a computer chip that matches the 802.11 standard, e.g. 802.11a, 802.11n and 802.11ac as well as other newer Wi-Fi standards.

The following factors impact achievable speeds:

- Network congestion
- The distance from antennas
- Overhead, which is the number of bits required in packet headers for information such as addressing and error correction
- Interference from thick walls or other material and glare from windows are factors that can also decrease range

Worldwide, the number of channels available in each standard varies. When governments set requirements for the number of channels that can be used for each standard, they do not always do it uniformly. The standards themselves often define flexible requirements.

Range and Capacity of 802.11n

The 802.11n standard is a Wi-Fi standard that is backward-compatible with 802.11a, b, and g networks. It enables Wi-Fi networks to cover longer distances by overcoming a certain amount of interference. It also increases achievable speeds, increases throughput (user data minus packet headers), and supports more users per access point than earlier Wi-Fi networks. Improvements in the number of users supported in a given amount of airspace are critical as the number of users and applications on Wi-Fi networks increase. 802.11n and 802.11ac mentioned below operate on 5Ghz frequencies.

Using MIMO Antennas to Carry More Traffic

Improvement in antennas is the reason 802.11n and 802.11ac use spectrum more efficiently and overcome many "dead spots." A dead spot is an area that access points don't cover because of interference from building materials or the distance from an antenna. The 802.11n access points use MIMO antennas, which were not available in earlier Wi-Fi networks to simultaneously transmit multiple streams at different frequencies within a single channel. 802.11n is being replaced by the higher-capacity 802.11ac described below. Access points that support both 802.11ac and 802.11n are widely available. These are compatible with user devices with only 802.11n computer chips.

MIMO antennas are classified by the number of transmit and receive antennas installed within access points and user devices.

- 2×2 antennas have two transmit and two receiver antennas.
- 2×3 antennas have two transmit and three receiver antennas.

- 3×3 antennas have three transmit and three receiver antennas.

- 4×4 antennas have four transmit and four receiver antennas.

- 8x8 antennas have eight transmit and eight receiver antennas.

Wi-Fi routers with more antennas support more capacity and higher data rates. To achieve the highest speeds and capacity, user devices as well as access points must have an equal number of antennas. See Figure 7-13 for an example of a Wi-Fi access point.

Figure 7-13 A Wi-Fi access point. (Courtesy of Linksys)

The increasing capabilities of Wi-Fi networks have resulted in greater dependence on wireless networks. This is particularly true in mobile environments such as hospitals, factories, and educational institutions where employees often do not have a fixed desk at which to send and receive data. In addition, staff members in organizations now assume that they can take advantage of wireless access for tablets and smartphones during meetings, at lunch, and wherever they are within their building or within their organization's campus.

Multi-User MIMO—Improvements in MIMO

Multi-User MIMO (MU MIMO) supports transmissions to more than one user device at a time. Without MU MIMO, transmissions are sent to different devices serially, one at a time. MU MIMO antennas operate at the 5GHz bands of spectrum that support gigabit data rates. MU MIMO equipped routers are referred to as Wave 2 or Wave 3 equipment.

802.11ac (Wi-Fi 5) Gigabit Data Rates, Beamforming, and Bonding

The 802.11ac Wi-Fi standard, now dubbed Wi-Fi 5 by the Wi-Fi Alliance supports bonding, Multi-User MIMO, and gigabit data rates. 802.11ac supports *beamforming,* the ability to focus a signal directly to the end-user device rather than transmitting wireless signals addressed to a particular device in all directions at once. Beamforming transmits separate streams to individual users within the same spectrum. This decreases congestion.

802.11ac achieves high data rates in part due to its modulation, the way bits are carried on the wireless streams. 256 Quadrature Amplitude Modulation (QAM) carries many more bits by varying the amplitude, the height, of each wave in the data stream.

Channel bonding enables high data rates by combining multiple streams into a single stream. However, bonding channels together results in fewer channels available to other devices in the network decreasing capacity to other devices in the Wi-Fi network.

 An *extender* is essentially a repeater. It "repeats" signals to extend their range, the distance they can travel before fading. For example, if a home has two stories, but the router is on the first floor, the extender will connect to the home's Wi-Fi routers and send Wi-Fi signals to, for example, the smartphone in the office on the second floor. In this way, both end-user devices on the first and second floor have good access to the Wi-Fi network. Extenders plug directly into electrical outlets. They are not equipped to attach to cabling.

User Devices—Capacity Requirements

The growing numbers of connected wireless devices require high-capacity Wi-Fi. It's not uncommon for families and students to have a total of five devices connected to Wi-Fi networks. This is an issue in student apartments where each person may have their own four or five devices. Thus, Wi-Fi networks able to support increases in wireless traffic are becoming crucial. The following is a list of wireless devices commonly used in homes, universities, and enterprises:

- Laptops
- Desktop Computers
- Connected environmental controls
- Networked light switches
- Cellular modems

- Smartphones

- Tablet computers

- Televisions

- Set-top boxes connected to HDTVs for streaming TV and movies from the Internet, via, for example, Roku, Comcast's Xbox, and Apple TV set-top boxes

- Printers

- Low-power medical devices used to monitor conditions remotely; for example, blood pressure and glucose monitors

Wi-Fi in Universities, Hospitals, and Warehouses

Large universities, hospitals, and warehouses have extensive Wi-Fi networks because their staff for the most part aren't at assigned desks where they are able to answer telephone calls, or in medical settings where they can look up patient records and reactions to medication. In large university campuses with multiple classroom buildings, access points are placed on every classroom's ceiling.

Students at these universities assume Internet access is available for research on topics covered in classrooms, and for research in the library. At one large university, the library has two floors with books, and another entire floor with carrels where students and faculty study, do research, and access the Internet. Wi-Fi is additionally available for guests and neighborhood residents who are able to hop on a "guest" segment of Wi-Fi where they can reach the Internet, but not any private, confidential files or databases. In a similar manner, hospitals have Wi-Fi throughout their administrative offices and patient floors. Like universities, they provide guest Wi-Fi for visitors and patient rooms. In warehouses, Wi-Fi is used for communicating with automated systems that track packages.

Wi-Fi Architecture in Enterprises

Wi-Fi networks are within buildings but are connected by cabling to the wired LAN. All Wi-Fi networks have access points and user devices. The computer chips in portable user devices must be compatible with that used in the base station and access point. For example, a user device cannot use 802.11ac capabilities without an 802.11ac chip in their device. Enterprise Wi-Fi networks have multiple access points and often controllers that direct traffic to particular access points. Central monitoring software can be used to remotely change access point configurations and monitor traffic on the Wi-Fi network.

Wi-Fi access points are connected to switches in each floor's wiring closets. See Figure 7-14 for an example of a connection between access points and the wired local area network. The point is, Wi-Fi is a way to connect internal wireless transmissions to enterprise LANs, which then transmit Wi-Fi–originated traffic to the Internet or to staff within the building or campus. A Wi-Fi controller or router is plugged into a port on Ethernet switches at enterprises.

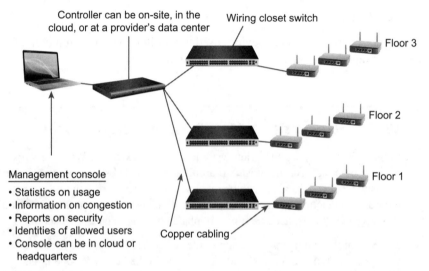

Figure 7-14   Wi-Fi connections to the wired LAN in an enterprise's wiring closet.

Wi-Fi in Homes

In a similar manner to enterprises, Wi-Fi access points connect to LANs within homes. However, LANs within homes are less complex and the access points are generally less robust, with fewer features and for the most part less complex security. In homes, Wi-Fi–equipped gear such as printers, laptops, and smartphones have internal Wi-Fi computer chips. The Wi-Fi router is directly cabled to cable modems or equipment associated with the fiber-optic cabling in the outside network.

Mesh Networks—Every Device to Every Device: Controller-Less Architecture

The main difference between centralized and mesh architecture is that in mesh networks traffic does not go through a controller. Rather, each access point has the intelligence to directly connect traffic to other access points. The software essentially establishes a point-to-point connection for the duration of the data session. It eliminates congestion at a central point while at the same time avoiding a single point of failure. If an access point fails, data is routed around the failure to another access point. The ability to route traffic around failures and coverage gaps and interference from thick walls or walls that contain wire, and large homes with three stories make them suitable for these environments and also for outdoor areas.

Moreover, access points in mesh networks filter out traffic from untrusted sources such as *rogue access points*. A rogue access point is an unauthorized access point installed by an employee. Figure 7-15 presents an overview of a Wi-Fi mesh network. In homes, people use a software app on their smartphone that is provided by their Wi-Fi vendor to set up the mesh network. The user selects a centralized location for the first access point and plugs it into power. The app then uses its intelligence to recommend locations for the other access points.

There is currently no mesh networking standard for all of the functions required in mesh networks. Thus, the entire network must now be provided by a single vendor. The current standard only specifies how the link layer puts the data on and takes it off the Wi-Fi network. A new certification program called *Wi-Fi Certified Home Design* is still evolving that may enable access points from diverse manufacturers to interoperate together. This will enable people and institutions to use equipment from different vendors to interoperate with each other.

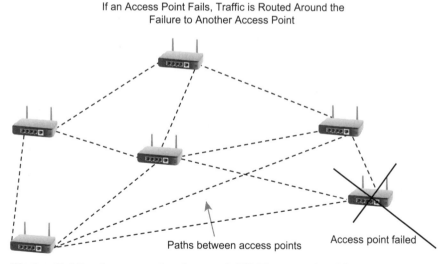

If an Access Point Fails, Traffic is Routed Around the
Failure to Another Access Point

Paths between access points   Access point failed

Figure 7-15 An example of a mesh Wi-Fi network with every access point to every access point connection. (Courtesy of NETGEAR)

Band Steering, Client Steering and Time Synch in Mesh Networks

Mesh networks include both band steering and client steering.

- In *band steering* the network is able to route the same traffic between 2.4GHz and 5GHz depending on band availability.

- *Client steering* connects clients (user devices) to the access point that has the strongest signal strength and the least congestion.

- *Time synch* is a Wi-Fi capability used in mesh networks to distribute and synchronize traffic. It enables clients to connect to multiple access points at the same time and an application in a server. Over-the-top streaming where speakers and audio are synchronized down to a microsecond so that characters' speech is coordinated with the way actors speak is an example of time synch.

Devices on Wi-Fi Networks—Access Points and Controllers

Access points translate between Wi-Fi wireless signals and Ethernet LAN signals and vice versa. An access point has an antenna and chips with 802.11a, 802.11b, 802.11g, and 802.11n, or 802.11ac protocols. Access points for the residential market also include routers with ports to which Ethernet cables are connected. The router aggregates traffic and sends it to the Internet via Gigabit Ethernet on fiber cable, or cable modems.

Access points for corporations are more expensive and feature-rich than those sold to residential customers. They contain higher-functioning security capabilities, such as intrusion detection and protection, the ability to detect hacker attacks, and Quality of Service (QoS) needed for voice and video. There are also robust access points for outdoor locations that are made to withstand harsh environmental conditions. For example, an enterprise might want outdoor coverage on a campus with multiple buildings. Each access point requires electrical power.

Cabling and Electrical Requirements

In a similar manner to cellular networks, all Wi-Fi networks require wired connections to switches, controllers and data centers, and electricity to power access points. Access points in organizations are connected to the LAN via a data jack and, from there, to unshielded twisted-pair (UTP) copper wire connection to the local wiring closet. Electrical and cabling requirements represent an often-overlooked cost in implementing Wi-Fi networks. The power each access point requires can be located remotely in wiring closets on each floor or locally by nearby electrical outlets. For local power, new outlets might be needed.

Wi-Fi Controllers

Non-mesh Wi-Fi in small and medium-sized organizations have controllers that manage access points and monitor the network. Non-mesh Wi-Fi networks require that traffic be routed through centralized controllers. The controllers are part of core switches or separate devices. If they are part of separate devices, they sit between the wireless and wired parts of networks. They are programmed with specifications of the level of access different staff are allowed. They act as gateways to the network, allowing access only to certain users. They often allow access to particular applications on a per-user basis. In addition, centralized controllers authenticate users and access points. Importantly, they can identify unauthorized rogue access points that staff may bring to work. They also pinpoint areas of congestion and gather statistics on usage into reports.

Cloud Service and Virtualization for Wi-Fi Management

Controllers can be installed as virtual entities represented in software on servers. This lowers the cost of Wi-Fi networks by eliminating a separate server and additional utility fees for air conditioning and electricity. This is often possible because more of the functions are distributed to access points rather than contained in central controllers.

Some Wi-Fi manufacturers provide an option called Software as a Service. This is a cloud offering in which the Wi-Fi manufacturer manages the controller and reporting functions at its own data center. For more information on cloud computing and virtualization, see the section "Computing and Enabling Technologies" in Chapter 1.

Securing Wi-Fi Networks—WPA3

The openness of Wi-Fi networks makes them vulnerable to hackers. Access points continually broadcast their network's Service Set Identifier (SSID) and Wi-Fi devices respond to these broadcasts. These broadcast messages are vulnerable to eavesdroppers and can result in attempted and successful logons by unauthorized users. Unlike wired networks, there are no natural boundaries such as those around fiber and copper cables. Thus, in apartment buildings and businesses, signals often easily leak into adjacent units and outside areas. This is why most users keep their Wi-Fi networks password protected. A password is a start, but other factors such as strong encryption and ease of implementing security are important ways to keep Wi-Fi networks safe from hackers.

The Wi-Fi Protected Access 2 (WPA2) security standard was established in 2004 and is currently used. In 2018, the Wi-Fi Alliance announced an updated security protocol, WPA3. The Wi-Fi Alliance is an organization supported by equipment vendors worldwide. It defines Wi-Fi standards and certifies equipment that meets the standards. The Wi-Fi Alliance specified the following WPA3 improvements:

- 192-bit encryption (a possibility of 192 combinations of zeros and ones for every bit that is encrypted). WAP2 has 128-bit encryption.

- Personal, individualized encryption on transmissions at places such as cafes, libraries, and airports. This will enable users to safely use Wi-Fi in public places.

- Simplified ways to set up security to ensure that more small organizations and households actually use and implement security.

- To block access to the Wi-Fi network after too many tries at guessing the password.

- Simplified ways to set up devices that don't have screens such as home assistants like Google's Alexa and connected light switches.

- Easier ways to test Wi-Fi networks when they are reconfigured.

Employees that don't have the newest smartphones and laptops won't be able to take advantage of Wi-Fi Protected Access 3. WPA3 was available in equipment late in 2018. User devices without WPA3 will be able to continue using WPA2. The same is true of older controllers, routers, and access points. For WPA3 to operate, each of these pieces of gear must have WPA3 computer chips. However, the Wi-Fi Alliance has announced that they will continue to support and enhance security and other features on WPA2.

Using Wi-Fi to Offload Traffic from Congested Mobile Networks

To ease congestion caused by increased tablet and smartphone traffic, carriers often supplement mobile services in densely populated areas with Wi-Fi in airports, train stations, and cafés where mobility is not required. In addition, Wi-Fi hotspots relieve backhaul congestion by transmitting traffic back to carriers' data centers over broadband links rather than on the mobile network.

Comcast and Charter operate large networks of Wi-Fi–equipped facilities. Instead of purchasing costly spectrum, these cable TV providers have built out a network of thousands of hotspots throughout the United States. The network is available to

Comcast customers that download the Comcast App to their smartphone, laptop, or tablet computer.

Wi-Fi equipment is less costly than base stations in mobile networks and spectrum is free. While cellular service excels at covering large areas, Wi-Fi service does extremely well at providing coverage inside buildings where it is relatively inexpensive to add access points.

This trend has been made possible by the advent of handsets with chips that support both Wi-Fi and mobile air interfaces. These interfaces are now tightly integrated and have the capability to automatically hand traffic off between cell sites and Wi-Fi networks. They additionally support both voice and data. However, using voice on Wi-Fi networks drains batteries more quickly than on mobile networks.

The downside of operating large numbers of small cell sites and hotspots is maintenance. Large carriers can have 50,000 of these sites to manage. Many mobile operators outsource management of their hotspots to other firms.

Worldwide Roaming on Wi-Fi

When people travel internationally or within the United States they expect Wi-Fi to be available so that they avoid the extra fees wireless providers charge for using cell phones over LTE and other mobile protocols in other networks.

Providers such as AT&T and Comcast offer large networks of Wi-Fi hotspots that are located mainly in the United States. However, using a smartphone in other countries can be problematic with the exception of hotels that offer in-building Wi-Fi either at no charge or at low daily rates.

Enterprises that have business in international locations often sign up for Wi-Fi roaming from aggregators such as iPass and Boingo. Wi-Fi aggregators have agreements with independent hotspots to manage their hotspots and for roaming between their locations. iPass manages over 64 million hotspots in more than 160 countries in which their customers' employees roam. Boingo has more than one million hotspots.

In addition to roaming internationally, Boingo offers Wi-Fi service in airports for travelers to download video and other content before boarding their airplane. The airport service is a collaboration with Comcast.

The Wi-Fi Alliance sets standards for roaming between Wi-Fi access points. Wi-Fi roaming involves middlemen. Intermediaries provide authentication that determines if the device belongs to a legitimate network provider. The intermediary also handles accounting functions related to billing.

Wireless Internet Service Providers

A Wireless Local-Area Network (Wi-Fi) hotspot is a public area where people with Wi-Fi–equipped laptops, tablet computers, and smartphones can access the Internet.

The Wi-Fi hotspot business is multilayered and includes aggregators, cellular providers, and companies that supply back-office services such as billing, roaming, and secure access to corporate networks from hotspots. Hotspot operators are also referred to as Wireless Internet Service Providers (WISPs).

The largest hotspot operator in the United States is AT&T Wi-Fi Services (formerly Wayport before AT&T purchased it in 2008). AT&T Wi-Fi Services is an aggregator. Aggregators install hardware and Internet access for hotspot services and resell it to other providers who provide billing, marketing, and customer service to end users. AT&T offers Wi-Fi access directly to its own subscribers as well as on a wholesale basis to other providers. These providers in turn offer it to their own customers. T-Mobile USA also owns an extensive number of hotspots. It offers the service at no charge to its subscribers.

SATELLITES—GEOSYNCHRONOUS AND LOW EARTH ORBITING ....

Geosynchronous satellites orbit 22,300 miles above the earth's surface. Because of this distance, each satellite can beam signals to a very large area; therefore, less equipment is required for coverage. This makes satellite service attractive for rural and difficult-to-cable areas.

Satellite Networks

Satellite networks are composed of a hub, the satellites themselves, and receiving dish antennas. Receiving antennas also are called *ground stations*. Receivers on antennas convert Radio Frequency (RF) wireless signals to electrical signals. The transmitter on the antenna converts electrical signals to RF signals. The point from which broadcasts originate is the hub on the ground. The hub has a large dish, routing equipment, and fiber links to the enterprise's headquarters for commercial customers. All communications broadcast from the hub travel up to the satellite and then down to the ground stations (the satellite dishes).

Satellites are used to broadcast television and radio signals and to transmit positioning information to aircraft and air traffic controllers. Satellites are particularly suited to broadcast signals to large areas for applications such as weather monitoring, mapping, and military surveillance.

NOTE The area satellites cover is directly related to how high in the sky they are located. Consider a flashlight: Holding it higher enables it to illuminate a large area. If the flashlight is held low, closer to a tabletop, for example, the beam and coverage area shrinks.

Low Earth Orbiting Satellites—Fewer Delays; More Satellites; 200 to 1,200 Miles High

Smaller, lower-cost satellites about the size of a shoebox have spurred an increase in the number of satellites launched into low earth orbits. *Low earth orbiting* (LEO) satellites are more suitable for broadband because they are launched into orbits 200 to 1,200 miles high, rather than geosynchronous satellites. Therefore, signals from low earth orbiting satellites travel a shorter distance than satellites in higher orbits.

Orbiting closer to the earth results in smaller coverage areas than for satellites located further from the earth. Thus, LEO companies invest in launching large numbers of satellites in order to cover more sections of the planet. LEO satellite owners include Aereon, OneWeb, and Viasat. Viasat is owned by satellite provider Iridium. Because of the multiple billions of dollars it costs to launch even a LEO satellite network, these companies often require backing from a variety of investors.

High-Frequency Satellite Service within Airplanes for Internet Access

Satellite service is used to transmit TV, movies, and data signals to Wi-Fi access points on airplanes. These satellites operate on the higher-frequency K_a band at 17.3–31.0 GHz spectrum. This enables them to support the high bandwidths required for on-demand services. There is essentially a Wi-Fi router with an antenna located on top of the airplane's fuselage. The antenna is protected by a 4-inch to ½-inch thin case called a radome. Wi-Fi antennas within the plane distribute signals to passengers' devices in the aircraft's cabin. Satellite providers with these higher-frequency satellites also market their services to rural areas for Internet access. Companies that provide entertainment and data services on airplanes include Gogo, Inmarsat Plc, iPass, Panasonic, and Viasat.

The challenge in providing data service in an airplane is the fact that both the airplane and the satellite travel at high speeds. This means that the airplane antenna must maintain contact with satellites that are also moving.

Satellite providers with these high-frequency satellites also market their services to rural areas and developing countries that have limited or no cable TV service. Dish Network and AT&T-owned DirecTV distribute television signals in rural areas where cable TV is not available. These services are prone to disruptions in heavy fog.

APPENDIX ....

Table 7-5 Mobile Services Worldwide

Technology	Frequencies	Features	Comments
Second-Generation (2G) Cellular Service			
Digital cellular service (CDMA, Time-Division Multiple Access [TDMA], Global System for Mobile Communications [GSM] and Integrated Digital Enhanced Network [iDEN])	UL: 824MHz to 849MHz DL: 869MHz to 894MHz	Digital service with more capacity than analog service. Provides advanced features such as caller ID and Short Message Service (SMS).	CDMA, TDMA, GSM, and iDEN are digital cellular air interfaces.
Personal Communication Service (PCS)	UL: 1.85GHz to 1.91GHz DL: 1.93GHz to 1.99GHz	PCS added more digital spectrum, competitors, and innovative services, driving prices down.	PCS refers to higher-frequency 1.9GHz services. Second- and 4th-generation services operate on PCS frequencies.
GSM	UL: 890MHz to 915MHz DL: 935MHz to 960MHz	A cellular digital technology. The same handsets can be used in all countries that use GSM multiplexing.	Standard used in Europe, the Far East, Israel, New Zealand, and Australia. Also used by T-Mobile and AT&T Mobility in the United States.
Digital Cellular System (DCS)	UL: 1.71GHz to 1.785GHz DL: 1.805GHz to 1.880GHz	DCS service added more digital spectrum for most existing carriers and a few new entrants.	DCS refers to higher-frequency 1.8GHz services in Europe. GSM is considered a DCS air interface.

Technology	Frequencies	Features	Comments
Enhanced Specialized Mobile Radio (ESMR)	UL: 806MHz to 821MHZ DL: 851MHz to 866MHz	Nextel (now part of Sprint Nextel) services operate on these frequencies.	Nextel and other SMR operators use iDEN technology developed by Motorola to support voice, paging, push-to-talk, and messaging on the same telephone. Also suitable for 4G service.
2.5-generation services (2.5G)		Many GSM mobile operators deployed these packet data services in the interim to 3G. They use the same spectrum as GSM. This is a lower-cost solution than 3G but with less efficient spectrum utilization.	
GPRS	Same as GSM, DCS, and PCS	General Packet Radio Service	Appropriates voice channels for data; 40- to 60Kbps.
EDGE		Enhanced Data Rates for GSM Evolution	Data speeds of about 110Kbps. Requires fewer voice channels for data than GPRS.
Third-generation services (3G)		3G packs more services into a given amount of spectrum than 2.5G technology.	

Table 7-6   3G Services and Spectrum

Technology	Frequencies	Features	Comments
WCDMA, also called UMTS CDMA2000 1X CDMA2000 1xEV-DO UMTS TDD TD-SCDMA	IMT-2000 bands: **UMTS:** Uplink: 1.885GHz to 2.025GHz (in the United States: 1.71GHz to 1.755GHz) Downlink: 2.11GHz to 2.17GHz (in the United States: 2.11GHz to 2.155GHz)	More capacity for voice, higher-speed data, acceptable video, low-latency applications, and so on. Standards bodies have specified all of these frequency bands for 3G services.	Carriers launched value-added 3G services to generate higher revenues. CDMA2000 1xEV-DO (data optimized) is always combined with CDMA2000 1X (voice and data) on a single chip.

Table 7-6   (Continued)

Technology	Frequencies	Features	Comments
	CDMA2000: 450MHz (NMT), 800MHz, 1.7GHz (Korea), 1.9GHz (PCS), and 2.1GHz (UMTS) **UMTS TDD:** 1.885GHz to 1.92GHz or 2.01GHz to 2.025GHz (primary), plus 2.3GHz to 2.4GHz (secondary) **TD-SCDMA:** TBD (China)		WCDMA is normally combined with GSM on a single chip for voice services. UMTS TDD uses one frequency band for uplink and downlink data transmissions. The Chinese government commercialized TD-SCDMA, a homegrown version of UMTS TDD.

Table 7-7   Releases and Revisions to 3G Cellular Services

Name of Service and Release	Downlink Data Rates: From the Network to the Subscriber	Uplink Data Rates: From the Subscriber to the Network
CDMA2000 Releases (1.25MHz Channel Bandwidth)		
CDMA2000 1X (Release 0) Doubles voice capacity	Peak data rate: 153.6Kbps Average data rate: 64Kbps	Peak data rate: 153.6Kbps Average data rate: 64Kbps
CDMA2000 1xEV-DO (Release 0) Data optimized High data rate (HDR)	Peak data rate: 2.4Mbps Average data rate: 500Kbps to 1Mbps	Peak data rate: 384Kbps Average data rate: 144Kbps
CDMA450 Same features as other CDMA standards but operates in lower frequencies so that fewer base stations are needed	Same as 1X and 1xEV-DO	Same as 1X and 1xEV-DO. Deployed mainly in rural areas because of its capability to cover large areas.
CDMA2000 1xEV-DO (Revision A) or CDMA2000 DO Rev. A Supports low-latency (delay) data in a single 1.25MHz channel.	Peak data rate: 3.1Mbps Average data rate: 1.8Mbps	Peak data rate: 1.8Mbps Average data rate: 630Kbps per sector (standard) Average data rate: 1.325Mbps per sector

Name of Service and Release	Downlink Data Rates: From the Network to the Subscriber	Uplink Data Rates: From the Subscriber to the Network
WCDMA Releases (5MHz Channel Bandwidth)		
WCDMA (Release 99)	Peak data rate: 2Mbps Average data rate: 220Kbps	Peak data rate: 384Kbps Average data rate: 64Kbps
WCDMA (Release 4) Enables operators to prioritize data services per customer subscription choices.	Peak data rate: 2Mbps Average data rate: 384Kbps	Same as WCDMA (Release 99)
WCDMA (Releases 5 and 6) HSPD/UPA (high-speed downlink/uplink packet access) Doubles the uplink speed	Peak data rate: 14Mbps Average data rate: 2Mbps	Uplink: 1.4Mbps

Table 7-8   802.11 (Wi-Fi) Standards

802.11 Standard	Description
802.11ac	A Wi-Fi standard designed to provide gigabit speeds on Wi-Fi networks. A replacement for 802.11n.
802.11ad	A Wi-Fi standard gigabit short range of only 30 feet, data rates over the 60 GHz spectrum bands. Envisioned as a replacement for HDMI cables and other short-range applications.
802.11af	A Wi-Fi standard designed to operate in the white space 700MHz spectrum freed up by TV broadcasters. It has low power requirements, supports longer-life batteries
802.11ah	A Wi-Fi standard for low sub-gigahertz bandwidth applications
802.11ai	A standard that supports the discovery and initial connectivity to the Wi-Fi network.
802.11ay	An IEEE draft of a standard that will have four times the data rates of 802.11ad. It uses bonding to achieve data rates of 20 to 40 GBPS. It has a range of 300 to 500 meters (327 to 547 yards).
802.11ax	A proposed standard that will operate in support of 10Gbps in the 5GHz bands and slower data rates in the 2.4GHz bands. It supports interoperability and *time synch*, which is used to synchronize timing in mesh architectures. 802.11ax gear is expected to be widely available in 2019. The Wi-Fi Alliance rebranded 802.11ax as Wi-Fi 6.

Table 7-8   (Continued)

802.11 Standard	Description
802.11aq	An IEEE standard to allow devices to detect which networks are available before users connect to these services.
802.11az	A proposed standard that will make it faster for Wi-Fi networks to locate devices and connect devices to Wi-Fi networks when they are moving. Uses power efficiently by reverting to sleep mode when not active.
802.11d	A standard that supports the capability for Wi-Fi devices to operate in different countries that require different power levels and frequencies. Enables equipment to be adjusted according to the rules of each country.
802.11e	A Quality of Service (QoS) standard, the Wi-Fi Multimedia (WMM) section of 802.11e that defines prioritizing voice and video. Was approved October 2004.
802.11f	A standard that supports the capability for access points from different manufacturers to interoperate in the same Wireless Local Area Network (Wi-Fi).
802.11h	A proposal that defines ways for 802.11a networks to dynamically assign packets to other channels if there is interference with other access points and services such as radar, medical devices, and satellite transmissions. In some countries, radar and satellite use the same frequencies as 802.11a.
802.11i	A standard for improved security. It's also referred to as Wireless Protected Access 2 (WPA2) and Wi-Fi Protected Access 3 (WPA3).
802.11k	A Wi-Fi standard for roaming between access points. Provides information to Wi-Fi management systems so they can balance traffic between access points.
802.11n	A standard to increase throughput—actual user data transmitted, and the range covered by each access point. Improvements achieved through enhancements in antennas that decrease effects of interference. In new devices replaced by 802.11ac.
802.11p WAVE (Wireless Access for Vehicular Environments)	A standard for vehicle-to-vehicle and vehicle-to-roadside structures, and vehicle safety services. It enables communications between vehicles and roadside access points or other vehicles.
802.11r	The standard that defines methods for switches to quickly hand off sessions between access points so that users don't have to be authenticated again. This is important to avoid delays for traffic between access points.

802.11 Standard	Description
802.11s	An IEEE networking standard used in mesh networks. It defines how access points access Wi-Fi in community-wide Wi-Fi networks, large homes, and buildings.
802.11u	An IEEE standard that enables automatic interworking between cellular and Wi-Fi networks. A user's mobile device with embedded Wi-Fi with 802.11u can automatically switch to Wi-Fi when it's in a Wi-Fi hotspot that has an agreement with the user's carrier. This is part of the Wi-Fi Alliance initiative known as Hot Spot 2.0 to simplify cellular devices' Wi-Fi access.
802.11v	Improves the ability to manage Wi-Fi networks by enabling statistics gathering and power management that will improve battery life. A must in client devices and access points.
802.11w	A standard used for security that protects Wi-Fi devices from attackers with spoofed (fake) addresses.
802.11x	A proposed security standard for authentication and security to prevent unauthorized packets from entering wired LANs from Wi-Fi networks. It's an alternative to creating virtual private networks.
Control and Provisioning of Wireless Access Points (CAPWAP)	An IEEE standard for Wi-Fi switches to control access points by centralizing intelligence in one device, a controller.
Unlicensed Mobile Access (WMA)	A way to route cell phone traffic over Wi-Fi networks. The cellular network maintains control of calls so that it can bill for traffic.
Wi-Fi Direct	A Wi-Fi standard that enables any device with Wi-Fi Direct software to communicate directly with another device. This allows a laptop to act as an access point so that nearby computers can also access the Internet. Can be used for printing directly from a smartphone to a printer.

Glossary

2G (second-generation cellular service)
Based on digital access to cellular networks. GSM and CDMA are 2G cellular technologies.

3G (third-generation cellular service)
3G mobile standards specify techniques that are capable of supporting more voice traffic and broadband mobile multimedia (speech, audio, text, graphics, and video) services. There are three main 3G services, including WCDMA, CDMA2000, and UMTS TDD. *See also* **3GPP** and **3GPP2**.

3GPP (3rd Generation Partnership Program)
A collaborative group that is developing an agreement to jointly create technical specifications for maintaining LTE, GSM, GPRS, and EDGE and for evolving WCDMA and LTE networks. European, Asian, and North American telecommunications standards bodies formed the 3GPP.

3GPP2 (3rd Generation Partnership Program 2)
An analogous group to 3GPP, but it is working on evolving technical specifications for CDMA2000 networks.

10base-T
An IEEE specification for unshielded, twisted-pair cabling used for Ethernet LANs that transmit at 10Mbps. The distance limitation for 10base-T networks is 100 meters.

100base-T
An IEEE standard compatible with 10base-T for transmitting at 100Mbps over unshielded twisted-pair cabling on LANs.

802.11
A set of IEEE standards for LANs. 802.11a, 802.11b, and 802.11g are the most common and are used in homes to share Internet access, in enterprises, and in hotspots.

802.15.4

The IEEE standards upon which the ZigBee Alliance tests and certifies equipment, and adds functions to sensor networks.

802.20

A set of IEEE standards for wireless technology based on OFDM. Flarion, which is part of Qualcomm, builds 802.20 equipment.

8YY toll-free numbers

An abbreviation describing the format of the North American Numbering Plan for toll-free numbers. The first three digits of toll-free telephone numbers must be the number 8 followed by 0 or 2 through 9 for the second and third digits. When central office switches see the 8YY format, they request a database check to determine where the toll-free number should be routed.

adaptive bit rate streaming

The capability of equipment (encoders) used to stream video and multimedia content from the Internet to computers and mobile devices to adjust the bit rate dynamically to the user's processing capabilities and bandwidth availability.

access fees

Carriers pay access fees to local telephone companies for transporting long-distance traffic to and from local customers. The FCC sets access fees for interstate traffic, and state utility commissions set access fees for intrastate traffic. They are intended to offset the costs that local phone companies incur in providing links to local customers, but these fees have been decreasing, and residential and business customers are paying some of the costs in the form of monthly charges called Subscriber Line Charges (SLCs). VoIP traffic is exempt from access fees.

ACD (Automatic Call Distribution)

Equipment and software that distribute calls to agents, based on parameters such as the agent who has been idle the longest. ACDs are part of telephone systems or adjuncts to telephone systems. ACDs are also referred to as contact centers. *See also* **contact centers**.

Active Directory

A directory of users on organizations' LANs. Provides authentication that people are who they claim to be and security by encrypting calls.

ANI (Automatic Number Identification)

The business or residential customer's billing number. Customers such as call centers pay for callers' ANIs to be sent to them simultaneously with incoming 800 and 888 and other toll-free calls.

APs (Access Points)

These contain antennas and chips with 802.11a, 802.11b, 802.11g, or 802.11n air interfaces for 802.11 wireless LANs. Access points translate between radio frequencies and Ethernet signals for cabled networks. An access point has similar functions to base stations for cordless home phones.

API (Application Programming Interface)

Software used to translate programming code between two different programs. An API can be used when an application at an enterprise accesses an application on the cloud.

architecture
Defines how computers are tied together. Some vendors refer to the architecture of their equipment in terms of the growth available and the hardware and software needed for their systems to grow.

ASCII (American Standard Code for Information Interchange)
The main 7-bit code personal computers use to translate bits into meaningful language. Most computers now use extended ASCII, which supports 8-bit codes. Each group of 8 bits represents a character. Computers can "read" one another's binary bits when these bits are arranged in a standard, uniform "language." ASCII is the most commonly used computer code.

ATM (Asynchronous Transfer Mode)
A high-speed switching technique that uses fixed-size cells to transmit voice, data, and video. A cell is analogous to envelopes that each carry the same number of bits. Used mainly in older networks.

backbone
A segment of a network used to connect smaller segments of networks together. Backbones carry high concentrations of traffic between on and off ramps to networks.

backhaul
A term used mostly to describe the links between antennas at base stations and mobile central offices, and services in the cellular networks core. Traffic and signaling information is backhauled from where it enters the network to the mobile core, and vice versa.

band refarming
The reuse of portions of spectrum for more advanced mobile protocols. Many countries are refarming spectrum originally used only for older second-generation services to newer fourth-generation technologies.

bandwidth
The measure of the capacity of a communications channel. Analog telephone lines measure capacity in hertz (Hz), the difference in the highest and lowest frequency of the channel. Digital channels measure bandwidth in bits per second (bps).

BGP (Border Gateway Protocol)
A routing protocol with more than 90,000 addresses. Used by carriers to route packets on the Internet. BGP enables routers to determine the best routes to various destinations.

bill and keep
A carrier-to-carrier billing method that eliminates the requirement for carriers to bill each other access fees. It is used by billing companies only to bill carriers that carry less traffic than carriers with whom they exchange traffic.

bit error rate
The percentage of bits received in error in a transmission.

blade
Circuit boards are often referred to as "blades" when they are dense, such as when they have many ports (connections) or software for a specialized application such as security.

Bluetooth

A set of standards for special software on low-cost, low-powered radio chips that enables devices to communicate with one another over a short-range wireless link. Bluetooth eliminates cable clutter between computers and peripherals in offices and supports wireless headsets for mobile handsets.

BOC (Bell Operating Company)

One of the 22 local Bell telephone companies owned by AT&T Corporation prior to 1984. Examples of Bell Operating Companies are Michigan Bell, Illinois Bell, and Pac Bell. Bell Operating Companies are now part of AT&T Inc., CenturyLink, and Verizon Communications.

border elements

Another name for media gateways. *See also* **media gateways**.

bps (bits per second)

The number of bits sent or received in one second.

BRI (Basic Rate Interface)

The ISDN interface made up of two B channels at 64 kilobits each and a signaling channel with a speed of 16 kilobits.

bridge

A device that connects local or remote networks together. Bridges are used to connect small numbers of networks. Bridges do not have routing intelligence. Organizations that want to connect more than four or five networks use routers.

broadband

A data transmission scheme in which multiple transmissions share a communications path. Cable television uses broadband transmission techniques.

broadcast

A message from one person or device forwarded to multiple destinations. Video and e-mail services have broadcast features whereby the same message can be sent to multiple recipients or locations.

BTA (Basic Trading Area)

A relatively small area in which the FCC allocates spectrum. There are 491 basic trading areas in the United States.

CAP (Competitive Access Provider)

Originally provided midsize and large organizations with connections to long-distance providers that bypassed local telephone companies. CAPs are now often referred to as Competitive Local Exchange Carriers (CLECs) or competitive providers.

CCIS (Common Channel Interoffice Signaling)

A signaling technique used in public networks. Signals such as those for dial tone and ringing are carried on a separate path from the actual telephone call. CCIS allows for telephone company database queries used in features such as caller ID, call forwarding, and network-based voicemail. CCIS channels are also used for billing and diagnosing public network services.

CDMA (Code-Division Multiple Access)

An air interface used to transmit digital cellular signals between handheld devices and cellular carriers' networks. CDMA assigns a unique code to every voice and data transmission by using a channel of a particular carrier's airwaves. CDMA is a spread-spectrum technology that is used by Verizon Wireless, Sprint, and South Korean carriers such as SKT.

CDMA2000 (Code-Division Multiple Access 2000)

A 3G technology for carrying high-speed data and multimedia traffic on cellular networks.

CDMA2000 1X (Code-Division Multiple Access 2000)

The earliest version of the CDMA2000 3G technology for carrying high-speed data and multimedia traffic on cellular networks.

CDMA2000 1xEV-DO (Code-Division Multiple Access 2000 Data Optimized or Data Only)

A later, higher-data-rate version of CDMA2000 1X 3G technology for carrying high-speed data and multimedia traffic on cellular networks.

central office

The site in the Public Switched Telephone Network with the local telephone company's equipment that routes calls to and from customers. It also has equipment that connects customers to Internet service providers and long-distance services.

channel

A path for analog or digital transmission signals. With services such as ISDN, T1, and T3, multiple channels share the same one or two pairs of wires or fiber.

CIC (Carrier Identification Code)

The four-digit code (previously three digits) assigned to each carrier for billing and call-routing purposes. AT&T's CIC is 0288. If someone at a pay telephone dials 1010288 and then the telephone number she is calling, the call is routed over the AT&T network.

CIR (Committed Information Rate)

A term used in frame relay MPLS networks to indicate the speed of the transmission guaranteed for a customer. *See also* **MPLS**.

circuit switching

The establishment—by dialing—of a temporary physical circuit (path) between points. The circuit is terminated when either end of the connection sends a disconnect signal by hanging up.

CLEC (Competitive Local Exchange Carrier)

A competitor to incumbent local telephone companies that has been granted permission by the state regulatory commission to offer local telephone service. CLECs compete with the incumbent telephone company. CLECs are also simply called local telephone companies.

CLID (Calling Line ID)

The number that identifies the telephone number from which a call was placed. For most residential customers, the calling line ID is the same as their billing number, their Automatic Number Identification (ANI).

CO (Central Office)

The location that houses the telephone company switch that routes telephone calls. End offices are central offices that connect end users to the Public Switched Telephone Network.

compression

The reduction in size of data, image, voice, or video files. This decreases the capacity needed to transmit files.

concatenation

The linking of channels in optical networks so that voice or video is transmitted as one stream. This is done to ensure that there are no breaks in the transmission.

connectionless service

The Internet protocol is connectionless. Each packet travels through the network separately. If there is congestion, packets are dropped. Packets are reassembled at their destination.

contact center

Another term for automatic call distribution. The term *contact center* implies that call centers have the capability to respond to e-mail and facsimile as well as voice calls.

containers

Application programs surrounded by software that enables a group of programs in the same container to work together.

convergence

The use of one network for voice, data, and video.

CORD (Central Office Re-architected as a Data Center)

Telephone companies that deploy CORD architect their central offices as data centers rather than as typical central offices. They use open source software and commodity servers and switches and software-defined networking. The goal is to be able to quickly add and delete features and services used by customers.

cordless

Cordless telephones provide portability, mainly within homes and apartments.

core networks

The portions of carrier and enterprise networks that carry the highest percentage of traffic, and where switches and routers connect to other switches and routers rather than to customers. High-speed core routers are located in core networks.

CPE (Customer Premises Equipment)

Telephone systems, modems, terminals, and other equipment installed at customer sites.

CSU/DSU (Channel Service Unit/Data Service Unit)

A digital interface device that connects customer computers, video equipment, multiplexers, and terminals to T1/E1 and T3/E3 lines.

CTI (Computer Telephony Integration)

CTI software translates signals between telephone systems and computers so that telephone systems and computers can coordinate sending call routing and account information to agents in contact centers.

CWDM (Coarse Wavelength-Division Multiplexing)

A multiplexing technology standard that enterprises and carriers deploy to connect corporate sites to public networks and to bring the capacity of fiber closer to residential neighborhoods. It carries up to eight channels of traffic on a single fiber pair.

dark fiber

Fiber-optic cables without any of the electronics (that is, multiplexers and amplifiers). Carriers can lay dark fiber and add SONET, Gigabit Ethernet, and wavelength-division multiplexers later.

DCE (Data Circuit-Terminating Equipment)

A communications device that connects user equipment to telephone lines. Examples include modems for analog lines and CSUs for digital lines.

dedicated line

A telephone line between two or more sites of a private network. Dedicated lines are always available for the exclusive use of the private network at a fixed, monthly fee.

de-duplication

A method of compression that removes changes in files sent between two sites where each site has a copy of the file as it was originally sent. De-duplication sends only changes each time after the original transmission. The receiving end adds the changes and puts the file back together.

DID (Direct-Inward Dialing)

A feature of local telephone service whereby each person in an organization has his own ten-digit telephone number. Calls to DID telephone numbers do not have to be answered by onsite operators. They go directly to the person assigned to the ten-digit DID telephone number.

DiffServ (Differentiated Services)

Used in routers to tag frames. The tags request a particular level of service on the Internet and other IP-based networks.

disk mirroring

The process of simultaneously writing data to backup and primary servers.

divestiture

In January 1984, divestiture deregulated long-distance service in the United States. It separated the former AT&T from its 22 local Bell telephone companies. Agreement on divestiture was reached by the Justice Department, which negotiated an antitrust settlement with the former AT&T, called the Modified Final Judgment.

DLC (Digital Loop Carrier)

Used to economically bring fiber closer to customers. Carriers run fiber cabling from central offices to DLCs and they lay twisted-pair copper cabling from DLCs to customers.

DNIS (Dialed-Number Identification Service)

The service used to identify and route toll-free and 900 numbers to particular agents or devices within a customer site. For example, if a customer has multiple 800 numbers, the network provider routes each toll-free number to a different four-digit number at the customer's telephone system. The onsite telephone system then routes the call to a particular group of agents, voice response system, or department.

DNSSEC (Domain Name Service Security Extensions)

An Internet security standard for preventing users from using other organizations' domain names, which is also known as *spoofing*. Disguising domain names makes it more difficult to track the origin of traffic.

domain name

Everything after the @ sign in an e-mail address. It includes the host computer, the organization's name, and the type of organization (for example, *.com* for commercial and *.edu* for educational). Both .com and .edu are top-level domain names. The domain name can also designate the country, such as .bo for Bolivia. A domain name is part of the TCP/IP addressing convention.

DoS (Denial-of-Service) attack
An attack by which hackers bombard networks with thousands of packets intended to disrupt the capability of the attacked network to function.

downlink (DL)
On broadband and mobile networks, the downlink portions are those that carry traffic from the carrier to the customer.

downloading
Receiving an entire file from another location. When music is downloaded, the entire music file must be downloaded to the computer's hard drive before it can be played.

DS-0 (Digital Signal level 0)
A transmission rate of 64Kbps. This refers to one channel of a T1, E1, E3, T3, fractional T1, or fractional T3 circuit.

DS-1 (Digital Signal level 1)
The T1 transmission rate of 1.54Mbps. There are 24 channels associated with DS-1 or T1.

DS-3 (Digital Signal level 3)
The T3 transmission rate of 44Mbps over 672 associated channels. (T3 is equivalent to 28 T1s.)

DSP (Digital Signal Processor)
Compresses (shrinks the number of bits required for) voice and video, performs digital-to-analog and analog-to-digital voice conversions, and packetizes voice and video in real time for IP networks.

DTE (Data Terminal Equipment)
Devices that communicate over telephone lines. Examples include multiplexers, PBXs, key systems, and personal computers.

DVB (Digital Video Broadcasting)
A standard approved by the European Telecommunications Standards Institute (ETSI). It has lower resolution than HDTV.

DWDM (Dense Wavelength Division Multiplexing)
A way of increasing the capacity of fiber-optic networks. DWDM carries multiple colors of light, or multiple wavelengths, on a single strand of fiber. Also known as Wavelength Division Multiplexing (WDM).

E1
The European standard for T1. E1 has a speed of 2.048 megabits with 30 channels for voice, data, or video, plus one channel for signaling and one for diagnostics.

E3
The European standard for T3. E3 has a speed of 34.368Mbps with 480 channels. It is equivalent to 16 E1 circuits.

E-911 (Enhanced 911)
The capability for agents who answer 911 calls to receive the callers' phone numbers and locations.

EDGE (Enhanced Data Rates for Global Evolution)
EDGE mobile services offered by cellular carriers have higher data rates than

second-generation cellular networks. EDGE is often used by carriers as they transition to higher-data-rate, third-generation mobile service.

end offices

The central offices connected to end users and to tandem central offices. Most end offices are based on circuit switching, but they are slowly being converted to *softswitch* technology to carry VoIP.

endpoint

Any device connected to LANs, such as computers, printers, and VoIP telephones.

Ethernet

Based on the 802.3 standard approved by the IEEE. It defines how data is transmitted on and retrieved from LANs. It is used by devices such as personal computers to access the LAN and to retrieve packets carried on the LAN.

exabyte (EB)

A unit of measurement to indicate the number of bytes in storage networks. An exabyte is equal to 1,000,000,000,000,000,000 bytes or 1 billion gigabytes. A byte is equal to 8 bits, or one character.

FDDI (Fiber-Distributed Data Interface)

An ANSI-defined protocol in which computers communicate at 100Mbps over fiber-optic cabling. FDDI can be used on backbones that connect LAN segments together. It is not widely used.

fiber-optic cable

A type of cable that is made from glass strands rather than copper wire. The key advantage of fiber-optic cabling is that it is non-electric. Thus, it is immune from electrical interference and interference from other cables within the same conduit. Fiber-optic cabling can be used for higher-speed transmissions than twisted-pair copper cabling.

Fibre Channel protocol

Used in storage area networks and data centers for gigabit-speed, highly reliable, short-distance access to devices such as disks, graphics equipment, video input/output devices, and storage devices that hold massive amounts of data.

firewall

Software and hardware that prevents unauthorized access to an organization's network files. The intention is to protect files from computer viruses and electronic snooping.

firmware

Special software embedded in hardware (routers, printers, cellular phones etc.) containing instructions that control the hardware on which it's installed. Firmware is non-volatile. It isn't lost when power is lost.

fixed mobile convergence

The capability to use the same handset or portable computer for Wi-Fi as well as mobile voice and data sessions. For voice calls, it is the capability to continue the call when moving; for example, from a hotspot or home to a cellular network, and vice versa.

fixed wireless

Wireless service between fixed points. Generally, these are between an antenna on a tower and a dish on a business or residential customer's building. It is also used to connect two buildings together as a lower-cost option than running cabling. Used most often in rural or hard-to-cable areas.

fixed wireless access
Provides similar data rates as Gigabit Ethernet technologies using wireless media rather than cabling. LTE and 5G can be used for broadband wireless access service.

fractional T3
A less expensive T3 access scheme in which the customer pays for a fraction of the 672-channel capacity of T3 lines. For example, it might have the capacity of 6 T1s or 144 channels. Fractional T3s are cheaper than a full T3 line.

FTP (File Transfer Protocol)
A part of the TCP/IP suite of Internet protocols. It is software that lets users download files from a remote computer to their computer's hard drive.

gateway
Allows equipment with different protocols to communicate with one another. For example, gateways are used when incompatible video systems are used for a video conference.

Gigabit Ethernet
A high-speed service used for site-to-site carriers' backbone networks, metropolitan area networks, Internet access, and in enterprise internal networks. These networks operate at 1- or 10Gbps.

gigabits per second
Billions of bits per second (Gbps). Fiber-optic cables carry signals at this speed.

GPRS (General Packet Radio Services)
A cellular data-packet network service. Upgrades to digital cellular networks are required to provision the service. This is an "always on" data service that users do not have to dial into to access. Its data rates are lower than EDGE and 3G protocols.

GPS (Global Positioning System)
Used for locational tracking purposes. For example, many wireless E-911 systems are based on GPS satellites along with equipment at a carrier's cell stations and special handsets.

GPU (Graphic Processing Unit)
Specialized computer chips able to manipulate graphics. GPUs are used in mobile phones, game consoles, and computers.

GSM (Global System for Mobile Communications)
The most widely deployed cellular service, worldwide. It is a digital service that was first used in Europe in the 1990s.

H.320
The standard for enabling video conference equipment from multiple vendors to communicate with each other by using ISDN service.

H.323
An ITU-based standard for sending voice via IP. H.323 was originally developed for video conferencing.

H.324
An ITU standard for sending video, voice, and data between devices over a single analog,

dial-up telephone line using a 28.8Kbps modem. Compression is used on the voice, video, and data.

HBA (Host Bus Adapter)
Used to connect Ethernet switches to networks running Fibre Channel protocols. *See also* **Fibre Channel protocol**.

HDTV (High-Definition Television)
A standard for digital high-resolution television video and surround sound audio.

headend
The control center of a cable television system where incoming video signals are received and converted into a format compatible for transmission to subscribers and combined with other signals onto the cable operator's fiber infrastructure.

home page
The default first page of an Internet web site. A home page is analogous to the first page and table of contents of a book.

hotspot
A public area where people with Wi-Fi–equipped laptops or personal digital assistants can access the Internet. Access might be free or available for monthly or daily rates.

HTML5 (Hypertext Markup Language 5)
A language for structuring browsers and web sites. The World Wide Web Consortium (W3C) specifies the standard. Its goal is to make browsing the Web from mobile devices faster, particularly for accessing video and other applications directly from browsers

without using specialized plug-in languages. Apple uses it on its mobile devices in competition with the proprietary Adobe Flash.

HTTP (HyperText Transfer Protocol)
The protocol used to link Internet sites to one another. For example, HTTP provides links to servers containing text, graphical images, and videos.

hub
Prior to the use of switches on LANs, each device (such as a computer or printer) was wired to the hub, generally located in the wiring closet. Hubs enabled LANs to use twisted-pair cabling rather than more expensive, harder-to-install and move coaxial cabling. Hubs are sometimes referred to as concentrators. In wide area network architectures, the hub is the headquarters, the central site, in the network of connected locations.

hyper convergence
Software to simplify data center architecture by tightly integrating computing devices, storage, network, and virtualization.

hypervisor
Software that monitors and supervises software on servers with virtual machines.

ILECs (Incumbent Local Exchange Carriers)
The former Bell and independent telephone companies that sell local telephone service. This term differentiates incumbent telephone companies that were the providers of telephone service prior to 1996 from competitors such as Paetec, XO Communications, and tw telecom.

IMS (Internet Protocol Multimedia Subsystem)

Enables applications for voice, video, and online games to be stored, billed for, and accessed on a common IP platform available from mobile as well as wired networks.

Indefeasible Right of Use (IRU)

Long-term lease for fiber-optic cable runs. IRUs are analogous to condominium arrangements. One organization lays the cable and leases it to another carrier for its exclusive use.

independent telephone company

An incumbent local telephone company that was never a part of the former AT&T's Bell system. Examples of independent telephone companies are Frontier Corporation and Cincinnati Bell, Inc.

instant messaging

The ability to exchange e-mail in near-real time without typing in an address. Users merely click an icon representing the user to whom the message is intended, type a message, and then click Submit (or press the Return key) to send the message.

intermodal competition

Competition between services based on different media and technology. For example, mobile services compete with wireline services for local and long-distance calling. Cable TV companies compete with telephone companies such as AT&T and CenturyLink.

Internet

The Internet—with a capital I—is an entity composed of multiple worldwide networks, tied together by a common protocol, TCP/IP.

intranet

The use of web technologies for internal operations. Intranets are used by organizations as a way to make corporate information and applications readily accessible by employees. An example is a corporate telephone directory that can be accessed by a browser.

inverse multiplexer

Instead of combining individual channels into one "fat" pipe, which is what a multiplexer does, an inverse multiplexer separates out channels into smaller "chunks." Inverse multiplexers are used for video conferencing, where the 24 channels might be transmitted in groups of 6 channels at a speed of 386Mbps.

IPsec (Internet Protocol Security)

A protocol that establishes a secure, encrypted link to a security device at the carrier or the enterprise. It is used for remote access to corporate services (such as e-mail) in conjunction with VPNs.

IPv4 (Internet Protocol version 4)

An older addressing format for networks. Each device on an Internet network is assigned a 32-bit IP address. This limits the total number of addresses available.

IPv6 (Internet Protocol version 6)

A newer Internet protocol format that specifies 32-bit IP addresses. This increases the number of addresses available in networks and on the Internet. IPv6 also has additional security.

ISDN (Integrated Services Digital Network)

A digital network standard that lets users send voice, data, and video over one telephone line from a common network interface.

ISP (Internet Service Provider)

An organization that connects end users to the Internet via broadband, mobile networks, and dial-up telephone lines. ISPs often own Internet backbone networks. ISPs supply services such as voicemail, hosting, and domain name registration.

IXCs (Interexchange Carriers)

The long-distance companies that sell toll-free 800, international, data networking, and outgoing telephone service on an interstate basis. They now also sell local telecommunications services.

Java

A programming language created by Sun Microsystems. Multiple types of computers can read Java programs. They increase the power of the Internet because programs written in Java (called applets) can be downloaded temporarily by client computers. They do not take up permanent space on the client hard drive. Interactive games can use Java programs.

LAN (Local Area Network)

Enables computer devices such as personal computers, printers, alarm systems, and scanners to communicate with one another. Moreover, LANs allow multiple devices to share and have access to expensive peripherals such as printers, firewalls, and centralized databases. A LAN is located on an individual organization's premises.

LATA (Local Access And Transport Area)

Upon divestiture in 1984, LATAs were set up as the areas in which Bell telephone companies were allowed to sell local telephone services. LATAs cover metropolitan statistical areas based on population sizes. For example, Massachusetts has two LATAs and Wisconsin has four, but Wyoming, which has a small population, has one LATA. LATAs are sometimes used for billing telephone calls in the United States.

Layer 4

One of the seven layers of the OSI model. Layer 4 is the Transport layer that routes and prioritizes packets, based on the source of the packet, the destination port number, the protocol type, and the application. For example, Layer 4 devices can prioritize voice and video so that networks using IP for voice and data can handle voice without the delays and lost packets associated with lower-level protocols.

LDAP (Lightweight Directory Access Protocol)

A directory protocol that describes a uniform way of organizing information in directories. Examples of LDAP directories include the address books in e-mail systems. LDAP enables companies to use one central directory to update multiple corporate directories. They also facilitate single sign-on to access different applications on corporate intranets.

leased line

Analogous to two tin cans with a string between two or more sites. Organizations that rent leased lines pay a fixed monthly fee for the leased lines that are available exclusively to the organization that leases them. Leased lines can be used to transmit voice, data, or video. They are also called private or dedicated lines.

LEC (Local Exchange Carrier)
Any company authorized by the state public utility commission to sell local telephone service.

local loop
The telephone line that runs from the local telephone company to the end user's premises. The local loop can use fiber, copper, or wireless media.

LTE (Long-Term Evolution)
A 4G mobile protocol that uses packet switching to carry voice, data, and multimedia traffic more efficiently than earlier protocols. It will eventually support broadband speeds of up to 100Mbps. LTE was developed by the 3rd Generation Partnership Project.

LUN (Logical Unit Number)
An identifier in Storage Area Networks (SANs). It identifies the particular database stored in a computer disk. LUNs are part of the Fibre Channel protocol used in SANs.

MAN (Metropolitan Area Network)
A network that covers a metropolitan area such as a portion of a city. Hospitals, universities, municipalities, and large corporations often have telephone lines running between sites within a city or suburban area.

Mbps (millions of bits per second)
A transmission speed at the rate of millions of bits in one second. Digital telephone lines measure their capacity or bandwidth in bits per second.

media gateways
Contain Digital Signal Processors (DSPs) that compress voice traffic to make it smaller so that it can be carried more efficiently. In addition, media gateways are equipped with circuit packs with ports for connections to traditional circuit-switched analog and T1 trunks. Thus, they are used to link converged IP networks to Public Switched Telephone Networks.

media servers
Specialized computers that play announcements and generate ring tones in corporate telephone systems and converged public networks. In corporate VoIP systems, they control call processing.

media servers for homes (home servers)
PCs or separate devices that store content, music, photos, movies, or TV shows that can be distributed over home networks to home entertainment equipment.

mesh networks
Networks in which every device is connected to every other device. Community wireless networks and sensor networks often use variations of mesh networks, as does the military when it sets up communications facilities in war zones. Mesh networks are also referred to as multipoint-to-multipoint networks.

microwave wireless services
Wireless services with short wavelengths operating in the frequency range of about the 890MHz to 60GHz bands. It is a fixed point-to-point wireless technology used to connect two points. Line of sight is required between microwave towers. For example, if there is a tree blocking the view between the towers, the service is inoperable.

middleware
Software used to translate between disparate systems. It translates between the hardware (set-top devices) and network protocols and the applications in satellite TV and cable TV networks. Middleware also enables interactive television applications from different developers to work with set-top box hardware from a variety of manufacturers. Thus, applications don't have to be designed differently for each type of device with which they interact.

millimeter wireless services
Operate at microwave and higher frequencies. Millimeter refers to the very short wavelengths of high-frequency services. Some next-generation, 5G, mobile services are implemented on millimeter airwaves. The wavelength is the distance from the highest or lowest point of one wave to the highest or lowest point of the next wave.

MIMO (Multiple-Input Multiple-Output) antennas
MIMO antennas simultaneously transmit multiple streams at different frequencies within a single channel. This improvement is analogous to the increased capacity on a multilane highway vs. a road with a single lane. MIMO antennas are used on 802.11n (Wi-Fi) WLANs, LTE, and WiMAX networks.

mobile wireless services
Provide mobility over wide areas by using services such as cellular, as in cities, states, countries, and in some instances, internationally.

MPLS (Multi-Protocol Label Switching)
Used to increase router speeds and prioritize packets. Short, fixed-length "labels" instruct routers how to route each packet so that the router does not have to examine the entire header of each packet after the first point in the carrier's network. Voice and video can have tags that classify them with a higher priority than data bits.

MSOs (Multiple System Operators)
Large cable TV operators, such as Comcast and Time Warner Cable, with cable franchises in many cities.

MTA (Major Trading Area)
A region that includes multiple cities or states. They are made up of some of the 491 BTAs. The FCC auctions off spectrum in both BTAs and MTAs.

MTSO (Mobile Telephone Switching Office)
A central office used in mobile networks. They connect cellular network calls to the PSTNs, and vice versa.

multicasting
The transmission of the same message from a single point to multiple nodes.

multicloud
Using more than one cloud provider to avoid dependence on a single provider or because a particular provider meets a customer's specific requirement, for example, using both Amazon and Microsoft.

multiplexing (muxing)
A technique in which multiple devices can share a circuit. With multiplexing, carriers do not have to lay cabling for each computer that communicates. T1 multiplexers and fiber multiplexers enable many devices to share strands of fiber, air waves, and copper cabling.

MVNOs (Mobile Virtual Network Operators)

MVNOs such as Tracfone and cable TV operators resell cellular service on cellular carriers' networks.

NAS (Network Attached Storage)

The use of servers for storing files that can be accessed directly by computers located on the LAN. NAS is less costly than traditional SANs.

NAT (Network Address Translation)

Translates external IP addresses to internal IP addresses, and vice versa. Carriers and enterprises use different internal and external IP addresses to conserve public addresses and to shield IP addresses from outside sources.

NFC (Near Field Communications)

A low-power, short-range protocol used for contactless payments via smartphones at retailers and at subway systems instead of tokens and credit cards.

NEBS (Network Equipment Building Standards)

Requirements published in a Bellcore (now Telcordia) technical reference for products placed in a central office environment. Bellcore is the former Bell Telephone central research organization. There are eight standards referring to issues such as environmental, electrical, and cabling requirements, as well as resistance to natural disasters such as earthquakes.

network

An arrangement of devices that can communicate with one another. An example of a network is the PSTN over which residential and commercial telephones and modems communicate with one another.

NFV (Network Function Virtualization)

Virtualizes the functions of devices such as switches, routers, load balancers, and firewalls and installs these functions as virtual machines in servers. Is used as an adjunct to software-defined networks (SDNs).

non-blocking

Switches that have enough capability for each connected device to communicate at the same time up to the full speed of the port to which it is connected.

number pooling

Allows local carriers to share a "pool" of telephone numbers within the same exchange. Number pooling is a way to allocate scarce telephone numbers more efficiently. Without pooling, a single local telephone company has rights to the entire 10,000 block of telephone numbers, but it might only use a portion of the block.

OSS (Operation and Support Service)

Hardware and software that carriers use for billing, maintenance, and changes to customer features.

packet switching

A network technique that routes data in units called packets. Each packet contains addressing and error-checking bits as well as transmitted user data. Packets from a transmission can be routed individually through a network such as the Internet and be assembled at the end destination.

PAN (Personal Area Network)
Operates over small areas within rooms and buildings. Bluetooth and RFID are examples of PANs.

PBX (Private Branch Exchange)
Computerized, onsite telephone system located at an organization's premises. PBXs route calls both within an organization and from the outside world to people within the organization, and vice versa.

PCS (Personal Communications Service)
Originally referred to 2G digital mobile services that use spectrum in the higher frequencies. PCS (or DCS in Europe) is now used in the industry to refer to all 2G cellular access technologies.

peer-to-peer network
Distributes intelligence over devices in the network instead of relying on central computers. Peer-to-peer networks are often used to download free music and movies from the Internet. In addition, companies such as Skype use the technology for voice calls and other services.

petabyte (PB)
A unit of measurement. One petabyte equals 1,000,000,000,000,000 bytes or 1,000 gigabytes. A byte equals 8 bits.

photonics
All of the elements of optical communications. This includes fiber, lasers, and optical switches and all elements involved in transmitting light over fiber.

ping (Packet Internetwork Groper)
A software protocol used to test communications between devices. To "ping" means to send a packet to another device or host to see if the device sends back a response. The ping also tests round-trip delay, the time it takes to send a message to another device.

plug-in
A small program that adds capabilities to a parent, usually larger, program. Plug-ins are used in browsers and in software defined networks and MANO (Management and Organization).

PoE (Power over Ethernet)
A standard that defines how power can be carried from wiring closets on floors to the computers and other LAN-connected devices using the same cabling that transmits packetized voice and data. Thus, every device does not need its own power or backup power.

PON (Passive Optical Network)
Technologies deployed to extend fiber to homes, businesses, and neighborhoods. PONs use non-electrical devices located in the access network that enable carriers to dynamically allocate capacity on a single pair of fibers to multiple homes, buildings in a campus, apartments, and small and medium-sized businesses.

POP (Point of Presence)
A long-distance company's equipment that is connected to the local telephone company's central office. The POP is the point at which telephone and data calls are handed off between local telephone companies, long-distance telephone companies, and the Internet.

POTS (Plain Old Telephone Service)
Telephone lines connected to most residential and small-business users. POTS lines

are analog from the end user to the nearest local telephone company equipment. People using POTS for data communications with modems are limited in the speed at which they can transmit data.

presence
The ability of users to know when someone within their community of users is available for real time or near real time messaging.

PRI (Primary Rate Interface)
A form of ISDN with 23 paths for voice, video, and data and 1 channel for signals. Each of the 24 channels transmits at 64Kbps.

protocol
Defines how devices and networks communicate with one another. For example, a suite of protocols known as TCP/IP spells out rules for sending voice, images, and data across the Internet and in corporate networks.

proxy server
Authenticates callers to ensure that they are who they say they are before they are sent to their destination. They serve as intermediaries between callers and applications or endpoints, telephones, and other devices connected to the LAN. For instance, a proxy server in a VoIP environment ensures that external devices requesting to communicate with an IP telephone are who they say they are.

PSAP (Public Safety Answering Point)
Groups of agents that answer and dispatch 911 and E-911 calls for their town, county, or cluster of towns. They are often located at police stations.

PSTN (Public Switched Telephone Network)
The global network of circuit-switched telephone services that telephone companies operate. The PSTN comprises traditional copper-based telephone lines, central office switches, fiber-optic cabling, undersea cable systems, cellular systems, microwave connections, communications satellites, and any other system connected via public telephone switching centers. It does not include the Internet or carriers' private data networks.

push-to-talk
A walkie-talkie type of service pioneered by Nextel (now part of Sprint) in which customers reach one another by pushing a button on the side of their phone. They also dial an abbreviated telephone number. Push-to-talk is used to reach individuals or predefined groups. Walkie-talkies are used on non-mobile spectrum between people that perhaps hike together or for parents to monitor children in other rooms of a house.

QoS (Quality of Service)
The ability to offer a number of priorities for various types of communications including voice, e-mail, and video on LANs and WANs.

radio
A wireless device with an antenna that converts signals to and from formats compatible with the airwaves. Wireless handsets are radios.

ransomware
A type of security attack where hackers encrypt organizations' files, and then demand payment to decrypt the files to make them readable again.

RBOC (Regional Bell Operating Company)

At Divestiture in 1984, the Justice Department organized the 22 Bell telephone companies into seven Regional Bell Operating Companies. As a result of mergers and name changes, the former RBOCs are now part of AT&T, CenturyLink, or Verizon.

reverse channel

In cable TV systems, this carries signals from the customer to the cable operator's equipment. Reverse channels are required for Internet access, on-demand TV, and VoIP.

RFID (Radio Frequency Identification)

A non-line-of-sight wireless technology used to control, detect, and track objects. Two common applications are merchandise tracking and automated tollbooth collection.

roaming

The capability in mobile networks to use the same handset on another carrier's network. Carriers set up roaming agreements to define terms such as per-minute fees that carriers charge one another.

router

A device with routing intelligence that connects local and remote networks together. Routers are also used to forward packets in the Internet.

RPKI (Resource Public-Key Infrastructure)

An Internet security protocol for routing packets on the Internet. It adds encryption between databases called Internet registries (centralized databases with Internet addresses) and network operators. Encryption is the use of mathematical algorithms to scramble data.

RSS (Really Simple Syndication)

A series of software standards that automates feeding updates from news sites such as Forbes.com and blogs to other sites and users. The use of RSS means that people don't have to continually check to see news headlines or updates to blogs.

RTMP (Real-Time Messaging Protocol)

A realtime streaming protocol developed by Adobe for using Flash servers to improve streamed audio, video, and data over the Internet. It is now used with other Adobe programs. According to Adobe, most of the RTMP specifications are open to developers to create applications compatible with Adobe Flash Player.

RTP (Real-Time Transport Protocol)

An IETF standardized protocol for transmitting multimedia in IP networks. RTP is used for the "bearer" channels, the actual voice, video, and image content.

SDH (Synchronous Digital Hierarchy)

A world standard of synchronous optical speeds. The basic SDH speed starts at 155Mbps, also called STM-1 (Synchronous Transport Mode-1) in Europe. SONET is a subset of SDH.

server

A specialized, shared computer on the LAN or in a carrier's network containing files such as e-mail or applications. It can be used to handle sharing of printers, e-mail, and other applications.

set-top box
A device connected to a television that allows access to various content, including pay-per-view programming. Set-top boxes can be used to distribute content to other TVs and devices. Newer models contain hard drives and multiple tuners. They can be used to watch one program while recording a different show, and to pause and rewind programs.

signaling gateway
A type of media gateway that converts signaling from IP networks to that compatible with traditional, circuit-switched networks, and vice versa.

SIM (Subscriber Identification Module)
A clip-on or internal card with microchips in mobile handsets that stores user identity and other information such as speed-dial lists and e-mail addresses. CDMA phones do not have SIM cards.

SIP (Session Initiation Protocol)
A signaling protocol used to establish sessions over IP networks, such as those for telephone calls, audio conferencing, click-to-dial from the Web, and instant message exchanges between devices. It is also used to link IP telephones from different manufacturers to SIP-compatible IP telephones. It is used in landline and mobile networks.

SLA (Service-Level Agreement)
Often provided to customers by carriers that sell MPLS. The SLA defines service parameters such as uptime and response time.

smart grids
Upgraded utility networks for metering that can carry two-way messages on cellular networks between customers and electric utilities. A goal is to use energy more efficiently by monitoring usage patterns.

SMS (Short Message Service)
Short, 160-character (including header address information) text messages that can be transmitted between digital cellular telephones.

SMTP (Simple Mail Transfer Protocol)
The e-mail protocol portion of TCP/IP used on the Internet. Having an e-mail standard that users adhere to enables people on diverse LANs to send e-mail to one another.

SNMP (Simple Network Management Protocol)
The Internet Engineering Task Force (IETF) protocol standard used to monitor devices on IP networks. SNMP is used on most LAN monitoring software packages.

softphone
Telephone functionality on a personal computer in VoIP systems. People with softphone-equipped laptops can use their VoIP remotely.

softswitch
Used in converged enterprise and carrier networks that carry VoIP traffic. Softswitches are built on standard computer processors and use standards-based protocols, which makes them less costly than proprietary switches based on circuit-switched technology. Softswitches manage and control traffic in IP networks.

SONET (Synchronous Optical Network)
An older standard for multiplexing high-speed digital bits onto fiber-optic cabling.

SONET converts electronic impulses to light impulses, and vice versa. Telephone companies use SONET to transmit data from multiple customers over the same fiber cables.

spectrum

Made up of frequency bands or airwaves that carry either analog or digital wireless signals. Spectrum consists of the multitude of invisible electric energy in frequency bands that surround the Earth and are used to transmit segregated radio waves. Radio waves carry signals as electrical energy on unseen waves.

SSAD (Solid State Drive)

Contains integrated circuits that store memory. SSDs are for the most part used as nonvolatile storage where data is not lost in power outages.

SSL (Secure Sockets Layer)

A newer type of security for VPNs than IPsec. It is embedded in browsers so that organizations aren't required to install special client software in each user's computer.

statistical multiplexing

Assumes that not all devices are active all the time. A statistical multiplexer does not save capacity for each device connected to it. It operates either on a first-come, first-served basis or on a priority basis in which certain streams of traffic have higher priority than others.

streaming video and audio

A means of starting to play a message while the rest of it is being received. Streaming uses compression to make the voice, video, and data files smaller so that they can be transmitted in less time. Streaming video and audio is used in broadcasting video and audio over the Internet.

switching

Equipment with input and output ports that transmits traffic and sets up paths to destinations based on digits dialed or addressing bits.

T.120

The ITU-defined standard for document sharing and white boarding. People using T.120-adherent software can participate in document-sharing conferences with one another over the Internet. For example, vendors can demonstrate their products to potential customers via computers connected to the Internet at dispersed sites.

T1

A North American and Japanese standard for communicating at 1.54Mbps. A T1 line has the capacity for 24 voice or data channels.

T3

A North American standard for communicating at speeds of 44Mbps. T3 lines have 672 channels for voice and/or data. Fiber-optic cabling or digital microwave is required for T3 transmissions.

tandem offices

Used in the core of traditional, traditional Public Switched Telephone Networks (PSTNs). Tandem central offices switch traffic between central offices. End users are not connected to tandem offices. Tandem central offices are being replaced by lower-cost, more efficient softswitches.

TCP (Transmission Control Protocol)

Includes sequence numbers for each packet so that the packets can be reassembled at their destination. The sequence numbers ensure that all of the packets arrive and are assembled in the proper order. If some packets are discarded because of congestion, the network retransmits them. The numbering and tracking of packets make TCP a connection-oriented protocol. Router-based LAN internetworking uses TCP.

TCP/IP (Transmission Control Protocol/Internet Protocol)
The suite of protocols used on the Internet and also by organizations for communications among multiple networks.

TD-SCDMA (Time-Division Synchronous Code-Division Multiple Access)
China Mobile uses TD-SCDMA, which is a homegrown version of UMTS TDD (3G mobile protocol), for its 3G mobile service.

tether
The ability to connect laptop or tablet computers that don't have Internet access to the Internet via a mobile handset's Internet connection. This is generally done by connecting the computer and mobile handset together through USB ports via USB-compatible cables.

throughput
The actual amount of user data that can be transmitted on a telecommunications link or on wireless networks. Throughput does not include headers, for example, bits used for addressing, error correction, or prioritizing packets with voice and data bits.

tier 1 provider
A loosely defined term for Internet service providers that own Internet backbone fiber-optic facilities in addition to ISP services

such as hosting and e-mail. Examples include AT&T, Level 3, Sprint Nextel, and Verizon.

TDM (Time-Division Multiplexing)
TDMs, such as T1/E1 equipment, save capacity for each device that is connected to the multiplexer. This is less efficient than other methods such as statistical multiplexing because capacity is unused when the device is not transmitting.

topology
The geometric shape of the physical connection of the lines in a network—or, the "view from the top"—which is the shape of the network, the configuration in which lines are connected to one another.

traffic shaping
A way for carriers to manage traffic to control congestion. Techniques include providing better QoS for particular types of traffic such as video, prioritizing traffic for higher fees, and throttling traffic (decreasing speeds) for subscribers who exceed allotted amounts.

transponder
Fiber-optic transponders receive, amplify, and retransmit optical signals on different wavelength channels on fiber cabling. They also convert electrical signals to optical signals and optical signals back to electrical signals where they connect to twisted-pair copper or coaxial cabling.

trunking gateway
Converts packet network circuits (such as T1/E1 and T3/E3), to those compatible with the Public Switched Telephone Network (PSTN), and vice versa, so that voice traffic

can be transferred between IP networks and traditional, circuit-switched networks.

trunks
The circuits (electrical or fiber paths) between telephone companies and enterprise telephone systems and between central office switches. A T1 is a trunk.

tuner
Used in televisions, radios, and set-top boxes to filter out all channels (frequencies) except the particular one at the frequency the tuner is designed to accept. The tuner then adapts the frequency to ones compatible with the TV or radio. Newer set-top boxes are equipped with multiple tuners so that one channel can be recorded while another is being viewed.

tunneling
A method of securely transferring data between sites connected by networks such as a VPN, the Internet, an intranet, or an extranet. Tunneling puts a new header in front of the data. This is a way of separating data from multiple companies using the same network.

UDP (User Datagram Protocol)
Part of the TCP/IP suite of protocols. UDP has less overhead because it does not have bits with packet numbers and acknowledgments. UDP is considered a connectionless protocol because packets arrive at their destination independently from various routes without sequence numbers. There is no assurance that all of the packets for a particular message arrive. UDP is suited for applications such as database lookups, voice, and short messages.

UMTS (Universal Mobile Telecommunications System)
A European standard for 3G mobile wireless networks that GSM networks generally use when they are upgraded. WCDMA is a UMTS technology.

UMTS TDD (Universal Mobile Telecommunications System/Time-Division Duplexing)
A high-speed wireless technology used for 3G cellular and broadband wireless access to the Internet. It is also referred to as TD-CDMA. It uses the same channel for sending and receiving, with small time slots to separate the sending and receiving streams rather than the larger guard band used in other 3G technologies.

UNE (Unbundled Network Element)
Parts of the incumbent local telephone company infrastructure required to lease out to other local exchange carriers. Examples of UNEs are the copper lines to customers' premises. Many UNE requirements have been eliminated.

unicasting
The transmission of one message from a single point to another point. This is also referred to as point-to-point communications.

unified messaging
Computing platform that contains voicemail, facsimile, e-mail, and sometimes video mail on a single system. Users can access all of these services from their computer inbox.

unlicensed spectrum
Governments specify portions of the airwaves for unlicensed services at no charge to

companies; 802.11 services are an example. Most governments issue certification, signal-spreading, and power-limitation rules to protect adjacent licensed spectrum bands from harmful interference from transmissions within the unlicensed spectrum.

Uplink (UL)
On broadband and mobile networks, the uplink carries traffic from the customer to the carrier's equipment.

URL (Universal Resource Locator)
An address on the World Wide Web. The address is made up of strings of data that identify the server, the folder location, and other information indicating the location of information on the Internet.

USF (Universal Service Fund)
Used to fulfill the commitment made by the United States government to affordable universal telephone service to all residential consumers. The Telecommunications Act of 1996 expanded universal service to rural healthcare organizations, libraries, and educational institutions for Internet access, inside wiring, and computers. The library and educational subsidies are a part of universal service known as the e-rate. Every interstate carrier, cell phone, and paging company must pay a percentage of its interstate and international revenues to the fund. A separate fund, The Connect America Fund, has been established for residential broadband.

UTP (Unshielded Twisted-Pair)
Most inside telephones and computers are connected to one another via unshielded twisted-pair copper cabling. The twists in the copper cables cut down on the electrical interference of signals carried on pairs of wire near one another and near electrical equipment.

UWB (Ultra-Wideband)
A wireless service that supports higher data rates than RFID and can be used for some of the same applications. However, widespread adoption is held up by a lack of an agreed-upon standard. It is also used by the military and by governments for tracking and for finding people trapped under rubble.

VLANs (Virtual Local Area Networks)
Groups of devices programmed in Layer 2 switches for special treatment in enterprise networks. They are not grouped together in physical networks; rather, they are grouped together in software for common treatment and programming purposes. They are "virtual" networks that act as if they were separate LANs.

VoIP (Voice over Internet Protocol)
The process of sending voice traffic in packets on IP-based data networks. VoIP digitizes analog voice, compresses it, and puts it into packets at the sending end. The receiving end does the reverse. Unlike circuit switching, no path is saved for the duration of the voice session. However, voice packets can be prioritized.

VoLTE (Voice over LTE)
A 3rd Generation Partnership Program protocol used to carry packetized voice (VoIP) on LTE networks.

VPN (Virtual Private Network)

Provides the functions and features of a private network without the need for dedicated private lines between corporate sites or between corporate sites and remote users. Each site connects to the network provider's network rather than directly to another corporate location.

VRU (Voice Response Unit)

Provides information to callers based on their touch-tone or spoken commands. VRUs query computers for responses and "speak" them to callers. For example, people often can call their bank or credit card company to find out their balance or to learn if a payment has been received.

WAN (Wide Area Network)

Connects computers located in different cities, states, and countries.

WAP (Wireless Application Protocol)

A protocol that defines how Internet sites can be displayed to fit on the screens of cellular devices and how devices access and view these sites.

WCDMA (Wideband Code-Division Multiplexing)

The 3G service that most GSM operators install.

WDM (Wavelength-Division Multiplexing)

Also known as *dense wavelength division multiplexing*, this enables multiple colors or frequencies of light to be carried on single pairs of fiber. WDM greatly increases the capacity of network providers' fiber-optic networks.

WebRTC (Real-Time Communications)

A set of IEEE and World Wide Web Consortiums (W3C) protocols for embedding software based codecs in applications and browsers for real time voice, video, and chat among disparate devices and operating systems.

Wi-Fi (Wireless Fidelity)

Wireless networks based on 802.11 IEEE standards. The Wi-Fi Alliance tests and certifies that products meet IEEE 802.11 standards.

WiMAX (Worldwide Interoperability for Microwave Access)

A forum whose goal is to facilitate interoperability of equipment based on 802.16 standards for high-speed fixed wireless service using the 2GHz to 11GHz frequency bands. Newer versions are used for mobile wireless service. WiMAX fixed wireless service is used for Internet access and for backhaul networks, which connect cellular towers to mobile central offices.

WiMAX 2

A 4G mobile protocol developed by the IEEE. It is not as widely used as LTE, but was available earlier.

wire speed

The capability of switches to forward packets equal to the full speed of their ports. Ports are the interfaces to which cabling is connected. Wire speed is achieved with powerful switch processors, the computers that look up addresses and forward packets.

wireless local loop
Uses wireless media to bring telephone service to a customer's premises rather than copper or fiber cabling.

WISP (Wireless Internet Service Provider)
Provides Internet access using non-cellular wireless technology.

WLAN (Wireless Local Area Network)
Local Area Network (LAN) in which devices are connected to other devices or the LAN wirelessly rather than with cabling; 802.11-based Wi-Fi networks are WLANs.

worms
Viruses that are programmed to start infecting networks and other computers at a predetermined future time and date. These time-released viruses are also referred to as *bots*.

WWW (World Wide Web)
Connects users from one network to another when they "click" links. It was developed in 1989 to make information on the Internet more accessible. A browser is required to navigate and access the World Wide Web.

XML (Extensible Markup Language)
A software language that was developed to make it easy for disparate computers to exchange information. XML uses tags to identify fields of data. XML is like a data dictionary in that uniform *tags* are attached to elements so that diverse programs can read the tags. For example, tags can be used to identify elements such as prices, model numbers, product identities, or quantities ordered.

ZigBee
Based on the IEEE 802.15.4 standard for wireless networks with devices that operate at low data rates and consume small amounts of power. The ZigBee Alliance is developing specifications for higher-level services to be used in sensor networks such as those that monitor and control heating and electrical systems in businesses.

Index

G

H

I

Q

R